"Ghada Karmi's stunning memoir is remarkable. Extraordinarily well-written, it is the amazingly honest story of a Palestinian woman of exceptional self-awareness. Hers is a story of exile and displacement ... rich in detail and human experience. Karmi is excellent on the quality of family and even communal life in Mandatory Palestine ... she also has a wonderfully subtle way of showing how in thousands of different ways the political and the personal intermesh, and this she does with a skill and insight that could be a novelist's envy." **Edward W. Said**

"One of the finest, most eloquent and painfully honest memoirs of the Palestinian exile and displacement, which western power and its creature, Israel, have *normalised*." *New Statesman*

"Ghada Karmi writes simply and poignantly. Hers is a story of our time, about exile and dispossession, and how she has come to be neither British nor quite Arab." *Jewish Chronicle*

"A very timely book in the current political situation ... This should serve to remind people just what the big fuss in the Middle East is all about." **Ahdaf Soueif,** *Times Literary Supplement*

"... an engrossing and remarkably frank account ..." *MultiCultural Review*

IN SEARCH OF FATIMA

A Palestinian Story

Ghada Karmi

VERSO

London • New York

This edition published by Verso 2024
First published by Verso 2002
© Ghada Karmi 2002, 2009, 2024

1 3 5 7 9 10 8 6 4 2

Verso
UK: 6 Meard Street, London W1F 0EG
US: 388 Atlantic Avenue, Brooklyn, NY 11217
versobooks.com

Verso is the imprint of New Left Books

ISBN-13: 978-1-80429-709-4
ISBN-13: 978-1-78960-482-5 (US EBK)
ISBN-13: 978-1-78960-483-2 (UK EBK)

British Library Cataloguing in Publication Data
A catalogue record for this book is available from the British Library

Library of Congress Cataloging-in-Publication Data
A catalog record for this book is available from the Library of Congress

Printed and bound by CPI (UK) Ltd, Croydon CR0 4YY

In memory of my mother
and for
her grand-daughter Lalla Salma

Contents

Acknowledgements

This book could not have been written without the generous help of my family, whose memories of events before 1948 were indispensable. I wish especially to commend in this respect my father and my sister Siham, but also my brother Ziyad and my cousins Zuhair and Aziza Karmi. I am also grateful to the late Mrs Leila Mantoura and members of her family. Many others, both inside and outside the family, helped also with their reminiscences of particular events and I am grateful to all of them. Any errors of fact or omission are entirely mine.

I am grateful to Iradj Bagherzade and Adel Kamal for their highly professional and painstaking editing of the manuscript. My thanks are due also to Jane Hindle and everyone at Verso Press for making the book become a reality. I owe a special debt of gratitude to Tariq Ali, whose initial interest and enthusiasm for the book set the ball rolling.

Critical and editorial work on the manuscript, which helped me in innumerable ways, was offered with unstinting generosity by several people to whom I owe special thanks: Karen Armstrong, George Joffe and Tim Llewellyn, whose help was invaluable in the later stages of

x *Acknowledgements*

the book. Many others encouraged and sustained me through the difficulties of writing this memoir with practical advice and useful suggestions: Gill Emberson, Cleeve and Barbara Mathews; Trevor Mostyn, Julia Hamilton, Alexandra Campbell, Selina Mills, Shelby Tucker, and other members of our reading group. Mrs Maureen Elliott gave me considerable self-confidence in the early stages and I am grateful to her and also to Amy Henderson who did much the same later on.

I am especially appreciative of the efforts of Hisham el Solh, Sami Alami and Bassam Aburdene in supporting the project and for their faith in me. I would also like to thank Adel Kamal and Said Aburish for their encouragement and help.

Edward Said has a special place in the genesis of this book for his marvellously inspiring support and friendship.

Last but not least, I owe enormous gratitude to my daughter, Salma, whose youthful enthusiasm and excitement about the book kept me going through many times of despondency and frustration.

Author's Note

Most of the people who feature in this memoir are known by their authentic names. In a few instances, however, to avoid professional or personal embarrassment, I have thought it best to alter the names.

Introduction

Ten years have passed since the events that conclude *In Search of Fatima*. The book ends in 1998, the year of Israel's fiftieth anniversary and, concomitantly, the fiftieth of Palestine's destruction. I remember how, at the time, an eager reporter from a local London radio station phoned on behalf of a Jewish programme to ask for a comment on Israel's anniversary celebrations. "Isn't it great!" she exclaimed. "Would you like to congratulate Israel for our programme?" Bemused that she should ask me, of all people, for an endorsement of Israel's "achievement", I cast about in my mind for something suitable. "Yes, certainly," I replied. "I would indeed like to congratulate Israel – for getting away with it for so long, like I might admire Al Capone or the Great Train Robbers!" I don't know what she made of this. I doubt that she ever used those words for her programme.

Looking back over the intervening years, I realize I had imagined that something would happen to improve the dismal reality of Palestinian life, blighted since 1948. I had little hope that the "peace process" between Israel and the Palestinian leadership, interminably and futilely pursued, would succeed. But there was still a feeling that things had to change, and that one day, perhaps soon, through some magical, unexpected event, this sad conflict would be resolved. In 1998, the Oslo Accords were just five years old. Many Palestinians still hoped for a positive outcome: for the recognition of a Palestinian state on the parts of the old Palestine that still remained. The international community encouraged them in this belief. Numerous organisations and aid agencies swarmed over the West Bank and Gaza in those years, helping to create the institutions of the putative state. People spoke of "Palestine" not as a sad, lost place of the past, but as a coming reality, a new beginning and the first step towards regaining the whole of the homeland. Sceptical of the Oslo Accords as I had been, even I could not help but warm to the enthusiasm of fellow Palestinians and the preliminary signs of statehood that made them so proud.

But as it turned out, it was a cruel deception. I have often wondered if the Western states that rushed so enthusiastically to prepare the people of the occupied territories for statehood knew in advance how empty their promises were, or whether they too were duped. Today, the Palestinian state is further beyond reach than ever. The Oslo Agreement is dead. The land that could have formed the Palestinian state is all but consumed by Israel's growing settlements. In 2000 the second Intifada erupted, an expression of Palestinian rage and disappointment at the reversal in their hopes. Israel's suppression of Palestinian resistance in all its forms has been the norm since then. After Israel withdrew its Gaza settlements in 2005, it turned Gaza into a prison and the focus of repeated attacks, sieges and blockades.

Similar Israeli tactics had rendered the West Bank a largely passive and quiescent entity, but Gaza remained the last outpost of resistance. For this, the region and its residents were ferociously punished at the end of 2008 and beginning of 2009 in an assault that left 1,400 Gazans dead and thousands wounded. Israel ruined the Palestinian infrastructure, destroyed homes and spread a blanket of devastation. Who knew when, if ever, Gaza's people would recover from this onslaught? Or how the complicated mess that had been made of their lives would be resolved?

When I wrote *In Search of Fatima*, I wanted to present this situation in a human, accessible form, in order to get away from the political treatises, research studies, economic analyses and dry histories which have become the norm for conveying the Palestinian experience. Such writings could never have expressed that other world of Palestinian feelings, personal stories, thoughts and aspirations. If people could understand Palastinians as human beings with names and life histories, rather than in terms of collectives such as "Arab refugees", "extremists" or Islamic "terrorists", they would begin to empathise with individuals caught within this most tragic of stories. I had grown up in a country, Britain, where the Jewish history of European persecution and the Holocaust was familiar to every schoolchild. It had not reached them through the medium of academic tracts and arid statistics, but through literature, memoir, film and stage play. So, too, I reasoned, must the Palestinian narrative be presented, if only because it is a consequence of the Nazi Holocaust, its sequel, and the last chapter in a catastrophe that started far away from Middle Eastern shores. In that sense, the Palestinian story is inseparable from the Jewish one; it is its natural and poignant heir.

Since this book's first publication in 2002, it has been touching and gratifying to see how many readers responded precisely in the way that I had hoped. Hundreds wrote to say how it affected them or resonated with their own experiences. Though I had aimed the book at a Western and, more specifically, an English-speaking readership, I was surprised by the number of non-Western readers who were touched by it.

Among these were other Muslims, who found in it an echo of their or their children's experiences growing up in a Western society. Many young Palestinians too identified with the book's narrative, and found it a source of knowledge about a historical period, before 1948 and the creation of Israel, they had known little about. But probably the most striking were the Jewish readers, who empathised with a tale of unbelonging and the search for home. The great American intellectual Noam Chomsky saw a parallel to his own Orthodox Jewish family in America. He wrote to me about this in 2002, jut after the book was published: "The account of your family and life in London . . . awakens many memories. You should have seen how my mother reacted to the marriage of her first son (me), and I was marrying 'a nice Jewish girl' . . . If it had been an Arab – words fail me. Or my grandfather who lived in Baltimore for 60 years and never learned a word of English, or, I suspected, even knew he was in the US.'

Since the book was first issued, many giants of modern Palestinian history, impossible to replace, have died. What a loss for a people in need of heroes. In 2003, Edward Said, the prominent intellectual and a personal friend who endorsed this book, passed away, followed, a year later, by Yasser Arafat, the embodiment of the Palestinian cause. In 2008 came two more great losses: the deaths of the influential radical thinker and activist George Habash, who had headed the Popular Front for the Liberation of Palestine since 1969; and the best known Palestinian poet and national figure, Mahmoud Darwish. A year before, in May 2007, I suffered a personal bereavement which accentuated all the others. My father, who was nearly 102 and whom I had begun to believe immortal, finally died, leaving a rich legacy of over ten English–Arabic dictionaries and hours of BBC recordings on Arabic literature.

These blows have only served to make me more determined than ever to preserve and document the Palestinian story, to save it from extinction, and to redeem the memories of those who suffered and died without seeing a solution. Palestine is not just a country or a name, it is an idea, an aspiration, and a symbol for everyone who has lost and longed for restitution and recompense.

In Search of Fatima is a testament to that hope.

Ghada Karmi
London, March 2009

Prologue

A mighty crash that shook the house. Something – a bomb, a mortar, a weapons' store? – exploded with a deafening bang. The little girl could feel it right inside her head. She put her hands to her ears and automatically got down onto the cold tiled floor of their *liwan* with the rest, as they had learned to do. Shootings, the bullets whistling around the windows and ricocheting against the walls of the empty houses opposite, followed immediately.

"Hurry up! Hurry up!" The danger in the air was palpable.

The taxi stood waiting outside, its doors open, to take them away to where she did not want to go. The little girl wanted to stay right here at home with Rex and Fatima, playing in the garden, jumping over the fence into the Muscovite's house next door, seeing her friends return, even restarting school, now closed since Christmas. Doing all the familiar things, which had made up the fabric of her young life. Not this madness. Not this abandoning of everything she knew and loved.

"Get into the car! Quickly!" A brief lull in the fighting. They must hurry, pack their two cases and the eight of them somehow into the taxi. The driver kept urging them to hurry. He was frightened and clearly anxious to get out of their perilous, bullet-ridden street. Rex could not come with them. He must stay behind. She held his furry body tightly against her and stroked his long soft ears. She wanted to say, "Please don't worry. It's only for a week. They said so. You'll be fine and we'll be back."

But she knew somehow that it wasn't true. Despite her parents' assurances, a dread internal voice told her so.

"Ghada! Come on, come on, please!" Rex inside the iron garden gate, she outside. The house with its empty veranda shuttered and closed, secretive and already mysterious, as if they had never lived there and it had never been their home. The fruit trees in the garden stark against the early morning sky.

Every nerve and fibre of her being raged against her fate, the cruelty of leaving that she was powerless to avert. She put her palms up against the gate and Rex started barking and pushing at it, thinking she was coming in. Her mother dragged her away and pushed her into the back seat of the taxi onto Fatima's lap. The rest got in and Muhammad banged the car doors shut. She twisted round, kneeling, to look out of the back window.

Another explosion. The taxi, which had seen better days, revved loudly and started to move off. But through the back window, a terrible sight which only she could see. Rex had somehow got out, was standing in the middle of the road. He was still and silent, staring after their retreating car, his tail stiff, his ears pointing forward.

With utter clarity, the little girl saw in that moment that he knew what she knew, that they would never meet again.

Part One

Palestine

One

On a cold autumnal day I stood with my mother, sister and brother in London airport. It was not then called Heathrow. "Oscar Wilde" were the only two English words I knew because one of the books in my father's library had borne this title, and when I was seven, he taught me to read the English alphabet.

It was September 1949 and I was nine years old. I didn't know exactly why we had come to London, or how long we would stay. In fact, I knew very little about anything. We were waiting for my father to meet us and I thought that that was why we had come, to see him again. The BOAC propeller plane we came on had taken all night to get us from Damascus to London and we had stopped in Malta on the way. Such new places, such new experiences for me who had hardly been anywhere before. The airport was a daunting place; it had immense halls with polished floors, vinyl and wood, which was the strangest sight of all. In Palestine, floors were tiled or made of stone. And there was such a crush of people, strangers pushing, rushing, jostling. Until then, I had never been anywhere in my life where I did

not know any single person. Even when we went to the big souk in
Damascus, which was the nearest thing to London airport that I had
ever experienced, we had gone with the rest of the family and some of
the neighbours as well. The people here looked different to the people
I was used to. They were taller and bigger and had pale skins. The
men didn't have moustaches and I wondered why none of the women
seemed to be pregnant; I could see no swollen bellies anywhere. Not
like Palestine.

We had not seen our father for over a year, not since he had left us
in Damascus in my grandfather's house. I missed him terribly at first.
Then I somehow began to forget about him. Everything was so
strange in Damascus. It wasn't where we normally lived, and we
scarcely knew our grandparents, although my mother had been born
and bred in Damascus. But I don't think she was ever happy there and
was glad to leave for Palestine when she married. "I never thought the
day would come when I would be relieved to come back here," she
had said on our arrival in Damascus. "I don't know what we would
have done without my parents to turn to at this terrible time."

And indeed it had been a terrible time, so terrible that I have
blotted many of its most painful moments out of my consciousness.
The troubles in Palestine started even before I was born, such that my
childhood (and indeed that of my brother and sister, who were both
older) was overshadowed by the great political events which were
happening around us in Palestine and in the world beyond. For a long
time, we did not understand their significance, nor why we, an
obscure Middle Eastern people, and our country, an undeveloped,
backward place, should have been chosen to play such an important
role in the affairs of the world.

My life began some two months after the start of the Second World
War. Later, my mother added this historical coincidence to her list of
reasons for not having wanted to have me, or indeed any child, just

then. Of course, this was not an unfamiliar situation for the women of Palestine at that time. Without contraception or access to abortion, many a woman was desperate not to add yet another mouth to feed on top of her already large family. But in my mother's case, where poverty was not a factor, there was another reason. Life in Palestine was very troubled at the time and no place, my mother said, to bring up a child. Hardly a day went by when there was not a shooting in the street or news of an ambush somewhere in the country. No one felt safe. "If it wasn't Jews after us, it was the British and finally other Palestinians as well."

Despite my mother's reluctance, I was eventually delivered at the government maternity hospital in Jerusalem, with the help of Dr Hajjar, her gynaecologist.

"Come on, Um Ziyad," he told her. "Cheer up. The troubles won't last for ever and things will be normal again." Um Ziyad is how my mother was known; it literally means "mother of Ziyad", after the name of her eldest son, my brother Ziyad, and is a usual form of address in the Levant for a woman once she has given birth to a boy; correspondingly, my father was known as "Abu Ziyad", father of Ziyad.

I was born possibly on November 19, 1939. I say possibly because my exact date of birth is not known. My mother had only an approximate memory of it – "it was winter, I know that." This is not as odd as it might seem because birthdays were traditionally not important in the Arab world. They were never usually celebrated in any way and certainly not with parties or presents. It was only in more modern times and with the advent of Westernisation that people began to adopt the foreign way of marking birthdays (accompanying which has appeared an absurd Arabic rendition of "Happy birthday to you" complete with the original tune and a rough translation of the words). Neither my mother nor my father knew their exact dates of

birth, which were not registered. They should have been because the
Ottoman authorities, who ruled Palestine when they were both born,
required all births to be notified. But it was not the custom and my
grandparents did not bother. This could be an advantage, allowing my
mother to make herself younger than she was without fear of con-
tradiction.

The British authorities who had succeeded the Ottomans, on the
other hand, rigorously registered my birth (and those of my brother
and sister). When she left the hospital, my mother collected my birth
certificate which had my full name on it, in English, Arabic and
Hebrew (Palestine's three official languages, as decreed under the
British Mandate): Ghada Hasan Karmi, after the name of my father in
accordance with Arab custom. It was blue in colour and she kept it
with all the family documents in the drawer of my father's desk in our
sitting room. She also put our photographs as babies and toddlers, and
then as schoolchildren, in an album in the same drawer. She liked to
keep them safe in our father's desk, but in the agitation and chaos of
fleeing from Jerusalem, she left them behind. "How could I have
remembered to take them?" she said afterwards guiltily. "All I could
think of was what clothes to pack for the five of us."

And there, I suppose, they remained until the Jewish family which
was moved by the Israeli authorities into our empty house found them
and, for all I know, threw them away. So, I never got to see how my
birth certificate looked or what my exact date of birth was, nor any of
my childhood photographs either. For many years, the first photograph of myself I ever saw dated from when I was eight, taken after
we had left Palestine for Syria. (Much later, one or two other
childhood photographs turned up in my uncle Taleb's possession.)
There I was with my brother, my sister, our mother and our uncle
Taleb, all looking posed and neatly arranged before the camera.
Whenever I looked at it as a child, I used to think that my real life

only started with that photograph. What went before left no record and had no reality except in my dreams.

On Christmas Eve, when I was only a few weeks old and while my mother was attempting to breast-feed me, shocking news came to our house. My eldest uncle Mahmoud, who was only fifty years old and had eight children, had been shot dead in Beirut. He was returning home at night when a masked man jumped up at him from beneath the stairs leading to his flat. It was dark and the lights were not working. "Are you Mahmoud?" the man demanded. "Yes," replied my uncle unsuspectingly. Whereupon the man shot him twice in the chest. No one heard it happen, as the family lived at the top of an apartment block. But the police caught the assassin and he subsequently confessed that he had been sent by Hajj Amin al-Husseini to kill him because my uncle did not support his camp, of which he made no secret since he was a journalist and rather outspoken.[1] Once before, in 1937 when he and his family lived in Nablus, Hajj Amin's men had come for my uncle. He fled just in time, leaving his eldest son, my cousin Zuhair, behind to look after the family. "So, they took me instead!" said Zuhair. "I was only fourteen, but they didn't care. They said, 'We'll take you hostage and get your father that way.' They pushed me up on a horse behind one of them and took me to their encampment outside the town. I was terrified, but I soon saw they were only a group of peasants, like our own peasants in Tulkarm, and

[1] At this time, there were two major Palestinian political parties in Palestine, one led by Hajj Amin al-Husseini, the Grand Mufti of Jerusalem and head of the Supreme Muslim Council, and the other by Raghib al-Nashashibi, the mayor of Jerusalem. Both aimed, but in different ways, to halt Jewish immigration into Palestine, which they feared would lead to a Jewish takeover of the country. The Nashashibis believed in a negotiated agreement mediated through the British, but the Husseinis rejected all negotiations. Their disagreement on method led to bitter enmity and internecine fighting between the two sides.

I didn't feel afraid any more. They kept me for two weeks and I think they felt sorry for what they had to do."

Another of my uncles, Abdul-Ghani, also a journalist and also opposed to Hajj Amin, whom he openly accused of being a British agent, had barely escaped an assassination attempt a few months before. Another man had been killed by mistake for him and he had taken to living in Tel Aviv where the Mufti's men could not reach him. "Why don't they fight the Jews instead of each other?" cried my mother. "God forbid that it should be you next," she said to my father. "I still haven't forgotten what happened last year."

A year before I was born, a man had come to our house. My mother had opened the door to him because it was safer – no one was after harming the women. He asked to see my father in a strange voice. He looked a rough sort of man, and when he came into the light, she could see that he had a bandoleer strapped around his chest. But before she could do anything, my father came out and the man suddenly said, "I was sent here to kill you by Hajj Amin's men. But God help me, I can't go through with it. You have nothing to fear from me."

This did not reassure my father, who was thoroughly alarmed. That very night he moved out, leaving my mother, sister and brother behind, and took refuge in the YMCA. This was nearer to his workplace, which was in the Russian Compound complex on the Jaffa Road and meant that he could take cover quickly if he had to. "For a while," my mother said, "he couldn't even come to visit us at home because he knew they were waiting for him." In order for them to see each other, he would have to go to the house of Muhammad Kamal, his cousin, which was in Qatamon and a safe distance away from the area controlled by Hajj Amin. And my mother would take my sister Siham and brother Ziyad and meet him there at night. She was a courageous, capable woman, but these stolen meetings and the danger my father was in taxed even her strength. Women did not normally expect to have to fend for themselves, there were no "single parents" in our society, and she started to feel the burden of bewilderment and insecurity. She sometimes wondered if it would ever end.

For, if life in Palestine was turbulent at the time of my birth, it was worse in the years which immediately preceded it. From 1936 to 1939, the Palestinian protests against the policies of the British Mandate authorities who governed Palestine were at their height. The uprising began with the General Strike calling for the suspension of Jewish immigration, which had reached alarming proportions. The whole country came to a standstill for six months. The British ended it by force. Its leaders were executed and hundreds of others were imprisoned. But even then the protests and violence continued, and what had started as a strike turned into a full-scale rebellion. Well over 3,000 Palestinians were killed in three years. Even decades later, my father could barely bring himself to speak of that time. Everyone thought they could see what the British were doing. They seemed determined to let more and more Jews into the country and stamp out any resistance. People became frightened, but their leaders could not agree on a common strategy to defeat either the Jews or the British. The rebellion involved enormous sacrifice for everyone; people were actually starving. But it came to nothing in the end. Jewish immigration continued and so, perhaps in frustration, the Palestinian leaders turned on each other and ordinary people like my parents paid the price.

In order to control the situation, the British brought into Palestine the much-dreaded *tatwiq* (round-up). This was a pernicious practice used by the authorities to root out Palestinian resistance fighters and to search for hidden arms. It formed some of my mother's bitterest memories of that time. "They would suddenly swoop down without warning and then round up all the men they suspected." At that time, our family lived in the Old City near the Palestine Archaeological Museum. "The soldiers would suddenly come and bang on all the doors with their rifles, looking for the men. They didn't care if they were guilty or innocent. They just dragged them out of the houses and rounded them up like animals. Then they took them off for questioning." They dragged my father away one day, and when she screamed her protests at the doorstep, the squad sergeant barked at her to shut up.

My father never spoke of the humiliation and the shame of these incidents. How depressing, I thought when I heard this, the selfsame brutalities, sickeningly re-enacted under every occupation and by every military regime and practised in identical fashion by Israelis on Palestinians today. And how strange and almost unbelievable to hear such terrible things said about the British, so many of whom I later grew to love and respect when I went to live among them.

My sister Siham learned to fear the British soldiers from a very young age. In the summer of 1935, when she was just four and our mother was expecting my brother Ziyad, the two of them saw British soldiers suddenly arrive in an army truck and spill out into the garden of the house opposite with rifles at the ready. Leaving Siham behind to look fearfully on at the armed men trampling the flowerbeds as they ran towards the house, my mother came out onto the street to find that they had surrounded the whole building. They had come to arrest Talaat al-Seifi, a good friend of my father, who lived there. When she realised this she rushed forward, but one of the soldiers turned round and, thrusting his rifle butt in her face, shoved her back into the house, trembling and shaken. For years afterwards, she swore that it was the terror of that occasion which gave Ziyad his bad childhood eczema.

One day, when my sister was seven years old, the soldiers came again to our road. They rounded up every adult they could find, including our mother, herded them together and cordoned them off at the end of the road. My father was at work and only my sister was left behind at home. As the soldiers marched my mother out, she shouted to Siham to tell them we had nothing in the house but books and not to search us. She said this because soldiers on such occasions were known to barge into people's houses, kicking furniture around and knocking things over. They particularly targeted the storage areas where people kept their staple foods like flour and sugar and olive oil. After a visit from the army, a kitchen floor would be left swimming in muddy puddles of oil and rice and flour. My mother lived in dread of this happening to us. Each year, she spent much money and effort to prepare and store our winter provision. To stand by and watch helplessly while the soldiers trampled over them with their great, heavy boots was a nightmare many of her friends had suffered and she prayed to avoid.

My father was an avid reader and book collector even then, and he kept several chests full of books in our house. These would have looked suspicious to a soldier searching for hidden arms, and indeed the man who came to our house suddenly stopped in his tracks and started to poke at them with his rifle. Siham was terrified and stuttered that the chests only contained English books. She stressed the word "English", thinking to placate him. He spoke a little broken Arabic and seemed to understand her. He tried to pat her head, but she shrank away in terror. He shrugged and turned to leave, virtually colliding with my mother who had broken through the cordon and was running towards the house screaming for fear that Siham was being murdered. She had grabbed another soldier who was standing outside by his jacket, oblivious of his heavy rifle, and was crying in the few English words she could muster, "Baby! My baby!" and pointing at our house. The man shook her off and strode inside our front door. Seeing my sister, he burst out laughing, "Good God, missus! Call that a baby?"

My mother sighed deeply, remembering. "Is it any wonder that I didn't want to bring a child into a world like that?"

ॐ

My uncle's body was taken from Beirut back to Palestine and to the town of Tulkarm for burial. This was because our family originates from Tulkarm, hence our name of Karmi (Arabic surnames often derive from their place of origin). It was then a small town, situated in the middle of Palestine halfway between Lydda and Haifa and to the north-west of Jerusalem. (Today, it is designated as being in the West Bank of the River Jordan and was from 1967 until 1995 under Israeli military occupation.)

My mother did not want to go to the funeral because she was breast-feeding me and could not take me with her. Also, for some time she had had her eye on a bedroom suite which was on sale at a store on the Jaffa Road in the commercial part of Jerusalem. The owner of the shop was a German Jew, who had immigrated recently to Palestine and was not doing well, which was strange because many of his fellow Jewish immigrants received generous help from the British Mandate government and prospered. As an English official in my father's department once quipped, "The Jews used to say they came here to help their brethren. But from what I can see, the majority of them are not so much doing good as doing well!" This sort of remark, my father said, was typical of the anti-Semitism so common amongst British officials in Palestine at the time.

My mother had managed to beat the shopkeeper down to a bargain price of £30 for the whole suite and was to take him the money and make her purchase. But my father said she had to do her duty and come with him to Tulkarm for the funeral. So, she dropped both me and the suite, and by the time she came back to Jerusalem, it had been sold.

In her absence, I had to drink diluted cow's milk with aniseed to make it more digestible. Our doctor advised that I should get accustomed to cow's milk as soon as possible, because in these troubled times, he said, powdered milk might run out. My mother had no one to leave us with because none of her family in Damascus could come to Jerusalem nor could any of our family in Tulkarm on account of my uncle's funeral. So she left us in Fatima's charge for seven days, "which was wonderful", said Siham years later, "because we could do what we liked and we loved Fatima. You cried a lot which was annoying and Ziyad said, why don't they send you back to the hospital. But we were happy all the same."

Fatima would put my milk in a concave glass bottle with two rubber teats at either end of it which she warmed over a small spirit-lamp. How antiquated such a device would seem to us nowadays, but nothing better was to be had at the time. Fatima did not normally live with us, but she had to move in on this occasion while our parents were in Tulkarm. Of course I did not know at that stage what Fatima meant to us children or what she would come to signify for me personally, how the precious memory of her after 1948 would merge with the rest of my irrecoverable childhood. To my mother, she was merely a hard-working village woman who cleaned our house and helped her with the cooking. It was usual then for the better-off Palestinian families in the cities to employ peasant men and women (fellahin) to do domestic work. For my mother, who came from a modest background, servants would have been an unthinkable luxury while she was growing up. However, having married a man with a reputable position and a promising career, she could now enjoy the advantages of her status.

Fatima al-Basha, as was her full name, lived in the village of al-Maliha, some three miles to the south-west of Jerusalem. In her early teens she had been married off to a man who treated her badly and from whom she escaped back to her parents whenever she could. She had two daughters by him and at some point he had either died or abandoned her, we never knew. When she came to work for us, she was about forty years old and lived with her children in the village close to her brother Muhammad. My father found him a job as a caretaker at the Umariyya school where Ziyad went. Each day, when he finished his work there, he would come over to tend our garden and do odd jobs.

Fatima's other brother had gone to South America to join the growing community of Palestinians and Syrians who had been emigrating there since the end of the nineteenth century. Many of these were Christians and had left because they saw no future for themselves during the turbulent last years of the Ottoman Empire. With the coming of British Mandate rule over Palestine which, far from giving the Palestinians independence, actually encouraged Jewish immigration into the country, the upheavals looked set to continue. And so some of those who could afford to take their families with them, or single men like Fatima's brother, set off for a new life. He was, like the rest of her family, illiterate and very poor and Fatima never said whether he did well or not.

At first, my mother took Fatima on to work for us just twice a week. But when we moved into our second house in Qatamon, where we lived until our departure from Jerusalem, she started to come daily. We wanted her to stay at night as well and would beg and plead with her, but she always went back to her own home. She used to walk from her village to our house every day which took about an hour. Halfway along the route, there was a large oak tree which she sat under to take a rest before going on. We knew this tree very well from when we went to visit her at al-Maliha. We loved going to her house – "though God knows why," my mother would comment – and always set out eagerly from Jerusalem with her and her brother.

Because Ziyad and I were still small, she and Muhammad used to carry us on their shoulders as they walked. But when we asked to get down and walk by ourselves, we soon got tired and wanted to be picked up again. And just as we were growing hot and thirsty, there suddenly would be the wonderful oak tree with its thick gnarled trunk and huge leafy branches. Seeing it, everyone would sigh with relief and run to sink down gratefully on the cool, shady ground beneath it.

Fatima lived in a tiny, square-shaped mud house with a wooden roof which stood, as is usual for Palestinian villages, in a close cluster of similar houses. It consisted of one room where everyone ate, sat, slept and conducted their business. Against one wall was a raised platform or ledge where the mattresses and covers were kept for the night-time. We all sat on the floor in the body of the room while Fatima cooked for us. She made simple vegetable stews, since meat for her and the other villagers was a rare luxury. At other times, she put out dishes of olive oil and ground thyme, crushed green olives and fresh sweet onions, all the staples of Palestinian peasant food. We ate whatever she made and the flat round loaves of peasant bread she baked, as if they were the most delicious foods we had ever tasted. After the meal, we would go with her daughters to the freshwater spring just outside the village. This spring served the whole village and next to it was a trough for animals invariably surrounded by a flock of goats pushing and jostling against each other to drink from it. Fatima's daughters would fill a large earthenware jug each from the eye of the spring and place them on the top of their heads. They always managed to walk upright, gracefully keeping their balance, without the full heavy jugs ever falling off.

From the start, I adopted Fatima for my mother. I knew of course that she was not my real mother, although my devotion to her was such that Ziyad and Siham used to taunt me with being a peasant child. "You're not our sister at all," they said. "We found you in the garden. Your real parents are peasants from Fatima's village and we're going to send you back to them." This used to torment me and I would wail loudly. "Leave her alone!" my mother would shout at them. But my distress was only partly because I did not want to be an outcast from the family. Most of it was to do with the idea of being associated with peasants. Even at my young age, I had already absorbed the prevailing social distinctions between the three major sectors of Palestinian society at the time: the peasants, the rural landowning families and the townsfolk, with the peasants at the bottom of the heap. In many ways, this was an unjustified snobbery since the fellahin of Palestine constituted the majority of the population and the backbone of the country. Palestine was above all an agricultural country and had scarcely a single industry until the twentieth century. Urban elites had always existed to a certain extent in the major cities, but they only really developed from the end of the nineteenth century onwards. The traditions and customs that distinguish Palestine from its neighbours derive not from these people but from its peasant class. The famous Palestinian handicrafts like the glass-making of Hebron, the cloth weaving in Majdal, the pottery making of all Palestine's villages; or Palestinian music and Palestine's folk dance, the *dabka*, or its traditional embroidery were all carried out by rural people.

And yet, there was a persistent snobbery amongst the better-off classes which relegated the peasants to a lowly and despised position. Even the word for peasant was used as a term of denigration. To call someone a fellah or a fellaha – the feminine form – was to imply that he or she was primitive and uncivilised. My father had a favourite description for people with peasant origins who had "jumped classes" and were trying to present themselves as something better. "So-and-so may call himself a university lecturer, but mark my words, the man is a peasant," he would say. "How do you know?" "Just look at his

trousers," he would answer. "They're round." As peasants traditionally wore a type of loose trousers, they were unaccustomed to
wearing city clothes and hence, according to my father, when they
adopted city wear they did not know how to iron their trousers
properly. Why he should have believed this, we never knew, since
none of us had ever seen any of these round trousers. But hearing him
say such things used to annoy my mother.

"As if your family were any better than peasants themselves!" she
would scoff. This was in fact rather harsh. Although my father's
family was indeed predominantly engaged in farming, my grandfather
was a well-known scholar and *qadi*, that is, a judge in the shari'a
courts (the religious institutions which regulated the life of Muslims).
His reputation for learning had spread well beyond the confines of
Tulkarm.

But he was also a landowner of considerable tracts of land in and
around Tulkarm (most of it later confiscated by Israel), which he gave
his brothers to farm on behalf of the family. He himself, however,
never engaged in farming but was primarily concerned with literature,
poetry and jurisprudence. My father used to say that it was his
influence which led to his own literary education and that of my
uncles. However, my mother, though of much humbler origins, was
nevertheless a daughter of Damascus, one of the Arab world's most
important capital cities. She never forgot that and would from time to
time taunt my father with his origins from what was, in her view, no
more than a large village.

Tulkarm was indeed a small agricultural place with a population of
no more than a few thousand in my grandfather's time. But its people
were proud to point out that the Ottoman authorities had seen fit in
about 1850 to grant it the status of a *qaimmaqamiyya*. This was an
Ottoman administrative category which made it into a township and
gave it precedence over the villages. In addition, it acquired a Turkish

*My grandfather, Sheikh Said
al-Karmi, photographed around
1920*

qaimmaqam, or governor, which was a further mark of distinction, since it brought the townspeople closer to the government. To be sure, it could not compare with Palestine's major cities, Jaffa, Jerusalem or Hebron. But neither was it totally insignificant, even in the nineteenth century, and when in 1908 it acquired a branch railway line and train station which connected it to the great Hijaz railway of Palestine and Syria people felt proud to be its inhabitants.

Although my mother would have unreservedly deprecated the people of Tulkarm and all others she regarded as fellahin, most Palestinians in fact had ambivalent feelings towards them. For the fellahin, judged uneducated and backward on the one hand, were also seen as symbols of tenacity, simplicity and steadfastness on the other. They represented continuity and tradition and the essence of what it was to be Palestinian. And people believe that it was these qualities which saved them from disintegration in the refugee camps after 1948 where so many of them were sent and still remain to this day.

In the immediate aftermath of the expulsions from Palestine, they showed themselves steadfast and stoic, especially the women. Having worked hard all their lives in the home and on the land, these women soldiered on in their tents in much the same way. One can see them from time to time on TV screens today in Europe and America, wearing their embroidered caftans and white headscarves, angrily berating Israeli soldiers or demonstrating outside the Israeli prisons where their menfolk are held. Whenever I have seen such scenes, I would remember Fatima and wonder where she ended up and how she died.

For she used to wear just such a caftan, black with a bodice of intricate dark red embroidery. Panels of this embroidery ran down its skirts in parallel lines and rode up its back to form a large colourful rectangle. She tied it round her middle with a broad black silken belt. Her hair was covered by a soft hat tied under her chin with straps, and over the hat she wore a fine white cloth. In winter, she had a long velvet jacket, also embroidered, with a ribbon to tie its lapels together at the top. It was quilted on the inside to keep her warm in the cold Jerusalem winters where it sometimes snowed.

This traditional dress was typical of the villages of Palestine, and each region had its own distinctive embroidery pattern and colours. People could tell at a glance whether a gown was from the Jerusalem area or from Bethlehem or Gaza, since most embroidered caftans were made in these places. Elsewhere, as for example in Tulkarm, the women wore plain dark-coloured gowns without embroidery. Village girls learned young from their mothers how to embroider their dresses according to the set patterns of their village. In the main, they were meant for daily use, but each woman also made a special caftan for her

My uncle Mahmoud, around 1929, and (right) my mother, just before we left for London in 1949

wedding. The stitching here was often remarkably detailed and highly ornamental.

At the time of my childhood in Jerusalem, no woman who was not a peasant would have been seen dead in such a caftan, however beautifully embroidered. Middle-class women like my mother were keen on the latest fashions coming from Europe, as portrayed in Egyptian films. They aped the hairstyles which Egyptian film stars sported, the dresses and the silk stockings they wore. A 1948 photograph of my mother shows her in a two-tone dress with large shoulder pads and wide lapels. Her permed hair is curled back at the forehead in a large roll and her mouth is finely outlined in dark lipstick. Her eyebrows are pencil thin and her eyes are accentuated with black, although this touch may have been added by the photographer later. For my mother, Fatima's caftan was a badge of her peasant identity and as much a part of her as the colour of her eyes. To wear Fatima's clothes would have been as unthinkable as becoming Fatima herself.

No one then could have known that after the loss of Palestine in 1948 this despised peasant costume would become a symbol of the homeland, worn with pride by the very same women who had previously spurned it. In exile, it became obligatory for each Palestinian woman to have her own caftan and to show it off at public functions. "Here, I brought you this," said Jane Willoughby, presenting me with a black embroidered caftan from Ramallah. It had a richly embroidered bodice and red velvet shoulders. This was in 1977 when Ramallah was a part of the occupied West Bank of Jordan. Jane, who was on the council of a British charity caring for refugees, had travelled out to the Occupied Territories, as this part of old Palestine was known. "They told me that every Palestinian girl has to have one of these and that it was the best present I could buy for someone like you," she said.

I wore it often and later found an embroidered jacket with the same patterns and colours which I bought from a Palestinian in Amman. It had been embroidered by his wife and sisters, and he made his living by selling their handiwork from his van. He parked this on the street, draped all over with gaily coloured caftans and embroidered cushion covers, and told me he dreamed of having his own shop one day.

Whereas embroidery had originally been an individual craft, after 1948 a whole new industry grew up employing village women to produce caftans for trade. Much of this work was centred on the refugee camps and helped raise revenue for the women who made the caftans. Later, it was developed to include the production of embroidered cushion covers, table runners, napkins, wall hangings and the like. The range of colours and fabrics has been expanded beyond what was traditional, but the basic patterns remain the same. It has become usual for well-to-do Palestinians who live in Britain or America to display these embroidered cushions and hangings in their lounges and to explain their origins at length to visitors.

After 1967, when the rest of Palestine came under Israeli rule, the embroidery trade increased, spurred on by the renewed feeling of loss amongst Palestinians. Specialists in Palestinian embroidery began to appear on the scene, lectures were given, embroidery books were written, exhibitions were held, and antique or rare caftans were avidly collected. What had started out as a solely peasant custom was now transformed into a precious national heritage.

Fatima, rolling up the sleeves of her caftan to clean our kitchen, had no inkling of course that what she wore would one day have such value. She was fair-skinned with hazel-coloured eyes and her hair was dark, although she usually had it covered up. I think her nose was aquiline and her mouth was full. But her face has a blurred dream-like quality about it because I cannot quite remember it. It was more the sense of her I retain, a kindly patient motherliness. When she came to our house in the mornings and before I was old enough to go to school, I used to follow her around everywhere. I would prattle away at her, telling her all kinds of stories to which she pretended to listen.

When it was lunchtime, usually about two o'clock when my father came home from work, she would lay the table for the family in our dining-room and retire to the kitchen to eat her own lunch. And I would always eat with her, sitting opposite her on a low wooden stool with a plate of food on the floor mat between us. She had a habit of eating the radish leaves which were left behind after the radish heads had been cut off and placed on the family lunch table. And I loved eating them with her; they had a crisp, slightly bitter taste. "You're a funny girl," she would say. "Fancy wanting to eat these poor leaves when you could have proper radishes like the others."

There was no particular reason for me to have had my lunch with Fatima, since no one had excluded me from sitting with the rest of the family. But I wanted to feel that she and I had a special bond, different from her relationship with my sister and my brother. When she lay down in our veranda sometimes to have a sleep in the afternoon, I would sit next to her and talk so as to keep her awake. She was good-natured and never objected but would nod with her eyes closed and I suspect that she often slept through my chatter. But I went on believing that I was very special to her and later, in memory, I appropriated her entirely to myself. But though I was devoted to her, in fact, Fatima cared for all of us equally and probably had no special favourite amongst us. Of course, she also had two daughters of her own, but I used to dismiss them as of no account because I saw her as being exclusively mine.

I hardly remember my mother at this time, I think because she went out so much. Ever since we moved to Qatamon, she had formed a large circle of friends with whom she exchanged daily visits. These were predominantly Christian because Qatamon was a mixed area where many foreigners lived alongside Arab families. We had English people who worked for the Mandate government around us, and also a small number of European Jews. Qatamon at that time was regarded as a desirable residential area where the better-off Palestinians lived. We were not particularly well-off ourselves, as my father had a modest salary which had to cater for our needs as well as those of his mother, brother and unmarried sister who all lived in Tulkarm and were entirely dependent on him. My father had only arrived at his position in the government education department after years of struggle and penury as a schoolteacher. Thus, we were distinctly at the lower end of the scale in terms of wealth, and could not compete with some of the other families who lived there.

Qatamon had wide streets and large detached villas built of sand-coloured Jerusalem stone with green shutters and tiled verandas. Many were surrounded by leafy gardens lavishly planted with fruit trees and flowers. We had five apricot trees in our garden, an almond tree, a plum tree, a pear tree and a lemon tree just under my parents' bedroom window. We also had a vine which bore heavy bunches of oval-shaped green grapes in the late summer. But my sister and I liked to pick them before they ripened when they were hard and sour. We would screw up our eyes in agony while we ate them and our teeth would feel sensitive for hours afterwards, but we still did it. Our neighbour's garden had a climbing rose-tree all over its walls. When the roses bloomed, they were huge and pink and scented and so beautiful that people passing by in the road would pluck them off the bush which annoyed our neighbours immensely.

Our house was similar to the others, stone-built, on one floor and raised above street level by steps which led up to a large veranda in front. Or at least, so it seemed to me because in my child's memory everything was large in comparison to my own small size. Once, many years later, when I tried to draw a picture of our house, all I could come up with was a huge structure with a tall front door and immense veranda with high steps leading up to it, as if it were being viewed from a crouching position. In the years of our absence after 1948, Qatamon underwent much depredation. For a while, it fell into disrepute and was regarded as undesirable and old-fashioned. Poor Jewish families moved in, many of them religious, and even its name was changed to "Gonen". However, in the 1970s, the fashion changed and middle-class Israelis began to find its old Palestinian villas appealing and stylish. House prices soared, and acquiring an old Qatamon house became increasingly difficult.

When we lived there, the fact that many of the people in Qatamon were Christian Palestinians was no accident. The Christian community in Palestine had a tradition of commercial and professional success, going back to the last days of the Ottoman Empire. At that time, various European countries had established their consulates in Jerusalem and had started to introduce foreign influence into Palestine. Soon after, missionaries from Germany, France, Russia and Britain came in the wake of this movement and set up denominational churches and hospitals and schools. Their aim was to convert the population to their own various Christian denominations – we had German Lutherans, Roman Catholics, Presbyterians, Anglicans and other smaller sects. The people of Palestine targeted for these conversions were predominantly Muslim, but even the ten per cent minority of existing, long-established Christians and the three per cent of Jews were not spared the attentions of the missionaries.

"It was a stupid idea and we left them to it," my father said. "Of course, none of the Muslims or Jews converted, so they worked on the Christians amongst us. Most of the old Greek Orthodox guard resisted, but a lot of them changed and became Catholics and Anglicans and I don't know what else."[2] A certain tension grew up between Muslims and Christians after these conversions because the latter drew closer to the European missions and consulates which had adopted them. These in turn favoured such Christian converts over their Muslim compatriots and encouraged them in trade and business. They learned foreign languages and foreign customs and even started to use European first names for their children. Hence it is that one finds such names as Edward, George and Philip, or Margaret, Mary and Patricia amongst Palestinians today.

---

[2] Palestinian Christians traditionally belonged to the Greek Orthodox Church. Until the nineteenth century, and apart from a tiny Catholic community which had survived since the Crusades, all of them were Greek Orthodox.

By the turn of the century, this process had brought forth a new and prosperous class of Palestinian businessmen, entrepreneurs, middlemen and professionals, most of whom were Christians. This lead over the Muslims was maintained under the British Mandate after 1920. People said that it was deliberately promoted by the British authorities as a part of the divide-and-rule policy which they used to keep the Palestinians disunited and unable to resist Jewish migration into the country. "Imagine," my father said, "in the education department where I worked, most of the others were Christians – that is, apart from the Jews whom the British also brought in. And it was the same in every branch of government. How could that have been when Christians were a minority and we Muslims were in the majority?"

None of this, however, impinged on my parents' socialising, especially my mother's. Our immediate next-door neighbours were a Christian family called Jouzeh who were in and out of our house all the time. We also made friends with the Tubbeh family, Christians who lived opposite our house. The head of the family, Abu Michel as he was known, was the *mukhtar* of Qatamon, a post dating from Ottoman times and something akin to a mayor. My mother's other close friends, Emily Saleh and the Wahbeh family, lived several streets away. She and Emily were devoted to each other and we were brought up to play with her children, the youngest of whom, Randa, was the same age as myself. I was also friends with the Wahbeh children, Lily and Nellie. Ziyad's best friend, Hani Sharkas, came from a Muslim family who lived two streets below. His mother, Um Samir, and ours were very close and he had a dark-haired sister called Lamis for whom my brother harboured a secret admiration; to his chagrin, even the poem he wrote her when he was ten failed to provoke any interest.

Though we saw a great deal of these largely Christian families because they lived in the neighbourhood, my mother also had a wide circle of Muslim friends who lived beyond Qatamon, in Sheikh Jarrah, in Baq'a and in the Old City. She socialised with some of the oldest Jerusalem families, the Husseinis, the Nashashibis, the Afifis. There was in Palestine at that time a certain snobbishness with regard to these established families. Each of the major cities had its own upper crust, but the Jerusalem families were considered to be of the highest order.

Their pre-eminence was due partly to wealth and to the ownership of extensive *waqf* property (pious Muslim endowments held in perpetuity for the benefit of the community, which included both land and buildings), but also to their having held high office under the Ottoman administration which ruled Palestine until 1918. In addition, some of them had traditional responsibility for Jerusalem's holy places. For example, the Nusseibeh family had held the keys to the Church of the Holy Sepulchre from the sixteenth century. In the scheme of things, our family, not being from Jerusalem and having little wealth, did not feature amongst the elite. But this did not prevent ordinary social interaction, and my mother was as popular with the wives in these families as she was with our less prestigious neighbours.

Families visited each other in the evenings after supper. Lunch being the main meal, supper was usually light and taken at about seven in the evening, after which people went out or entertained. Socialising and mixing with people was my mother's principal pastime, indeed her main activity in life. Like the other women, she regularly engaged in the practice of what was called the *istiqbal*. This was a women-only reception, held in the afternoon, when the men were out of the house. Once it so happened that my father was at home and sitting reading in the *liwan* (the main reception room) as the women began to arrive. They were quite horrified at seeing him and told my mother so in no uncertain terms, whereupon he took himself off chuckling into his bedroom.

Each woman had a certain day for her *istiqbal*; I think ours took place on Tuesdays. There was a routine to these events. First, we were made to keep out of the way while our mother spent the morning making savouries and sweetmeats. (The best thing about that from our point of view was the wonderful food left over for us to feast on after everyone had gone.) Then, the front room, or salon, to the right of the *liwan* was dusted and swept to be ready for the occasion. There was an air of excitement as the women began to arrive, all dressed up and bejewelled. A great hubbub arose that echoed throughout the house as they greeted and kissed each other. Everyone admired and commented on each other's clothes, which was the main aim of the exercise. At *istiqbals*, no woman adorned herself for men; it was a practice meant only to excite the envy or approbation of other women.

When they had assembled in our salon, the smell of their various perfumes wafted outwards powerfully. I gawped at them through the open door, they looked so glamorous. The talk was all about their households, children and husbands. They exchanged news, gossiped and let off steam. Someone asked if anyone had noticed how one of the Nashashibi women never ate a thing whenever she came to visit. It was a waste of time going to the trouble of making or offering her anything. She would just smile primly and say that she would have loved to, but her appetite was so poor she hardly ever ate.

"I thought there was something fishy about it. I mean you only had to look at her waistline to know it wasn't true." The women were agog, as they all thought that some of the Nashashibis were snooty and condescending. "I was determined to get to the bottom of it. So, I walked in on her just before she was due to visit me one day and least expecting it. And there she was, stuffing her face with cakes and pastries! That's what she does each time she goes out."

"No wonder she had no appetite! Fancy that, trying to make us feel like gluttons," exclaimed the others.

If there was one place where a woman could complain about her husband, it was here. The others usually advised caution and patience, as well they might, since a disaffected wife had few other options in our society. In some of these gatherings, although not in ours, women sang or danced for each other. The ones who were especially good at it were usually egged on by the others to perform. A western eye might have seen something erotic in this, but it was nothing of the sort. It was joyous, uninhibited fun and everyone who could joined in. The dancing they did was that known in the West as belly-dancing, which we all learned as children. No one taught us how to do it, we just picked it up. I used to sway my hips and twist my hands around in rhythm with the music when I could barely walk, and by the age of three or four, I was dancing quite adeptly and entertaining the neighbours. My exhibitionism used to distress my brother who would drag me off the table where I was performing and take me home. "You should see your daughter," he would exclaim to our parents, pushing me angrily towards them, "dancing and singing like a . . . like a . . . " and he would run out of epithets.

Although by the 1940s several women's organisations had come into being in Jerusalem, my mother was never attracted to join, even when friends like Tarab Abdul-Hadi were involved. This woman, whom I was to meet living in exile in Cairo many years later, had been one of the founders of the first women's organisation, the Palestine Arab Women's Congress. This was established in the late 1920s and was political in nature, a remarkable phenomenon for the conservative Arab society of that time.

The women who joined Tarab Abdul-Hadi in setting it up came from those very same notable Jerusalem families with whom my mother mixed, but she found their overt political activism not to her liking. From the start, they made clear that they would protest against the Zionist presence in Palestine and would support their men's national struggle for independence. My mother was uneasy about their bold declaration that they had left the traditional female arena of the home to engage in public life. Shockingly, many of them went on to discard the veil which was then ubiquitous and which my mother also wore. They wrote hundreds of letters and telegrams to anyone they thought might be sympathetic to the Palestinian plight.

But they also had a humanitarian side to their work which my mother did support. They ran a campaign on behalf of the prisoners whom the British authorities had incarcerated for resisting government policy on Jewish immigration into the country. They entreated

One of the Jerusalem women's organisations active during the 1930s (reproduced courtesy of the Palestinian Academic Society for the Study of International Affairs)

the British High Commissioner to reduce or commute harsh sentences and they collected money, clothing and food for prisoners' families who had been impoverished by the loss of their breadwinners. Some of them even sold their jewellery to raise money for their work. In 1938, they sent representatives to the Eastern Women's Conference in Cairo to defend Palestine. This had drawn women from the Arab countries and also from Iran, and demanded an end to British rule in Palestine, a prohibition on Jewish immigration and land sales to Jews. "Good for them!" my mother said approvingly at the time. "If you ask me, they're better than the men."

Towards the end of the 1930s, the Arab Women's Congress split into a political and a social branch. The latter proved more appealing to ordinary women and, in the early 1940s, my cousin Aziza, who was then married to Zuhair and living in Jerusalem, joined the social branch. Soon, this association developed branches in other Palestinian cities, including Tulkarm, and Aziza was able to continue her membership when she went back there. She never tried to interest my mother in joining. She was content to socialise in a more informal way.

Socialising came naturally to my mother, as she was talkative and vivacious and in her element when telling stories and anecdotes. Had she been born in another society and at another time I think she could have become a professional comedienne. As it was, her audience consisted of our friends and us. My father's one form of relaxation was listening to her gossip about our neighbours or people we knew. He would pretend to be reading his book while she talked. But if she stopped her narrative for a moment, he would look up and say, "Yes? What happened next?"

Those early years of the 1940s were probably the best of her whole life. The general troubles besetting Palestine had calmed after I was born and did not resurface to affect our area until after 1945. In that brief period, my mother could enjoy her comfortable social position attained after many years of hardship with my father's straitened circumstances and struggling career. He was now set to rise in his job and could look to a better salary. With her maid and her gardener and all her friends about her, she felt contented, and the last thing in the world she wanted was for it all to come to an end.

The fact that men and women mixed freely in our area on social occasions was by no means the norm for the rest of Jerusalem. Society was predominantly Muslim and conservative, and men and women did not meet socially. Indeed, many women in the Old City wore the veil and, unlike my parents, people performed all the Islamic rituals of daily prayer and going to the mosque on Fridays. This was in keeping with the traditional life of Jerusalem which had always been viewed by Palestinians as a holy Islamic city and a great religious centre. During the major part of Ottoman rule it was even something of a backwater to which only pilgrims and religious scholars went, many of them hoping to die there. "I suppose in those days, you could best describe it as a large village with a religious atmosphere," said my father. Jerusalem only began to change in the nineteenth century when the Christian missions established themselves there. In just fifty years, they built over a hundred churches, schools, hospitals and other institutions. From 1900 onwards, European Jews came to join the rest of the new arrivals and establish their own institutions. Twenty years later, the British made Jerusalem what it had never been, the seat of government and the de facto capital of Palestine. As a result, it became the most important city in the whole country.

The change in Jerusalem's character which ensued was not uniform throughout the city, but occurred in patches, reflecting the pattern of foreign and immigrant settlement. The Old City and its environs remained Muslim, but newly built suburbs like our own had a more mixed population, including a number of Jews who had come to live

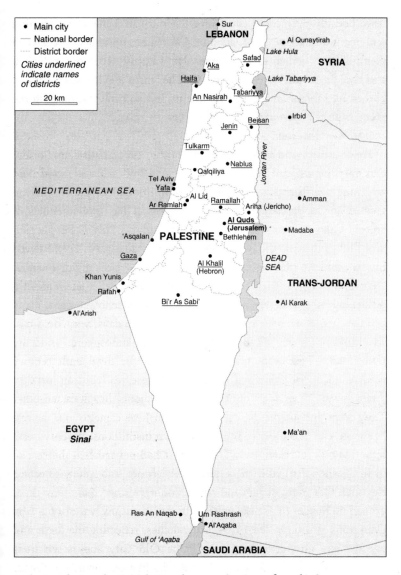

Palestine during the British Mandate, at the time of my birth

there because they could not afford the rents in Rehavia, the Jewish settlement directly next to Qatamon. Otherwise, Jews usually confined themselves to certain areas in Jerusalem like the Hebrew University complex on Mount Scopus, or the part behind the King David Hotel known as Montefiore (after the British Jewish philanthropist Moses Montefiore who founded it), and the Jewish quarters in the Old City and at Mea Shearim.

Mea Shearim was an odd orthodox Jewish enclave very near to the Old City, established in the early 1900s and full of black-coated men with long beards and ringlets for sideboards. Some of them wore what seemed to us outlandish round fur-trimmed hats and knee-length breeches and formed a bizarre sight amongst the Arabs. People said they looked dusty and unwashed. They were immigrants from Eastern Europe, and we often wondered how they could bear going about in their heavy clothes during Jerusalem's hot summers. There was little residential mixing between Jews and Arabs, but in commercial areas like the Jaffa Road people mingled, usually without friction. "In fact," chuckled my father, "all the young Arab men liked to go down to the Jaffa Road to look at the Jewish girls. They found them attractive and used to whistle at them and try and chat them up." But my mother disapproved. "Yes and you know why. Because they were all easy. They were anybody's."

By the end of the 1930s, Jerusalem had acquired a cinema, cafes and something of a social life. The Zion Cinema (which was Jewish-owned) was also used as a stage for shows and plays. Visiting Egyptian film stars, singers and comedians performed there to packed, excited audiences of Jerusalemites who felt themselves part of a new glamorous world. In the 1940s, several other cinemas appeared, and one day my mother took us with her and the neighbours and their children to see a film. It was showing at the Rex Cinema, which was Arab-owned, and soon displaced the Jewish cinemas for Arab audiences. I must have been no more than four years old at the time. We saw the film *Frankenstein* with Boris Karloff, now considered a cinema classic, but then something of which my mother knew little except that it was foreign (she was used to seeing only Egyptian films). The effect on me was quite horrific and long-lasting. I had nightmares for months afterwards, not helped by my brother's Frankenstein impersonations. We would sit in the deep window seat of the *liwan* and he would pull down the shutters to make everything go dark. And then he would invent stories on the Frankenstein theme to make me scream.

The YMCA of Jerusalem opposite the King David Hotel also had an auditorium for concerts and lectures. Young people loved to go there because it offered a variety of entertainments. It had tennis and squash courts, a large swimming pool, a library and a cafeteria. Not the least of its attractions was that it provided a venue for young men and women to meet. This of course was nothing like the sort of mixing between the sexes to be found in Europe and was based much more on people meeting together in families, but nevertheless it enabled the sons and daughters to see and talk to each other. These were predominantly Christians, who also had other opportunities of meeting each other at picnics and gatherings organised by the various Christian churches to which they belonged. Social custom amongst Muslims did not encourage such activities, but many Muslim men and the more modern amongst the Muslim families also used the YMCA. Our cousins Zuhair and Iyyas, who normally lived in Tulkarm but came and stayed in Jerusalem with us frequently, used to take the three of us to see plays there, but Ziyad and I were too young to join in the sports and other activities.

The most popular cafes in Jerusalem were Jewish-owned. "They had tables on the pavements and some of them had a real Viennese atmosphere," Leila Mantoura, a Christian Palestinian friend, told me. "You could eat the most delicious chocolate cake there." Iyyas sometimes took Ziyad to such cafes on the Jaffa Road. They had ice-cream and sat outside, watching people go by. This was a new feature in Jerusalem's life imported by the European Jewish immigrants. The traditional Arab coffee-house, a feature of every city in Palestine and indeed every city in the Arab world, was of course a place where only men went to talk, play backgammon and smoke a narghile (or hookah).

Our father used to take us out to a Jewish European place in Baq'a which served ice-cream. When we walked back and it was dark, we could see the sky lit up with a brilliant patchwork of stars. Our father would then give us a small lesson in astronomy, telling us the names of the stars and the constellations. One day, while scraping the bottom of the ice-cream bowl in his eagerness to get at the last mouthful, Ziyad dropped the bowl onto the floor and it broke. As our father was about to tell him off, the owner, who was a Hungarian Jew, held up his hand and hurried over. "Never mind, never mind," he said, bending down to sweep up the mess. "If all our worries were so small, what a good world it would be!"

Families often went to the new garden cafes outside Jerusalem, in Ramallah and around the village of Beit Jala. We went for outings to the Grand Hotel in Ramallah, except that everybody still called it the Odeh Hotel after the name of its owner. It had a large garden res-taurant with shady pine trees where they served charcoal-grilled meat, tasty salads, olives and freshly baked bread. But well-to-do Palesti-nians still preferred to go to Jaffa for picnics, to swim and saunter about. This had traditionally been Palestine's major city, where the best families lived, where the first Palestinian newspapers were established, and where the intelligentsia met. "The bride of the sea," people called it; "bride" in Arabic is used to denote a thing of great beauty.

Jaffa had wide roads, big houses, picturesque views over the Mediterranean and a lively, busy harbour. It was a place for fun, for business and, as Palestine's major port, for travel. Before Jerusalem livened up, people went there to get away from its fusty religious atmosphere. Whenever my father went to Jaffa to work at the Near East Broadcasting Station established by the British, he would take Siham and Ziyad along with him. As soon as they saw the sea, they would beg to go swimming and then my father would leave them trustingly in the care of one of the men who looked after the beach.

Jaffa also drew Jews from nearby Tel Aviv who went there because the food was cheaper and better than any they could get in their own European restaurants. From the 1930s onwards, they had taken a special shine to two of our most prosaic national dishes, falafel and hoummos. These were easy to make, cost little and were generally eaten as snacks. Most neighbourhoods had a local falafel shop where you got them hot and freshly cooked. For many of the poor people, they were often the main staple foods, along with bread and olives. The Jews who came to Palestine in the late 1920s and early 1930s were often so impoverished that they used to come into the restaurants where people were eating and beg for money and food. They soon discovered the cheap, yet nutritious Arab foods, and learned to make falafel themselves. However, they never tasted as good as the original and they still came to the Arab restaurants to eat. Many years later when visiting Israel, I was told, to my astonishment and irritation, that falafel, hoummos and some others of our recipes were regarded as authentic "Israeli dishes", and few people seemed to have any idea of their real origin.

There was an active intellectual side to life in Jerusalem. Prominent Palestinians and visitors from other Arab countries gave public lectures and poetry readings. I remember my father talking about the poetry evenings at the Arab Orthodox Club in Baq'a where my uncle Abu Salma and his fellow poet Ibrahim Tuqan read their nationalist verses. This kind of poetry was new to Palestine, since it concerned itself with political subjects and expressed opposition and resistance to what was happening in the country with a passion which drew enormous sympathy from the audience.

His nationalist fervour landed Abu Salma in trouble. At a time when he was employed as a teacher by the department of education (my father's same employer), he published a poem called "Jabal al-Mukabbir" – the name of the hill just outside Jerusalem which was famous in Arabic history for being the place from which Jerusalem's great conqueror, Umar ibn al-Khattab, surveyed the city for the first time in 638. On seeing it, the Muslim troops cried out, "Allahu akbar!" from which it thereafter acquired its name.[3] In the 1930s, it was the site of the British High Commissioner's house. Using a mixture of allegory and symbol, the poem vowed that no Palestinian would rest until he had brought the British citadel of power in Palestine crashing down. The literary and historical allusions which aimed to disguise the verses' real intent did not fool the authorities, and my uncle was dismissed from his government job forthwith. But Abu Salma's literary reputation was not harmed by this. Far from it; he gained respect and admiration for what people saw as his patriotic stand against British colonial rule and Zionist infiltration. My father was never invited to give a lecture himself at the Orthodox Club, but his close friend Khalil Sakakini, who was a neighbour of ours in Qatamon and a well-known Palestinian intellectual, was a frequent speaker there. Such people also travelled to literary clubs in Jaffa, Haifa, Nablus and Gaza.

As Jerusalem's general character changed, so in particular did our part of it too. Whereas it had at one time been a predominantly Arab

---

[3] Jabal al-Mukabbir literally means the mount which proclaims Allah *kabir*, great.

neighbourhood, Qatamon was becoming increasingly settled by Europeans, many of them Jewish. In our street alone, there was a German Jewish doctor and two other foreign families – one White Russian and one Jewish. The latter were called Kramer and had come from Eastern Europe; we did not know exactly where, but Mrs Kramer was Scottish. They had two children, David and Aviva, who were closest to my sister in age. Their parents spoke to them in Hebrew, but they had learned English from their mother and the father also spoke Arabic. He was a soldier in the Haganah, the underground Jewish army in Palestine which, though supposed to be illegal, was in fact semi-officially recognised by the authorities, and which the Palestinians regarded as nothing less than a branch of the British army. After all, the British trained, armed and paid for them, people said. Siham became friendly with Aviva and her brother David who was quite cheeky and used to tease the Palestinian girls, especially the daughters of the Farraj family who lived directly opposite.

"I don't remember any feelings of animosity towards Jewish people," Siham said. "Once when I was a girl guide, we decided to invite the Jewish girl guides to our school. They spent the day with us and then invited us back to their school, which was all-Jewish. They were friendly and we all got on quite well. We knew they were different from 'our Jews', I mean the Arab Jews. We thought of them more as foreigners from Europe than Jews as such." (By "Arab Jews" she meant the small Jewish community who had lived in Palestine for centuries and who spoke Arabic and were physically indistinguishable from Arabs. Before the start of European Jewish immigration to Palestine in 1880, they numbered some 3,000 people out of a total population of 350,000.) "I don't know that anyone thought much about why they'd come to Palestine in the first place. They were just visitors like so many other people in Jerusalem and we accepted them."

Many of the Jewish immigrants who came to Palestine in the 1930s were Germans fleeing from Nazism and included a number of doctors, like the man who lived at the end of our street. Local people were soon impressed with their standard of medical practice, even though the Mandate administration had provided a range of medical services for the population. Despite this, people sometimes consulted the German Jewish doctors without demur. My father took Ziyad to see a German doctor in Rehavia, the new Jewish settlement to the West of Qatamon. "He was really good and Ziyad got better," my father reminisced. "The German Jews were a class apart. They kept to themselves and looked down on all the other Jews as inferior."

The German Jewish doctor in our road often went out of his way to speak to us and to the other Arab families. He said he wanted to live peacefully with the Arabs and he knew many other Jews who felt the same. But the Jewish leadership wouldn't let them, he said, they had other plans. "Many of them were afraid of their leaders," my father said. "I actually felt sorry for them. I can remember a German Jew called Roth who worked with us at the education department, coming to see me and after making me promise that I would tell no one what he said, asking how he could convert to Islam. He never explained why, but this was 1941 just after Rommel's success in North Africa, and I suppose he was thinking, as we all were, that the Germans would win. And if they reached Palestine, then the Jews would be in danger, and so he was better off being counted amongst the Muslims. I could understand how he felt."

At about this time, two other Jews, Leon Blum and Shlomo Goitein,[4] who worked in the education department with my father, invited him to one of their meetings. The Jews in the department were responsible for Jewish education in the country and, astonishingly,

<hr>

[4] This was the same S.D. Goitein who was later to edit and translate the famous Geniza collection of manuscripts held at Cambridge University Library. His work was subsequently published in the three-volume book entitled *A Mediterranean Society*.

they had a standing at least equal with that of any Palestinian and often higher. "How could this have happened when they were only a minority amongst us?" demanded Salim Kattul angrily. He was a school teacher and friend of my father. Goitein's knowledge of Arabic was so good that he once corrected an Arabic draft of a report which my father had been writing. He and Blum belonged to a small organisation called Brit Shalom, established in Palestine in the 1920s. This had a membership of European Jews dedicated to coexistence with the Arabs. "Didn't you mind going?" I asked my father years later. "Not at all", he answered. "In fact I went to address them twice. There were about twenty-five to thirty people each time and I found them pleasant and friendly. They were not like the hard-line, aggressive Jews who wanted to pretend that we did not exist. I thought that at least they were trying to find a solution to the problems which were being created between us and them in Palestine."

We remained friends with the Kramers until the end of 1947. One evening, in November of that year, Kramer came to see my father at our house. "Mr Karmi," he said in Arabic, "I have come to tell you at some risk to myself to take your family and leave Jerusalem as soon as possible. Go to Tulkarm while you still have time, it will be better for you. Please believe me, it is not safe here." Life in Jerusalem had by then become turbulent. There were armed incidents virtually every day. But no one believed it could get much worse and no one contemplated moving. My father thanked him for his advice and tried to pump him for more information. But Kramer would say nothing else and shortly after took his leave. My father shrugged his shoulders and ignored the whole incident. Why should he have believed him, seeing that Kramer was working for the other side? But I wondered, years afterwards, if my father looked back on that conversation as we were leaving in panic and haste and remembered Kramer's prophetic words.

My father met many English people at his work. One of these was a

man called Clayton who lived near us in Qatamon, and whose son
Philip we were friendly with. Philip was an amiable boy of seventeen
who attended the school established by the government for English
children, but kept failing his exams at school because he was poor at
mathematics. Since my father taught mathematics at the school, beside
his duties as an education inspector, Philip used to come to see him for
private coaching. I liked it when Philip came round because he had a
dog called Peter which was frisky and affectionate. Philip always used
to bring presents for us with him, but whether this was in lieu of
payment for my father's help or not, I never found out.

One day, he brought me a toy dog and then a big teddy bear which
I named Peter, but because I could not pronounce the "p", as the
letter does not exist in Arabic, I used to say, "Beta". This Beta slept in
my bed, sat up with me in the morning, got dressed with me – he had
a pair of blue pants which Fatima made – and even sometimes had a
wash. I kept him right up to the time we left Jerusalem, bedraggled by
then, with one of his yellow bead eyes missing. Eventually, Philip
stopped bringing toys and gave us a real dog. This was a saluki, a
skinny hound which Arabs use for hunting, and we called him
Snooky. We loved him but he did not last long with us, for he
disappeared one day. Whether he was run over or taken in by the
British authorities, which was a common fate for dogs assumed to be
strays and hence a potential source of rabies, we never knew.

Heart-broken as we were, it was not long before we acquired
another dog. This one was a mongrel, half saluki and half spaniel. He
was short-haired and tawny-brown in colour. Ziyad found him
roaming about in the street, apparently without an owner, and
immediately befriended him. In no time, he became a well-loved
member of the family except for my mother who never liked dogs.
She refused to let him come into the house and would chase him out
with the broom if he ever tried to, which was why he ran off as soon

as he even saw the broom handle. My father chose an English name for him, Rex, since an Arabic name would have seemed odd in a society where it was not customary for Arabs to rear dogs.

Rex had a habit of following my sister to school, and when she shooed him away he would make as if to go and disappear from view long enough to fool her into thinking he had really gone home. But when she came out at lunchtime she would find him on the school steps waiting for her. "I couldn't tell him off," she said. "He had a way of looking at you pathetically and swallowing hard, and so I ended up patting and hugging him instead and telling him feebly not to do it again."

Once, he followed my father going to work on the bus. As my father climbed on he could hear cries of consternation from the passengers because, much as we might have liked dogs, the majority of Palestinians did not. They regarded them as unclean, and if they needed to use any as guard dogs they kept them in a shed well away from the house. The commonest expletives in Arabic all refer to dogs or to sons of dogs; to call someone a dog is to imply that he is a bastard or to indicate that he has no pride or dignity, as in the old English use of "cur". So my father, seeing people's reactions, turned round to find Rex close on his heels. He had to get off the bus and take him back to the house, telling Fatima that the garden gate must be closed at all times to keep the dog in. In fact, he did not need to say that for we were all afraid that what befell Snooky would happen to Rex. So we were all assiduous at keeping him from running out into the street. But he was smart and had ways of slinking out when no one was looking.

Ziyad loved him dearly and used to play with him for hours in the garden. Many years later, and living in a country far away from Palestine, he acquired a dog. It was a large labrador and nothing like our dog in Jerusalem except for his tawny colour. But my brother chose to call him Rex.

Two

It seems incredible that in the Palestine of the 1940s we could have had anything like a normal life. But the fact was that for several years our particular part of Jerusalem remained immune from the revolt erupting in every Palestinian city. We lived in a sort of fool's paradise. After my parents moved to Qatamon, in 1938, there was no further harassment against my father from the Arab factions who had been so threatening before, and the British army searches and interrogations also ceased. "The worst time was the General Strike," my mother said later. "We didn't think there could be anything as bad as that again. It all died down after Ghada was born and we thought the worst was over." The General Strike clouded my sister's early childhood and gave an unhappy backdrop to her life. She was only four when it began in April 1936. "Of course I didn't understand what it was all about," she said , "but father said it was because people had begun to see what was happening and they felt a terrible sense of betrayal."

At that time, our parents lived in a rented house in Wadi al-Joz, just outside the Old City. My mother was expecting my brother Ziyad who was due to be delivered in hospital. However, because of the General Strike, a total curfew was imposed by the British authorities which meant that people could not leave their houses. So, in August of that year, Ziyad was born at home with only the local midwife in attendance.

"I wanted to stay with mother, but the neighbours came into our house to help and they pushed me out," said Siham. "They only let me back in when the baby was born and already being washed in a basin." Our father was reading in the sitting room and the midwife went to give him the good news that he had a son, an important event for Arab families, and stood around waiting to be tipped, as if it had all been her own doing. "But father paid her her fee without giving her a tip and told her to go." Ziyad's birth was the only exciting event of that time. Because of the Strike, shops and offices were closed, and children could not go to school. "It was so boring," said Siham. "When the curfew was on, we couldn't go out to play and no one could come to visit. The only excitement we had was when we were sent out to get things from the shops opposite Bab al-Sahira [Herod's Gate in the Old City]. We used to have a lookout kid with us to make sure there were no army jeeps or cars around, and when he said the coast was clear, we all went to the shops. They had grilles on them to look closed, but there were people inside and they sold us things."

"Sometimes, the kids threw nails or sharp stones on the ground to puncture the wheels of the British army cars and the police. And if they were spotted, the soldiers came after them with sticks. We particularly had it in for the lorries of the Potassium Company. It was owned by foreign Jews, Germans I think, and the lorries had permission to go around even though no one else did. The drivers were Jews as well and one day the kids threw a lot of nails in our road, just as the lorry was coming. It stopped and the driver began to shout at

the kids. Mother ran out and started to pull them away off the road."
Later, describing the occasion, she shuddered slightly. "It was quite
frightening really if you think about it, but at the time it also seemed
like fun." After six months of this, the Strike ended and Siham went
back to school. It was called al-Ma'mouniyya al-Jadida at Wadi al-
Joz, the school I would also eventually attend. But though, to
everyone's relief, the strikes and curfews were over, the basic conflict
was not resolved.

The pro-Husseini and pro-Nashashibi parties leading Palestinian
opposition to the widely feared takeover of the country by European
Jews were even more at loggerheads than before. And now they
began to attack each other more and more viciously, with uninvolved
or apolitical people like my father increasingly caught in the crossfire.
Unlike my uncles, he had never been a member of a political party or
a political activist at any time. Of course, he cared passionately about
what was happening and, like most other Palestinian men, spent much
time discussing the political situation.

"Let's leave the men to their politics," my mother would say when
people came to visit, and the wives would all sit together and talk
about other things. When we went to live in England after 1949 this
practice continued amongst the men but, if anything, with greater
intensity. As in Jerusalem before, all that I learned about Palestine in
those days was picked up from the conversations which took place at
home between my father and our Arab friends. My mother might send
me with the coffee tray into the lounge where they sat, and it was then
that I would hear snatches of conversation. Brought up to believe that
political discussion was men's natural activity, I was amazed to find
that in English society of the 1950s hardly anyone mentioned politics
at all. In fact, I learned that it was considered bad taste, like talking
about religion or one's voting intentions at the next election. What a
difference, I thought to myself, between this country and my own. It

never occurred to me that societies not torn apart by conflict, as mine had been, did not have the same incentive to care about politics.

Despite my father's interest in politics, he preferred reading and scholarship to anything else and was mainly concerned with furthering his career. And indeed, at about the time of the General Strike, he was promoted to inspector of education and could leave behind his lowly job as a schoolteacher of mathematics and English in Jerusalem. In the next year, 1937, he was sent to London by the Mandate government on a six-month training course in education. He could not leave my mother and the children without ensuring that she either join his family in Tulkarm or her family come to stay with her in Jerusalem. Women in our society were not normally left to live on their own; they always had to have a male guardian, father at first and then husband. In the absence of either, their brothers or brothers-in-law were responsible for them. When my father came to leave for England, my uncle Mahmoud, who was the eldest in the family and therefore had the greatest say, pronounced that my mother would have to go and stay with our grandmother in Tulkarm. By the normal standards of the time, a woman in this situation would have had to comply, since women had little power to affect their own lives. But my mother was different because my father, although brought up in a conservative household, had a liberal outlook. From the beginning of their marriage he had allowed my mother to run the home freely and, what was most unusual, to have money of her own to spend. As a result, she had acquired the habit of independence and refused to move to Tulkarm. Because of the curfews, the family could not come to Jerusalem to stay with her, which would have been the alternative in normal times. So she managed with help from the neighbours.

"What a terrible time we had," she said, "what with the *tatwiq* and the armed men and everyone protesting about the Jews coming in. It was only when we moved to Qatamon that we began to feel normal again."

In the winter of 1938 the family moved into a rented house in Qatamon. The landlady was a woman called Um Jabra whose son had married a Polish Jewish immigrant. Marriages between Arab men and Jewish women (but not the other way around) had become increasingly common with the advent of European Jews into the country. In cases where the husbands were Muslim the women often converted to Islam, but the couple was then in danger of reprisals by the wife's family and the wider Jewish community. After 1940, and the increase in tension between the two sides, the Arabs also began to disown these unions, and the couples either escaped or went into hiding. My mother didn't much care about Um Jabra's son and she didn't like the house either, so they moved again after a year into our last Qatamon house, the one which we occupied until the end. And here at last my mother could build a family life for the first time since she had married in relative prosperity and free from disruption.

She was an enthusiastic home-maker and wanted a well-furnished home, generously stocked with staple foods, as was the prevailing custom, and having all the necessary facilities for entertaining. My mother kept her stock of provisions in what might be called a loft. This was a large open shelf built into the space below the kitchen ceiling and usually reached with a ladder. Here my mother kept sackfuls of rice, flour and *burghul* (ground wheat). Huge jars of olive oil and olives stood against the wall. Smaller jars held lentils and chickpeas and dried pulses. She stocked salt and *samn* (clarified butter for cooking), soap and candles. She also made different kinds of jam and pickles, and during the summer she dried vegetables like *bamia* (okra) and *mulukhiyya* (a spinach-like leaf vegetable) against the winter. To see our food stores, one might have thought she was catering for an army. But her obsession with stockpiling only led in the end to all that food falling into the hands of the Jewish family which took over our house, whoever they were. "My God, they must have had food to last them for a year," my mother said. "And when I think that I left them all my best blankets as well. I took some old ones with holes in them because I didn't think we would stay away for long in Damascus." Nevertheless, hoarding was a habit she never lost. In England, with shops on her doorstep to go to every day if she wished, she still stocked up supplies as if everything were about to run out.

Our house was ideally suited for entertaining. The front door opened directly into our *liwan*, a spacious square room with two large windows on either side of the door. It opened through double doors at the back onto the rest of the house. My mother mainly enjoyed the fact that it could hold a large number of people and was roomy enough for the women to sit well apart from the men. Not that there was any formal segregation, merely that men and women automatically sought the company of their own sex. This was considered natural because each had similar interests which were not shared with the other. On either side were two rooms: the first acted as the main sitting room where people were entertained on formal occasions – what might be called the parlour in England. It was also the place where the men sat when they came to visit my father, and at other times the women who came separately to see my mother. The second was my parents' bedroom. At the back of the villa was our bedroom, the family dining room, kitchen and bathroom. A corridor which separated the *liwan* from the bedrooms opened onto the garden from the side of the house. The three of us shared a bedroom, but I don't remember feeling crowded; the two beds in which my brother and I slept stood against the wall on opposite sides of the room and my sister's bed was in between. Two large windows opened onto the back garden. The floor was tiled throughout, but in winter my mother put rugs down to keep the house warm; in spring they were removed, beaten, washed and folded away.

On summer nights, people sat out on the veranda, where it was cooler than staying indoors. My father used to say that the Jerusalem climate was the best in the world. "We had proper seasons, a cool autumn, a cold winter, a warm rainy spring and a hot dry summer. And even at the height of summer, it always cooled down at night, so much so it could actually get cold." When we went to live in London, his chief complaint was that there were no seasons in England. "It seems to be about the same the whole year round," he would say. "Or maybe there are two seasons here, cold and less cold." When I close my eyes and think of that time in Jerusalem, I can feel the still summer afternoons when the adults were sleeping and the heat of the day lay heavy on the empty streets and the quiet houses. After lunch, when I played in the garden with Leila and Najwa, my friends from nearby, one could almost touch the warm stillness.

Our mother had a daily routine which was enforced rigidly on the household. In the mornings she did the cooking, with Fatima helping. This meant that Fatima washed the meat, crushed the garlic, peeled the vegetables, washed and strained the rice and got everything ready so that when my mother entered the kitchen, all she did, master-chef-like, was to put the ingredients together in her uniquely magical way. And indeed she was a good cook. She brought to Palestinian cuisine a special quality from her Syrian background. This expressed itself in a general increase in the use of clarified butter and garlic and in richer flavours which produced delicious results. Her stuffed vine-leaves were legendary; she rolled them up into small neat rows on top of a layer of lamb, mint and tomatoes and cooked them slowly until their varied flavours mingled and they melted in the mouth.

However, alone amongst us, our father never ceased complaining about these dishes. For years, he blamed his various abdominal symptoms on her fatty cooking. But as far as I know, it never deterred him from refusing a single mouthful. At mealtimes, it was always the same with him. After eating heartily what she had prepared, he would begin to frown and mutter and pull at his trouser belt, grumbling that he was overfull and distended and would my mother stop using so much *samn* and oil. But she never took any notice and he never stopped eating. We became so used to the rich flavour of her cooking that all other foods seemed bland and boring by contrast.

Sometimes she made bread which we loved because it was hot and tasty as it came out of the oven. Previously, each household made its own bread, since there were no municipal bakeries. The women would prepare the dough and then take it for baking to the public ovens which were present in every neighbourhood. But by the time we lived in Qatamon, things had changed, and we had a baker who came to the door every day with freshly baked bread.

When she had finished cooking, my mother would leave Fatima to clear up and go out to have coffee with her friends. She returned home just in time for lunch, Fatima having laid the table. After lunch in the summer, she and my father had their siesta which lasted until about six o'clock. When they woke up they drank strong sweet coffee, after which my father would usually sit at his desk in the *liwan* reading. It was at this time and into the evening that, if they were not going out or receiving visitors, we got a chance to talk to our father. I was very attached to him and considered myself to be his favourite. Just as I believed that Fatima was there exclusively to look after me, so it was with my father who I thought loved me the best. He was certainly indulgent and patient and often put me on his knee and kissed me. I would tell him what I had been doing that day and bask in his apparent interest in my prattle, even though I noticed that he went on reading his book while I was talking. In some ways we all felt closer to him than we did to our mother because she often went out in the evenings while he stayed at home quietly reading. When she came back, she made sure that we went to bed early, having first washed our feet. This was a strict rule which was never to be explained or disobeyed.

It was partly to get away from her rigid discipline that we loved to go to Tulkarm to see our family. This happened principally on the occasion of the two Eids, the major Muslim festivals. These trips were thrilling from beginning to end because they started with an exciting journey on the train which took us from Jerusalem to Tulkarm, all dressed up in our new Eid clothes. Once arrived, we were met by a variety of uncles and cousins at the station who walked or carried us to our grandfather's house. He had died in 1935, leaving our grandmother, our uncle Hussein (who was my father's twin) and his family, and our unmarried aunt Zubeida, all living in the house. It was crowded but we never minded because it was so different from the relative solitude of our own house in Jerusalem.

Although our relatives were always coming to stay with us, sometimes for weeks or even months (much to my mother's annoyance), it was not the same. The houses in Tulkarm were nothing like those in Jerusalem. They were domed and made of grey mud-bricks. The streets were really alleyways that ran between the houses, and where goats, hens and donkeys often roamed. This was not surprising, since Tulkarm was in the midst of a heavily agricultural area and its people were almost all engaged in farming.

Because there was little room at our grandmother's, we children stayed at our aunt Souad's house. This had a flat roof and when it was summer and very hot, our greatest pleasure was to sleep on the roof. Ziyad and I fought hard to be allowed to do this, since there was not enough room for everyone. It was cool on the roof at night and one could lie down and look at the stars shining in the clear sky and smell the jasmine tree which grew against the wall. We chattered and told stories to our cousins until, tired out, one by one, we fell asleep. Our family was so large and our aunts, uncles and cousins so numerous that there was a seemingly inexhaustible supply of playmates. And most important of all, our mother could not make us wash our feet or sleep early or perform any of the other rituals we had to observe at home.

When I was nearly six, I started to go to school. This was in September 1945, at about the same time that my father left for England once more. He would be going to London for another training course and was to stay away longer on this occasion, until the next summer. We did not mind so much when he said he would come back with wonderful English presents for us, and I was in any case too excited about going to school for the first time to think of much else. My school was the same al-Ma'mouniyya which my sister already attended. We would wake up at seven in the morning while our mother was still asleep and make a packed lunch to take with us. Ziyad went to the Umariyya school by the bus station, not far from the King David Hotel. Siham and I had to take two buses to reach our school, first a number 4 to the Old City and then a number 33 to Sheikh Jarrah.

School started at eight and ended at half past three, and as I came out before Siham did, I would wait for her at the school gate and then we would take our two buses back home. Unknown to us then, this process would repeat itself in London, both of us going to the same school, leaving our mother in bed in the morning and returning home together for lunch. I liked my school in Jerusalem where we played more than we did anything else. Our teachers were all young, except for Miss Zuleikha. She was an elderly, forbidding lady who waved her arms around when she got cross which made the loose folds of skin on her upper arms sway back and forth most alarmingly.

I loved it when my sister and I came back home in the afternoons. On days when Fatima wasn't there, Siham would wash the floor of the sitting room while our parents were sleeping. I am not sure why she

My mother, Siham, Ziyad and I in our Qatamon house and (right) with my classmates at al-Ma'mouniyya school, around 1946

did this; perhaps my mother, who was not fond of housework, asked her to. While she cleaned the floor, she often taught me how to do simple sums and how to read. I recited back what she taught me and got to be so proficient that they let me skip a class at school. Some twenty years later in London, when I was studying for my specialist medical exams, I remember revising out loud to her as she sat sewing in the bedroom at home. I knew she could not understand my subject, but reading it to her was evocative of that time and somehow comforting and familiar.

I suppose Siham acted like a little mother to me during my childhood, and I loved her devotedly in return, second only to Fatima. It was a role she would assume even more after we left Jerusalem

because, being the eldest, she took responsibility for me and Ziyad. This was not an uncommon arrangement in Arab families in that the eldest children were expected to look after their younger siblings. Presumably, it originated in the fact that people had large families where the mothers could not have coped without some such arrangement. The burden usually fell on the eldest daughter who became her mother's deputy in the family. My father for example, being one of thirteen children, was brought up by his elder sister, my aunt Souad.

From the age of five, when Ziyad was born, Siham had had to help look after him. And when I was born, she was eight and she started to look after both of us. This remained her role for all of my childhood and adolescence and I often wondered whether she herself had had much of a childhood.

I suppose that the illusion of tranquillity we lived under during those final years abruptly came to an end in the summer of 1946. It was not that nothing at all was happening until then, but rather that it had seemed remote from our part of Jerusalem. Not only that, but the Jewish "terrorists", as the British called them, were more engaged at that stage in fighting the British authorities than the Arab population. The Jewish forces in Palestine consisted of the Haganah, the underground army, and the dissident Jewish groups – most notably the Irgun Zvei Leumi and the Lehi (better known as the Stern Gang). These last two organisations were known in Palestine as the terrorists and were responsible for a spectacular campaign of violence against anyone who stood in the way of their aims. (It is ironic to think that the term "terrorist", which has now become virtually synonymous with Arabs, especially Muslims, started life as an appellation for Jewish groups in Palestine.) Despite the illegal character of the Irgun and Stern groups, the Haganah participated in a number of their operations, although it was always careful to disown them afterwards. To many Arabs, however, all the Jewish forces in the country were tarred with the same brush and they did not often distinguish the one from the other.

From the beginning of the year, the terrorists had been attacking British military jeeps and trucks with bombs and flame-throwers. Many roads used by the army were mined, British buildings and installations were bombed, and the bridges over the Jordan river were blown up. My father wrote from London that none of this had gone unnoticed in England. "It's very strange," he said in a letter to my mother, "I feel sometimes as if I were still in Palestine because people here talk about the events just as we do. I went into a pub yesterday (which is like a coffee-house, I'll explain to you when I get back), and ordinary people were saying that it was time to pull the army out of Palestine. They said it wasn't fair because the Jews were killing British soldiers. And the British newspapers are full of it as well. Nearly every day, there is some story about Palestine."

One day in March, Jewish terrorists held up a military train carrying British soldiers' pay and seized £30,000. "I can't understand these Jews," said Khalil Sakakini to my father when he returned from London. "You should have seen what they've been up to, fighting the very people who let them come into the country and gave them ideas about staying here. They should be dancing in the streets, not biting the hand that feeds them."

Though terrible, these incidents were for us more topics of conversation than anything else. They did not touch us personally – until the day that terror struck closer to home. It happened during the school holidays in July. We were out playing in the garden under the trees because it was the middle of the day and very hot. Rex was lying down with his tongue hanging out, clearly overheated. "Come on Rexy," my brother kept calling out, "come on, lazy dog!" And Rex, making no effort to get up, acknowledged my brother's invitation with a slow thump of his tail on the ground. Suddenly, we heard a dull thud in the distance and minutes later our mother, who had been out visiting, came running home. She shouted out to Siham who was inside the house, saying she'd seen smoke in the distance which seemed to be coming from Mamillah, close to the office where my father worked.

"I know something terrible's happened," she said. "Switch on the radio." The neighbours rushed in saying there was an explosion in the centre and God knows who had died or what the damage was. Shortly afterwards, the radio announced that bombs had exploded in the King David Hotel and many people were killed. "Please God your father's not gone there for some business or other," said our mother. The King David Hotel was the headquarters of the British government in Palestine and it was always bustling with people who went there for all kinds of business. My father had once worked in the translation bureau on the ground floor of the hotel in 1937 when he helped translate the Peel Commission report on the conflict in Palestine into Arabic.

By the end of that day, the full story became clear. Jewish terrorists had blown up a whole wing of the hotel by posing as Arab delivery men and smuggling explosives hidden in milk cans into the basement. My father saw the fire and smoke from his office. He went out onto the balcony of the building and into a great cloud of dust which had drifted across from the site of the explosion. Nearly one hundred people, mostly Arabs but also British, and a small number of Jews, were killed. The dead included a number of our neighbours or acquaintances, since Jerusalem society was small and most families knew each other. "Poor Hilda," my mother said. "Her poor, poor parents." Hilda Azzam was a young secretary employed at the King David Hotel who was pretty and well thought of at work and my parents knew her family. She had perished in the explosion, as had Mr Thompson, an English official who worked for the British authorities at the hotel and lived in the next street to ours. "Diabolical," exclaimed old Mr Jouzeh, our next door neighbour. "These people aren't human. They're devils from hell!"

All those who came to our house spoke of nothing else for what seemed like weeks. They said it took four days to dig out and move the bodies of the dead and wounded to the government hospital in the Russian Compound, right next to the maternity hospital where I was born. Those who were Jewish went to their own hospitals. There were funerals in Jerusalem for weeks afterwards, five or six a day, as some of the wounded joined the ranks of those who had died in the initial explosion. The social customs over bereavement, which were already elaborate in our society, became more so in the aftermath of these deaths. The women in our street, my mother amongst them, were all busy visiting the relatives of those who had died after the incident. Poor Mrs Thompson, who was Greek and used to visit us from time to time, became utterly distraught after her husband's death in the explosion and would often come weeping to our house.

For the men who visited my father it became the major topic of conversation. "They say it was the Jews taking revenge on the British." At the end of June, just before my father came back from England, the army had tried to control Jewish terrorism by clamping down on all Jewish settlements in the country. They were closed off, placed under curfew and their telephone lines cut. From all accounts, the army found a huge quantity of arms, explosives and mortar bombs, and they arrested about two thousand people, members of the illegal terrorist groups, but also of the Haganah. The Arabs looked on bemused. "Let's hope it stops these lunatics," people said. But Mr Thompson, describing the British anti-terrorist campaign to my father on his return, had shaken his head at the time and said, "I am very afraid that it won't work. I think they'll strike back." "Poor man," said my father later. "As it turned out, he was only too right."

Nothing was the same after the King David incident. The authorities were furious and instituted a huge search operation for the terrorists centred on Tel Aviv. This made my father and his Palestinian colleagues at work feel slightly better, for, as employees of the British administration, they had also begun to feel hunted. There were soldiers everywhere and a big detention camp went up outside Jerusalem where hundreds of Jewish suspects were held. My father said that the British were determined to stamp out Jewish terrorism because they were worried that the Arabs would be tempted to join in the fight against the Jews. "Better for the Arabs to stay out of it," said my uncle Abu Salma who was on a visit from Haifa. "Knowing the mess they make of everything, they'd be guaranteed to turn the British pro-Jewish again." It was noted that the British soldiers had become more and more hostile to the Jewish population as the attacks on them increased.

"It's funny, Mr Karmi," said Philip's father. "If anything, we were all rather sympathetic to the Zionists when we first came here. But now most of us feel quite differently, some would say even anti-semitic." Abu Suleiman, the grocer whose shop was in the road behind ours next to the Semiramis Hotel, said that the soldiers sometimes dropped in to buy something from him. "You're all right, you Arabs," they used to tell him, "not like the other lot."[1]

When in London, my father had made friends with a certain Henry Dodds who lived in the same building in Sussex Gardens where my father was staying. It so happened that he had a nephew in the Palestine police whom we had never met because he was stationed in Haifa. Henry Dodds introduced my father to London life, took him to the pub and generally helped him to settle in. After my father's return to Palestine, they wrote to each other from time to time. In the wake of the King David Hotel bombing, Henry Dodds wrote anxiously to enquire after our well-being. He said that the whole of England had been rocked by the event. The House of Commons had met in emergency session and, for the first time, members had begun to speak of a British withdrawal from Palestine. "You are not alone. People here are disgusted with the violence in Palestine," he wrote. "The press is full of it, they've even begun to compare the Jewish gangsters to the Nazis. But others, more charitable perhaps, are saying that what the Jews suffered in the war has deranged their minds. Who knows? I can only hope that you and your family may escape the worst of it."

---

[1] It was no secret that the British army and the British-staffed Palestine police were generally pro-Palestinian while the government and its administrators were pro-Zionist. Many Palestinians thought to exploit this division in British ranks by making contacts within the army and police. Their efforts were of limited value, however, against the implacably pro-Zionist policy of the government.

He ended by saying that he was thinking of us and also of his nephew who had so far escaped the attentions of the terrorists.

For a while, there were no further incidents of that magnitude close to us, people were on their guard, and the authorities were determined to take no chances. The government divided Jerusalem, Haifa and Tel Aviv into security zones, A, B and C, with checkpoints at each. Area A, which was the British zone, was especially well guarded with high walls and barbed wire. You had to have a special permit and your papers checked by the soldiers before you could enter. This was because the government had to protect its buildings and personnel from further attack by the Jewish terrorists. The latter regarded the zones with contempt and referred to them as "Bevingrads", after the British Foreign Secretary, Ernest Bevin, who had drawn up the policy.

There was a checkpoint at the bottom of our hill, past the Wahbehs' house, which led to a security zone and was manned by British soldiers. We were told never to go there, but of course this made us want to all the more. So one day after lunch while everyone was asleep, my friend Randa and I walked down the hill until we came up close to the checkpoint. There was only one soldier on duty and he was bending down to do up his bootlace. We crept up on him so quietly that he did not hear us, but we could see his red neck below his beret. Suddenly he straightened and spotted us. He was fair haired and had bright blue eyes which lit up in a smile. "Hallo!" he said, shifting the barrel of his rifle away from our direction. We giggled and ran away as fast as we could and once safely over the top of the hill, we shouted, "Hallo! Hallo!" back at him.

To our delight, we found when we returned that no one had discovered our little escapade. And so we started to visit the young soldier on other afternoons when everyone was asleep and he was on duty. His name was Jack and he would smile a lot and say things we could not understand. But we knew they were friendly. And then one time, he asked us where we lived. We knew what he meant by the gestures, and we said, "Come and visit us," covering our faces with our hands and giggling as we said it. We thought he understood because he nodded hard and smiled at us. And we wondered what we would say at home, if he really did come. But nothing happened and we did not see him again until the day Randa and I went to Abu Samir's shop. And there he was with another soldier, buying cigarettes. He saw Randa first and said, "Hallo!" and bent down to pat her head.

Abu Samir looked amazed. "That's my friend Jack," he said. "How do you two know him?" We were covered in confusion, but we explained and begged him not to tell our parents. "It won't matter very much anyway now," he said. "Jack's going to leave us. Aren't you?" Jack's friend, who knew some Arabic, translated. "That's right," said our Jack, as we had begun to think of him, "*khalas*, finished, had enough."

"We've all had enough," repeated the other soldier to Abu Samir.

"But we are friends," said the latter. "We like you. Why go?"

Both men shook their heads. "We like you too, Mr Abu. If it was up to us, it wouldn't be like this, believe me." And Jack nodded. "It's a shame what's happening in this country. It shouldn't be allowed, but no one listens to us. We don't make the rules, only wish we did. That's our government does that. And they say you've got to live with the Jews, like it or not."

"We don't like it," said Abu Samir. Jack's friend clapped him on the shoulder and said he was sorry. And then Jack bought Randa and me some sweets and, to our great excitement, shook our hands. "Goodbye, young ladies," he said, gravely. "We probably won't meet again". We didn't know what to answer, but his friend smiled and told us what he had said. And then we felt sad and wished we could have spoken English.

That autumn, I went back to school on my own because my sister had left and gone to Dar al-Mu'allimat, the government secondary school. She would stay here until her matriculation exam, something akin to the old English School Certificate. It was strange going to school without her and I used to hang around a little in the morning, hoping that Rex would follow me, even though he was not supposed to. But when he slipped out of the garden gate behind me, more often than not he abandoned me soon after and took himself off for a walk round our road instead. Those few people who kept dogs were not in the habit of walking them outside the house, and when my brother was not there to take Rex out with him, which he did as often as he could, Rex was expected to get his exercise by running around in our large garden. But from early on he took matters into his own hands and simply went off whenever anyone left the garden gate open. Then, after having completed his walk, which consisted of sniffing round other people's gardens and barking at other animals he met on the way, he would return home wagging his tail and asking to be let in.

Rex was the only one to remain unaffected by the atmosphere in Jerusalem as the year drew to a close. It was not that anyone at that stage experienced the panic and insecurity which were yet to come, but things had definitely changed. My father's friends talked incessantly about the political situation and even my mother's coffee mornings and *istiqbals* were overshadowed by the events. The British army continued its operations against Jewish targets with searches and arms seizures, one of them in the Montefiore district of Jerusalem, not far from Qatamon. But nothing seemed to have any effect on the terrorists who went on attacking buildings and kidnapping British soldiers. And then, as the new year came in, Mr and Mrs Clayton came to see us. Visits from English people to our house were exceptional because my mother did not speak English and my father confined his contact with them to the office. So, when they came over one evening, we knew something was up.

"My wife has come to say goodbye," said Mr Clayton. "She's going back to England with the children. We want to thank you for looking after Philip so well."

"Why do they have to go?" my mother asked through my father.

"The situation isn't safe here," he told her. "It doesn't look to us as if the terrorists are going to stop and anyone British is fair game to them, you know. I can't have my family threatened like that. I mean it's dangerous to let the boys out to play or to let my wife go anywhere in case she gets caught up in some awful attack."

"All the other wives are leaving," said Mrs Clayton. "It's very sad, we didn't want to go like this." She smiled warmly at my mother and told my father to explain that she had been very happy in Palestine. "I'll never forget the kindness and hospitality of people here. We've made so many wonderful friends." She suddenly burst into tears. "It's awful, awful what the Jews are doing."

That January, all British wives, children and other people whose presence in Palestine was not considered essential were evacuated back to England. This would give the authorities greater freedom to control terrorism, it was said. "But you know," commented my uncle Abu Salma who was staying with us at that time, "it also means that the English" – or, as he put it, *al-Ingleez*, which was the usual way Palestinians referred to the British authorities – "are expecting much more trouble from the Jews." My father agreed. He said one could tell that from the general air of apprehension in his office. "But the Jews are jubilant, you know," he informed my uncle. "I know a German Jew at work, Roth, who says that the Jewish irregulars are celebrating because they think they've got the English on the run. He's not much happier about this than we are. He says 'you Arabs can't tell the difference between us and them.'"

By "us", my father explained, he had meant the Jewish Agency and the Haganah, as opposed to the Irgun and the Stern Gang. "That's because they're all the same," retorted my uncle. "Everyone knows that Ben-Gurion approved the King David Hotel bombing [David Ben-Gurion was the head of the Jewish Agency in Palestine] and most of the other incidents as well. They pretend to be shocked every time an atrocity occurs and deny they had anything to do with it, just as they did after the King David. But take it from me, secretly they're all dogs in collusion with each other."

My father said that at least the Jews were not aiming their aggression at the Arabs. Many of them in fact went out of their way to say that they had nothing against us, it was the British they were after. And indeed in the very next month, February, and following the evacuation of civilians, the terrorists increased their campaign of bombings and sabotage against the British military. The worst of this was the effect on the railway system. The terrorists saw to it that most of the routes were mined which meant that the trains could not travel and all rail transport in the country was paralysed. The army put out all its men to clear the mines and patrol the train lines. But it was difficult to keep them protected at all times, so the government tried to enlist Arab help.

My aunt Zubeida who came to see us from Tulkarm said some of the villagers had been approached by British army officers offering rewards for information about Jewish terrorists. There were two major Jewish settlements in the vicinity of Tulkarm, Hadera and Petah Tikva, which might harbour them. Fatima also came saying that some of the people in her village had been approached with the same request. "And are they going to do it?" my mother asked her. "Well," replied Fatima, "they're not rich and they could do with the money."

By the end of the month, the British Mandate government calculated that it had lost nearly half a million pounds due to the damage to the railways and the loss of traffic. And as soon as the danger from mines abated, the Irgun and Stern terrorists turned their attention to attacking British army vehicles. Gangs sped by in fast-moving stolen cars lobbing bombs at army trucks. "Like those American gangster films," people said. "No wonder the English can't cope." Indeed, the British authorities seemed overwhelmed by the ferocity of the Jewish assault on them. They tried to bring in a requirement on all vehicles to display the name and photograph of their drivers on the windscreen. But it was widely ignored and had to be abandoned. Then, at the beginning of March, there was another major bombing in Jerusalem carried out by the Irgun. Goldsmith House, the radio announced, had been bombed and the whole building reduced to rubble. There were many casualties, between fifty and eighty dead and wounded it was thought, all British.

Now Goldsmith House was the British officers' club and an important centre for army personnel. It stood inside the British security zone and should have been safe from attack. Nevertheless, a terrorist unit had managed to get in, no one quite knew how, and throw explosives through the windows of the club. The British took this attack very hard, especially back in England. My father's office was buzzing with talk that the view from there was of an incompetent Mandate government, unable to control the situation. "Trying to handle the terrorists with kid gloves instead of applying the law of the Old Testament," British newspapers were saying. "An eye for an eye, that's what they understand." In desperation, the government, we learned, had declared martial law in Jerusalem and Tel Aviv. This was centred on the Jewish areas, where the terrorists were presumed to be. They were cordoned off and guarded by soldiers. Under the new law, the Jews who lived there would lose all government services and henceforth would have no postal deliveries, no law court sittings, no tax collection, no working telephones and hardly any traffic in and out. Food distribution was under the control of the army.

Everyone said we Arabs were not the target of these measures, but life in Jerusalem was badly disrupted. By 1947, there was a great deal of mixing between Arabs and Jews, not socially, but in terms of commerce and professional services. The sight of so many soldiers on the streets – by then the British army in Palestine amounted to 100,000 men – all heavily armed, was quite frightening. They were grim and business-like and very few looked like our nice smiling guard at the Qatamon checkpoint. It was said that they had started to hate it in Palestine and just wanted to go home. Life in the city was not normal, and no one knew when it would become so again. In fact, as it happened, it was only to last for two weeks. Martial law was lifted, having failed miserably to stop the terrorists from striking again; far from it, at least twenty operations were mounted against British targets during the two weeks when it was in force.

"What idiots these English are!" our neighbours commented. "They managed to terrorise all of us in the Great Strike and now they can't control a bunch of Jews?"

Because my father worked for a government department, many people came to ask what he thought was really going on. Increasingly, we children sensed that important matters were afoot though we did not know what they were exactly. Though I understood little of what I heard when people came to see us, it was not the content of what they said but their manner and expression which I noticed. But I was merely intrigued and occasionally concerned. Not for a moment did I think it could touch me or Rex or our home.

"What is the matter with them?" Rashid Khayyat asked my father. He and his wife lived nearby and were frequent visitors to our house. Everyone that evening was talking about the Irgun's recent attacks on the British. "What do they want?"

"It's not a mystery," replied my father. "They want the English to get out of Palestine. They think that if they make life here bad enough for them, they'll be forced to leave."

"They must be mad if they think that a bunch of Jewish lunatics can get the whole of the British government and British army to move out!" scoffed my mother's friend, Emily.

"I'm not sure," said my father. "Don't forget the English moved their wives and children out in January and they've now turned the subject of Palestine over to the United Nations", he went on. "And there are calls in England for them to pull out of the country altogether."

"But what about us?" asked Vladimir Wahbeh, who came from a Greek Orthodox Arab family. "What's supposed to happen if they leave us with the Jews here?"

No one knew. But everyone decided that the Jews couldn't throw the English out and the English were not going to leave us just like that. "It simply isn't possible," they said.

But as matters between the Jews and the British continued to deteriorate, it was impossible not to think the unthinkable. Acts of revenge and counter-revenge accelerated in an underground war of attrition which seemed to get more and more violent. Even though the Arabs were not directly involved in any of this and did not have much sympathy for either side – "one oppressor fighting another", as they put it – they nevertheless felt a sense of unease.

In July, another terrible incident took place which was to have far-reaching effects. The radio broadcast its details day by day, almost as if it might have been a thriller. It all started with a British decision to execute three Jewish terrorists, all members of the Irgun, for their part in breaking into the maximum security government prison at Acre. Whereupon, the Irgun kidnapped two British soldiers and threatened to execute them in retaliation. The authorities refused to give in to what they saw as blackmail and the terrorists were duly hanged. At this, the more moderate Jewish Agency and Haganah tried to deter the Irgun from carrying out the revenge hanging of the British soldiers. They urged the Irgun's commander, Menachem Begin, to exercise caution, but to no avail. The two sergeants were strangled and then strung up on trees. When the army came to cut down the bodies, they did not realise that the area had been booby-trapped by the Irgun who hoped in this way to increase British casualties. One of the bodies exploded right in the face of the soldier who was trying to bring it down.

All the English we knew were in a state of shock. The Arabs said, "It's got nothing to do with us. They let them in and now they're paying the price. Let them fight it out." In the next week, we had a letter from Henry Dodds, my father's friend from London. "This has really done it," he wrote. "The country is in an uproar. You should see what is happening here. People are saying that the Jews are Nazis, and Jewish shops and Jewish homes have been attacked up and down the country. I don't defend that myself, but I do feel disgusted about the booby-trapping of the bodies. Everyone here is saying that our boys will have to get out of Palestine." In the aftermath of the hanging, the army could not control the furious reaction of many of its soldiers. They smashed Jewish shops and Jewish buses in Tel Aviv and even shot at Jews from armoured cars. Our neighbours the Kramers said they were only too glad that they did not live there.

"You know, most of us don't approve of what the dissidents are doing," Mr Kramer said to my father. "Dissidents" was the term the Jewish community used to describe what everyone else called terrorists. "If they go on like this, they will destroy everything we have worked so hard to create here. Actually, the Haganah leadership has called on everyone in the Yishuv [the Jewish community in Palestine] to work against them."

My father told this story the next evening to a group of his men friends. "It's their insolence that annoys me," Vladimir Wahbeh commented. He worked as a civil engineer in the Jerusalem municipality. "I mean, this man Kramer talks about what the Jews created here, as if they were doing it for us."

"Or," Hatim Kamal, another good friend of my father, added, "as if this was their own country they were building."

"But they think it is," said my father, who had been hearing such things from the Jews he came across at work.

No one could accept this. "Really?" Hatim laughed. "All those Poles and Russians and Germans, in all shapes and sizes, jabbering in all sorts of languages – making out this is their country? What a joke!"

"They want much more," said Vladimir. "From what I hear at the municipality, they won't give up until they've taken over the country for themselves."

"Well, it won't happen," Abu Ahmad asserted with finality. "First of all, the English are in power, and second there's all of us living here. How are they going to get rid of us and of the English government? It's a nonsense." Everyone agreed vigorously. "Mark my words," he continued, "this will blow over. The English are back in control now and they will sort out the mess."

తెన్స్

To me, that summer was chiefly memorable for the business of the "doll-babies". Before school had ended for the holidays, one of the girls in my class, Hala by name, had come to say that she had an exciting secret which could only be shared with a chosen few. I was not one of these and had to wait until given the information second hand. It turned out that Hala knew of a place where they had "doll-babies", small living toys which looked like babies. They did not talk or cry but they had to be fed and washed and put to sleep like real babies. As children we were all abundantly familiar with babies because there were so many of them around us. But one could rarely play with them because they always started to cry and their mothers invariably took them away when they did. So the idea that there was a kind of baby which never cried and one could keep for one's own was irresistibly attractive.

We all wanted to know how to get one and Hala took our orders. She said they came in all sorts of hair and eye colours, from blond to black. I wanted one of the blond and blue-eyed variety, as did most of the others. This was because, even at that age, we had already adopted the prevailing Arab prejudice against brunettes. Blondes were unusual amongst a predominantly dark people and were considered highly desirable. So, girls longed to be fair-skinned and have light-coloured eyes. Because my sister Siham was the darkest of us all, my mother used to make her drink lots of milk in the hope that her colour would lighten. When Hala said that she would get a doll-baby of the required description for me during the holidays, I was overjoyed. I could see it already, about a foot and a half long, swaddled in a white blanket, with a head of pretty blond curls and two bright blue eyes, like those of the English soldiers. I told Fatima all about it one hot afternoon when she was trying to have her siesta on the veranda.

"And Fatima," I said excitedly, "it's like a nice quiet baby, just lies there and looks at you. I'm going to look after it and it's going to love me." Fatima nodded with her eyes closed. "Fatima, you're not listening. Wake up, wake up." And then Fatima opened her eyes and smiled. "Yes, my darling, yes," she said soothingly. I waited all that summer for the doll-baby to arrive. I dreamed about it at night and often during the day. But the holidays came to an end and the doll-baby never arrived. And when I went back to school in September it was to find that Hala had left because her family had moved out of Jerusalem, leaving me with an anguished sense of loss.

Meanwhile, the conflict in the country was beginning to change direction as the Arabs prepared to join in. It was not that they had been wholly inactive throughout the months of anti-British terrorism. But their resistance was relatively muted, not least because they were divided amongst themselves. Although their aim was supposed to be the fight against Jewish immigration into the country, in reality the power struggle to secure leadership of the resistance movement sapped much of their energy. Only very late in the day, at the beginning of 1947, did a more united front emerge in the shape of the Arab Higher Committee, the AHC. This was predictably headed by Hajj Amin al-Husseini and brought together the various Arab parties which had until then been fighting independently. Many complained that it was dominated by the leading Jerusalem families and in particular by the Husseini clan and as such did not represent the ordinary people of Palestine. But no one took any notice.

As talk of a UN decision on the future of the Mandate increased throughout the summer of 1947 and the unthinkable – a British withdrawal from Palestine – began to be whispered aloud, Arab resistance came to the fore. In September 1947, just a few weeks after we all went back to school, the British made a stunning announcement. The UN special committee on Palestine had found the Mandate to be unworkable, it said, and recommended that it should end. In response, the British declared that they had accepted the UN verdict and would terminate their rule in Palestine in May 1948. At the same time, a new and dreaded word entered the political vocabulary: partition.

Partition meant that the country might be divided into Jewish and Arab parts. "God forbid!" everybody in the neighbourhood said as soon as they heard it. "No, no. It can't happen. The English can't leave, whatever they say now. It's a long time to next May and by then God may create what we do not know." This was a well-known saying taken from the Quran, "And God creates that which you know and that of which you have no knowledge yet". My father said very little at this time. But we could see that he was worried. When my mother pressed him, he said he was thinking about the future of his job if the Mandate were to end. At the beginning of the year, he had been approached by Abdul-Majid Shuman, the head of the Arab Bank, with an offer of a job. He had invited him to become director of the bank in Amman, a well-paid job with a commercial future. But my father had hesitated to make such a move which would not only take us away from Jerusalem but also direct him towards a very different career. So he asked his head of department, a man called De Bunsen whom he had first met during his second spell in England and whom he trusted, what he should do. "I don't advise you to take it up," De Bunsen had replied without hesitation. "Stay with us because I can promise you we have you in mind for a substantial promotion."

My father must have wondered what would happen to that promise. Many others who worked with him were also worried. Sometimes they came to our house and spoke in low voices. Always they came to the conclusion that the British could not possibly leave. This was reinforced by government officials who stated repeatedly that they would settle the conflict before making any move. And it was not only Palestine which was perturbed, other Arab countries became involved. When in October their leaders met to consider sending troops to Palestine's borders in case the partition plan was ever adopted, my mother refused to be downhearted and behaved as normal, and life continued in the same way.

Not for long though. In November of that year, when I had just turned eight, the bombshell exploded. It was announced over the radio early one morning that the UN had met in New York and decided on partition. Palestine would be divided into two states, Jewish and Arab. Jerusalem would become an international city under UN trusteeship and not part of either the Arab or the Jewish state. The effect on the Palestinians was electric. Siham went to school to find a scene of grief verging on hysteria. Many of the teachers and girls were crying and classes were suspended. Because our parents were not in the habit of explaining political events to us – what we knew about the situation around us was picked up from overhearing snatches of conversation – she was unsure about the significance of what she had heard over the radio. She knew it was something serious and that it involved the creation of a Jewish state, but little else. So she asked what was the matter with everyone.

"We all know the Jews have taken lots of our land," she said. "Surely it's only a way of recognising that they have?" Siham did not really understand the issues and was trying to work it out for herself.

"Are you a traitor or just stupid?" demanded her teacher angrily. "It's a good thing I know who your family is or I would have suspected your loyalty. Don't you understand that our country is being destroyed?" And her other teacher said, "You live in Qatamon, next to the Jews, don't you? Didn't you hear them singing and dancing all night?" Indeed we had not, but over the next few days our friends spoke of scenes of wild jubilation in the Jewish areas as they celebrated the news from New York. "We have a state! We have a state!" they sang.

Ziyad came back from his school, saying that everyone seemed short tempered. The atmosphere all around us had changed and we knew that terrible, frightening things were happening. As soon as partition had been announced, Arab snipers were out onto the streets shooting at Jews and attacking Jewish shops and cars. The Jews were shooting back and in some places no one seemed to be in control. My uncle Abu Salma, who had come to see us, said that in Haifa, which had a large Jewish population, it was just the same. We normally looked forward to his visits because he was the merriest and wittiest member of our family. He was an attractive man who had quite an eye for the women and was a well-known flirt. Even when heatedly discussing the most serious political topics, he could always be distracted if a pretty woman came into the room.

People excused his flirtatiousness because he was a poet and they said that poets were romantic and could not help themselves. It was after all through his love sonnets that he had won his wife, who had not wanted to marry him. She was the daughter of the mayor of Acre and a beautiful, cultivated woman who played the piano and spoke French. Before meeting him, she had decided never to marry anyone, and strenuously resisted his advances at first.

But on this visit, my uncle was not his usual merry self, and my father and he fell into an intense and serious conversation almost immediately on his arrival.

My father wanted to know what was happening on the Arab side.

"You know that the AHC have ordered the whole country to come out on strike, so that we can be free to fight against partition," replied my uncle. "They've set up local committees in all the towns to coordinate activities."

My father was afraid it would merely be a repeat of the shambles of 1936, and worse, since the leader was directing operations from Cairo. (Hajj Amin al-Husseini had been banished from Palestine by the British authorities in 1946 and lived in Egypt.)

"And the rest are more interested in settling scores against each other than in fighting the Zionists," said my uncle.

"At this rate," said my father, "things can only get worse."

"Well of course. What can you expect when we don't rule over our own country?" demanded my uncle. "When we are ruled by people who promote our enemies?" My father took this to be an allusion to his government post, as if my uncle were accusing him of colluding with our oppressors. This was a sensitive issue for all those who worked for the British administration, and a source of shame. "What else could I have done?" he said angrily. "There was no other administration, no other structure here to work for except the English. How could I or you have known that they would do this to us? How could anyone imagine that they would want to give half of our country to immigrants?" The UN had decided to accord the proposed Jewish state 55 per cent of the land and the Arab one the remaining 45 per cent, although Jews made up only one third of the population. "I mean it isn't conceivable by any standard of fairness or human behaviour. All right, we accepted a Jewish homeland. But this?"

As children we had often heard them talk of the so-called Balfour Declaration. The British had promised the Zionists to help set up a "Jewish homeland" in Palestine. This was apparently the basis of the problem in Palestine. By doing that, the British government had in effect promised to give away the land of one people to another when it did not own that land. Even we, as children, could see what a bitter bone of contention it was between the Arabs and the British that the people of Palestine, who were to host this Jewish homeland, were never consulted nor their agreement obtained.

"What was a 'homeland' but an excuse to create a Jewish state here?" said my uncle bitterly. "The English are treacherous bastards. They never had me fooled!"

My father was stung. He must have resented the implication that he was either stupid or worse, that those who worked with the authorities were tarred with the same brush. "Of course it's always satisfying to be wise after the event," he snapped.

They had started to quarrel. My mother came in and intervened. "Now stop it, you two," she said. "That's how the Arabs always end up, fighting each other. That won't help us now, and I still say that the

English don't mean it. They must have some plan but they're not telling us everything."

The word betrayal was on everyone's lips. People were saying, "The English tricked us. They must have planned this all along." When my father went to the office, he found himself faced with a smiling Mr Roth, the very same man who only a few years before had wanted to convert to Islam. Roth tried to be friendly but my father could not bring himself to speak to the man. "We don't have to fall out over this, Karmi," he said. "You know, the Jewish state we're going to have will really be shared between us and you. I mean we're only a third of the population. There aren't enough of us to go round." "And", said my father afterwards, "he had the insolence to laugh. As if I didn't know that they've no intention of leaving it at that." Everyone around us was saying that the Jews were after a state devoid of Arabs and were unhappy with the UN offer as it stood. My father heard that David Ben-Gurion had made a speech to his party soon after the partition plan was announced in which he did not hide his anxiety about the number of Arabs in the state to be allotted to the Jews.

When people heard about this, there was much alarm and wild speculation. The riots got worse. Throughout December, central Jerusalem became a battleground for angry mobs who burned and attacked Jewish buildings and property and Jewish militias who responded with shootings and bombings. The British army kept a noticeably low profile, except for the imposition of curfews. Suddenly, shrill sirens would sound over the city and everyone who could scurried indoors. Increasingly, as this happened while we were at school, they would despatch us home as soon as the curfew was announced. And I would rush back anxiously, longing to be in the house in the warm with Fatima with the door closed, roasting chestnuts and letting Rex into the *liwan* with us.

The curfews could happen at any time and we never knew when we left in the mornings whether we would be home as usual or not. Sometimes, it meant that Fatima could not come to us, or if she did, she could not return. On the days she did not turn up, I would feel desolate. What if a sniper had got her as she walked along the road? I started to think like this after Randa said that people in lower Qatamon had seen a man shot dead in front of their house. If I said as much to Siham or to my mother, they said, "God forbid, don't say such things." Getting to the shops was becoming difficult, and the village women who used to come to our house selling vegetables often did not appear. My mother complained about having to cook without the proper ingredients, but we managed. And amazingly, all three of us still struggled to school every day, although I retained nothing of the lessons we were taught. All the time we heard at school of the conflict spreading; every town centre was disrupted and the villages became bases for Arab fighters and irregulars, soon joined by volunteers from neighbouring Arab countries.

The unrest continued until we broke up for the winter holidays. At the end of the term it was announced that all government schools were to close until further notice, as the situation was too hazardous for children to be out in the streets. Some people relocated their children to other, usually private, schools nearer home, but we could not afford that. So we were all grounded at home "until the troubles die down". But no one knew when that would be, since the situation was deteriorating day by day. The Rex Cinema, where my mother used to take us, was set on fire by the Haganah. "My God, we could have been there," she said. Shortly after that, the Irgun gang threw bombs at a crowd in front of the Damascus Gate of the Old City, killing four Arabs. All that day, the neighbours were desperate for the names of the dead in case they included someone we knew. The Irgun likewise bombed Arab cafes in Jaffa and Haifa. Villages were attacked; at al-

Tireh just outside Haifa, twelve villagers were shot dead. Meanwhile, the Arabs had managed to cut off the major roads leading to Jewish settlements and Jewish transport was severely affected. The traffic going from Jerusalem to Tel Aviv was so disrupted it had to take diversionary routes to avoid the Arab attackers. The British army sometimes provided protection for Jewish convoys, but in general they seemed content to leave the protagonists to it.

"Do you think the Arab riots will die down soon?" asked Mr Kramer. "I mean, we" – by which he meant the Haganah leadership – "think that it might be just a repeat of the 1936 Arab riots which eventually came to an end. We hope there will be no war."

"Perhaps you are right," replied my father without elaborating. "Why should I tell him anything?" he said afterwards. "Let them think it's a only a minor matter and will soon disappear." But the Haganah were not sanguine for long. As the Arab fighters looked to have got the upper hand in the struggle, the Haganah unleashed its forces on civilians. They blew up Arab houses in towns and villages and attacked Arab transport, including a bus in Haifa full of women and children.

My aunt Zubeida, who often used to come and stay with us, could no longer make the journey from Tulkarm. Nor could anyone else of our family because the roads were too dangerous. We missed them, especially our aunts, because they were so different from any of the people in Jerusalem. I think my mother was never too pleased to have to entertain them, as they never came in ones and twos, but always with a variety of small children in tow. My aunt Zubeida frequently brought my two cousins Sharif and Sawsan, the children of my uncle Hussein. Sharif was a pale, skinny three-year old and Sawsan was a year younger. They both whined a lot and my aunt, who had no children of her own and looked as if she never would, spoilt them. I used to end up having to play with them, since Ziyad quickly made himself scarce as soon as they arrived.

Domestic telephones were few and far between at that time and we had no news from Tulkarm for weeks. And then, Abu Jasir, a distant relative of my aunt Souad's husband, came to see us. He had come in a hired car through Nablus and the journey had not been easy. "Don't expect to see anyone from Tulkarm for a while," he said. He had only come to Jerusalem because he had urgent business there; otherwise, he would never have taken the risk. My aunt Souad had sent him with a message for us which she insisted he deliver to my father in person. "She says that you and the family should leave Jerusalem and come to Tulkarm as soon as possible. She has a room furnished and ready for all of you." My father smiled one of his rare warm smiles. He and my aunt Souad were very close. She had brought him up and he considered her the most intelligent of his sisters. He used always to bemoan her lack of education, forced on her by the prevailing social custom in her youth when girls were not allowed any schooling. If she had been educated, there's no knowing what she could have achieved, he used to say.

Abu Jasir advised my father to take up the offer. "Tulkarm will be safer than here," he said. "You see, we've had assurances from the Jews." There had been meetings between some of the *mukhtars*, the village heads, and Jews from the Hadera Jewish settlement just north of Tulkarm. "The *mukhtars* told the Jews we didn't want any trouble, just to be left alone. We only want peace and to stay good neighbours. And you remember," he added, "we never had a problem with them in the past when your father Sheikh Said was alive. They didn't bother us and no one ever bothered about them. There was never any of this fighting and shooting."

"And what did the Jews say?" asked my father.

"Well, they said they would keep the peace as long as we did. But some of our men from Tulkarm didn't agree with talking to the Jews and they tried to stop the *mukhtars* from going to the meeting. 'What, begging Jews for mercy? The Jews will kill all of you when the time comes, and God will be the witness,' they said. But they couldn't stop them and the meeting went ahead. I didn't go, but they said there were people from the Jewish Agency there as well and they said that the Jews in Hadera would give us flour and other things if we ran short because of the troubles."

"And you believe them?" asked my father. Abu Jasir shrugged his shoulders, "Well, it's still better than being here right on top of the volcano," he said. But my father shook his head. "Thank my sister Souad and tell her from me that, if anything, it will be Tulkarm which will fall to the Jews first and Jerusalem will stay."

December, which was a nice month usually because it was the time when we broke up for the holidays, was a sad one that year. Ziyad and I had initially been excited by the prospect of not returning to school, but that soon evaporated. The atmosphere at home was tense and my mother was worried each time my father went to work. There were so many incidents and so much hostility with the Jews that no one felt safe. Even so, it was unimaginable to us that our father was in any real danger; to think that would have been to demolish the very foundation of our existence. Fathers in our culture were crucially important. They were the central figures of authority, the source of the family's reputation, the sole means of economic survival and the basis of identity. When people were introduced to each other, almost the first question was "whose son or daughter are you?" And the nature of the ensuing relationship was often determined by that information. In our case, both our father and grandfather were figures of public esteem and admiration. And so, we could not think that our father was seriously threatened. Nevertheless, we could not help but be influenced by the general uncertainty and unease.

Among the very few good things about that time was the fact that Fatima had begun to stay with us more frequently as the danger on the roads increased. She slept on the floor in our room. Although she got up early every morning to pray, long before we were awake, having her there all through the night was comforting. My mother, who was distracted and worried, provided no comfort or reassurance; my father was preoccupied with the news. He spent his time at home either listening to the radio or reading the newspapers. So Fatima became our anchor.

The other good thing was that we started to let Rex into the house most of the time because my mother was out and we stayed at home. As if Rex knew that we were doing him a favour, he was more affectionate than usual. Ziyad and I played games together sitting on the floor and Rex tried to join in. But he usually managed to knock things over with his tail, which he wagged vigorously to show his approval of the whole arrangement. I associate those early months of 1948 with Rex and with Fatima who had become full members of our family and who were now as important to me as my parents or Siham and Ziyad. Life was unthinkable without them.

It was cold that year and it began to snow in early January. The summer, when we played in the garden and ran out to the shop for sweets, seemed to belong to another century. Despite the prevailing gloom, the neighbours prepared for Christmas on January 7. This is the date when the Eastern Orthodox church celebrates Christmas, not on December 25. Because hardly any of our neighbours belonged to the converted Christian sects, such as Anglicanism or Roman Catholicism, Christmas was always in January. They usually had a Christmas tree and made special cakes, *ma'moul*, round or oblong shapes of baked semolina stuffed with dates and nuts. We also made *ma'moul* during our Eid, but my mother started to make them at Christmas time too, because she did not want us to feel left out. Ziyad and I went next door to the Jouzehs' house and offered to help decorate their tree. We got there by crossing over from our garden to theirs at the back because it was too dangerous to go on the road. As it happened, they had already decorated the tree, but they were pleased to see us and as we were leaving, they said to make sure to come back on Christmas day. It was the custom in Palestine for Muslims to call on Christians on their feast days and the other way around.

As it turned out, however, no one would be celebrating anything on January 7.

Three

On the night of January 4, 1948, three days before Christmas, we went to sleep as usual. It was raining heavily with occasional bursts of thunder and lightning. Fatima was staying with us that night and was sleeping on her mattress on the floor of our bedroom. Suddenly, at some time in the night, I awoke from a deep sleep and found myself in the middle of a nightmare crashing with thunder and lightning. For a few seconds, I could not distinguish dream from reality. The bedroom seemed to be full of strangers until I realised that they were my parents. There was a tremendous noise of shattering glass, shootings and explosions which seemed to be coming from our back garden. Rex was barking wildly. My mother dragged me off the bed and sat me up with Ziyad against the bedroom wall. The floor was cold against my warm body. She sat in front of us, her back pushing against our knees. The room was strangely lit up and as I twisted round towards the window I saw that the sky was orange, glowing and dancing. "Is it dawn?" I asked. "Is that the sun?" No one answered and I could feel my mother's body shaking in her nightdress. My father was on the other side of Ziyad, sitting against the wall with Siham and Fatima squeezed in next to him. They all stared ahead and Fatima was intoning in a whisper the words of the *Fatiha*, the opening chapter of the Quran, over and over again:

In the name of God, the Merciful, the Compassionate. Praise be to the God of the worlds, the Merciful, the Compassionate, Lord of the Day of Judgement. You do we worship and to You do we turn for help. Guide us to the true path, the path of those whom You have favoured. Not those who have incurred Your wrath. Nor those who have strayed. Amen.

I thought that my mother was whispering something too, but I did not know what it was. A shattering bang shook the windows as a great clap of thunder exploded overhead. And then I knew that I was afraid, more afraid than I had ever been in my life before. As Ziyad turned his face towards the window, I saw that his eyes were enormous but he never made a sound. After who knows how long, the noise outside began to abate. And with that, my mother started to move forward. "Stop!" my father hissed. "There may be another explosion." He made us wait a little longer until the sky stopped being so red. It now had a far-away glow, like the embers in our charcoal stove. My leg was numb and the palm of my hand hurt where I had pressed it against the floor. We got up and groped our way out into the *liwan*. It was about two o'clock in the morning. Torrential rain lashed against the shutters. Fatima made coffee, but neither I nor Ziyad wanted anything, and our mother made us go back to bed. Siham followed soon after, but I don't think our parents slept at all the rest of that night.

By morning, when we got up, jaded and tired, we found no one in the house and the street looked deserted too. Everybody had gone to the scene of last night's explosion, the Semiramis Hotel in the road directly behind ours. This hotel was owned by a Palestinian Greek and had been fully occupied on the night when it was blown up. We decided to go and see for ourselves, walking through the wet, slippery streets in a howling icy wind with Rex close on our heels. The windows of several houses in the vicinity gaped, their glass shattered by the explosion of the night before. There was a great crowd around the devastated building which was still smoking and there was a strong smell of kerosene. Their faces were cold and pinched and many people were crying.

Municipal workers and British soldiers were trying to clear the rubble and still dragging bodies out. Some of these were very dark-skinned, Sudanese kitchen workers. As the crowed surged forward to see the bodies, in case there was a relative or friend amongst them, the soldiers pushed them back. Because Ziyad and I were small, we had got right to the front and they shouted at us to go back home. All the dead and wounded who were accessible had been taken away in the small hours, but the search was now on for others still buried beneath the slabs of concrete and stone and unlikely to be alive. An elderly couple next to where we were standing pressed forward repeatedly to get close to the digging. "They must find him," the man kept saying. But she said, "No. It's no use, he's gone. He could have been alive, standing and watching just like these people, but he's not."

We pulled away to go back and noticed for the first time that amongst the debris on the ground was a large quantity of headed hotel stationery, some of it grubby, and stacks of wet envelopes. Ziyad bent down and started to pick it up and I followed suit. "Stop that!" cried Siham but we kept hold of what we had picked up. Neither of us could take in the enormity of what we had just seen; to us this was an opportunity for play and mischief. But the images would remain to haunt us one day. Later that morning, it emerged that it was the Haganah which had planted the bombs in the hotel, thinking that it was being used as a base for an AHC unit, "a hotbed of armed Arabs", as they called it.

In fact, this was not the case, although Arab journalists were in the habit of staying at the Semiramis and it was a well-known meeting place for activists of all political persuasions. Some thirty people perished in the bombing, amongst them the hotel owner and the Spanish consul. The rest included several families all of whose members were killed, except in one case where the parents died and their three children lived. We saw them wandering about in the rubble looking dazed.

The Haganah command expressed condemnation of the incident and regret and said that it had been carried out without its knowledge by a splinter group. But everyone around us said, "Liars and sons of dogs!" People demanded that greater protection be provided by the AHC or from the Jaysh al-Inqath (the army of salvation), which consisted of volunteer soldiers from Arab states recruited by the Arab League. The AHC had national committees in the towns all over the country, but the defence of Jerusalem was part of a special force. A unit of this force arrived in Qatamon at the beginning of the year and took up residence in Abu Ahmad's house in the road above ours, which had stood empty ever since he and his family had left for Egypt.

It was headed by a man called Ibrahim Abu Dayyeh who had a reputation for bravery, but the men he commanded were few in number and poorly armed. Jewish soldiers, who were better armed and better trained, frequently chased them around and, though they assured everyone that they would defend us against all odds, it was obvious to everyone that they did not have the capacity. One evening, we even found one of them hiding in our garden shed, having been chased by an armed Jewish unit. He was very young, not much older than Siham, and trembling with fright. "It's no good. We can't compete with the Jews. They've got more men, more arms and more money," everyone said.

We heard that the men of the area met at the house of Khalil Sakakini to discuss what security measures ought to be taken. After the devastating attack on the Semiramis, it was clear to everyone that we were vulnerable and alone. The men decided to put up barricades at both ends of the roads and to have them manned. But only five people had guns and the rest did not know how to use weapons. There was consternation and in the end they drew up a rota of the people with weapons whose job it would be to guard the defence posts every night. Our father did not share in this rota, but he and others who did not take part paid a monthly fee towards the costs. This effort did not last long, however, for one night, Jewish gunmen shot and killed the man on duty.

There was terrific shock and mourning and then recriminations. "For God's sake, who is there left to guard anyway?" asked Daud Jouzeh sadly. He said this because in the days which followed the bombing of the Semiramis, there was a panic exodus from Qatamon. The months of instability and fear, culminating in this incident, had finally broken people's resistance. Those of the Arabs who were still holding out murmured, "They ought to be ashamed of themselves. They're doing just what the Jews want them to." The National Committee tried to persuade them not to go. They had received orders from the AHC on no account to allow anyone to leave. "If you go, the Mufti will only order you to return," they warned. "Or he will bring in Arab fighters to take your place. So, better for you to stay."

Whether because people heeded this or not, they first tried moving only from one part of Qatamon to another, hoping it would be safer, but others like my mother's friend Emily went to the Old City for the same reason. Yet others went out of Jerusalem or Palestine altogether, and often in such cases the women and children were evacuated first and the men stayed behind. But as the danger grew without any visible support from anyone, least of all the AHC and its local committees, many of the men followed their families and the majority left Palestine. "Fine for them to talk, but who will care when our children get killed?" they said as they came to say goodbye to us. "Still, it won't be for long. Just until the troubles die down."

But far from dying down, the troubles continued to get worse. It was as if the Jewish forces no longer felt restrained from unleashing all-out attacks against our neighbourhood after the small number of Jews who had lived amongst us departed. The Kramers went to Tel Aviv at the end of 1947 in the wake of the turbulence which followed the partition resolution, but the Jewish doctor hung on into the new year. When Arab snipers shot at him as he walked along the road soon after the Semiramis bombing, he left for Tel Aviv too.

At the end of January, the Haganah blew up another building in our vicinity, this time the big Shahin house on the edge of Qatamon. The Shahins were a wealthy family and had a beautiful villa standing in open ground at the top of Qatamon; no one could think why they had been targeted, except perhaps that the house might have been used at one point as a base by Arab snipers. Ever since one such sniper had shot dead a Jewish cyclist in Rehavia, the Haganah had instituted a policy of blowing up any Arab house which they suspected of harbouring gunmen. As February came, the sound of gunfire in the air was a frequent occurrence. From time to time, it was punctuated by explosions which vividly brought back the memory of the Semiramis. We had found this difficult to forget and whenever anyone even banged a door shut in the house, Siham would jump and start trembling.

Word came to my father at his office from a family friend of ours in Tulkarm, Hamdan Samara, urging him to move his books out of Jerusalem. "I will store them for you in Jenin where they can be safe," he wrote. Jenin was a town to the north of Tulkarm. "You may be forced to leave your house, and you never know, the Jews might

pillage your library." My father had an extensive and unusual collection of books in Arabic and English, lovingly bought over the
years, which he treasured. "Will you take up his offer?" my mother
asked. "No," he laughed. "We're not going to be leaving and no one
is going to harm my books."

By now, Ziyad and I were told not to go out onto the road because
it was too dangerous. He and his friends took no notice of this,
however; they found the whole thing rather exciting, especially when
they went out on patrol with Abu Dayyeh's men like real soldiers
looking for Jewish snipers. They never found any, but usually came
back with a collection of the spent cartridges and used bullets which
had been fired by the snipers. These had foreign markings, Belgian,
French, Czech and others, and Ziyad would line them up excitedly
according to shape and place of origin. "What do you want with those
horrible things?" our mother said. "Get rid of them!"

At other times, he went out on his own with Rex in tow, apparently
unafraid. On one such jaunt, he ventured as far as Talbiyya which was
a mixed Arab-Jewish neighbourhood. As he walked down a street
which, unknown to him, was mostly inhabited by Jews, he saw a
foreign-looking man on a balcony above him suddenly spring up and
aim a rifle directly towards him. Rex started to jump up, barking and
growling, and the man shouted out in broken Arabic, "Go away! Get
out!" He was so threatening, and the street so empty, that Ziyad
turned and ran off as fast as he could. He arrived home, panting with
fear. After that, he never tried going to Talbiyya again.

The assault on our part of town was especially concentrated
because, in company with other West Jerusalem neighbourhoods like
Talbiyya, Sheikh Jarrah, Romema and Lifta, we formed the "seam"
with the Jewish areas to the west of us and thus came under repeated
attack by the Jewish forces. All these districts were either mixed or
predominantly Arab, and the news which reached us from there was

all grim. Because of the attacks, people were frightened and were starting to leave their homes. All through January and February, long queues of cars packed with people and luggage filed out of the streets on their way to safer places. The AHC were worried; they issued threats through the local committees and imposed punishments against anyone leaving. But as had happened in Qatamon, no one took any notice. What was a verbal threat from the AHC compared with the reality of a Jewish sniper shooting at you from the rooftops as you walked along the street? Or with the Haganah van which toured your neighbourhood, as happened in Talbiyya, with loudspeakers blaring, urging you to leave or you and your house would be blown up?

All the while, the Arabs retaliated by attacking the Jews and trying to cut off their supplies, and the more they did this the more inflamed the situation grew. The Jewish neighbourhoods had been the object of Arab snipers for months. The Jews complained bitterly about us in Qatamon from where their neighbourhood of Rehavia was under attack. They also protested about Sheikh Jarrah because the Arabs fired on Jewish traffic going to the Hebrew university or to the Jewish Hadassah hospital from there.

My mother had friends in Sheikh Jarrah, the Mansour family, whom she used to visit frequently. The father, Abu Ya'qub, was elderly and sick, but before he died in January of that year, he would sit up in his bed and call out to his children, "Get me my rifle from under the bed!" He had had this old rifle since Ottoman days and it was rusty from disuse. "By God, I'm going to get up and shoot those Jews myself!" After his death, his sons, as if not to let him down, used to stick pumpkins on tall poles which they covered with a *kuffiyya*, the traditional Arab head-dress. They would then hold these pumpkins aloft and juggle them about, as if to make out that they were men. This invariably fooled the Jewish snipers on the other side who would start to shoot frantically at the pumpkins and, it was hoped, exhaust their ammunition.

In response to Arab sniping from Sheikh Jarrah, the Jews used armour-plated vehicles to get their patients and students through, but it was still unsafe. So the Haganah invaded the area and terrorised the Arab residents, more of whom now prepared to leave. The British ordered the Jewish army to withdraw on the promise that they would forbid Arab fighters from re-entering Sheikh Jarrah. But the Haganah complained that the British reneged on their promise and that the Arabs were back in no time. Both sides accused the British of helping the opposing camp. In our neighbours' house, they said the same, but Mr Wahbeh said, "I tell you the British don't care about us or them. All they want now is to get out and then they'll leave us to it. Look at them, all they do is keep the route to Haifa open for their troops to clear out when the time comes."

Since the start of the new year, everyone had finally begun to face the unthinkable, that we would indeed be abandoned by the British without proper arms or a proper army. What a tragic turnabout, that those who had been oppressors were now seen as saviours, the malady and its cure rolled into one. And even then, they would betray us again. That, I suppose, was the essence of what it meant to be colonised.

"They say the Arab League is sending in a big army," said my mother hopefully.

No one was impressed. "If you mean that small band of irregulars from Syria," said our neighbour, "I don't call that an army." In January, several hundred Arab volunteers under the leadership of the Syrian commander, Fawzi al-Qawaqji, had come across the Syrian border into Palestine in order to help in the resistance against the Jews. People thought highly of Qawaqji and of the Syrians. They believed in him and said that he would save the situation. His forces joined local Palestinian troops which by then had begun to organise better than had been the case before. They had now formed themselves into three separate groups with headquarters in Jaffa, Jerusalem and Gaza. But they had no proper arms, no training and little idea how to organise effectively.

It was no secret that the weaponry possessed by our side was out of date and far smaller in quantity than that of the Jews. There were no Arab weapons factories in Palestine and no way of making anything other than simple bombs. The Haganah, by contrast, had several arms factories producing bullets, grenades, sub-machine-guns and mortars. When, in addition, the Jewish forces later received shipments of modern arms from Czechoslovakia, everyone looked on in envy and alarm. There was a belated attempt to organise a country-wide Arab defence. The AHC's network of national defence committees, which functioned in towns and cities, should have provided a coherent organisation. But it was undermined by the fact that each locality had its own militia which usually ignored AHC orders and behaved autonomously. Likewise, the Palestinian villages had their own armed defence bands, untrained and acting independently of each other. To make matters worse, the whole arrangement was constantly undermined by internal feuding and rivalry.

"Well, you can't blame people for taking matters into their own hands," said Mr Jouzeh on one occasion when he and his wife had come across to our house for coffee. "The Jews are trying to take over the country, that's all there's to it and we can't rely on anyone. Everyone has let us down."

"Even if the Jews succeed – and they haven't yet –" said his wife, "they won't last long in this land. Look at what happened to the crusaders. They stayed in Palestine for a long time, but in the end, they were thrown out. And that's what's going to happen to the Jews now if they try it."

"And who's going to get rid of them?" asked her husband.

"Oh, all the Arabs and all the Muslims together," she answered firmly, looking at us, since we were the only Muslims in the gathering. My parents fidgeted uneasily and looked away.

But as February slipped into March with no sign of relief for our plight, hopes that the Arab states were going to leap to our defence were dwindling fast. Everyone said that the Mufti had received volunteers and arms from Egypt to continue the war effort, but we saw no change in our lives, which remained as isolated and defenceless as before. The rumour was rife that the Arab League had no real intention of helping to rescue the Palestinians, but only wanted to control the future of Palestine for its own ends. The exodus from Qatamon continued relentlessly, as from elsewhere in the country. By March, people had fled from large parts of the coastal plain area between Tel Aviv and Hadera, north of Tulkarm. Everywhere the story was the same, that the Jewish army and the Jewish irregulars attacked the peasants, village by village, and threatened them with worse. So they ran for their lives either in the immediate aftermath of a Jewish attack or because they feared that their turn would be next.

They poured into Tulkarm and its vicinity, since this was the first safe haven they could find. The panic they brought with them infected the people of Tulkarm, some of whom began to fear that the Jewish advance would not stop at Haifa. There was no one to tell people what was happening, why the Jews were on the attack and who, if anyone, would defend them. My aunt Souad gave refuge to one family from a village outside Haifa who came saying that Jewish soldiers had suddenly entered their village, shooting at anyone they saw. No one had any arms and so they fled. They never knew how many people had been killed. These and similar stories fuelled the terror in Tulkarm, and some began to flee towards the villages further inland. News from our family was increasingly hard to get, but we heard that the Bedouin outside the town brought out their machine-guns, which had been with their fathers since the days of the Ottoman Empire, in readiness for the Jewish attack. They were soon joined by Bedouin from Wadi al-Hawarith, a village by the coast near to Tulkarm, who had fled before the Jewish forces. The situation was said to be chaotic.

"To think", my cousin Aziza said afterwards, "that those Jews in Hadera who were our neighbours in good faith, as we thought, should have turned on us like that. We should have remembered that the Jews can never be trusted. Did they not betray the Prophet himself?" Aziza was referring to that time in Arab history when Muhammad made an alliance with the Jewish tribes to ensure their neutrality, an agreement which they then broke, going to the aid of his adversaries. Neither Aziza's mother nor that generation would ever have said such a thing. But after Israel's creation, such anti-Jewish sentiments became common amongst Muslim Palestinians in a futile attempt to find explanations for their defeat.

Hadera was a rural Jewish settlement, established at the end of the nineteenth century, which lay to the north-west of Tulkarm and whose lands adjoined those of Aziza's family. "We never thought of them as enemies until then. And then we began to be afraid of them when we saw how they were putting up the barbed wire fences around their land and bringing in arms and big dogs."

Matters got worse and there was shooting in the streets of Tulkarm. The old people were bewildered by it. They remembered how it was in the Great War and thought it was happening all over again. "But even the Great War came to an end," they said, "and so will this. The Jews will leave us alone." But no one else believed that. Talk was rife that the Jews wanted to take over the whole of Palestine. Our cousins bought rifles, which they did not know how to use, in readiness to defend the town against the Jews. My mother and father worried a great deal about our family in Tulkarm but were powerless to help.

The news from my uncle Abu Salma in Haifa brought no relief either. Here, the battle for the city had been raging ever since the beginning of the year. Many people had already left because of it, perhaps 20,000 or more. Businesses and shops were closing down and being eagerly bought up by Jews at a fraction of their true value. My uncle said that the Jewish terrorists had started a campaign of intimidation. This and the constant sniping, bombing and demolition frightened people so much that they were leaving in panic.

He himself did not know how long he and my aunt could hold out. He was disgusted with the Arab defence forces in the city because they were disunited and undisciplined. The National Committee could not control the irregulars who did not obey orders and attacked Jewish targets in an unruly and impulsive fashion. The Jewish attacks, by contrast, were organised and effective. And each time the Jews struck, they caused a fresh wave of flight from the city. The AHC were not firm enough in telling people to stay where they were, even though they knew the Jews were aiming to seize Haifa for themselves.

In Jerusalem, we were feeling more and more besieged. By March, the neighbourhoods in our vicinity were emptying fast. People had left in large numbers from Romema, Lifta, Sheikh Jarrah, Musrara and Talbiyya, and many among these were friends or acquaintances. My mother put her head in her hands. "Oh God, they say the Jews are taking over all the empty houses." The villages on the outskirts of Jerusalem, Beit Safafa, Abu Dis, al-Aizariyya and Beit Sahour, were also being evacuated as people fled. Sometimes at night, when there was a thunderstorm and we imagined that the Semiramis bombing was happening all over again, Fatima would shake her head and say, "I wonder which poor village the Jews are attacking now."

My father came home and told us that the Jewish leaders were celebrating "the new Jerusalem". You can go through the western part of the city, they were saying, without meeting a single Arab, thank God. "Surely that's not true," Siham said. "What about us then?" We were still hanging on, but it was dismal to realise that so many people we knew had already left. Our road seemed more and more deserted. The Khayyats had gone just after the Semiramis bombing, and so had my mother's old friend Um Samir al-Sharkas. Emily and her family had gone too. Before they left for the Old City they gave us the keys to their house and told us to stay there if we needed to. This was because it stood inside the British zone and as such was more secure than where we lived, exposed to direct attack. Emily and my mother embraced and hung on each other weeping, as if they would never meet again.

"It will be over," said Emily to my mother. "It must end soon, and we'll be back." Randa and I did not hug each other or cry, I think because we did not fully comprehend what was happening. The Old City was not far away and it was not such a long time since we had gone there to see my aunt Khadija. It did not seem possible that we would not be going there again. And Randa's departure in the bewildering and extraordinary situation of our lives at that time did not seem especially dramatic. More worrying was the fact that Abu Samir, the grocer to whose shop we went for sweets and nuts and drinks, closed down. Many of the houses on the opposite side of our street were now empty.

Ziyad and I had nowhere to go and few friends to play with any more. In March, even the Jouzehs, our neighbours for all the time we had lived in that house in Qatamon, finally left. They cried when they went, for leaving their home and for leaving us. "How much longer do you dare stay?" they asked. "The Jews are not going to drive me out of my house," my mother declared staunchly, but she said this only afterwards in order not to upset them. "Others may go if they like, but we're not giving in."

The only people to agree with her were the young couple who had moved into the old Muscovite's house next door to us on the other side. This was a truly amazing event, given that everyone was deserting Qatamon as fast as they could. The couple who bought the house came from the village of Ain Karim, just outside Jerusalem, and, strangely enough, were also called Karmi, but written differently to our surname in Arabic, with a long "a". No one could credit such a purchase in the dangerous, besieged place that Qatamon had become. But they had got it for a very low price and were delighted. My mother said to them, "How can anyone buy in Qatamon at a time like this?" But they were unperturbed. "It's a good investment. People say that the Jews are going to take over Qatamon, but it won't happen, wait and see." And my mother felt vindicated in her own view.

One evening not long afterwards, we were sitting in the *liwan* after dinner. The radio was on, and both our parents were listening intently as usual. It was the only link we had with outside events, since most roads from Jerusalem and even from Qatamon were dangerous or impassable. Suddenly, Rex started to bark and there was a sound of scuffling at the back of the house. All our shutters were tightly closed, as had become our habit since the Semiramis bombing, and so no one could see out. But my parents froze and my mother turned the radio off. We sat absolutely still, listening. There was no doubt about it, someone was in our garden. There was a sound of heavy running feet, and as we sat scarcely breathing, the silence was shattered by a loud bang of gunshot followed by shouting. Fatima, who came up behind me where I was sitting on the floor, put her hands tightly over my ears and curled my head over my chest. But this frightened me even more and I wriggled out of her grasp. My father sprang up towards the door and my mother called out, "No! Please, no!"

By now there was a sound of running feet everywhere, as if an army had descended on our house. Although it seemed close, in fact the sound came from behind the wall at the back of the garden. There was a great deal of shouting which we could now make out as something like, "Not that way! There, over the wall!" The running sound seemed to change direction. It came alarmingly close to the side of our house and then moved towards the garden gate. My father went to the front door and began opening it cautiously. And as he did so, I noticed with sudden anxiety that Rex was not barking any more. I rushed to the door and tried to look into the dark outside. "Sst!" my mother shouted and pulled me back. "But Rex ... " I implored. "Is this a time to worry about dogs?" she demanded.

A while later, as we tried to calm down, Abu Dayyeh from the Defence Committee came to see us. He said that a few of his men had been pursuing a group of Jewish irregulars who ran into the garden – "like the cowards they are" – behind the Jouzehs' house. From there they had crossed into our garden where the Arab soldiers caught up with them, and that was what we had heard. He said he was sorry for the disturbance it had caused us, but it was necessary in the war against the Jews, and he wondered what my father was doing, letting his family stay on in the house. The AHC had now advised everyone in the neighbourhood to evacuate all women, children and old people. Did we realise that Jewish snipers had been occupying the empty houses on the opposite side of our road from where they were preparing to shoot at people? To me, this instantly conjured up a nightmare image of menacing shadows lurking unseen behind the dark windows of Abu Samir's deserted shop. "And will your men evict them?" asked my father. "Of course," Abu Dayyeh answered confidently, "you and your family can be assured of that". As soon as he went, my father said, "Hmm, I wonder who was chasing who." On several occasions in the last few weeks we had almost got used to the sight of Abu Dayyeh's men being pursued by armed Jewish men who ran through our garden and even onto our veranda, as if our house were a public highway. We found these pursuits terrifying, but they usually happened in the daytime and no shots were fired.

The very next morning, as if the Jewish snipers had heard Abu

Dayyeh's boast, a Bedouin walking along the road was shot dead right in front of our house. He was one of the dwindling numbers of street peddlers that still braved the danger to come round the houses, selling foodstuffs. The chaotic conditions prevailing in the country had hit the poor hardest of all, and they were obliged to continue what trading they could despite the hazards. This Bedouin had come into our street with a great sack over his shoulder, the kind his people usually used to carry their wares: yoghurt, *samn* and goat cheese. In the time before the troubles, my mother had always bought such things from the Bedouin, which she said were the tastiest of all. We were out on the veranda and Fatima was hanging out the washing at the back when it happened. He was rather dusty and bedraggled, wearing a brown cloak and *kufiyya* on his head and he walked in the middle of the road as there were very few cars about. As he drew level with our gate, shots rang out from the houses opposite and, as if the two events were unconnected, he suddenly crumpled up and fell down hunched over his sack. There was screaming from somewhere, perhaps from our house. Someone, I think Fatima, dragged me and Ziyad back inside and closed the door tight.

That night, we decided to start sleeping at Emily's house in "the zone", as the British sector was usually known. Although it was not far away in terms of distance, getting there seemed interminable. We tried not to walk along the road as far as possible and crossed over the gardens behind the houses. Most of these were deserted and it was a strange, ghostly experience to see them so dark and still and to remember how noisy and full of people they had been. When we arrived, it was to find a cold, unheated house, its shutters closed and the carpets all rolled up, not covering the floors like ours. The place had a look of complete abandonment which my mother and Fatima tried to dispel by lighting the fire and turning on the radio and bustling about. Emily's house, where Randa had lived and where we had had such fun, now filled me with gloom. I hated going there, especially as we had to leave Rex behind. Every time we left in the evening, he leaped up all over me and Ziyad. "Silly Rex," Ziyad would tell him and ruffle the fur around his neck and ears, "don't worry, we'll see you tomorrow." And each time we returned home, he would be standing behind the garden gate, waiting for us to appear. And each time he would realise too late that we were coming through the garden route and not the road and would run around maniacally, as if to hide his embarrassment.

Throughout this turbulent time, Siham was trying to study for her examinations. She was nearly eighteen and in her final matriculation year. The government decided that students like her should not be deprived of completing their education, even though the situation made normal schooling difficult. They further decided that the matriculation exam would be brought forward to April from its normal date in June. This was because the British Mandate would be ending in May and no one could guarantee what might happen after that. From the beginning of the year, she and her classmates started to go for their lessons to the British Council which was in the German Colony and relatively safe. To get there, she walked through the back gardens to avoid the open road. She became quite adept at finding a sheltered route, along which Rex occasionally followed her until she shooed him back, and for a while never came across any danger.

However, by the end of March, many parts of Jerusalem had become too unsafe to travel through, and the government arranged for all those taking the matriculation to become boarders until they sat for the exam. This was to be held in al-Ma'mouniyya, our old school, which, being in Wadi al-Joz, was in the Arab zone and hence considered safer than either the British or Jewish zones. The students were to board in a nearby house which had been rented for the purpose. She packed a small bag with her clothes and her books went into another, while Ziyad and I looked on. She said she would be away for about two weeks, just over the period when they would be revising and then sitting for the exam.

No one in our house talked about what was to happen or what we were going to do, at least not in front of me or Ziyad, who were nine and seven at that time. We still went out into our garden when it was not raining or too cold, but we did not often venture out into the road. Hardly any children came to see us, but Ziyad still went out with Rex whenever it seemed quiet. At about this time he developed a cold and sore throat. It seemed trivial at first, but when his temperature rose and he developed severe earache, our mother got alarmed. Cut off as we were, she wondered how to get Ziyad to a doctor. As he continued to get worse, she turned to Fatima's brother for help. He was in the habit of looking in every few days with news of Fatima's daughters whom she had not seen since she came to stay with us.

"Muhammad," she said, "you"ll have to get to our doctor somehow and bring him back with you. The boy is getting worse by the minute." Muhammad said it might not be possible to bring the doctor and wanted to know what was wrong. Ziyad was usually uncomplaining, but he was clearly in great pain, his face flushed and his hand held against his ear. Seeing him, Muhammad told my mother to stop worrying as he had a remedy for such things. No one was particularly surprised at this, since folk treatments and herbal recipes were a familiar part of life in Palestine at that time, especially amongst villagers like Fatima and Muhammad who had no access to doctors or hospitals. Many a time I remember a bellyache or an attack of diarrhoea settling with nothing more than a concoction of Fatima's herbs.

We now all looked on while Muhammad went to the kitchen and warmed some olive oil in a pan. He then sat Ziyad up and gently took him in his arms. Bending over him, he poured the oil into his ear and waited for a few minutes. He then clamped his mouth over it and began to suck vigorously. After a minute, he moved his mouth away and spat a cloudy mixture of blood-stained oil, mucus and saliva into the bowl. It acted on my brother like magic. The earache seemed to stop instantly and as Muhammad lay him down again slowly on the bed, Ziyad closed his eyes and fell into a deep, natural sleep. The next day, his temperature was down and in a week he was completely cured.

In the meantime, we had begun to run short of fresh food. Fatima was going daily to those shops in our vicinity which were still open and also to the great souk in the Old City for vegetables. My mother stocked up with staples whenever she could, although we already had a large store of food in the loft. But now she augmented it further in case the half-siege we lived in got worse. The village women who used to come from the places just outside Jerusalem like Battir, Beit Safafa, Beit Jala, al-Walajeh and Fatima's own village of al-Maliha, still called to sell vegetables and fruit, but these occasional visits were nothing like they had been.

There was one woman in particular who always used to call at our house, sometimes alone and at other times with her sister. She wore an embroidered caftan like Fatima's, but grubby with soil and dust, and had a white veil draped loosely over her head. Her figure was ample and her face was ruddy from being out in the open. She used to walk barefoot, balancing a great wide basket full of vegetables on her head. Whenever she reached our house, she would rattle the front gate and call out, and Fatima would come out to her. She then came up onto our veranda and put down her huge basket of vegetables and fruit. I remember rich bunches of parsley, fat, blood-red tomatoes, shiny, taut-skinned aubergines and the hugest radishes I have ever seen. She took the same route every time, coming from al-Walajeh through to West Jerusalem and to Qatamon, then to Baq'a and on to the German Colony, finally ending up in the Old City souk, where she disposed of what had remained in her basket unsold.

Only now, she and the others came to our house less frequently and because our road was virtually deserted, they often missed us completely, thinking there was no one living in the houses at all. Eventually they stopped coming altogether. The baker had long ceased to come to the house and my mother started to bake bread once again. As in the past, she would prepare the dough and Fatima would take it down for baking to the public oven which was still functioning. We were eating more or less normally, but many luxury items were now unobtainable.

This was more than could be said for the Jews in Jerusalem at that time. The Arab forces had managed to gain control of the road which ran between Jerusalem and Tel Aviv. As this was the main highway along which the bulk of the Jewish community's supplies and transport moved, they began to face real hardship with shortages of food and fuel. Their leaders imposed severe rationing of bread, flour, sugar and fuel. Baths were a luxury since there was no fuel to heat the water, and even the dogs which many Jews kept could not be fed. Water itself was in short supply, since the springs outside Jerusalem and the water pumping stations were all within Arab-controlled territory. The Arabs attacked the railroad as well as the highway, stopping trains and removing from them supplies destined for the Jews. The Jewish leadership complained angrily that the British did not interfere because they were too busy preventing Jewish immigration into the country. The ships carrying Jews from Europe were still coming to Palestine despite a British ban on immigration, and many Jews tried to enter the country illegally.

Nearly one year before, in June 1947, a ship full of European Jewish immigrants called the *Exodus*, had sailed for Haifa and tried to force its way past the British authorities but was turned back. It became something of a *cause célèbre* amongst the Jews, who made much of the plight of the Jewish immigrants thus denied entry to

Palestine and who accused the British of callousness and brutality.[1] But for the Palestinians, it hardly featured at all; people saw it as but one example amongst many of the Jews' determination to invade the country.

"We wouldn't want to deny a haven to ordinary refugees," they said. "The problem with these refugees is that they're not coming here just for safety. They're coming to take over the country."

We suffered in no small measure alongside the Jews. For, as well as enduring the perils of warfare, we witnessed a decline in the public services of Jerusalem throughout March. The post barely reached us and letters we wrote to Tulkarm and Haifa took at least a week or, more frequently, never arrived at all because the mailbags were stolen on the way. Letters to and from Damascus were totally suspended and my mother no longer had news of our grandparents or uncle there. Jerusalem's telephone lines were often out of action and, although we ourselves had no telephone, we used to use the one at Abu Samir's shop until it closed. There was a general breakdown in law and order; theft was commonplace and Jews and Arabs carried arms openly, although if they were caught, the British authorities disarmed and punished them. But the British police were more and more reluctant to enforce the law and this attitude encouraged further independent action on the part of each side.

It was in any case now tacitly accepted that within their respective zones, both Arabs and Jews were responsible for the security of their communities. Apart from the so-called mixed neighbourhoods like Talbiyya, where Jews and Arabs lived uneasily together, neither community was welcome in the territory of the other and people went

---

[1] The story of the *Exodus* later became the subject of a best-selling novel by Leon Uris, published in 1959, and a Hollywood epic. Both book and film contributed enormously to presenting the birth of Israel in a positive light, depicting the Jewish heroes as plucky fighters, many as displaced victims of the European Holocaust, while making short shrift of the displaced Arabs, usually shown as shifty, violent and crazed.

only if it was strictly necessary. But Sami Haddad, our neighbours' friend who lived in Upper Baq'a dismissed this as so much scare-mongering. "The Jews don't frighten me," he said when visiting with his wife one evening. "You know they put these rumours about on purpose to make us nervous and think they're stronger than they really are."

One day, he was in the middle of Jerusalem in a Jewish area known as Zion Square. This was a major commercial centre just off the Jaffa Road where Arabs and Jews had conducted a great deal of business before the troubles, and where Arabs bought merchandise from Jewish shops which stocked European goods new to Palestine. With the outbreak of violence, most Arabs suspended such dealings with Jewish businessmen and generally observed the boycott of Jewish merchandise. Arabs tended to stay out of the Jewish-controlled zones of Jerusalem and vice versa. But Sami Haddad worked for the American airline TWA which had an office in Zion Square, one of these Jewish zones. He had gone there that day on an errand as requested by his office, although he did not much want to.

Sami belonged to his local Civil Defence Committee which orga-nised nightly rotas, rather like those we had had in Qatamon. As chance would have it, the day of his visit to Zion Square had followed the night of his turn to stand guard. Thus he still had on him the gun which he had carried during his night's vigil. Inevitably, he caught the attention of a Jewish patrol which stopped and searched him. Finding the gun, they arrested him and accused him of being an Arab spy. "It would be hard to find anyone less likely to be a spy than Sami," said his wife afterwards. "It was ridiculous." But the Jews wouldn't let him go and locked him up. They then told him he would be released only if he agreed to spy on the Arab camp for them. They promised him large sums of money for his services, but as he continued to refuse, they gave him some food and left him to think about it. "I've never been so scared in all my life," he confessed afterwards. And as he racked his brains for a way of escape, there was a sudden explosion nearby which made the Jewish guard scatter, and, in the mêlée that followed, he was able to run off. "I never thought the day would come when I'd be glad to hear a bomb going off, but at that moment it was the sweetest sound in all the world!"

The situation in Palestine was so bad that the UN met to discuss it. We heard on the radio that the United States considered the 1947 partition plan unworkable and the country should be placed under UN trusteeship. The few people left in Qatamon heaved a sigh of relief. "Well, now maybe we will see some order restored in the country instead of this madness." The Jews, however, rejected the American proposal out of hand. They were furious at the United States which they accused of betraying them "for the sake of Arab oil". The Jewish Agency declared that the trusteeship idea represented an assault on the rights and sovereignty of the whole Jewish people. We did not know it, but the idea that the Jews of the world had an unassailable right to Palestine was by then deeply entrenched. Since Jews had been deserted by the world, the Agency argued, it meant that they would have to fight on alone and the struggle for Palestine would be that much harder. And indeed we heard that Jewish schoolteachers, doctors and dentists who had never contemplated military action before were lining up at Haganah headquarters asking for guns and rifles.

The news from the UN was a fillip to the Arab side which now succeeded in gaining control of the communications between Haifa, Tel Aviv and Jerusalem, the three main cities where Jews were concentrated. The part of the Tel Aviv–Jerusalem road which passes between Bab al-Wad and Jerusalem was under the control of Abdul-Qadir al-Husseini. This man was one of our few charismatic and popular commanders, a relative of the Mufti (whom, however, he did not get along with) and a leader of an irregular Arab force called

Jaysh al-Jihad al-Muqaddas (the army of the holy jihad). He had started life as a surveyor in Ramleh where my father first met him when he and my mother lived there. He thought him decent and loyal with a reputation for being brave, perhaps foolhardy, but totally dedicated to fighting the Jews. In the course of this effort, Husseini had tried to incite the villages outside Jerusalem to attack Jewish settlements. But many of them were too afraid of Jewish retaliation to do so and refused. But though he failed in this, he redeemed himself by holding the road into Jerusalem, strangling Jewish traffic and attacking their convoys successfully. "Perhaps he will save the city for the Arabs," people said in hope.

Life for our aunt Khadija in the Old City was also becoming troubled. Ever since the partition resolution was announced, there had been clashes around the Jewish Quarter, not far from her house. They were not too worried at the beginning because the British intervened repeatedly to keep order. But the Haganah were not satisfied and sent in their own soldiers to protect the Jewish Quarter. They made out that the British wanted the Jews out of the Old City to leave it all in Arab hands. This was unthinkable, they said, because the place was sacred and a holy trust for the Jewish people. The Arabs heard this with considerable scepticism. "No one believes a word of it," said my aunt. "They're only looking for an excuse to get themselves a foothold in the Old City." My aunt's husband Abu Isam, whose shop was in Mamilla near my father's office, told him much the same thing. "They say the Jews want to take control of the Old City." But my father reassured him that it could not happen.

The Haganah started smuggling arms and ammunition into the Jewish Quarter. When the British discovered this, they confiscated the arms in the face of fierce Jewish resistance. At the same time, Arab irregulars continued to attack the Jewish Quarter and the Haganah forces who were based there. Fighting then broke out between the

Haganah and the British army. Several British soldiers were killed, and at the end of March a cease-fire was agreed. However, this turned out to be only temporary and the hostilities started all over again. By then my aunt's family was finding life difficult, especially as my cousins were all very small. My aunt's husband was getting few customers in his shop and they did not know what to do. They could no longer come to see us because of the danger on the roads, nor could we visit them for the same reason. "What a situation," my mother said to us, shaking her head. "Your aunt is not more than ten minutes away from here, but she might as well be in Syria for all the chance we have of seeing her."

As March drew to a close the violence in Qatamon was worse than ever. Sometimes we found it hard to sleep at night for the whistling of bullets and the thunder of shells. We were now sleeping on the floor most of the time, which was hard for my father who had recurrent back pain (he called it "lumbago" and continued to suffer from it intermittently for much of his life). He would groan loudly every time he laid down or got up. There was little respite from the shooting in the day either, when machine-guns could be heard firing, sometimes continuously. Explosions shook our house without warning and we spent our time in anticipation of the next attack. None of this seemed to worry Ziyad who was still collecting bullets and playing at being soldiers in the garden.

But to me this was terrifying and bewildering, so far removed from anything I recognised as normality that I think I became a little shell-shocked. After a while, I accepted each blow silently without protest, as if we were fated to live like that. I learned to adapt by clinging to the small routines of our life which still went on despite everything. Siham had gone to board at her school which left me and Ziyad and Fatima in our bedroom at night. A suspicion bordering on conviction had taken hold of people's minds that the Jewish forces meant to take over Qatamon and that the battle to repel them would get fiercer. Everyone was afraid, especially the children who screamed and wailed uncomprehendingly through the bombing and the shooting. And so more families packed up and left. But still we hung on, like the Sakakini family and a few others, because we simply could not imagine leaving our home and still believed that somehow a last-minute rescue by the British or the Arabs would take place.

Our parents said no matter what happened, Siham had to take her exams. And in any case, we had nowhere to go. Many of the families who had left had gone to relatives elsewhere, or the men had found temporary work, or they were wealthy enough to bide their time away from Jerusalem in comfort. For everywhere the word went out that, until the problem was solved, leaving the danger zone was only a temporary measure.

My mother kept saying that help must come soon, that the English, the Arab League, the UN or some combination of these could not stand by and allow the Jews to drive us out. In saying this, she echoed many other people who waited impatiently for the Arab armies to enter Palestine and defeat the Jews. But whenever she said this, my father dismissed her hopes with a show of cynicism. "You can believe what you like. They've not done much for us so far." But perhaps he secretly also looked for some such salvation.

At that time, there was much talk of a separate status for Jerusalem when the Mandate was terminated. The city would be put under UN trusteeship and, even if the rest of Palestine was divided into two states, Jerusalem would not be part of either and might continue more or less as it was. The Jews had never accepted this and people around us said that they secretly planned to make Jerusalem their capital. But everyone discounted this as Jewish wishful thinking and further evidence of their greed for our country.

Four

When I look back, I see how that time in my life is overlaid with areas of silence, impenetrable to memory. I was aware that everything had gone wrong with us, but did not know why, or whether my world would ever come back again, the sunny times, the friends, the going to and coming from school. Around me, events succeeded each other with a relentless momentum, heading for some cataclysm. And we were being pushed uncontrollably by this momentum, powerless to stop it. The worst of it was my instinctive sense that my parents were frightened and did not know where we were headed either. Ziyad often ignored orders and went out riding his bicycle. Otherwise, he and I played with Rex desultorily in the garden, for there was nothing else to do.

But the fearful days and nights continued, and all the time the things which were familiar in our lives receded. Now Fatima hardly ever went to the souk and we waited for the village women to come to the house. When they didn't, we had no vegetables or eggs. Siham was not with us any more, something which had never happened before. She had always been there for as long as I could remember, and though everyone else had gone away at one time or another – Fatima, our father, and our mother who was out so much she might as well have been away – Siham never had. Her absence was deeply disturbing and yet also in keeping with the other bizarre events taking place. My father had little to say when he came home; he just read the newspapers or his books and listened to the radio intently.

Amazingly, the Palestine Broadcasting Service in Jerusalem was still operating, albeit with difficulty. A short while later, however, its transmitters in Ramallah were shot away in fighting on the Jerusalem-Ramallah road. All this time, Ziyad seemed oblivious to everything; he just read and re-read his old comics, *Superman* and *Captain Marvel*, since there were no new ones to be had. Rex was the only one to remain the same. In fact, I think he was happier than he had ever been because we were always at home with him now, playing all the games he loved best.

It was now spring in Palestine. With the coming of April, all the trees in the garden came out in blossom. Although it was still cold, the weather was variable and some days were brilliant with sunshine. For me, the world had shrunk to the confines of our garden and our house in a private enclave, which I made magically immune from the bombing and the shooting. I invented games to play on my own and told my toys stories loosely based on *The Arabian Nights*, such as our mother used to do when we were younger. People still came to our house to see my parents, and my mother went out visiting those neighbours who remained near us. "I'm stifling," she would say. "I must get out." The talk was always the same – terrible things happening all over the country, more people leaving (my uncle Abu Salma among them), no one to save us from the Jews and so on.

And then Fatima's brother appeared at the house one morning looking agitated. He and Fatima stood at the kitchen door talking in low voices. Then my mother came out and Fatima said that something terrible had happened. They all went inside the house and, after a while, Muhammad came out again with Fatima and they both went off together. We found out that they had gone to the Old City. When Fatima came back, she told my mother that this terrible thing was true, everyone was talking about it. The poor people had fled first to the nearest village, Ain Karim, and then to Beit Safafa, and to al-Maliha, which was how Muhammad got to know about it. Some of them escaped into Jerusalem itself, to the Old City, where they told their terrible stories. Incomprehensible snatches of sentences came across to me and Ziyad, all about fearful happenings and killings of women and children.

My father came home and they talked more, but in such hushed voices that we could not hear them. What was this terrible thing? Fatima would not say and neither would our parents. A few people came over to our house that evening, saying that the Jews were threatening to do it again and that everyone believed them. The next morning – was it then? It seemed so, and yet when I looked back long after, I was not so sure and, amazingly, no one in our family could remember the exact date of that momentous day; my father thought it later in April, my sister said it was earlier. A baffling amnesia has enveloped that time. I woke up that morning with a feeling of nameless dread, as if I had had a bad dream which I could not recall. Fatima and my mother were long since up, and I heard them pushing furniture, opening drawers and cupboards in my parents' bedroom. No one said anything to me, not even Fatima, and so I went and woke Ziyad up.

He was bad-tempered and tried to push me away. "There's something going on," I said urgently. "There always is," he grumbled and turned away, covering his head with the bedclothes. Siham was not back yet, although the two weeks she said she would be away were up. Perhaps I could ask about that, but when I went into my mother's room I saw that there were suitcases on the bed and clothes on the floor. Before I could exclaim she pushed me out and told me in a tense, irritable voice to go and play, but to "stay inside the house". A panic began to seize me and I went out to the back of the house and through the garden door to the shed which served as Rex's kennel. He was lying down in front of it sniffing the air. As soon as he saw me he sprang up, his tail wagging. Though I knelt down and hugged him and tried to draw comfort from him, it did not still the anxiety welling up inside me. I went back inside and now my mother was in the *liwan*, wrapping up our china plates in newspaper. "Against the bombs", she was saying to Fatima. "They might not break this way."

"Have you had your breakfast?" asked Fatima. I shook my head. I had no appetite at all; I just stood there looking wanly at what they were doing. They ignored me and my mother went on wrapping the plates and handing them to Fatima who put them into a cardboard box. After a while, Muhammad appeared and told my mother that he had found a car, but it would not be available before evening. "Are we going somewhere?" I asked in sudden alarm. Someone finally spoke to me, "No, it's just to fetch your sister back from school," said my mother. I was overjoyed with relief. Siham was coming home and all would be well. Whatever this strange thing was which had overtaken our house, Siham would explain and we would go back to normal.

When Ziyad finally got up, I told him everything that had happened that morning. "When Siham is here, she'll tell us what's going on," I finished. "You're just stupid," he said testily. "How can she know? She's been in school taking exams. I'm going to get to the bottom of this." But as the day wore on, he was little wiser than I had been, except that my mother said we would know everything later when Siham got home. There was more packing, this time it was blankets from the big chest where my mother kept such things. We discovered that she had also taken some of our clothes away from the cupboard in the bedroom.

"Fatima, please tell me what's going on," I pleaded. "Are we going somewhere?" But Fatima only answered, "Don't worry, your mother will tell you very soon."

When my father came home in the afternoon we all had lunch as usual. I sat with them at table in the dining-room – not with Fatima – because her brother Muhammad had stayed overnight and the two of them were eating in the kitchen. The atmosphere was full of tension and unspoken anxiety and I wished I was eating with Fatima as I had always done. But I told myself that I would do so tomorrow. After lunch, my mother and father went silently to their room, having evaded our questions by saying we would know later when we were all together. Ziyad and I took the remains of our half-eaten food out into the garden and gave them to Rex. Because the butcher in the road had closed down we could no longer give him all the leftover meat and bones which he was used to. So he ate whatever we could spare and my mother gave him bits and pieces while she was cooking.

It was late afternoon. We sat around aimlessly, uneasy and apprehensive. There was the sound of occasional shooting, but it was far away like the sound of distant thunder; thus far the day had been relatively quiet. I kept going to the garden wall which looked out on to the road and watching for Siham. It was windy and I got cold, so I went back into the house, but as soon as I warmed up, I went out again. It was while I was warming up inside that Siham arrived. It seemed like a year since I had last seen her and I rushed to put my arms round her. But she was upset and crying. "I knew it," said our mother. "You've gone and failed your exams!"

"No, I haven't," sobbed Siham. "But why couldn't you have waited at least until we'd had our party? We've worked so hard and we were going to celebrate the end of exams tonight. I was really looking forward to it. Please, please, can't we wait just one more day?" Muhammad had turned up at the school without warning, since there was no way of making contact beforehand, and had announced that she must come home with him in the taxi without delay. "And anyway, what is all this Muhammad says about us leaving?"

"It's true," replied my father. "Your mother and all of you are leaving in the morning. It's not safe here any more, not after Deir Yassin."

What was he saying? We could not be leaving. It could not be true. I followed Siham into our bedroom, full of agitation. "Where are we going? What does it mean? Why won't they tell us anything?" She took my arm in her hands. "God, why are you so thin?" she asked. "They didn't want you and Ziyad to know in case you told anyone else." (At this time, the AHC had given strict instructions again that no one was to leave the country, and people who intended to go were therefore careful to avoid discovery.) "And besides, they didn't want to upset any of us. I think we're going to Damascus to our grand-parents' house."

"But why do we have to go?" She started to explain that it was not safe to stay on, but, as she spoke, the words suddenly lost meaning. A numbness began to come over me and I had a sudden feeling of utter helplessness. I had never met my grandparents and I didn't want to. I wanted to stay here at home, despite Deir Yassin (whatever that was) and however bad the shooting got. Siham suddenly put her hand to her mouth and gasped. "Oh no!" she cried, "My watch. It's still at the watchmaker's. How am I going to be able to get it before we leave?" The watch, which was being mended, had been given to her by our parents, she was proud of showing it off. "It doesn't matter. I'll pick it up for you when I come back," said my father. He was intending to escort us until we had arrived safely in Damascus and then return to Jerusalem. He had informed them at the office of his intention and had been given a short leave of absence. But the head of his department hinted that this might be longer than my father thought. When he asked what this meant, the other smiled and replied cryptically, "Oh, well, you know how it is. In Jerusalem these days anything can happen." My father chose to ignore this and said he would be back to work in two or three days, long enough to cover the time of the journey to Damascus, an overnight stay and the journey back. On this basis, my mother had not packed a separate suitcase for him and had taken only a few summer clothes for us because, as she kept saying, "We won't be gone for long. It's not worth taking much more." But even though she had packed so little, the house already had an empty and deserted look, rather like Emily's house had been.

I do not remember how we spent that evening nor how we slept afterwards. That time belongs to one of those impenetrable areas of silence. I do not know if my parents took their leave of our neighbours or if anyone came to say goodbye. But the next morning, when we got up, events moved rapidly. Whatever the reason for the respite in the fighting the day before, it had now resumed with vigour. In recent weeks, mortar bombs had been added to the usual gunfire and shooting, and we could hear heavy thudding from the direction of the St Simon monastery. This was a large and ancient place surrounded by trees which stood at the top of the Qatamon hill to the other side of our road. The Jews said it was a stronghold of Arab soldiers and arms and had been planning to attack it for weeks. In the interval between explosions there was an eerie silence. The street outside was deserted. My mother said, "I hope Muhammad can make it." He was supposed to bring up a taxi for us from town, an enterprise that would be something of a miracle to carry through, given the danger of reaching Qatamon. No cars ever came here any more, but Muhammad said he was confident he would find one.

And indeed, in a short while, the taxi appeared with him sitting in the front seat next to the driver. The latter was clearly nervous and told us to hurry. My mother had our case and the old blankets ready in the *liwan*, and Ziyad, who had been very quiet that morning, now said he wanted to take his bicycle along. "Don't be silly," snapped my mother. "But I want to take it," he insisted. Everyone ignored him. Siham had a winter coat which our father had brought back for her from London. It had been too big for her when he bought it but now it fitted and she had scarcely ever worn it. She now tried to pack it with the rest of our clothes, but it was too bulky. "Never mind," said our mother, "leave it for when we come back."

Muhammad and Fatima took down our cases over the veranda steps towards the gate, leaving the front door of the house open. Through the door, Rex now ran in, undeterred by his usual fear of my mother and started to jump up all over us in great agitation. He made a high-pitched, keening sound I had never heard before.

"He knows we're going," Siham said. "I don't know how, but he does." Ziyad and I could not catch hold of him long enough to pat his head and calm him down. He kept rushing from one to the other so fast that his hind legs slipped on the floor. But I managed to grab him and hug him tightly to me. Fatima came back in and tried to say that the car was now ready, but she started to cry. My mother put a hand on her shoulder, "There, there, we'll be back. It won't be long." But Fatima just went on crying. Then she said, "I've got to cry now because I'll be too shy to cry when we say goodbye at the depot." She meant the place in town where we would stop to change cars for Damascus.

There was a loud explosion outside. My father said we must now leave. He had a heavy brown overcoat on his arm which he now gave Fatima. He had bought it in England for himself and it had a label inside the collar which said Moss Bros.

"This is for you." And as Fatima started to cry again, my father said hurriedly, "Here, take the key and keep it safe." This was the key to our house where Fatima was going to stay until we all returned. She put it in the side pocket of her caftan and wiped her eyes. "I'll look after everything, have no worry."

We came out with Rex still running round and my father locked up. We put Rex into the garden and closed the gate on him in case he ran out into the road on his own. I lingered, looking back at the house. The shutters were all closed and silent and the garden seemed to hug the walls, as if to retain their secrets. Enclosed in that space was all the life that I had ever known and I thought what a dear, dear place it was.

A deafening burst of shooting. My mother ran forward and dragged me away. My father got in the front of the car with Muhammad and Ziyad and the rest of us squeezed into the back. I sat on Fatima's lap and wondered whether I dared ask if I could go back for my teddy bear, Beta, which no one had thought to pack for me. I thought of him left all alone with Rex in that silent, shuttered house. Ziyad was quiet in the front seat. He too was thinking about Rex and whether he could have managed somehow to smuggle him into the boot of the car. But as we were about to move off, my father suddenly said to the driver, "Wait!" A soldier from the Arab defence unit which was encamped at the British zone checkpoint was striding purposefully towards us. He was armed with a rifle and had a gun at his side and there was no doubt that his business was with us.

My father got out of the car and greeted him politely. Rex started to bark and jump up against the gate. The soldier peered into the taxi and examined each of us in turn. "Where are you going?" he demanded. "Don't you know it's not allowed to leave. AHC orders." "It's all right, I understand," said my father calmly "but this is my wife and these are my children. I'm simply taking them to my father-in-law's house for safety. I will be coming back straightaway." "All right," replied the man, "make sure that you do." He checked the suitcase and then, apparently satisfied that it contained nothing but our clothes, he nodded to my father. "God be with you."

My father got back into the car and my mother said, "Why can't they make up their minds? One minute they tell us all the women and children are to leave and now they're saying we shouldn't. And anyway, what's the point now with everyone already gone?" My father told her to keep her voice down. As we started to move off, I twisted round on Fatima's knee and looked out of the back window. And there to my horror was Rex standing in the middle of the road. We can't have closed the gate properly and he must somehow have managed to get out. He stood still, his head up, his tail stiff, staring after our receding car.

"Look!" I cried out frantically, "Rex has got out. Stop, please, he'll get killed." "Shh", said Fatima, pushing me down into her lap. "He's a rascal. I'll put him back when I return and he won't come to any harm. Now stop worrying."

But I stared and stared at him until we had rounded the corner of the road and he and the house disappeared from view. I turned and looked at the others. They sat silently, their eyes fixed on the road ahead. No one seemed aware of my terrible anguish or how in that moment I suddenly knew with overwhelming certainty that something had irrevocably ended for us there and, like Rex's unfeigned, innocent affection, it would never return.

The short journey to the taxi depot in the Old City opposite the Damascus Gate passed without much incident. We were stopped again at the checkpoint outside the zone, and my father explained once more why we were leaving. When we reached the depot, we got out and transferred our luggage to a taxi which would take us to Damascus by way of Amman. To reach Damascus from Jerusalem, one would normally have taken the northern route through Ras al-Naqura. But all that part of Palestine was a raging battleground and no car could travel that way. Hence we had to take the longer and more roundabout route through Amman. The taxi depot was bustling with people leaving Palestine like us. There was a different atmosphere here to the one we had got used to in Qatamon. As it was a wholly Arab area, there was no sound of gunfire and, though it was full of crowds of people crying and saying goodbye, it felt safe and familiar.

Fatima stood by the car which would take us away. For all her efforts at self-control, tears were coursing down her cheeks. She embraced and kissed the three of us in turn. My father said, "Mind you look after the house until I come back," and she nodded wordlessly. I clung desperately to the material of her caftan but she gently disengaged my fingers. As we got into the taxi and the doors were shut, she drew up close and pressed her sad face against the window. We drove off, leaving her and Muhammad looking after us until they were no more than specks on the horizon, indistinguishable from the other village men and women who were there that day.

No doubt my parents thought they were sparing us pain by keeping our departure secret from us until the very last moment. They also believed we would be away for a short while only and so making a fuss of leaving Jerusalem was unnecessary.

But in the event, they turned out to be woefully wrong. We never set eyes on Fatima or our dog or the city we had known ever again. Like a body prematurely buried, unmourned, without coffin or ceremony, our hasty, untidy exit from Jerusalem was no way to have said goodbye to our home, our country and all that we knew and loved.

I did not know until much later that, although my parents had accepted for some time that we would have to leave Jerusalem, if only for a while, there were two major events which had finally persuaded them to go. The first was the death of Abdul-Qadir al-Husseini and the second, close on its heels, was the massacre at Deir Yassin. In the first week of April, the battle to control the road to Jerusalem had raged between Jewish and Arab forces. Fighting was particularly fierce at the strategically important village of al-Qastal, ten kilometres to the west of Jerusalem. This was built on top of a hill and derived its name (castle) from an ancient fortress whose remains still stood there. It was there, as the Arab side was winning the battle (in which Husseini was joined by our Qatamon commander Abu Dayyeh and his unit), that he was killed by a Jewish soldier from the Palmach. This was a special unit of the Haganah whose men were highly trained for difficult or dangerous assignments.

While Abdul-Qadir's death meant little to the Jews it had a profound impact on the Arab side. Even my father, who was sceptical about the Arab forces' chances of success, shared in the general hope embodied in Abdul-Qadir's courage and commitment. His death was therefore seen as an omen of impending disaster. In the wake of his killing, it was said that the Arab fighters were so overwhelmed with grief that most of them escorted his body back to Jerusalem. This emotional send-off left al-Qastal unguarded and enabled the Jewish forces to regain it later that day. They were exultant and claimed that the Arab fighters were deserting in droves and returning to their villages. Traces of that triumphalism are still evident today. When I saw al-Qastal on a sad, windswept day in 1998, Israeli flags were fluttering from its old castle walls and placards declaring it to be the site of a major Israeli victory.

So great was people's shock and grief that Abdul-Qadir's funeral at the Dome of the Rock in the Old City on April 7 drew a crowd of

30,000 mourners. Two days later, on April 9, Irgun and Stern Gang gunmen perpetrated a massacre at Deir Yassin, a small village on the outskirts of Jerusalem. This was the unmentionable thing which Ziyad and I were not allowed to know. The people of Deir Yassin were mainly engaged in stone quarrying and had been peaceable throughout the troubles besetting other parts of Palestine. They had even concluded a non-aggression pact with the nearby Jewish settlement of Givat Sha'ul, approved by the Haganah, at the beginning of April 1948.

The accounts of what the Jewish attackers had done to the villagers were truly shocking. The survivors who fled came with stories of mutilation, the rape of young girls and the murder of pregnant women and their babies. Some 250 people were massacred in cold blood (though recent estimates have put the number at between 100 and 200). Twenty of the men were driven in a lorry by the Irgun fighters and paraded in triumph around the streets of the Jewish areas of Jerusalem. They were then brought back and shot directly over the quarries in which they had been working and into which their bodies were thrown. The surviving villagers fled in terror, and the empty village was then occupied by Jewish forces. The worst of it was that the gangs who had carried out the killings boasted about what they had done and threatened publicly to do so again. They said it had been a major success in clearing the Arabs out of their towns and villages.

In this they were right, for news of the atrocity, disseminated by both the Jewish and the Arab media in Palestine and the surrounding Arab states, spread terror throughout the country. But because of Deir Yassin's proximity to Jerusalem, the news reached us first and led to an accelerated exodus from our city. The rest of the country was powerfully affected too. Menachem Begin, the leader of the Irgun, said with satisfaction that the massacre had helped in the conquest of places as far away as Tiberias and Haifa. He said it was worth half a dozen army battalions in the war against the Palestinian Arabs.

On April 30, the Palmach unit of the Haganah launched a huge attack on the St Simon monastery. They overcame the contingent of Arab fighters inside and within twenty-four hours had taken control of the monastery. Fierce fighting ensued between them and the Arab battalions defending Qatamon for a full two days before it was brought to an end by the British army. Ibrahim Abu Dayyeh fought and was wounded in this final battle. A twenty-four-hour truce was agreed between the two sides, but before it ended the Jews had occupied the whole of Qatamon up to the boundary of the British zone. The Sakakini family had been the last to stay on, but on April 30 they too left their home.

Throughout April, the Arab League was deliberating over plans of invasion to defend Palestine. These involved various combinations of Arab forces which would cross into Palestine from the neighbouring states and rescue the Palestinians. But none of them came to anything, while the Jews continued to consolidate their hold on the parts of the country they had conquered. In Jerusalem, they had control of most of the new city, which included our neighbourhood, while the Arabs retained the Old City.

We heard that Fatima kept going back to check on our house for as long as she could brave the journey. But in the end, it was too dangerous and she could go no longer. Her own village, al-Maliha, was conquered by the Jews (Israelis by then) in August 1948 and its people were made refugees. She escaped to the village of al-Bireh, east of Jerusalem and still in Arab hands, where we presume she stayed. After that news of her died out. In the chaos that attended the fall of Palestine and the mass exodus of its people, lives were wrenched apart, families brutally sundered, life-long friendships abruptly severed. No organisation existed to help people trace those they had lost.

And so it was that we too lost Fatima, not knowing how to pluck her from the human whirlpool that had swallowed her after our departure.

As for Rex, whom we last saw that April morning in 1948, no news of him reached us ever again.

Five

My father escorted us as far as Damascus, a journey of which I have no memory. Siham says that when we reached Amman, we went to the house of my mother's old friend Um Samir who had left Jerusalem long before we did. She tried to give us lunch but no one had any appetite and my father was in a hurry to reach Damascus. So we got back into the car and drove on into Syria crossing the border at Der'a. And as we drove towards Damascus, Siham marvelled at the sight of people here looking normal, strolling about, sitting in the sun, even picnicking on the banks of the river. "Why don't they look sad?" she asked. "Don't they know what's happened to us?" We looked with wonderment at the signposts, which were all in Arabic. We were used to seeing them in English and Hebrew as well in Palestine. We reached my grandparents' house in the evening. They were warm and welcoming, my grandmother hugging and kissing us repeatedly. Ziyad, who had been excited by the journey to Damascus and agog to see new places, looked pleased with our new surroundings. Our grandparents had only known us by our photographs before and they made much fuss of meeting us in the flesh. They gave us supper, bread and a sort of hard ball-shaped cheese immersed in olive oil.

The next morning, our parents returned to Amman (our mother had decided to go as well), intending to continue at once to Jerusalem. But they were advised to go no further, for all of West Jerusalem, especially Qatamon, were virtually impassable. Taxis were unwilling even to go to the Old City. Government offices, including my father's employer, the education department, were being closed down one by one, it was said. They stayed for four days in Amman, hoping to find a way back and unwilling to believe that they could not return. It was at that moment that my father first started to feel a sense of finality, that somehow and with what seemed like incredible speed, it was all over, not just for Jerusalem but for all of Palestine. While in Amman, they met by strange chance the Karmis, the couple who had bought the house next to ours in Qatamon. They had a sad story to tell. Soon after we left, the attacks on the district, especially on our road, had escalated. One night, a bomb landed just behind their house and they fled in terror, still in their night clothes. "If only we'd gone when you did," they said, "at least we would have left with dignity."

Our grandparents' house was very different from the one we had left in Jerusalem. It was situated in Harat al-Akrad, an old run-down suburb of Damascus with rubbish tips and a maze of narrow, unpaved alleyways, a world away from the prosperous roads and spacious villas of our part of Jerusalem. Some alleys were so impenetrable that cars could not pass through and people were dropped off at the open space outside and had to go the rest of the way on foot. The house was old-fashioned and had a central open courtyard with rooms around three sides of it; "inverted", Ziyad called it, because the windows looked in instead of out. To get from one room to the other, one had to cross the courtyard, which could be unpleasant if it was raining or very cold. There were flower-beds against the whole length of one wall and potted plants against the other walls.

The kitchen was built of rough stone and it was dark and gloomy. Opening directly into it was a small toilet, a common arrangement in old houses of that type. This was a traditional toilet, a pear-shaped cavity in the ground with two ridged tiles on either side to prevent slipping. One placed one's feet over the tiles and squatted over the cavity. In the corner was a water jug and a cloth for washing and drying oneself afterwards. I dreaded using this toilet because it was so dark and the hole in the ground so black that I always imagined something unspeakable would arise from it and grab hold of me. It symbolised for me all that was hateful and different about Damascus. We had had two toilets in our house in Jerusalem, white-tiled and fresh and clean, and both had seats. We used one and Fatima used the second one, but she always squatted over the seat as if it had been a toilet in the ground to which she was more accustomed.

The only other relatives we had in Damascus were my uncle Abu Salma and his family. They had preceded us into Syria by a month or so, driven out of Palestine like us by the increasing danger. The fighting in Haifa had forced them to move at the beginning of March to nearby Acre, to take refuge with my aunt's family. They waited to return, but things in Haifa got worse and more and more people kept flooding out of the city. Seeing how rapidly the situation was deteriorating, my uncle decided after a week to withdraw his family "temporarily" to safety in Damascus.

Soon after we arrived in Damascus, my aunt Khadija's family joined us, having reluctantly accepted that they had to leave Jerusalem as well. Abu Isam's business had declined to the point of extinction. In the end, they were forced to leave their house and their shop with all its furniture and fittings behind. They had four children, three boys and a girl, and from the moment they arrived they seemed to be all over the place. I hated them because they crowded us out and the youngest two cried a lot. This did not worry Ziyad who had played with Isam, the eldest boy, when we were in Jerusalem. They now resumed their friendship. But I had no special playmate and felt differently. Before we came, my grandparents slept in the room opposite the entrance lobby and my uncle slept in one of the two rooms at the back of the courtyard. The other back room was used as a sitting room in winter when people could not sit outside. The house was not large, but adequate for the three of them. And at the time when we came my uncle Taleb was away in Belgium, training as a telephone engineer, and my grandparents had the whole house to themselves.

However, with the arrival of two families every room was taken up. My parents slept in the bed in my uncle's room and my brother and I slept on a mattress on the floor. In July, my father left for England and my uncle came back home a month later. He appropriated his old bed, and so my mother joined me and my brother on the floor. My sister slept in my grandparents' room, on the floor separating their two beds. They woke her up early every morning when they got up to perform the dawn prayer, but she thought them sweet and did not mind. All six of my aunt's family occupied the second back room, opposite my uncle's bedroom. They all slept on the floor on mattresses borrowed from the neighbours when my grandparents had run out of bedding.

Since the room my aunt's family slept in had ceased to be a sitting room, and the April weather was still cool, everyone sat outside in the *liwan* all muffled up. The classic *liwan*, unlike ours in Jerusalem, which had merely meant lounge, was a feature of old Arab houses like my grandfather's. It was positioned between the two back rooms and was walled on three sides with the front opening onto the courtyard. It functioned as a semi-formal reception room; benches covered with cushions were built against the wall on its three sides so as to seat a large number of people, although they had to sit in rows. This seating arrangement derives from that of the traditional Arab *majlis* going back to the Bedouin tribal tents where the men sat together along the sides with the sheikh at the top. It is still to be seen today, upgraded and opulently furnished, but essentially the same in the palaces of sheikhs and princes throughout the Gulf countries.

I could not get used to sleeping on the floor alongside my mother and brother. It was uncomfortable and my mother would come to bed late and wake me, or Ziyad would push me off the edge of the mattress in his sleep. As soon as my uncle returned from Belgium, I would leave them and crawl into his bed whenever I could. This disturbed his sleep, but he didn't have the heart to throw me out. "You were such a poor frightened little thing," he said years later. Even today, I can still recall the feel of his flannel pyjamas against my face and the warm smell of him as I snuggled into his back. He seemed to me like a safe and tranquil island in a sea of madness. We had all warmed to him from the first moment we saw him. He was an attractive, likeable man with long-lashed brilliant green eyes, and fine handsome features. I remember how many of the women in the neighbourhood eyed him surreptitiously.

Both my uncle's departure to Belgium and his return caused a great stir in the neighbourhood. For anyone to travel so far afield was a great event and when he returned home in August 1948 the whole street turned out to greet him. The women ululated from the doorways, a high-pitched sound made by flicking the tongue rapidly up and down against the roof of the mouth which traditionally accompanies all Arab celebrations. People thought he had brought a touch of European magic with him and everyone wanted to see him. And indeed he did seem to have a magic tape recorder which he proudly displayed. "It recorded not on tape but on a sort of thin wire" Siham remembered. "It was like nothing anyone had ever seen before."

Of course, it would have been unthinkable for either of his sisters, my mother and my aunt Khadija, to have had a similar educational opportunity. As was the custom, they only had had an elementary education, enough to read the Quran and be able to write in a rudimentary way. Girls were only there to get married, went the prevailing wisdom, so why waste too much effort in teaching them what they would never use. In addition, there was the constant fear that once a girl knew how to write, she might start to correspond with men and be led into improper ways. My mother had barely learned enough before she was removed from school at the age of ten.

I particularly had it in for my two youngest cousins, Hisham, who was three years old, and Hind, who was about eighteen months. She was pretty and chubby with black hair and red cheeks, where I was thin and hollow-eyed. My mother made a great fuss of both of them, hugged and kissed them, especially Hind, and gave them chocolates to eat, but no one took any notice of me. I felt ugly and scraggy and jealous of both of them. Hisham once followed me climbing a ladder up to the flat roof. I turned to see his skinny, pallid figure clinging on to it fearfully. In a fury of jealousy, I pushed hard at his scrawny chest and tried to kick him off. It was a miracle, said my aunt afterwards, that he did not fall to his death. He managed to cling to the rung of the ladder when my mother rescued him.

No one had a good word to say for me after that. Guilt was now added to my sense of exclusion and misery. Child psychology was not an art known either to my mother or any of those around her. Children, like adults, were expected "to get on with it" and I was left to fend for myself. Nor could I turn for consolation to my brother, as had happened sometimes in Jerusalem. Things had changed between us and I had grown increasingly resentful of him ever since coming to Damascus. Much of the previous harmony when we played together in Jerusalem had been dispelled. In those days, he was amiable and easygoing and I could often get the best of him. And we had Rex to share. But here it was different.

People thought he was special and better than me because he was a boy. They said that as he was the only son, just like his uncle, he must be treated especially well. My mother would now make me lay the table and also clear up, whereas the arrangement in Jerusalem had been that one person would lay the table and another would clear up. When I complained that it was unfair and he ought to do half, she told me that he was a boy and sisters must serve their brothers. Siham said, "Don't worry, that's how it is and we must get used to it." When Ziyad was born, the family in Tulkarm had slaughtered a sheep to celebrate the birth of my father's first son. But when I was born, she said, no one killed any sheep for me and it used to make me cry. This was of course the traditional Arab position. Sons were prized over daughters and women were reared to indulge and look up to the males of the family. In return, the males were expected to protect and support their mothers and sisters. But at the age of eight, this did not cut much ice with me. It just seemed an arrant injustice and I resented and hated my brother for it, as if it had been his fault.

But I did not envy him one ordeal, regarded as a celebration and affirmation of my brother's nascent manhood. This was the ceremony of circumcision, which Ziyad had to undergo while we were in Damascus. When Grandfather found out that, at twelve, Ziyad retained his foreskin, he was outraged. He questioned our father as to how this scandal had been allowed to happen, since it was the custom for Muslim boys to be circumcised in the first years of life and certainly before the age of ten. (Today, Muslim babies are circumcised soon after birth.) Our father lamely explained that it had slipped his and our mother's attention, what with the troubles in Palestine and the fact that he was away in England for some of the time. But this did not mollify our grandfather who proceeded to make urgent arrangements for the circumcision.

Such occasions were dominated by the men of the family. The women's role was to make the special foods and sweets which were served at the end of the "operation". On the morning in question, Ziyad was awakened early and dressed in his circumcision gown. This was a long and loose white tunic made of silk from which his dark head and bare feet protruded comically. The men of the family began to arrive, my mother's cousins and more distant relatives all in their best clothes, until the courtyard of the house filled up. Ziyad was sat on a chair at the base of the *liwan*, where he was soon surrounded by the men, joking and jollying him along. I watched him from the window of our uncle's bedroom, for none of the females could attend. He looked scared and alone there on his chair.

The man who was to carry out the circumcision now appeared. He was the local barber, and looked none too clean. The implements he was to use on my brother, a shaving knife from his shop and a long-handled hook, looked grimy. My father asked if his instruments were clean and if he wanted to wash his hands first. "None cleaner!" the man answered cheerfully, declining the offer of a wash.

Without further ado, he turned towards Ziyad and lifted the hem of his gown to expose his small penis. He grasped it in his hand and using his long needle, he hooked the foreskin with it and pulled it right down. He then severed it with one cut of the shaving knife. Blood seeped down Ziyad's thighs as the barber held the piece of flesh aloft for all to see. At this point, the women ululated from inside and Ziyad looked as if he was about to faint. Watching in horror, I thought I would faint too. His face had a greenish tinge and his jaws were clenched, but he never uttered a sound. The barber put a bandage over his bleeding penis and pulled down his gown over his legs. My grandfather gave him a jug of water which he took to the flower-bed and poured over his instruments, but he still did not wash his hands. He then looked round for his fee which my father had ready, and having pocketed this, he nodded his head at the assembly and went off.

Ziyad was now congratulated and patted on the head by the men who all had presents for him. After a while they withdrew, and the women could bring out the food and sweets. These were delicious, but Ziyad looked dazed and ate nothing. When the men had gone, it was the turn of the women of the family to come and visit with more presents for Ziyad. My grandmother picked up the foreskin, which the barber had thrown carelessly on the ground, and buried it in the flower-bed beside the kitchen. To her dismay, Louliyyeh, the cat, tried to dig it up again and was shooed off angrily. I do not know how much of the ceremony Ziyad took in, for he was in pain and when he stood up, he had to hold his gown away from his body to keep it from touching his sore and bandaged penis. Even looking at him made me shudder anew at the memory of what I had just seen, and I thanked God fervently that I was not a boy. It was a fortnight before he had healed sufficiently to wear his usual clothes once more.

Although many of my memories of that time are clouded, I remember that I was not sorry to leave Syria. It seemed to me that in the eighteen months we spent there nothing good ever happened except perhaps for the cats. My grandmother and uncle were devoted to cats, an unusual thing in the Arab world, where both cats and dogs are considered unclean and objects of revulsion. The figure of the scrawny cat scavenging for food in rubbish piles and evading the odd kick, is a familiar one throughout the Middle East, even today. Yet, in my grandfather's house cats were kept as pets, fed and relatively cosseted. My mother had grown up with a succession of cats, most of whom were feral and tended to run off. My grandmother's cat Louliyyeh – meaning pearl – was a handsome grey tabby with a white breast and grey-blue eyes. My grandmother had a habit of shoving the cat into bed with her to keep her warm in winter. She would push the cat down to the bottom of the bed and place her feet on it, as if it had

My grandparents and Uncle Taleb in the liwan *of their house in Damascus, 1949, clutching members of Louliyyeh's litter*

been a hot-water bottle. The cat would object violently, miaowing and struggling, and my grandmother would shout and curse her and tell her to lie still. This irritated my grandfather who would scold both of them and swear that no cat would enter his house again.

But the worst thing about my grandfather was the way he made me and my brother pray with him as near to five times a day as he could. Everyday, we would spread our prayer mats and stand obediently behind him, while he led the prayer. When Muslims pray, they go through a set of prescribed motions which involve standing, bowing down to the ground and sitting on the haunches. The worshipper may not turn round or look away or be disturbed until the prayer is over, and this ritual is repeated five times a day. After a while, Ziyad and I devised a way of relieving the monotony of the prayer, especially when we were not at school and had to pray the full five times. Once my grandfather had turned his back to us to commence the prayer and we knew we were safe, we would quickly spread our children's comic on the floor between us. Each time we prostrated ourselves in the prescribed ritual, we would turn over the page of the comic, and by the time the prayer ended, we would have managed to get through half of it. This worked well enough until one day, to our horror, my grandfather turned round unexpectedly and saw what we were doing. Without further ado, he delivered us each a ringing blow to the head and went angrily in search of my mother. "This is what comes of bringing them up like heathens," we heard him snort.

Tears stung my eyes. I didn't want to be there in this poor, overcrowded, miserable house. I wanted to be back in Jerusalem with Fatima and my toys and our dog. I pined for them and thought about them every day. I hadn't wanted to come to Damascus and I didn't know why my father had gone away barely three months after our arrival. Our mother had even less time for us than she had had in Jerusalem, but it had not mattered then because I had my home and Fatima and all the familiar things. Now all that had evaporated as if it had never been, and I could not guess whether we would ever return, or whether we would live in Damascus for good, or whether I would see my father again.

It was a curious thing, when I look back, that not long after we reached Damascus no one spoke of our home any more. Our parents did not talk about Fatima or Muhammad or the house or even Jerusalem. It was as if only I preserved their memory. They seemed wholly preoccupied with the immediate present, as if we had materialised out of nowhere in my grandparents' house. No one questioned this strange turn of events, least of all Siham and Ziyad. And so, bewildered and lost, I took my cue from them and kept my confusion to myself. My allegiance to Fatima, to our house and to my childhood became a private affair, my secret to cherish and protect. It was a world away from Damascus which I thought then was a horrible place, or at least the part of it which I knew. It was poor and the streets were dirty and full of grim, unsmiling people. Once, when I went running off with my cousin to the market to buy my mother a bag of sugar, a man with a beard and a long robe darted out of the crowd and grabbed hold of my hair. I had long plaits and he pulled them so hard, it hurt. "Cover your head, you shameless girl!" he cried. "Have your parents no shame?"[1]

When we had first arrived in Damascus, my father used to go out every day looking worried. When he came back, I would hear him telling my mother that he had found nothing. We had left Palestine with £330, a sum which was dwindling fast, since my grandfather could not provide for us and soon more money would be needed. Some of my father's friends who had left Palestine at about the same time had managed to find work out of Damascus. They went to the smaller Syrian cities, Homs, Hama, a few to Aleppo, where they became schoolteachers but all were unhappy. These were men who had progressed beyond school teaching, no less than my father, and each had developed his own career in Palestine. They had all had high hopes for their futures and going back to teaching in small schools was a setback none had ever anticipated. "They're lucky to get any work at all," said my grandfather. "God knows Syria is flooded with Palestinians looking for jobs, and every day there are more and more coming in. How will we ever cope?"

Desperate-looking men came to the house and spoke of nothing except their predicament: no work, no jobs, no money. Many of these

---

[1] In Islam, women are enjoined to dress modestly – a preference that has often been interpreted to mean that they should cover their hair, arms and legs. This form of dress is supposed to be adopted only after puberty, but Muslim fanatics will often insist on veiling pre-pubertal girls as well.

were people from Safad who had come to Syria in early May, less than
a month after we did. They had come suddenly in a terrible crush,
10,000 of them or more, the whole population of Safad, it was said;
old people and women and children, soon to be followed by the men
who had stayed behind in the hope of a truce with the Jewish army.
They had nothing but the clothes on their backs and they spoke wildly
of being pushed out of their homes in the night with guns and mortar
bombs. The rains were unusually heavy in Palestine that year – we
would have had a wonderful crop, people said – and they had waded
through deep mud and rivers of water to reach the Syrian border eight
miles away. They arrived dazed and exhausted, their clothes and shoes
sodden with water.

"Poor souls," said Um Said, my mother's cousin who lived in the
street above us. "There was nowhere for them to go. We heard that a
lot of them were being put in tents while the government worked out
what to do with them. Their tents were swimming in water. They said
the Jews would never let them go back, but God knows best." The
local mosques and schools were given over to the refugees and
everyone in the neighbourhood went with their blankets and sheets
and mattresses, clothes, food and whatever they could afford. My
grandmother cooked for them every Friday and the men of the family
took the pans of food down to the mosque. "What a terrible thing is
happening in Palestine," said Um Said. "God help us all". The
government started to distribute staples to the refugees and, as soon as
this was known, a number of the poorest amongst the local inhabitants
began to claim that they were Palestinians too. "What a shameful
disgrace," said my grandfather.

Some of the Safadi people turned out to be relatives of my mother's
family whom they had not seen for many years. For her ancestors
came from Safad and one branch of the family later moved to
Damascus where my grandfather was born. Now a few of his relatives

found out where he lived and came to visit, but were in such a sorry state that it made my grandmother cry.

"We woke up one night to see the house opposite on fire," said Mustafa, a distant cousin of my grandfather. "And then we heard the bombs. They were so loud and made such a flash we thought they were atom bombs. The children started screaming, I opened the windows to see what was happening but we were all so panicked we didn't know what to do. 'The Jews are coming', people were shouting, 'the Jews are coming.' I went outside and the street was full of people pushing against each other trying to get away. I rushed back in and got Nahla and the children. We dressed them quickly, but there was no time to take anything with us, just the clothes on our backs. My father couldn't get up – he's been ill and he can't walk far. So we had no choice but to leave him behind. But I told him I'd be back to get him."

"What a terrible thing, what a terrible thing," said my grandfather, shaking his head.

"Anyway," continued Mustafa, "we walked along with everyone else in a great crowd. The children kept falling down and it was raining and bitterly cold, but we had to keep on walking because the Jewish soldiers were behind us."

"Where were the Arab fighters all this time, the AHC, the Arab Liberation Army?" asked my father.

"What Arab fighters?" said Mustafa bitterly. "They were as scared as we were. I don't suppose they'd ever heard bombs like that before either. Even the battalion from the Arab Liberation Army which was supposed to defend us actually pulled out with the Jewish soldiers on our doorstep. We asked the Jews for a truce, but they refused, and so we were just left to our fate. Mind you, they didn't have it that easy. When the assault began, some of our men fought them as hard as they could. In some streets, the Jews had to get them out house by house, but in the end, what could we have done? We're just ordinary people, no match for an army." He paused and everyone looked at him. "All those who could walk went in the end. The very old ones, like father, were left behind because they couldn't move and there was no way to move them out. God knows what happened to them."

It later emerged that the Jewish troops rounded up these old people, whose average age, according to the Jewish military commander in Safad, was eighty and who were all Muslims, and expelled them to Lebanon in early June of 1948. That left a small number of elderly Christian Arab Safadis still clinging to their homes. But these were also removed, driven in lorries to Haifa, where they were placed in the care of two convents there. Not one of the inhabitants of Safad was ever allowed back and, in the chaos of their various expulsions, I don't know if Mustafa ever saw his father again.

Out in the street, the talk was all of Palestine and Palestinians. Men in pyjama trousers stood around and talked of Safad and of politics in general. The custom in the poorer parts of Damascus was for men to wear their pyjamas in the day as well as at night. Sometimes, they "dressed up" by wearing a shirt over the pyjama trousers and if it was cold they might slip a jersey over the shirt.

∂∞∂

After a few months of looking fruitlessly for work in Syria our father left us to go to England. This had not been an easy decision for him to make and only arrived at after much hesitation and disappointment, not to mention opposition from my mother. Finding that he could not return to his job in Jerusalem, he realised he would have to find new work, "until the situation in Jerusalem settles", explained our mother. He searched in Jordan, but Amman in those days was a small provincial place with little capacity for absorption of qualified people like him, and he had already turned down the only good position with the bank the year before. Abu Ahmad, our old neighbour who had ended up in Cairo, wrote to my father through his cousin in Damascus, urging him to come. He said that Cairo was a paradise on earth, there were jobs to be had and money to be made. My mother was excited when she heard this.

"Perhaps it's true," she said. "Perhaps that's where we should go until we can return to Jerusalem." Egypt was the home of glamour in the Arab world. It had a film industry, produced the most famous singers and entertainers and published the best-known newspapers and magazines. Cairo was the foremost centre of style and fashion, but also of intellectual and political life. Every Arab aspired at least to visit there and many would have liked to stay.

But my father did not agree. "I wouldn't trust Abu Ahmad if he were the last man alive," he said, "not after that business in Palestine." There had been much talk in Jerusalem that Abu Ahmad was one of those who sold land to Jews. He worked as an estate agent and made a reasonable living but no more. When he suddenly got rich, the rumours started that there was only one way this could have happened – by selling land to Jews. My father once saw him slipping into the offices of the Zionist land agency in Zion Square in Jerusalem. It was well-known that the Jews who came to Palestine from the 1880s onwards were desperate to acquire land. They would have paid any price to get hold of it, often backed by wealthy Jewish sources from Europe and America. And at first, some Palestinians sold them land and became wealthy in the process. But gradually the realisation grew that this was not as innocent as it seemed.

"They've got a plan in mind," people said. "They want to take over our country." Selling of land to Jews after 1946 became an act of treason in the eyes of the AHC, even on occasions punishable by death. One night in the summer of 1947, when our neighbours were all congregated at the house of Abu Ahmad and there was much laughter and merriment, masked men suddenly appeared. They barged in and immediately separated the men from the women whom they pushed roughly into a back room. Shots rang out and a man was wounded, but it was not Abu Ahmad, "although that's who they were after", asserted my father. He meant the Boycott Committee, which was one of the AHC's units set up to fight commercial dealings with the Zionists. He had also been invited to Abu Ahmad's that night, but had somehow lingered on at home, lighting a narghile and looking through his books. "As if he'd known what was going to happen," remarked my mother.

After that, Abu Ahmad lived in some trepidation. He and his family were terrified that the AHC would come after him again. But nothing further happened and they stuck it out until the beginning of 1948. They then packed their belongings and headed off for Cairo. Before long Abu Ahmad succeeded in establishing himself there and setting up a prosperous business "with tainted Jewish money", said our neighbours in disgust. As we knew no one beside Abu Ahmad in Cairo who could advise us, and my father had little money to spend on going there to find out for himself, he had to think of something else. He spoke to my uncle Abu Salma, although he did not set much store by anyone's advice.

Abu Salma advised my father to wait for the situation in Syria to settle after the first rush of refugees, or else think once again of working in Jordan. They had both accepted by now that an early return to Palestine was not realistic. My uncle's city of residence, Haifa, had fallen to the Jewish forces at the end of April. Nearly all its Arab inhabitants had fled or been evicted and it had become what it had never been before: a Jewish city. Shortly after, in May, my aunt's home town of Acre met the same fate. Other Palestinian cities were similarly overrun during that period. When Jaffa, the largest of the cities fell, its Arab inhabitants reduced from 80,000 to 4,000 in just a few weeks, there was immense shock and gloom. These stories all had the same ending, thousands of people on the move, destitute, walking towards safety wherever they could find it. The Arab leadership and sometimes the British authorities as well ordered them to go back, but no one was prepared to provide them with any protection.

Meanwhile, in Tulkarm, events had worsened for our family. In order to defend the town against Jewish attack, armed young men had stationed themselves in the school building just above our aunt Souad's house. From there, they could see the road leading up to Tulkarm and could shoot at the Jewish soldiers. Aziza was by then living with her mother because her husband Zuhair was away studying in London on a government scholarship. She had three small children, two girls and a boy, and her main anxiety was how to keep them safe. From the beginning of 1948 the situation had become more and more unsettled and dangerous with displaced people pouring into Tulkarm. There was not enough food for them all and everyone's stores ran out. Even the tobacco was finished and people started rolling herbal cigarettes. Eventually they were all eating dates, the staple diet of the Arabs from ancient times, and hence that time in Tulkarm was known thereafter as "the year of the dates". It was a long time before the town's food stores were replenished.

By April, shooting was an everyday occurrence, and Aziza lived in daily terror of her children being hit. One morning, a bullet whizzed through the window of the house and lodged itself in the door just above the place where her three-year-old daughter was playing. In that moment, she said afterwards, she felt that she had lost her reason. The food shortages, the constant danger, the absence of her husband – news of him had not reached her for months because of the troubles – all combined to make her determined to escape the hell they were living through. She packed a bag, mainly with her children's clothes and nappies, and told her mother she was leaving for Amman. Seeing

her so distraught, our aunt Souad pleaded with her to stay, but Aziza
would not be swayed. She had little money and only a vague idea of
where she would go once she reached Amman. During her time as a
schoolteacher, she had been friends with another teacher whose father,
she remembered, owned a restaurant there. She thought to go and find
it and throw herself on their hospitality. She bundled her children on
the bus, whose driver was a relative of ours, and he took her to
Amman free of charge.

In London, Zuhair, who had been studying at Imperial College
since 1947, was living in constant apprehension as the news of the
disturbances in Palestine came through. Towards the middle of April,
he and forty Arab students who had come from all over the Arab
world decided they could no longer stand by while Palestine was
being torn apart. They made up a delegation and went to ask their
professors for leave of absence from their studies to go and help in the
struggle. This was no mean sacrifice for Zuhair, since government
scholarships were hard to obtain and much sought after. Breaking
such contracts incurred the risk that they would not be renewed. In
addition, the students were uncertain of their professor's reaction,
since the British had a confused and ambiguous attitude towards
Palestine. To Zuhair's pleasant surprise, however, his professor was
sympathetic and understanding. He let him go and wished him luck.

Zuhair reached Tulkarm on April 14 to find Aziza and the children
gone. No one could tell him where she was, except to say that she was
probably in Amman. And then there followed a nightmare quest for
her whose memory remained with him all his life. Having left
Tulkarm as a relatively tranquil place, albeit under the encroaching
shadow of events in the rest of Palestine, he was totally unprepared
for what he saw on his arrival. The town was unrecognisable, teeming
with thousands of refugees who had come from the north and the
coastal villages. They were living in schools, mosques, public build-

ings and even in people's houses. There was little food and no authority to organise the flood of displaced people. The National Committee was undermanned and wholly taken up with defence. Outside Tulkarm, battles were raging between armed Jewish and Arab groups, but the fighting seemed chaotic and uncontrolled. Zuhair tried to leave for Jordan, but the National Committee stopped him, since they were under orders to allow no one to flee. He told them of his plight and begged them to let him go. The Committee's commander was the father-in-law of Aziza's sister and so he agreed, but only on condition that Zuhair should promise to return. He told him to look in Salt (a city to the west of Amman), since the refugees coming out of Palestine went there first.

On his way to Salt, he was stopped numerous times by Arab fighters to check that he was not a Jew. When he got there, he found the situation far worse than the one he had seen in Tulkarm. Here again, thousands of refugees lived wherever they could find a place, families separated from each other by bed sheets hung on washing lines to give them some privacy. He looked into a mosque full of refugees and saw a woman giving birth in one of the corners. The local people had all become volunteer social workers. They fed the refugees and gave them what shelter they could. But, as in Tulkarm, there were no government representatives and no public authority here to provide services. It was a scene of breakdown and chaos.

Zuhair looked desperately for Aziza and his children amongst the horde of people and it seemed to him that none of them could have been his family, for thousands of village men and women wore similar clothes and had the same wretched and anxious expression. Someone had drawn up lists of the names of the refugees and they gave him these to search through. People were kind and wanted to help; they said he was not the only one to have lost relatives and, God willing, he would find his.

With increasing desperation, he left for Amman, only to be met again with sights like those in Tulkarm and Salt. He searched fruitlessly amongst the refugees here and began to think that he had lost Aziza forever. So angry and dejected did he feel that he decided there and then to join any group, any army, so long as it was engaged in fighting the Jews. He would give up his training and his hard-won education and dedicate his life to that fight. Unknown to him then, Aziza had found her schoolteacher friend and was staying with her. She had returned to her senses somewhat and now longed to see Zuhair again. She knew that our uncle, Abdul-Ghani, was based in Amman and went to seek his help. When Zuhair also ran into our uncle at one of his usual haunts, the Philadelphia Hotel in central Amman, the couple were re-united and the next day they went back to Tulkarm.

&c&

On May 14, 1948 the news went out everywhere that a new state called "Israel" had been set up in our country. Its people would henceforth be known as Israelis. "Now you see," said my uncle Abu Salma, "this is what the Jews were aiming at all along." And he kept shaking his head. No one took the new state seriously and it was universally referred to in the Arab world as "the alleged state of Israel". At the same time, everyone castigated the British and the Arab states for having allowed matters to get this far, for having encouraged the Jews in their conceit. There was talk of British betrayal and that it was the British who were the real enemy – and not the Jews – for having permitted them to enter Palestine. The talk at my grandfather's house was full of anger and disappointment and it reminded me of how it used to be in Jerusalem with all the neighbours constantly complaining about the same things.

The next day, May 15, the armies of five Arab countries, Jordan,

Syria, Lebanon, Egypt and Iraq, moved in to attack the "unlawful entity" erected, as they said, on pillage and the theft of Arab land and property. They would overcome the Jews, they boasted, and return the refugees to their homes. People rejoiced at this and the refugees began to have hope. "Give them hell!" they said, "Let the Jews eat shit!" The Iraqi army moved to the western front line with the Jewish forces and encamped outside Tulkarm. As one of its first acts, it let off a million shells, firing continuously for over thirty minutes. The Jewish advance in the direction of Tulkarm was halted immediately. "Those shells were like music to our ears," said Zuhair. "For the first time we started to feel that deliverance was at hand." Until the start of 1948, the people of Tulkarm had shared the general Arab view that the Jews were cowardly and would not succeed against the Arabs. The ferocity and effectiveness of the Jewish attacks had taken them completely by surprise and so they were overjoyed at seeing the Iraqi soldiers; they lined the streets and applauded them enthusiastically. Zuhair had bought a rifle after returning from Amman to defend the family, but with the arrival of the Iraqis he put it away.

In Damascus our father only said, "We'll see, we'll see." He seemed at this time more depressed than ever. For the reality we had to face was that we had lost our home in Jerusalem and we had no money. The sense of finality he had felt in Amman returned more vividly after the State of Israel was declared, as if it were the last chapter in the story of Palestine. He no longer planned on an imminent return there and continued to look for work. Nor did he accept our uncle Abu Salma's advice to stay in Syria or Jordan but went back to thinking of other possibilities.

By June, it was clear that the combined armies of five Arab states, however grand that sounded, had failed in the war against the Jews. Most people at the time did not realise what became clear after the recriminations had died down, that the total number of troops of the

five Arab countries scarcely amounted to those of the Jewish army and
that they were inexperienced conscripts, poorly trained and unmoti-
vated. They were no match for the more sophisticated, highly dedicated Haganah, many of whose men were Second World War
veterans who had fought with the Allies and had been trained by the
British. Moreover, the Jewish leadership had been preparing inten-
sively since 1947 for the war it anticipated with the Arab states and
had reorganised its army in line with professional British advice well
in advance of May 1948. It was well-armed with modern weapons and
had bought over twenty warplanes from the British. By contrast, the
Arab side was ill-prepared and did not decide to go to war against the
Zionists until the very last minute. The arms their soldiers carried
were inadequate and out-of-date. The only exceptions were the Iraqis
and Jordan's Arab Legion, especially the latter, which was British-
officered and British-trained. These advantages were however dissipated by the lack of coordination between the Arab commanders of
each country, the absence of a united strategy against the Zionists and
by the fact that Jordan (or Transjordan, as it was known then) had
entered the war with an agenda of its own.

Rumours abounded that Jordan's King Abdullah had made a secret
agreement with the Zionists to carve up Palestine between the two of
them. The Jews could have the area assigned to them by the UN in
the partition resolution and the king would take the densely populated
Arab regions and make them part of his kingdom. Consequently, the
Arab Legion was said to be under orders not to attack the Jewish
army in that part of Palestine which would form the Jewish state – to
the frustration of its well-trained soldiers, who were made to withdraw each time they thought they were winning. But Jordan was not
alone in its designs, for Syria, it was thought, had entered the war in
order to take Tiberias, which was in the north and close to the Syrian
border, for itself. The Iraqis too were said to have their own agenda.

If all that were true, then the Arabs were fighting with one hand tied behind their backs, everyone said.

In June, a truce was drawn up between the two sides, but not before the Jews (or Israelis) had halted the Syrian advance in the north and been inexplicably left to do so by the Iraqis, who were still in the vicinity of Tulkarm. Having succeeded in pushing the Israelis back from Jenin, they suddenly stopped fighting. They said they had no orders to continue. "We couldn't understand it," said Leon Blum, my father's old colleague in the education department when he came to visit us in London in 1950. He was by then an Israeli citizen and had changed his name to Gideon Binor to fit in with his new identity. "All the Iraqis had to do was extend along to Tel Aviv and they would have cut the country and our forces in half. We would have been in real trouble then. Why didn't they do it?"

During the fighting, the Israelis had attacked the Old City of Jerusalem trying to secure the Jewish Quarter. In doing so, they had shelled the Dome of the Rock, and this provoked widespread horror and outrage. The women of our neighbourhood in Damascus, some of them my mother's relatives who came round to visit my grandmother, were angry. They turned their anger four-square on my mother.

"If the mosque is harmed it will be your fault, God's punishment for your lack of religion," they said. "All of you in Jerusalem, going about with your heads bare and without shame, it's no wonder!" They were referring to the fact that neither my mother nor my sister had worn the veil in Palestine. This was not strictly true, for my mother had only discarded the veil when we moved from the Old City to Qatamon. Since coming to Damascus, she had been forced to wear it again in deference to social custom, but this did not satisfy any of the women who knew it was not genuine. Admittedly my mother shook off her veil the moment she was out of my grandfather's neighbourhood. My grandmother, who always tried to keep the peace, shushed them all and said they weren't being fair and it was nothing to do with my mother. "God knows, she's upset enough as it is by the news," she admonished. And indeed my mother looked unhappy and cried a lot. She was thinking of all her friends who lived in the Old City. "Please God, they're safe," she said, turning her palms up to heaven in prayer. "Please God, that no one has harmed them."

Following the first truce, fighting broke out again and a second truce was declared a month later without the Arabs being able to defeat the Israeli army, although the Arab Legion had managed to prevent an Israeli conquest of eastern Jerusalem. People were furious. "How can it be that the armies of five countries, *five countries no less*, cannot defeat a bunch of Jewish gangsters?" There were bitter complaints that each truce seemed only to benefit the Jews who took advantage of the lull in the fighting to replenish and illegally stock up their arms, while the Arab side was prevented from doing so by a UN arms embargo.

In Tulkarm, apathy and a feeling of helplessness set in. Its people had worked ceaselessly to help in the war effort, but apparently to no avail. In the battle outside Qalqilya, for example, they had sent as many men as they could muster to fight the Jews alongside the Arab army. When they arrived, they were ordered to advance against the enemy under cover of cannon fire. But they were largely untrained and the Arab army was outnumbered in men and fire-power by the other side. Inevitably, the battle was lost and Tulkarm's single hospital was inundated with the wounded and the dying. The town's pharmacy offered all the medicines it had for the care of the wounded. Zuhair, who had never treated anyone in his life but had studied biology in London, offered his services to the hospital with the other volunteers. Amongst his first patients was a severely wounded man whom he started to tend energetically until he realised with horror that the man was dead.

At the same time and under cover of the war, the Israelis continued to empty the towns and villages of Palestine of their inhabitants. In June, scores of villages in the vicinity of Haifa, Tel Aviv and Acre were entirely demolished, levelled to the ground as if they had never been. Both my father and my uncle knew many of these places because they were all near to Tulkarm or Haifa. By July, the Israelis had taken all the land outside Tulkarm up to the railway line. In this takeover, my uncle estimated that our family had lost 100 dunums[2] of its land and Aziza's family 200 dunums. He and my father listened to the radio together in grim silence when it was announced that the Israelis were doing this in order to prevent the inhabitants from ever returning. But the Arab states, it said, were aware of these evil manoeuvres and they would avail the Jews nothing in the end. Egypt and Syria declared that they had already won the war against Israel. People, listening, just shook their heads and sighed. The atmosphere of gloom and dismay was almost palpable and it somehow served to decide my father on what he should do next.

My father never made any secret of the fact that he had a love–hate relationship with the British. On the one hand, he admired their culture, their language and their organisational skills, but on the other, he hated them for what they had done to Palestine. "But for them", he was fond of repeating, "there would never have been a Jewish invasion of our country and there would certainly never have been an Israel." In 1938 and again in 1946 the Mandate government in Palestine sent him on a training course at the Institute of Education in London. This engendered in him an abiding love for the city which never faded. "London grows on you," he used to say. "It's not a place you like at first. You have to live in it to appreciate it." So, when from Jerusalem he applied to the BBC in London for a posting, he had had

---

[2] 4 dunums = 1 acre

in mind the simple idea of spending more time in the city which he
admired.

The dire situation in Palestine and the difficulties of finding suitable
work in the Arab world, or at least those parts of it he was prepared to
consider, now acted as an incentive to revive his old interest in going
to London. He reapplied to the BBC and received a favourable
response. He was asked to go in June to Cairo for an interview, which
made my mother hope that he would find other work there. And he
did indeed look up our old neighbour, Abu Ahmad, who tried to
persuade him to stay in Cairo. But after his interview the BBC offered
him the job of language supervisor in its Arabic service and he was
keen to accept. Shortly after his return to Damascus they wrote from
London advising him to come alone at first, without the family. "We
are still recovering from the war," they wrote. "There is food
rationing here and we cannot recommend that you bring your children
into the country at the present time." My father secretly determined to
go, but he first convened a meeting of our family and friends to
discuss the matter. My grandfather was strongly against it and my
uncle likewise urged him to reconsider, "Your wife is a conservative
woman, not used to living outside our society, and your children are
too young to be taken so far away," he said. Most of the friends
agreed, but a few said there might be no harm in his trying to see how
it was.

In the end, my father decided to go on his own for one year to
begin with. If all went well, Siham would join him so that she could
go to university. Ziyad and I would remain with our mother in
Damascus until she felt ready to go to London as well. On hearing
this, our mother became greatly alarmed. For her, his decision to go
to England was the worst thing that could have happened, second only
to our flight from Jerusalem. She made clear that, whether he went to
England or not, neither she nor any of us was going to join him. For

her, the prospect of going to a remote country whose language and customs she knew only sketchily from meeting a few English people in Palestine, distant from her family and friends, was unthinkable. She was a daughter of the Arab world and content to be so and her plans for our future had been quite different. She had hoped for my father to settle in a job in one of the Arab countries close to Palestine, preferably Egypt, but possibly Jordan. "At least the children will be able to grow up Arab, as if we had still been in Palestine, and the girls will eventually find husbands," she said. "But if we go abroad, what will happen to them?"

However, she could see that my father was determined and she also recognised that we could not go on much longer without more money coming in. My father had been a prudent saver and had set aside funds for contingencies in the Arab Bank in Jerusalem. On the day before we left, he took out all his savings because of the uncertainty of the situation. Afterwards, he said that some sixth sense must have guided him in this, for many of his friends lived to rue the day they had not done the same. Not having withdrawn their money before May 1948, they found that after that date their bank and its contents had been taken over by the new Israeli state. All Palestinian bank accounts were appropriated by the Israeli government which did not reimburse their owners until years later. It took a concerted and prolonged effort on the part of the UN and a loan from Barclay's Bank in Amman to persuade Israel to hand over Palestinian bank accounts they had frozen. Even then, not everyone was reimbursed and some lost their money, which presumably went to fund the new Jewish state.

So, much against her will, my mother agreed and my father spoke with my grandfather about his decision. "I will send Amina fifty pounds a month," he told him. "She and the children will not want for anything."

"In gold?" queried my grandfather, whose financial accounting was still grounded in the Ottoman era. My father laughed, "No, no, not gold, but it will be enough, you need not worry."

He left at the end of July, just after the start of the second truce in Palestine and just after we had received word that the Israelis had begun moving Jewish families into the empty, pillaged Arab houses in Qatamon. The Israeli army had by now conquered more areas of the country; a large part of the Galilee and the towns of Nazareth, Lydda and Ramleh, where Siham was born, had all fallen. "Perhaps it's good that you're leaving now," Abu Salma told him when he and his family came to say goodbye. "You won't have to see the wolves feasting on the corpse." A further 100,000 people became refugees and flooded out of Palestine. A few families tried to return when the truce commenced, but they came back saying the Jews had pushed them out at gunpoint. Many of the roads out of Palestine were mined by the Israelis, making them hazardous. It was becoming clearer that the newly established Israel was determined to do everything to keep those who had fled from ever returning. But though everyone talked of these things, my father seldom joined in. He just quietly made his preparations to depart.

At first I did not understand that he would be away for a long time to come. I vaguely remembered his visit to England before in 1946 when I was six and it had not seemed too long then. So I thought it would be the same this time, although I did not fully know why he was leaving us again. My sister was sad but also excited about his going because he had promised to have her join him as soon as he could. Ziyad, however, looked unhappy. For him, all that mattered was that the family should stay together. He had accepted leaving Jerusalem because we had done so together and were still one family at the end of it. But now, it was different. For the first time he began to feel that we were truly being split up. He let our father kiss him goodbye but showed no emotion.

Father kissed the rest of us, except for our mother with whom he shook hands only. That was because our grandfather was standing by, and it was not the custom for men and women, even married couples, to kiss in public. I don't know what he felt when he said goodbye, except that I noticed he had tears in his eyes. Were they, I wonder now, for his parting from us, or for the parting from his roots and memories of Palestine that he believed irretrievable? It was impossible to tell because he never talked about his feelings. Throughout that difficult time, I remember how he always appeared preoccupied, but it was with the practicalities of our situation, never with its human significance. It was almost as if our leaving Jerusalem was nothing more than an inconvenience, albeit a serious one, which meant his having to make some tiresome arrangements. Accordingly, he made those arrangements and did what was necessary with a minimum of fuss, as if there were nothing more to it than that. Who knows what private anguish he endured for the loss of his career, the home he and my mother had struggled to create, the destruction of his ambitions and the plans he had made for his future and ours?

On arriving in London, he sent us a temporary address while he looked for something else. And at first he was as good as his word; our mother would go to the British embassy every month and collect the fifty pounds he had promised. And then, suddenly, nothing more was heard from him and no money arrived. Our mother became worried. It wasn't like him, she said, he had always done his duty by us and by his mother and sisters and brothers who all depended on him. She could not understand it. Eventually, she made Siham write to him and ask him to send us some money, as we had none and my grandfather's means were limited. "Ziyad has to walk to school because there is no money for his tram fare," she wrote affectingly. "And we are still wearing our old clothes which are now full of holes." "Where did you get all that from?" demanded my mother when Siham read her what she had written, but she was not displeased. And it worked. A short while later, our father answered. He had been busy, he said, finding somewhere to live and settling into his new job. Finding accommodation in London was not easy and he had had to move from one bedsitter to the next. Family houses were next to impossible to obtain, but he was still trying. He was not coming back but would send money very soon.

After this letter, our mother had even less time for us than before. She went out visiting people all the time and came back just as we were about to have lunch, or sometimes after. In Jerusalem, she had also liked to be out seeing her women friends, but she never left home without cooking first and she always returned in time to have lunch ready laid out for our father and us. But now, she often did not cook at all, leaving it all to my grandmother or even Siham. Not infrequently, she stayed the night at people's houses and only appeared the next afternoon. One day, she had a shouting match with my sister.

"What's the matter with you?" said Siham angrily. "What about us, what about Ziyad and Ghada?" "Leave me alone!" my mother screamed. It was only when our uncle Taleb, who had also noted her absences, commented that as she no longer did the cooking he would henceforth go to my aunt's house for lunch, that she started to cook for us once more. There had always been a slight rivalry between her and my aunt, and she was stung by my uncle's implied criticism. But for him I think she would have continued to go out every day.

Thinking back on my parents' behaviour during that period, I realise now that it was bizarre. It was as if each one of them had been attacked by a temporary madness, an abnegation of responsibility that would have been inconceivable before. Perhaps the trauma of what they had been through went far, far deeper than any of us realised, and the prospect of having to build their lives and ours anew led them somehow to lose control – to want to escape the bleak reality we all faced. Hence my mother went gadding about in Damascus as if she had been a young girl, while far away in London my father put us out of his mind and behaved as if he had no ties.

Soon enough, however, he started to send us money on a regular basis once again. He wrote that he was getting used to working for the BBC where he had met a number of other Arabs and a small number of Palestinians. Ziyad and I were sent to school in September of that year and life began to acquire a certain normality. Ziyad's was at a government school to which he usually walked as we could not afford the tram fare. The tram was the commonest form of transport in Damascus at the time, one that we found strange when we first arrived. In Jerusalem we used buses and had never seen trams before. When he was late for school, he climbed on the back fender of the tram and hitched a free ride until the conductor saw him and shooed him off. It was a wonder the trams managed to move at all, weighed down as they were by the large number of youths who clung on to the back. At other times he rode pillion on Um Said's son's bicycle.

I think he was quite happy at his school, but I did not like mine. It was nothing like my school in Jerusalem. It was full of impoverished-looking girls, many of them Palestinians who had come with the exodus from Safad. They were poorly dressed and talked about nothing except that there was not enough to eat here and how they wanted to go back home to Palestine. Some of the Syrian teachers were sympathetic to our plight, others less so.

"You should be grateful that you found us to take you in. It wasn't our fault that the Jews threw you out," was a point often heard. Whenever they said this, Zeinab, who was a Safadi and the only friend I made at that school, would hang her head and say nothing. I remember how she looked, thin like me, but sad with large green eyes and long chestnut hair braided in two thick plaits. Her clothes were shabby and she wore black boots so big and heavy that her spindly legs could scarcely lift them up when she walked. "Your friend with the boots," my grandmother would say. I used to take her back with me to my grandfather's for lunch because I felt sorry for her. She was one of a large family who lived near us – I think there were eight or nine children – and she said they never had enough food in the house. She sometimes brought her youngest brother with her, a boy of three or four who looked pale and sickly. The children used to make fun of him because he passed blood when he went to the toilet, "just like a girl", they mocked. "Only girls pass blood from their behinds." And at this, he would cry and bawl while his sister put her arms round him. "Poor thing," my aunt said, "he looks half starved." A year later, all of Zeinab's family were registered with UNRWA[3] and I suppose they finally did get enough to eat. After we left Damascus, I forgot all about her, and for over thirty years we never met nor heard of each other again.

And then one day, to my astonishment, she found me in London. She came with a man she introduced as her husband and told me they were on their way back to Canada where they now lived. Theirs was a typical Palestinian diaspora story: moving from one Arab state after another. A little studying here, a job there, visas, expired work permits, running after residency permits, again visas, passports. Finally, despairing of the Arab world and the Middle East, they ended up emigrating to Canada. "It's not home," Zeinab said, "but what can you do?"

∂∽∾

The months went by and our father never mentioned when he would be coming to see us. To me, he became a distant memory bound up with the now unreachable past in Palestine. Although he had been

---

[3] The United Nations Relief and Works Agency was set up in 1949 specifically to provide assistance to the Palestinian refugees.

with us when we first came to Damascus and stayed at my grand-father's house, it seemed to me that he had actually been left behind in Jerusalem along with Fatima and our house and Rex. He now belonged to the lost world where he would go on existing separately with the other memories. When Siham read out his letters from London to me and Ziyad I had no image of him in my mind nor of this place called London. He could have been writing to us from heaven for all I could imagine. I certainly never thought we would ever go there, and perhaps we may never have done if it had been left up to him. In January 1949 he wrote suggesting that Siham should come alone and join him. He said that he had still not found a house but had managed to rent a small flat. So Siham could come to London and start her university studies which were overdue; the rest of us would follow once he had found a suitable place for us to live in.

Our mother would have none of it. "Either we all go together or no one goes," she said adamantly and, unable to write well enough herself, got Siham to write and tell my father so. Better still, she said, he should try to come back and resume the search for a job in the Arab world. Things might have changed since it seemed that the dreadful exodus from Palestine had finally come to an end. Thousands of refugees were now living in temporary camps put up in the countries where they had ended up – Jordan, Syria and Lebanon – waiting until they were allowed to go home. It was grim but, at least, the first scramble for jobs had died down and there may well be some work for our father now. But he had other ideas: we must consider coming to London to join him. It would only be temporary, he wrote, just while the UN and the Arab governments sorted out the problem. We would return to our homes soon, but in the meantime, where would he get a job and we a decent education outside England? "Even when England was the cause of our problem in the first place?" retorted our mother.

By the spring of 1949, it seemed inevitable that it was only a matter of time before we all went to London. We had been in Damascus exactly one year. After Ramadan, our father wrote that he had now found a family house, passed to him by an Egyptian colleague who was returning home. Our mother began reluctantly to accept that if our family was to be re-united at all it would have to be on my father's terms in London. She knew she had no real choice in the matter. "Perhaps it won't be for long," she said wistfully. Siham wrote to tell him the news and he wrote back after a while with the instructions for our travel.

Ziyad and I knew that we would be going to London, but it was in some remote future time and we played games in which we imagined how it would be over there and what we would do. No one spoke about the actual journey or the date of travel. And so it was with surprise and shock that in the summer of 1949 we received the news of our impending departure to this unimaginably far-away place.

With my mother, Uncle Taleb, Siham and Ziyad in Damascus, February 1949

We had to have visas for entry into Britain and so our uncle Taleb took us into town to be photographed. Ziyad had got over his initial shock and was now excited about going to London, where we would see our father again and be one family as in the past. He perused his comics intently for clues about how English people dressed. They all wore long trousers, not short ones like his, and when our mother took him to the shops she bought him a pair of plus-fours because the salesman told her these were typically English. (Later, when he wore them in England, the other boys laughed at him and he threw them away.)

At last the time came when we had to leave for England. My mother and sister had been packing for days and we ended up with some six or seven suitcases. These were full of bulky winter clothes because everyone warned of the cold and fog which they said was the permanent state of the English climate. My father had sent my mother and sister a fur coat each, one brown and beige, and the other brown, which Ziyad and I loved to stroke, as if the coats had been two cats. To the clothes in our suitcases my mother also added great quantities of dried foods, spices, nuts and sweets. "Who knows where in that God-forsaken place we'll ever find decent coffee or spices for cooking," she said when Siham objected. Finally, the packing came to an end and it was our last morning in Damascus.

Munthir, who was a cousin of my mother and worked at the Arab Bank in the centre of Damascus, came to say his goodbyes. He was a thin, earnest young man who, it was rumoured, had taken a shine to my sister. "You know, I suppose," he said self-importantly, "that you're probably never going to see Jerusalem again." Everyone looked shocked. "God forbid!" said my mother. "Oh yes", he persisted. "They say that thousands of Jews are pouring in from all over Europe, and they're being settled in all the houses and buildings and farms you left behind. There's probably someone in your house right now." He did not realise that we had heard some such rumour before in July of 1948, when we were told that a family of Yemenite Jews had moved in. My uncle shushed him angrily. "If you've got nothing good to say, better keep your mouth shut," he exclaimed. Munthir looked as if he could say more, but decided against it. I heard him incuriously, as if he were speaking of events and places occurring in some remote country, far away from the one I knew. I had no feeling that any of it was connected with our home in Jerusalem and no image at all of some anonymous Jewish family sitting in our *liwan*, eating in our dining room, walking in our garden.

I was only dimly aware that on that September morning in 1949 we left behind a Palestine ravaged beyond recognition. A new, Israeli government ruled there now and more than half of its area was in Jewish hands, virtually emptied of the Arabs who had once lived there. All over its land, new Jewish settlements had sprung up, replacing the old Palestinian villages. Some 200,000 new Jewish immigrants arrived, mainly from Europe, and were being settled in what had been the Arab districts, towns and houses. Following the armistice agreements which ended the war between the Arab states and Israel in the first half of 1949, the Palestine we knew was fragmented. More than half became Israel and the rest come under Jordanian and Egyptian rule. Tulkarm was now part of the "West Bank of Jordan", ruled by King Abdullah. Our city of Jerusalem was split down the middle. Its western half, where we used to live, was left in Israeli hands, while the other half was annexed to Jordan. "At least", our friends in the Old City commented, "we're all Arabs together here." In the process, three-quarters of a million people lost their homes, like us, and were living temporary lives in other places, some in Syria, some in Lebanon and some in the part of Palestine which was now under Jordanian rule.

Palestine in 1949, at the time we left the country

As we were standing by the door with our suitcases ready to go, my grandfather, who was normally stern and not given to displays of emotion, suddenly put his hands on my mother's shoulders. His pale blue eyes were shiny and the tip of his nose was red. "Don't go, my daughter, don't go," he entreated. "Don't take your children to the land of the unbelievers.[4] They will grow up heathens, ignorant of their faith."

"It's too late, father," she said. "What choice do I have? I never wanted for this to happen as God is my witness, but we need to be together again as a family and Abu Ziyad cannot come back. There is no work for him here, as you know, and with so many others from Palestine looking for work as well, he didn't have much chance."

My grandfather shook his head from side to side, unconvinced. "Even so, it is wrong, it is wrong," he repeated.

"It will not be for ever," said my mother, "don't worry. We will be back, Palestine will not be lost to us and we'll go to our house again in Jerusalem and look back on this as if it were a bad dream, you'll see." But he continued to shake his head. Without another word, he turned on his heel and went into his room and we could hear him crying.

A great crowd of family, neighbours and friends came to see us off at the front door of the house where the taxis were waiting. The alley leading up to the house was narrow, like all the roads in that neighbourhood, and the cars had found them difficult to negotiate. As we got into the taxi, I saw that many of the women were crying. "Don't forget all about us when you're far away over there in England," they said, "and come back soon." The last contact any of them had had with foreign travel had been the time when my uncle came home from Brussels, and it was still an unfamiliar happening for them.

---

[4] Literally translated from the Arabic expression, *bilad al-kuffar*, a designation commonly used in the Arab world for Europe and the West.

It was arranged that we would go first to our uncle Abu Salma's house in downtown Damascus, and would later drive from there to the airport. Our uncle Taleb was to come with us. Our grandmother, weeping all the time, kept slipping her hand under the heavy black veil covering her face to wipe her eyes. Our grandfather was left behind in the house with our aunt Khadija who had hugged and kissed us goodbye, and I saw Siham look back and suddenly burst into tears. She cried on and off all that day.

"I do want to go to London," she said, "but I don't want to leave you behind." She had grown deeply attached to our grandparents, our aunt and our uncle in the eighteen months we had spent in Damascus. My uncle Abu Salma put his arm round her when we reached his house and made her dry her eyes. My aunt had prepared us a light lunch and soon we re-boarded the taxis, with the addition of Abu Salma this time. No one spoke much as we squeezed into the cars and resumed the short journey to Damascus airport. I remember very little of the farewells which took place at the airport, for the prospect of boarding an aeroplane was so frightening and exciting that it was all Ziyad and I could think about.

෫෧

All that seemed unimaginably far-away as we stood in London airport. After getting off the plane, we were accompanied by a pleasant and smiling air hostess. We had to walk in the open air to get to the terminal building, and then through long corridors until we reached immigration. My sister was the only one who could speak English because she had learnt it at school. While on the plane, she had been given forms for all of us to fill and, walking through the airport, it was she who could read the signs that told us where to go. Thanks to these, we found ourselves standing in a queue at the immigration desk, which was the first time any of us had ever been in such a thing as a queue; we were used to people pushing their way to get ahead of others.

I thought the immigration officers looked like the British soldiers I had seen at the bottom of our road in Jerusalem – with uniforms and pink necks. My sister gave them our two passports, hers and my mother's, which included Ziyad and me. They were dark red and had a white window at the top, and on the inside page it said "Government of Palestine" in English and Arabic. Of course, by 1949, there was no Government of Palestine any more, and the officers examined our passports and our visas slowly and carefully. They asked Siham many questions, but in the end they let us go. We went through to the baggage hall and collected our cases. And there, by the customs counter where we were told to take them, stood our father.

The authorities had given him permission to come to the customs area because he had explained that we knew no English and had never travelled this far before. Without thinking, I ran forward towards him, Ziyad behind me. He kissed the top of my head and hugged Ziyad awkwardly, but he was smiling. "Wait, wait till we're outside," he said pushing us back. He turned to mother and Siham and kissed both of them, which was the first time I had ever seen him kiss our mother.

I could not take my eyes off him, for he did not seem like my father at all. His hair was all white and he was thinner and smaller than I remembered. I tried to fit the image of this stranger with that of my father, the one I knew in Jerusalem who was not white-haired and was bigger and somehow nicer and who had spoiled me and loved me, but I couldn't. The customs officer asked us to open our cases. While my father struggled with the locks, he asked if we had brought in any cigarettes or tobacco. My mother who was a smoker and had brought her tobacco with her said nothing. She normally rolled her own cigarettes and used only Turkish tobacco. "Do you have to take that?" my sister had asked in Damascus. "Of course!" my mother had replied indignantly. "Where on earth am I going to get this tobacco in London?" And she had stuffed a great packet of it into her coat.

The customs officer immediately asked for her coat and searched its pockets, whereupon he came across the tobacco. "And you," he said to Siham, "when did you get that watch?" This was a parting present from my uncle Taleb which he had given her just before we left and she was very proud of it. "Last week," she answered truthfully. Meanwhile, the cases had been opened to reveal a variety of foods – dried *mulukhiyya*, mint, saffron, pine nuts, garlic, coffee and sweet-meats – the like of which the officer could never have seen in his whole life before. My father was looking annoyed and embarrassed. He tried to explain that my mother knew nothing about London, had never left her native land and was worried about the rationing. There was a twinkle in the customs officer's eye, "If you don't mind my saying so, sir," he said, "even without the rationing, I don't think your wife would ever find anything like this over here." And with that, he told us to pack our things, said he would not be charging duty for the watch and my mother could enjoy her tobacco in peace. My father looked greatly relieved and we took our cases out into the arrivals hall.

"Well," he said, "here we are". No one answered and he continued, "Let's get a porter to carry all these things." And as the porter struggled with the cases, my father said, "Good heavens, have you brought the whole of Syria with you?" Our mother said something about heavy winter clothes for the cold and the fog. We carried our smaller bags and the porter took the rest. Out in the fresh air, we found a taxi and our father packed my brother and me in the back first, then my sister next to us, and he and our mother sat opposite. "All set?" our father said. My sister nodded and he tapped the window behind him for the driver to start the journey to our new home.

So, for the third time in my short life, yet another taxi was to transport me from one world into another. But though I did not know it then, this time would be the strangest and the last.

Part Two

England

Six

London looked like nothing that I had ever seen. Neither Jerusalem nor Damascus had prepared me for this cold northern city. In fact, the weather was fine and sunny and, did we but know it, quite mild for the time of year. Siham said, "Why isn't it raining? They said it always rained in London." I remember thinking when we were in the taxi driving towards our house that all the cars were driving on the wrong side of the road. And how green everything was! I had never seen such greenness in my life. The garden of our house in Jerusalem had its varied trees, its vine and flowers, but the colours of everything there were muted by contrast to the rich verdance of England. I was overwhelmed by the strangeness.

"Goldans Green", Ziyad and I intoned slowly. "No, Golders Green", laughed my father, stressing the "r". "Never mind, you'll soon learn." Our house was one of a row of almost identical houses stuck to each other on both sides, "terraced", the English called it, and nothing like our "detached" house in Jerusalem. In front, it had a wooden gate and a hedge which acted like a wall. Beyond this was the front door with the number 133 on it and a small window with a frosted glass pane to the side. Inside, it was dark and cold and there were stairs leading to the upper floor. Downstairs, there were two rooms, a kitchen and a scullery. The back room had a 1930s fireplace with a lacquered wooden surround, later to be a "feature" prized by middle-class English house-hunters, but which at the time left my mother utterly indifferent.

Accustomed as she had been to our stone villa with its tiled floors and open veranda, this cramped house with its wooden floorboards and small rooms did not appeal to her. The door of the scullery at the back of the house opened onto the back garden, which was long and narrow and bordered on both sides by wooden fences. Thus, everyone could see into everyone else's garden. Ours was overgrown with a mass of weeds and long grass out of which struggled two mature apple trees against the end wall. Backing onto the scullery wall was an outside toilet, which used to be a feature of English houses of that age, but was not now in use. Its door was barely hanging on its hinges and we started to use it as a repository for junk of all sorts.

I try to remember now when I first saw our new home in London: did I look at that dreary suburban street with its small, dark houses, all standing in monotonous rows, and its humble little strips of land pretending to be gardens and compare it to what I had known in Jerusalem? Did I feel the stark contrast between the two and grieve for what had been lost? I don't think I did, because I had by then already closed off the Palestine of my childhood into a private memory place where it would always remain magically frozen in time. My mother, on the other hand, had decided to recreate Palestine in London – as if we had never left, had never gone to Damascus afterwards, or come to live in England now. Like some Palestinian Miss Havisham, for her, the clock stopped in Jerusalem in April 1948.

My parents having their morning coffee in the back of our house in London

She started first with the floors. In the Arab world, floors are usually made of stone or tiles because of the hot summers. Housewives, or their servants if they had them, washed the floors regularly to clean them but also to keep the houses cool. In no time, and despite England's cold weather, my mother removed the carpets which covered the kitchen and the hall and had the floor laid with reddish-brown, shiny tiles to simulate our house in Jerusalem. She would fill a bucket with soap and water and slosh it all over the floor, exactly as Fatima used to do in Palestine, get down on her knees and mop it up vigorously with a cloth.

Upstairs there were no carpets and the floor was covered in linoleum. This was in the days before central heating, and on some winter mornings it was so cold that our bedroom windows were covered with a layer of frost on the inside. Likewise, the linoleum on the floor was ice-cold to the touch of our warm feet. So, we would curl our feet over onto their sides to minimise contact with the floor and hobble over to get our slippers. "Just like Dr Seckbach," we said. This was a German Jewish doctor who lived in the house next door. He was a thickset, elderly man with frizzy grey hair and large, brown-framed glasses which magnified his eyes. We found out that he had come to England as a refugee from Germany in 1946. He had a practice in Golders Green Road with which we registered soon after arriving. He seemed lonely and sad, and of course we had no way of knowing how he got up in the morning. But we were convinced that he had a linoleum floor and had to curl his feet over to avoid the cold, just like us.

Our house was supposed to have four bedrooms, but in fact one of the rooms was tiny. I shared one room with my sister, my brother had the boxlike room to himself, and our parents slept in another room. The fourth room was used as a spare bedroom and was soon filled with clutter, suitcases, boxes and surplus objects of all kinds. Later, it became Ziyad's bedroom, and the boxlike room he vacated was turned into my father's study. He retreated into this room every evening after dinner and at weekends.

Our main meal was now taken in the evening, not in the middle of the day, as it had been in Palestine. No one slept in the afternoon here; the working day just went on without a break. Except, that is, for "tea". This did not mean a cup of tea, as we first thought, but something altogether more complicated. I found out the true nature of this English tea soon after our arrival. My father had befriended an English couple whom he had met at a BBC function, called Heathcott-Smythe, pronounced "Hethcott". They invited us all to tea, my first social encounter with the English, which made a vivid impression on me.

On a damp and chilly Sunday afternoon in October we made our way to their home. They lived in a block of flats off Baker Street which we reached, I remember, by taking the Number 2 bus from Golders Green station. Their sitting room was full of furniture and bookcases and had a fireplace with a coal fire burning in it. Such fires were new to us, and my mother had only just learned how to make one up. She always overloaded it with huge lumps of coal that burned fiercely and rolled dangerously over onto the hearth. By contrast, the Heathcott-Smythe's fire was well-behaved and stacked with neat, small pieces of coal which glowed quietly and emitted a low bluish flame. I thought it was a beautiful fire, warm and safe. They made us welcome, which could not have been easy, as three of us spoke no English at all. They were both very tall and bland-looking with fine mid-brown hair and light blue eyes. But for Mrs Heathcott-Smythe's shoulder-length hair and pleated skirt, she and her husband could have been twins. She looked nothing like the women I had grown up with who were dark and vivacious, much shorter and often quite plump. But she had kind eyes and she took my hand and sat me on a low stool by the fire. My brother sat awkwardly next to me in the middle of a large armchair with a frilly cover, like a curtain, and we looked at each other.

In a while, the tea tray was brought in, bearing a pretty floral china teapot and matching teacups, a jug of milk and a bowl of small square sugar lumps, along with what seemed to be a pair of tweezers. We had sugar lumps in Palestine too, but they were large, flat and rectangular and looked nothing like these. I leaned across and started to whisper to Ziyad, pointing at the sugar lumps. Mrs Heathcott-Smythe smiled, but my mother, who was sitting next to my brother and looking unhappy, shushed us sharply. She had never been on a visit before where she could not speak to her hostess, and she would lean across to my sister from time to time and tell her to translate something to Mrs Heathcott-Smythe.

My sister and my father were meanwhile chatting quite animatedly with Mr Heathcott-Smythe, who was wearing a V-neck woollen pullover under his check jacket and the shiniest brown shoes I had ever seen. Our hostess put her tray down on the highly polished dark wood table with its starched white tablecloth and then brought in a plate of round sponge-like objects which she placed on the hearth. Smiling at my staring face, she knelt by the fire and proceeded to impale the sponge-like objects, one at a time, onto a large, long-handled brass fork. She then put the fork over the flames of the fire and toasted the sponges. When these turned golden brown, she put them down on the plate and took them to the table, where she spread them generously with butter.

These were in fact crumpets, an English pastry whose charms quite eluded most Arabs. I like them to this day, but my mother, whose taste in food never deviated far from our native Arab cuisine, clearly did not. Later, she adapted the English crumpet into something more fitting to an Arab palate. The crumpet was fried in butter and then soaked in syrup and finally topped with a large dollop of thick cream. The result was so fundamentally different from the conventional crumpet that it was unrecognisable as such. When English visitors came to our house and were served this dish by my mother, they had no suspicion that what they were eating was a homely English crumpet. Mrs Heathcott-Smythe then brought several cakes to the tea table which she said she had made herself. We were given slices of these which we ate while we drank our tea. The tea tasted quite horrible because it was mixed with milk, a combination unheard of for us. Arab tea is strong, dark and very sweet and drunk from small glasses. To make this tea drinkable, we put in lots of sugar. Astonishingly, however, our hosts did not take sugar at all.

So, I thought, this is English tea: with milk and no sugar, and lots of cakes and grilled sponges. "Why didn't you tell us about English tea?" we asked our father afterwards. He laughed, "I suppose I forgot that you never saw English people in Jerusalem in the way I did. The English officers I worked with all drank their tea just like that. They used to complain about the milk, which was not as good as the milk in England, they said. 'Well, why not do without and drink tea as the Arabs do?' I would ask. But they'd look at me pityingly, as if to say that someone who was not English couldn't possibly understand."

"Well, English or no English," my mother grumbled, "it tasted quite horrible and especially those lumps of buttered dough." My father looked annoyed, "Do you realise that they probably used their whole week's supply of butter and sugar on our tea today? One should show a little gratitude."

Britain in 1949 was still in the grips of postwar food rationing. We were given five ration books, one for each of us, which had pages of coupons that could be exchanged for food. We collected them each month. The books came in different colours. Everything was rationed, milk, eggs, flour and, until a few months before our arrival, even clothes. Allowances were quite sparse; the weekly meat ration, for example, was down to half a pound per person. It was as if we were back in besieged West Jerusalem all over again.

There were different types of coupon for different items, including ones for sweets. Neither Ziyad nor I understood much about this, but I recall that soon after our arrival in London we took our two ration books and went down the road to the newsagent's shop. There, we offered them to the woman behind the counter with the one important word we knew in English, "chocolate". She looked through the books and shook her head. Evidently, we did not have the appropriate coupons. But we must have looked so crestfallen that she smiled and gave us a toffee each. Our ration books also had a pork and bacon allowance. Since we did not eat any kind of pig-meat, because it is forbidden to Muslims, my mother gave our pork coupons to the greengrocer at the bottom of the road. His shop was next to the newsagent and opposite the butcher's shop across the road. Used as we were to the profusion of fresh fruit and vegetables in the markets of Jerusalem and Damascus, the sight of orderly rows of lemons, cabbages and pears displayed as if they were pieces of jewellery was strange indeed. "Their fruit and vegetables have no taste," my mother would grumble. "Like eating water. But what can one expect when they all come out of refrigerators?"

The pork coupons which she gave to the greengrocer ensured his lasting devotion. He picked out his best fruit for her or kept it aside until she came round. Sometimes he would put off taking payment if she did not have enough money on her; and all this was conducted in sign language, mixed with English on his part and Arabic on hers. Her success with the butcher was even greater, though only after an initial battle. He had been with the British army in Egypt and spoke a few words of Arabic. Realising that my mother was unfamiliar both with the country and the rationing system, he helped himself to one of her ration books one day when she innocently offered them to him to locate our meat coupons. When she found out what he had done there was much consternation. My father went to our local police station. After this incident, the butcher was utterly repentant and could not do enough for my mother. Eventually, they made friends again and she won his heart by giving him our bacon coupons. This enabled her to teach him how to cut up meat the way we liked it.

The cuts we use are different to those for English meat dishes. Stews are the norm in Arab cooking, while roasts are unusual. Hence, meat needs to be boneless and diced into cubes. Not only did the butcher learn how to cut up the meat in the required way, he also learned more Arabic words, and he and my mother would converse together after a fashion in this pidgin language.

And then there was the man who delivered the coal. He used to arrive every Tuesday with a grimy face and a heavy black coal bag

over his shoulder. With a great heave, he emptied all this into our coal
bunker at the back of the house. This manoeuvre used to raise a great
cloud of black dust which we ran to avoid if we were in the vicinity.
On one such occasion, my mother took pity on the man and offered
him a cup of coffee. This was Arab coffee, strong and sweet and
served in small cups. The man thanked her and when she handed him
his cup, he exclaimed, "I know this coffee! I've had it before. And
here," he continued, "what's that language you're all talking?" Siham
said that it was Arabic. Whereupon he said with satisfaction, "I
thought so. I've been wondering about you for weeks." It turned out
that he had served in the British army in Palestine and had been
stationed in Jerusalem. He had only returned to England at the
beginning of 1948. "Lovely people, the Arabs," he said. "I had a lot of
time for them." And he sat reminiscing over his experiences in
Palestine, asking Siham to interpret. When he finally left, our mother
said, "Look at him, delivering coal. I bet you in Palestine he was a
colonel or something grand, lording it over us."

She made no secret of the fact that she resented being in London.
She complained endlessly that there was no decent food to cook, none
of the vegetables we were used to, and even garlic, the staple of all
Arabic cooking, was a luxury. She hated the cold weather and the rain
and complained she could scarcely keep the house warm. She was
lonely and longed for company. In the Arab world, you were never
alone for a moment. Your neighbours or friends were always there to
call on every day and, in any case, there was the family around you at
all times. In London, she had no neighbours she could talk to, no
family and few friends. In the late 1940s and throughout the 1950s,
there was only a small number of Arabs in England and hardly any
Palestinians beside us. My mother had been a gregarious, sociable
woman who depended on the company of other people almost for her
very survival. "Try and read something," my father would say. "It

will help to pass the time." But she did not agree. She said reading only made her restless and miss the company of people even more.

With our coming to London, she had changed. Whereas in Jerusalem, she had been house-proud and energetic, rushing noisily round the house in the mornings, organising the cooking and the cleaning, here in London she sometimes found it hard even to get out of bed. We might come back at lunchtime and find her still there. She took no interest in the house and, apart from the obsessional blitz on the floors, did not bother to clean it at all. No one understood what had happened to her or why she had changed so. Perhaps we should have realised that her whole life had collapsed around her. In coming to England, my mother had lost everything that to her made life normal and worthwhile. Its whole fabric had been destroyed and she could not come to terms with that loss. She never expressed any of this overtly, and each of us, trying to cope with one's own sense of loss, was in no position to help her. Today, we would call it depression, but none of us understood such a concept at the time.

She often sat in the kitchen in the dark with her ear pressed against our second-hand radio, trying to tune into Arabic stations on short wave. This radio, which my father had obtained from the BBC, was a large brown wooden box with a circular speaker covered in beige matting. It did not work well. When my mother complained, he replaced it with a succession of others, all BBC rejects and all equally scratchy. A few years later, he took pity on her and bought her a modern, black, sleek-looking Grundig radio which was much better at receiving short wave.

She listened avidly to the news coming out of the Arab world about Palestine and she and my father would talk to each other about it in the evenings. Once, a month or so after we had arrived, I heard them say that there was still no word from the Jews – they never once used the words Israelis or Israel to the best of my knowledge – about

allowing us all back to Palestine, and that the UN was doing nothing
about it. It was at this time that I first heard them refer to the *nakbah*,[1]
a word I would hear over and over again throughout my life. When I
asked what it meant, they fobbed me off with, "Never you mind about
that. It's something that happened in the past."

When there was no news on the radio, my mother would listen to
Arabic songs or to recitations of the Quran. Traditionally, the Quran
is not supposed to be read out like ordinary prose, but recited
melodiously with long pauses between phrases. The men who recited
the Quran were specially trained and chosen for the beauty of their
voices, and Egyptian reciters were recognised as being at the forefront
of this art form. Probably nothing is more evocative of the Arab
world than hearing recitations of the Quran. I remember a Christian
Jordanian friend once telling me how in the 1960s he had gone on a
visit to Munich. While there, he saw a mosque and entered it out of
curiosity. As he heard the Quran recited (quite badly by a Turkish
imam, as it happened), he suddenly felt a surge of nostalgia for home
stronger than any that had assailed him in all the beautiful, old
churches that he saw there. It was customary at that time for radio
stations in many Arab countries to run a half hour of Quranic reading
every day, and wherever one went one could hear it on people's
radios. Coming into our house in London with my mother's radio
emitting Arabic songs or Quranic recitations, albeit that the sound was
crackly and intermittent, had an uncanny effect. In an instant, I could
feel myself transported back to Palestine, as if the key to our front
door was all it took to send me there.

The daily routine of our life at home was as Arab as my mother
could make it, just as if we had never left Jerusalem at all. Our food
was entirely Arab, difficult though this was to achieve at first, since

---

[1] Meaning disaster or catastrophe. This is the word Palestinians use to describe the exodus of 1948.

few of the ingredients needed were available. Britain had not at the time acquired its Indian, Pakistani and Cypriot immigrants whose cooking was similar to ours or at least used the same spices and vegetables. So, my mother had to be ingenious and use what was available from the street market in Soho. My father went there every week on his way home from work and bought aubergines and peppers and garlic at inflated prices. But as it was the only place where such things could be found we had no option; for the alternative, that is modifying our cuisine to become more English or European was, for my mother, wholly unthinkable.

It is ironic that the only non-English foods which were available in Golders Green at that time were those eaten by the Jews who lived around us. This was where I first learned of the existence of such a thing as a delicatessen offering the hitherto unfamiliar salami and pickled gherkins and smoked salmon. I later ate these things at the homes of my Jewish friends from school and got a taste for them which I have never lost. The delicatessen sold other things eaten by Jews, gefilte fish and chopped herring and latkes, but I never learnt to like any of these. Because many salamis contained pork, I used to eat the kosher type made for religious Jews, and later, my father and brother acquired the same taste for this salami. But my mother would have none of it and for years Ziyad and I ate such foods only outside our house.

Our home soon became a refuge for lonely Palestinians. These were often young unmarried men who, like my father, had found their way to a job at the BBC Arabic Service. Some of them also brought their friends to our house and in no time we had acquired a reputation amongst newly arrived and homesick Palestinians for being a home-from-home. My mother would cook them Palestinian dishes and find out where they came from and who they were related to. This sort of inquiry was always important amongst Palestinians, but it became obligatory after the exodus of 1948. People were eager to define each other's exact town or village of origin in Palestine, as if to affirm to themselves that the country was still there in spite of what had happened. Their families were no less important, since this was the way in which people traditionally assessed each other's social position and, more significantly, established any family links there might be.

Kinship ties have always played a major role in Arab society, but for Palestinians dispersed after 1948 establishing their exact identities by reference to family and lineage became crucial. Palestine was a small place with a settled population. Because of this, families became associated with specific places, and surnames were usually all that was needed to establish someone's geographic origin. People of peasant stock, for instance, were recognisable by the fact that they used the father's first name as their surname. Rendered into English, this would

With Arab friends in London soon after our arrival

go something like Mary Alfred or Derek Philip, where Alfred was the father of Mary and Philip the father of Derek. Christians were equally recognisable because their surnames were usually distinct from Muslim surnames.

"Are you the Canaans of Nablus or the Canaans of Jerusalem?" my mother would ask. My father often joined in because he prided himself on knowing every inch of Palestine. But sometimes he was stumped when someone cited the name of a small village which he did not recognise. He would worry at it until he found it. "Ah," he would suddenly say, "it's just outside Jaffa, why didn't you say so at first?"

For years, I thought this obsession with places and family names and "who was related to whom" was just a quirk of my parents. My sister and I used to imitate them in our bedroom after a particularly gruelling interrogation with some hapless Palestinian visitor, and laugh and shake our heads. It took me years to realise that after 1948, establishing a person's origin became for Palestinians a sort of mapping, a surrogate repopulation of Palestine in negation of the *nakbah*. It was their way of recreating the lost homeland, as if the families and the villages and the relations they had once known were all still there, waiting to be reclaimed. And indeed, for Palestinians in the immediate aftermath of the 1948 exodus, the prospect of return to Palestine was very real. Who can believe, they used to say, that we won't be allowed to return to our homes? It's our country, they're our homes. The UN, the Americans, the British will never allow such a terrible injustice to happen. Of course we're going back!

This was my mother's conviction too. "I'll put up with being here," she would say about living in London, "because I know it won't be for long. And you, children," she would continue, "don't get too used to things here, we're not staying." And she put this philosophy uncompromisingly into effect. She refused to learn English, she had no English friends, she would reject any suggestion of decorating

our shabby house, or even of buying such a basic thing as a refrig-
erator. "I never had such a thing in Palestine where it was hot, why
should I need it here where it's freezing?" Agreeing to any house
improvement other than cleaning would have meant that her stay in
England was no longer temporary. Since this possibility was not
remotely acceptable, we struggled on living in a cold house (for
central heating was another rejected improvement), with peeling
walls, a dilapidated bathroom and a damp, old-fashioned kitchen.

But despite herself my mother became friends with the English
people next door. They lived at no. 131, the house to the right of ours
and identical to it in layout and external appearance. Our neighbours
were an elderly man called Mr Nunn and Mrs Brinkhurst, his
housekeeper. In all the years we knew them we never found out their
first names. Nor did we understand the concept of a housekeeper. We
decided that she must be some sort of a wife to him. There was no
such thing as a paid housekeeper in our country. When a man needed
someone to look after him, he usually had his mother or his sisters to
turn to. For a woman to live with a man who was not a close relative
would have been unthinkable. "It just shows", my mother said, "what
miserable lives they lead here, no family or friends, they've got to pay
someone to keep them company."

There was a gap in the fence between our back gardens and so it
was easy for us to cross over into each other's houses. Not that it
looked as if either Mr Nunn or his housekeeper wanted to have
anything to do with us when we first moved in. But such aloofness, as
we discovered later, was due to English reserve rather than hostility.
For us Arabs, the idea of the neighbours keeping to themselves so as
not to annoy others was bizarre. In our understanding, neighbours by
definition were supposed to be friendly and helpful, very much concerned with other people's affairs. My mother ignored these English
proprieties, and soon after we moved in, she sent me across the fence

with a dish of food which she had cooked that day. I shyly offered it to Mrs Brinkhurst who was in the kitchen.

I found myself looking at an old lady with permed white hair, held flat against her head with a hair net. Over her clothes, she wore a sort of body apron, a floral sleeveless garment which crossed over round her middle and was tied in a bow at the back. Her skin was pale and lined and her hands were swollen at the joints with what I did not recognise then as arthritis because I had never seen it before. She looked surprised to see me and even more so at the plate I was offering her. She started to say something. But she could see that I did not understand and smiled at me. Behind me, standing in our scullery door was my mother, calling out "hallo" and gesticulating to her to take the plate.

Looking bewildered, Mrs Brinkhurst gave in. She disappeared into the house and reappeared with a frail-looking old man wearing a dark suit. He had thin wispy hair and thick-lensed glasses. He waved awkwardly and smiled at me and my mother and tried to say something, but Mrs Brinkhurst shook her head, as if to say it was no use talking to us. That night, the plate was returned empty and washed clean with expressions of gratitude. And from that time on we became good friends. When they found out that we were Palestinians who had been displaced from our country, Mr Nunn, missing the point and in an effort to please us, said, "To tell you the truth, I don't like Jews either. Never used to feel anything about them until I ran across them in business." Before he retired, he had owned a small plumbing firm. "They were always complaining and haggling to get the price down. If you'd charged them nothing at all, it would still have been too much. Got on my nerves, so I can imagine how you must have felt."

Such explicit anti-Semitism was not uncommon in Britain at the time. Pejorative remarks about Jews, which would be unthinkable today, were made freely then, though usually in more oblique and subtle ways that often puzzled us. That gut anti-Semitism which had become so embedded in European culture over the centuries was quite alien to us. Although ignorance about Palestine was widespread, it often happened that when we mentioned we had lost our homes because of what the Jews had done to our country, people became sympathetic, but on the basis of their instinctive anti-Semitism rather than any love for the Arabs. Such sympathy left my mother cold. She said, "These English! If they dislike the Jews so much, why did they give them our country?"

"Because we don't want them over here!" chuckled Mr Nunn with unashamed and startling candour. "Sorry, but there it is!" Our neighbours' affection for us was, however, genuinely unfeigned. My mother regularly passed plates of food over to them which, as we later discovered, they devoured with relish; though how their English palates accepted the strong garlic, spices and herbs which were our regular seasoning, I never understood. In return, they helped us settle in in innumerable ways, taught us about our ration books, advised us on how to tend our garden and put us in touch with workmen when something went wrong in the house.

In time, Mrs Brinkhurst got too old and ill with her arthritis to continue with her household duties. She left and went to live with her sister in the country. And very shortly afterwards Mr Nunn sold the house and went somewhere else too. It was sad when they left, especially for my mother, who had grown attached to Mrs Brinkhurst. After a few years in London, she had managed to learn some words of English and they could carry on a sort of conversation together. "Presently" was a word Mrs Brinkhurst used often. When you asked her to do something, she would invariably reply, "Presently, dear, presently". And my mother who had no idea what this word meant, nevertheless added it to her tiny English repertoire and would repeat it proudly at intervals, pronouncing it "brezinly". The day Mrs Brinkhurst left, my mother embraced her and cried and said she would never have such a good neighbour again. But her warm feeling for Mrs Brinkhurst did not make her like the English better or wish to know them any the more. For my mother, it was an isolated experience without relevance to anything else, and she never made another English friend after that in all the forty years she spent in England.

ॐ

"What's your name?" said the nun bending over me. She was large and had a round face framed by a starched white head-dress shaped in a stiff rectangle with upturned ends. She wore a grey habit and a long rosary round her neck with a crucifix at the end of it.

"She's asking you your name," my father said in Arabic. I sat on a chair next to him, staring up at her.

"Ghada al-Karmi",[2] I said in a rush.

"What's that?" The nun looked at my father inquiringly.

"Ghada Karmi," he said. The Gh in my first name is not a "G" at all, but is a transliteration of an Arabic letter not found in the English language and sounds like the French "R"; the "ada" that follows is supposed to have an open sound, as in Anne or Dan. But the nun, unable to pronounce these sounds, said, "Garda. I see. Well, that's nice." She made me sound like a different person. In an instant, I was no longer the Ghada I had known all my life, but this alien creature, "Garda". To my dismay, I found that it was not only the nun but virtually everyone else who pronounced my name in the same way. For years, whenever anyone asked me my name, I would feel the need

---

[2] The "al-" prefix, meaning "the", is used automatically in many Arab surnames. Because it was unfamiliar to English people for many years, most Arabs living in England, including ourselves, dropped it.

to preface my answer with, "I'm afraid my name is hard for an English person . . . " I found all this so distressing that for a long time I hated my parents for choosing a name that was so difficult for English people to pronounce – as if they could have foretold the future.

My father and I were sitting in the Mother Superior's office of La Sagesse Convent School in Golders Green, where he had taken me to apply for admission. Ziyad was accepted into a boy's school in Mill Hill and Siham was to be enrolled with me at the Convent. The school occupied an imposing set of buildings at the lower end of the Golders Green Road, away from the station. Inside, it had schoolrooms, a boarders' dormitory and a chapel. Outside, there was a tennis court and a garden which the day girls were not allowed to use. Over the heavy front door was a large cross bearing the figure of Christ. My father thought that the nuns would be kind to us and patient with me.

The idea of sending Muslim children to Christian religious schools was not unfamiliar to a Palestinian like my father. From before the beginning of the twentieth century, Jerusalem had been the centre of a vigorous missionary movement by European Christians of all denominations. Aiming to convert the local population to Christianity, they made themselves useful through a variety of good works, including the establishment of schools. Palestinians believed that these provided a better education than the government schools. Many families who could afford it sent their children, whether Christian or Muslim, to Anglican or Catholic or German Lutheran schools. Girls in particular were enrolled in convent schools which could be relied on to protect their modesty while giving them an education. Muslim parents did not worry about the proselytising influence of these places which they said had never been known to convert a single Muslim to Christianity.

So, in placing me at La Sagesse Convent School, my father was merely following a well-established Palestinian tradition. It never for a moment occurred to him that I could be lured away from Islam into the arms of Roman Catholicism. He did not understand that in London things were different. The Muslim children who went to missionary schools in Palestine might have been immune to Christian influence because their environment was largely Muslim. In London, our family was isolated and alone, without the support of a Muslim community. In addition, he underestimated the nuns' subtle influence over me. From the very beginning, they were the epitome of kindness to me, to the point of indulgence.

They chose me to clean the statues of the Virgin Mary and the saints, for which I was rewarded by being given time away from lessons. This was justified on the grounds that, as I knew no English, I was better employed in tasks which did not require the use of language. They gave me only the prettiest statues to clean, milky white marble figurines small enough to hold in one's arms. I used to have a comfortable little seat and table to work on and as I polished the features of the Virgin's lovely face and they started to gleam like satin, the nuns would pat my head and speak in kind voices. At times they would take me into the chapel which, like the other non-Catholic girls in the class, I did not normally enter. Its colours were all turquoise and gold and it seemed to me the loveliest place I had ever seen. The statue of the Virgin in the chapel was larger than life-size and her robes were edged in shining stars. Candles burned everywhere and filled the room with a magical radiance. The nuns would take pleasure in my evident delight. On Christmas eve, many of the girls stayed on after school because, as I found out, they were all going to midnight mass in the beautiful chapel. I wished I could have gone too.

Every lesson began with a Hail Mary, which the girls recited with the teacher. I did not join in and as soon as I understood that this was a Catholic prayer I began to close my eyes each time and say the

Fatiha prayer in my head. I saw this as the only way to preserve my identity from being overwhelmed by the Christian forces around me. At the same time, I started to pray at home in the way which my grandfather had taught me, completely setting aside my previous aversion. My parents found the whole thing very amusing. Neither of them observed religious ritual, but they believed in God and identified themselves as Muslims. They approved of my new religiosity although they did not understand it.

I continued to pray in this fashion until the age of sixteen when I began to change. The nuns of La Sagesse were never able to convert me in the end, but they succeeded far more than they knew. To this day, I cannot enter a Catholic church without feeling a special tug of affection at my heart. And, when I went to an Anglican school after the convent, I could not warm to the Protestant version of Christianity. It seemed to me ineffably dreary and had no Virgin Mary or pretty statues. In addition, there was an emphasis on the Old Testament, the Hebrew prophets and Jews as a whole that I had not met before at the convent. "And God gave the land of Israel to the Jews," our scripture teacher intoned reverentially. "This, girls, means that it used to belong to them and happily they have now returned to it." This was in 1953 when the State of Israel was five years old. Although I still knew little about the *nakbah*, which my parents would never discuss, I felt a stirring of obscure anger when she said this. I went home and told my father about it. "Protestants!" he exclaimed angrily. "What do you expect? They and their Old Testament are the root of our problem. But for them there would have been no Israel and no *nakbah*."

I had a best friend at the convent school. She was the only Jewish girl in my class or possibly even in the whole school. Her name was Leslie Benenson and she was a plump, fair-skinned girl with curly brown hair and green eyes. We became firm friends at the end of my first year at the school. Until then, I had struggled to learn English and to keep up with the rest of the class despite my handicap. The nuns had arranged for me to have private English tuition from a Miss Buchanan who had her own rooms at the convent.

This was a lady of advanced years with snow-white hair and ill-fitting false teeth which made her lower lip jut out. She had lived in India for many years and treated me with slight distaste, as if I had been another of the coolies who had no doubt served her there. Evidently, she was at a loss to know how to teach me and on that first day took me to the nuns' dining room. This was the room where the Mother Superior and the nuns took their meals. The dining table was covered with a starched white table cloth and matching napkins. Here, Miss Buchanan tried to teach me the names of the cutlery and crockery on the table, pointing to each with a thin shrivelled finger and intoning its name with slow enunciation. And hence it was that the first words of the English language I ever learned (after Oscar Wilde, that is), were "soup tureen" and "soup ladle", terms I would never use in my life again.

I cannot remember so much misery as I felt in those early months. The very first day at school had been particularly harrowing. Understanding no English at all and not knowing how to find my sister at lunchtime, since we were in different classes, I had wandered into a large dining-room full of girls. This was the boarders' dining-room and, had I but known it, I should not have been there at all. But I could ask no one where to go, nor could I see any sign of Siham amid the chattering, laughing girls and the clatter of plates and cutlery. I felt as if the end of the world had come, but a nun found me sobbing and somehow managed to make something out of my distressed and breathless Arabic and took me to find Siham. After that, I would wait for her in a certain spot every lunchtime to avoid getting lost again, and every day I would cry because I could not understand what people were saying and because the other girls didn't speak to me. "I feel like a deaf man at a wedding,"[3] I wailed, but my mother laughed and said, "You'll be all right".

After three months, and despite Miss Buchanan, I had learned sufficient English to be able to cope, although not always with the proficiency I would have liked. My first public foray into the English language ended in ignominy when, during the class which I was now allowed to join, I had boldly asked if I could read out loud from the book we were studying. The teacher smiled at me encouragingly and I proceeded. I recall that the subject of the passage I attempted concerned the history of the British flag, the Union Jack. And so, reading phonetically, I began, "The Onion Jack . . . ", but before I could go any further the girls and the teacher dissolved into gales of laughter. I was so distressed that I did not try to read again for months.

Meanwhile, Siham had left at the end of the first term and had gone to a tutorial college in Tottenham Court Road to study for her university entrance exam. She had set her heart on studying medicine. I was now expected to join in all the classes and could not go to Sister to be excused any time I wanted to, as had happened at the beginning. The lessons were still too hard for me. Only when it came to arithmetic did I feel any measure of confidence. At my first lesson, we were given an exercise to do which looked quite easy, several multiplication and division sums as I recall. After we had handed in our books the teacher marked them. But instead of the 9 or 10 out of 10 which I was expecting to get, since I had always been top of the class at school, both in Jerusalem and Damascus, I got only 6 out of 10. I was so mortified that tears filled my eyes in front of everyone. When the other children started peering curiously at me, I said defiantly in my halting English, "It was not like that in my country. It was different

---

[3] This is a translation of a well-known Arabic saying, *mithl al-atrash bi'l-ẓaffeh*.

there." They laughed jeeringly, "Ooh, it's not like that in her country! It's not like that in her country!"

I turned away, filled with misery, and went outside where I found Leslie Benenson waiting by the door. She said nothing, but stood with me in the school yard and, although she never mentioned the mathematics test, I felt that she was on my side. From that moment on we became friends. She was the first Jewish friend I made, not that I ever thought of her as such. In fact, the only reason I knew she was Jewish at all was that the sisters made such a point of telling everyone to which religions the non-Catholic girls in the class belonged. There was myself as the only Muslim, Leslie as the only Jew and four others who were Protestants. All the rest were Catholics.

By the summer of 1950, when I was ten, my English was fluent and I could hold my own in class with anyone. Leslie invited me to her home for tea, a meal I was now familiar with and enjoyed whenever I was invited to it in someone's house. Leslie was an only child, her father was Belgian, her mother English, and they were devoted to her. Mr Benenson was a kindly, humorous man who often played the clown with me and Leslie as if we were all of the same age. When the horseplay got too boisterous Mrs Benenson would call out from below, "Marcel, stop that! Behave yourself!" And he would wink at us and make faces of mock terror. One day, Mrs Benenson decided to invite a few of the nuns from the convent to tea, something which my mother would never have dreamed of doing. In fact, to my sorrow, my mother never once visited the convent in the three years I spent there. I was invited along as well and found it a strange experience. I remember that after the nuns had finished their tea, blessed Mr and Mrs Benenson and taken their leave, Mr Benenson went to the toilet. As he emerged, he said, "There's a distinct odour of sanctity in there!" We burst out laughing and Mrs Benenson said, "Marcel! You are terrible!" But she was smiling.

Leslie and I became very close. Occasionally, she came to my house, but there was no tea there unless I went and bought a cake or a few pastries, and there was nowhere for us to be alone. So we ended up more often at her house. Her parents accepted me without demur. They knew my origins but whether that signified anything to them or not I never discovered. That they were Jewish themselves seemed to play little part in their lives. Leslie's mother – whose name, as she stressed, was pronounced Irene and not Ireen – was proud of her Englishness. She often boasted of her "English skin" and her "English colouring", even the "English shape" of her head, whatever that meant. Only once did she betray any prejudice towards me. I was telling them that my parents had had ten people to dinner the night before, which was not unusual in our house as my mother had by then collected a motley group of Arabs around her, when she laughed in disbelief. "Oh come on, don't tell awful whoppers, like Arabs do. Ten people indeed! You know that's not true." I was doubly hurt because I had indeed been telling the truth and I didn't know why she should think that Arabs were liars.

"Do you want to come and visit my grandmother?" asked Leslie one day. "We're all invited to tea on Sunday afternoon." Her grandmother lived in a big house in Temple Fortune, which was just beyond Golders Green station in the direction of Finchley. Leslie did not usually mention any of her family to me and I knew little about them. But I was pleased to be invited and somehow felt included and accepted. That I should feel like this, unfazed by the seeming incongruity – a Palestinian child amongst a Jewish family – never struck me. I had no sense at all of them as Jews at the time. When I arrived with Leslie and her parents I found a houseful of people, apparently Leslie's uncles, aunts and cousins over from Belgium. They were gathered in the sitting room, a spacious split-level room with a grand piano and much dark polished furniture. There were candlesticks and cut glass decanters and large velvet armchairs. Leslie's grandmother was a diminutive woman dressed all in black. She had a bun of snow-white hair on the back of her head and wore long, old-fashioned earrings and a cameo brooch at her neck. The family spoke to each other sometimes in French and sometimes in English, and when Leslie's grandmother had kissed and hugged Leslie, as had her aunts and her cousins, she turned to me. "And who is zis?" she asked in a strong French accent.

"Mother, this is Ghada, Leslie's Arab friend from school," said Mr Benenson. He pronounced my name correctly, with the French "R" at the beginning as did Leslie, but her mother always said "Garda" like everyone else. I thought she might ask which country I came from, but she didn't. No one mentioned the words Palestine or Palestinian. Leslie's grandmother took my hand and said, "Come on Leslie, look after your friend." She smiled at me and said, "Soon we will 'ave tea." Leslie's uncle, who looked much older than her father, also smiled at me. "Maman, je t'en prie, assis-toi," said Leslie's father and helped her back into her chair. I gathered it was a family reunion and some of them had not met for a long time. "They surely don't want me here," I whispered to Leslie. "I don't care what they want," she whispered back. "I want you here to keep me company. They're all terribly boring." But I did not agree. They were different and interesting and did not conform to anything I knew. At that stage I had hardly met any European Jews at such close quarters, although so many of them lived in Golders Green.

"Are all the people here your relatives?" I asked.

"What's left of them, yes," she said.

"What do you mean?"

"My father says they were all killed in the war." I had an image of bombs exploding and people being shot as had happened in Jerusalem. I nodded sympathetically, "I'm sorry," I said. "Thanks," said Leslie, "but I never knew any of them, so it doesn't feel very bad." Amazing to think now, amid the current and intense public prominence given to the Holocaust everywhere, that Leslie and I could have had such a conversation. The truth was that neither she nor I knew anything about it then, even though it had taken place but a few years before.

When tea was brought in it was nothing like the tea at Mr and Mrs Heathcott-Smythe's. There were open sandwiches of salami and sliced gherkins on rye bread. There was smoked salmon and cream cheese and potato cakes. "Yummy!" said Leslie. "Come on, let's tuck in, it's not every day we get this sort of grub. They've brought it over with them from Belgium."

After a while, Leslie's elder uncle announced that Raymond had agreed to play the piano. Raymond, I gathered, was a friend and not one of the family. Everyone clapped enthusiastically and egged him on towards the piano seat. He was a short, insignificant-looking man with thinning hair and narrow shoulders, not my idea of what a pianist should look like, at least according to Hollywood films. "He's awfully good," whispered Leslie to me, "he's a professional pianist and he doesn't often play in people's houses like this." Everyone sat down on all the available chairs and stools and Leslie and I perched on the arm of the large sofa next to her father. "What do you want me to play?" asked Raymond. No one answered immediately and so he said, "Very well, I will choose something myself." At that, he flexed his fingers athletically back and forth a few times and then started. I think that he played Chopin but, whatever it was, I found it beautiful, and when I glanced round at the faces of the others, all raptly listening, I could see that they thought so too.

At that time, I had just begun to appreciate classical western music, which was no mean achievement, for I had been brought up on something entirely different. Throughout my childhood, it was the songs of Um Kulthum and Abdul-Wahab, famous Egyptian singers of the Arab world, or the lute playing of Farid al-Atrash, the Lebanese musician, I had heard. This kind of music, with its quarter-notes and special instruments, had nothing whatever in common with Chopin or Beethoven. It was the music I still heard in our house in London, thanks to my mother and her radio, one that would haunt me for the rest of my life. Because of this association, I cannot hear an old song of Um Kulthum without a sense of aching nostalgia for my mother and a vanished past I never shared with her. Nor can I listen to the 1920s and 1930s music of Abdul-Wahab without instantly visualising my father as I imagined him in his youth strolling through the streets of Jerusalem.

Ignoring our mother and her radio, Siham and I had begun to listen to classical music on the BBC Third Programme and to like it. Our parents never understood this or learned to share our interest. If Siham or I had the radio on to a Mozart symphony or a Beethoven piano concerto and our mother happened to pass by, she would switch it off immediately, exclaiming, "What a dreadful racket! How can you stand it?"

When Raymond's playing came to an end and tea was finished we helped to clear the dishes. Then it was time to leave. Some of the family and friends went with us, but others stayed on. The time I had spent there seemed too short. Leslie's family and I parted with great warmth, as if we had known each other for ages. Her grandmother hugged and kissed me, her small bright eyes disappearing into her cheeks as she smiled at me and told Leslie to bring me round again to see her. And I went home thinking how I wished I had a nice large family like that to come over from Palestine and visit me.

By the time I was eleven, life in London had acquired a certain stability. Ziyad and I were fluent in English and able to cope with school. He had made several friends in his class, all of them Jewish, his school, like mine, being in a largely Jewish neighbourhood. I would have had more Jewish friends myself had my school not been a convent intended for Catholics. Even when Ziyad moved schools, it was to another Jewish part of London. Some of the Jewish friends he made at those schools remained his friends for life, devoted to him despite his later wanderings and travel abroad. One of the first and most devoted of them had been a boy called Martin Weiss. Martin came from a family of German Jews and was strikingly blond and blue-eyed. He had liked my brother from the beginning, even when Ziyad could hardly speak any English, and they soon became firm friends.

But one day, Martin told Ziyad that their English teacher had advised his parents to stop them associating because Ziyad would be a bad influence on their son. My brother was the only non-European boy in the school and he got very upset at this. But Martin said, "I don't care what they say. I'm not going to take any notice." And he was as good as his word. He came home with Ziyad sometimes and stayed with us for as long as he dared. When I was turning fifteen and beginning to be aware of my looks he had said to Ziyad admiringly, "Gosh, isn't your sister pretty?" To which my brother replied, "Her, pretty? You must be mad!"

At the convent, I became especially proficient in religious studies. In fact, both Leslie and I, a Jew and a Muslim, were top of the class in scripture. The nuns indulged me quite outrageously and I started to really enjoy life at school. It became a sort of second home. I knew every inch of its polished corridors, high windows and stairways, even Mother Superior's forbidding doorway, with loving familiarity. Some of the older girls were beginning to talk about feeling a sense of religious vocation and about becoming novice nuns. But no one in our class took this seriously and in so far as any of us thought about the future, it was only to see it as a far-away time when we were grown up. Never for a moment did it occur to me that I would not stay on at La Sagesse until then.

Unknown to me at the time, my father had other ideas. He had by
then already planned that none of our future careers would lie in the
pursuit of "useless subjects" like history and literature which, he
argued, could only lead to some low-paid teaching job (or no job at
all) which would neither feed us nor pay the rent when the time came.
"But why should such a time ever come?" my mother protested. "The
girls will get married, a job is not that important for them." "Oh
yes?" my father retorted, "And what happens when they don't get
married or they end up with some bastard who walks out on them?" I
wonder sometimes at the effect this jaundiced view of marriage had on
me and my sister. He would sometimes say to us when the matter of
careers came up, "You must never become anyone's employee,
anyone's slave, as I have been." And occasionally he would add in the
closest allusion to the loss of our country he ever permitted himself, "I
want you all to have a skill in your pocket to take with you wherever
you go. That way, you will always survive, no matter where you are
forced to live."

Meanwhile, with the exception of our mother, we had all started to
explore London. When we had first arrived, our father took us on
outings to London's most famous places. But our very first and
possibly most memorable visit was to the Woolworth's store on
Golders Green Road. We had never seen anything like it, for it
seemed so big and so full of all the things one could want, toys and
comics and sweets, even a stamp counter for Ziyad's stamp collection.
Woolworth's became an indispensable part of our lives, even our
mother's, for of course it sold household goods which were of great
importance to her, but of no interest to us. When we went to see
historic places, she stayed at home in her half-dark kitchen, saying
that she wanted to see living people (meaning Arabs), not piles of
stones.

The most striking feature of London was its size and scale. We had never known a city of such dimensions, such large buildings and such wide streets. It was when we went to Madame Tussaud's waxwork museum that I experienced the first panic attack I had ever had. This happened in the museum's Chamber of Horrors, which showed scenes of bloody historical events, torture and death. One of these, a tableau of Admiral Nelson's last hours, depicted a life-like group of men bending over his dying form. Next to him was a basin full of what looked like real blood and I noticed with horror how his eyes were rolled up and how sickly pale he looked. I began to feel stifled and my heart started to pound. The place seemed suddenly intolerably hot and I tugged at my father's hand. "Let's go, please, please," I begged urgently. My father said, "Wait a bit, we've only just arrived." But I pulled and pulled at his hand until he gave in and we got out into the fresh air, the others grumbling that they had hardly seen anything.

I went on getting these sudden inexplicable attacks for years afterwards, but fortunately never in the one place where they might have been expected to occur, the London Underground. The underground train system features high on the list of exciting discoveries of those days. The idea that one could travel in something which was plunged deep under the ground traversing dark, lonely tunnels and from which one could emerge at the other end unscathed was little short of miraculous. The thought of this continued to fascinate me for years, as did the thrill of impending fear of being on the train during one of its brief sojourns in the open air overground – knowing it would soon be swallowed up in the deep, dark, claustrophobic tunnel.

The names of the stations had a special magic for me and each acquired a character of its own. Thus the stations on our line, the Northern Line (Edgware branch), were friendly and familiar. But stations like Hainault, Cockfosters or the sinister Ongar were places of unbelievable obscurity which one never went to. (It didn't occur to me that the people who used those stations might have felt similarly about ours.) But even on our own Northern Line there were areas of darkness, like Collier's Wood or Morden, which were at the extreme southern end of the line and seemed to lie in another country.

In general, however, the limit of my travelling on the underground was at Leicester Square in the centre, from which one could reach Trafalgar Square and all the major West End cinemas. I learned to estimate the distances between the stations on the way there with some accuracy, knowing which were short and which long and between which stations the train was likely to make one of its inexplicable stops. I also learned to be adept at using the escalators, which at that time had slatted wooden steps. The trick was to make sure one's foot did not go over the line that separated two steps at either end of the escalator because these would separate as soon as it started to go up or down. The other trick, which came later when I started to wear such things, was to avoid getting one's stiletto heel stuck in between the slats.

The London of the early 1950s was a safe, dull place with a strong atmosphere of austerity. As children, we went about at night without the slightest nervousness on our parents' part or on ours, a situation unthinkable in today's London. But there was little to do, and without television people passed the time by listening to the radio – or wireless as everyone called it – and going to the cinema. Siham and I were devoted listeners to what was then known as the BBC Home Service and where we used to listen to "The Archers", the longest running radio serial in the world. Started in 1951 (and still going strong), it depicted the daily lives of farming people in the English countryside – a world of which we knew nothing and which could not have been more different from the landscape of our family in Tulkarm.

At the same time, on the BBC Light Programme, there were a number of comedy half-hour programmes, the funniest of which was without doubt "The Goon Show". The three of us were soon hooked on this strange programme. It was impossible to describe it to anyone who had never heard it. It was zany, crazy and to us extremely funny, though how on earth any of it related to our culture or experiences no one understood. "Look at them. What on earth can be so funny?" our mother would remark to our father as they watched us in bafflement reeling about with laughter, imitating the voices and repeating the jokes to each other. No Arab could have understood the English innuendos and allusions in the programme, certainly not our parents, and it was like a bond between us children, recreating the ties that had existed in Palestine. "The Goon Show" had a large cult following throughout the 1950s of which we three were part, probably the only three Palestinians to have had this distinction in Britain.

There were several cinemas in Golders Green and Hendon – the Gaumont, the Odeon, the Lido and the Ionic, where we frequently went. The longest of these to survive was the Ionic which underwent several name changes, but it too finally closed after 51 years. "Going to the pictures" was an exciting activity in those days, seeing famous film stars whose names had been transliterated to Arabic back in Damascus and Jerusalem and sounded like "Jon Craford", "Lana Teerner", "Bet Dafees" or "Irl Fleen" and "Clark Jeebel". We were amazed to hear these properly pronounced in English for the first time. In the Arab world, western film stars seemed to us like glossy gods and goddesses, inhabitants of another planet. But seeing them on screen in our local cinema in London, they became more human and accessible.

Going to the cinema in the 1950s was a real treat, for there were always two films in the programme, a major one and a second feature, the so-called B-movie. They played continuously, and Ziyad and I never minded going in after the film had started because we knew we could stay on and watch it again. Most often, we went with Siham when the film censor permitted. The British Board of Film Censors of the time was much more stringent than it is today. Ziyad and I could see all "U" films on our own, but had to be accompanied by an adult to watch "A" films. But "X" films, which were reserved for people over eighteen, were out of bounds for us, and it became our ambition to look older than we were so that we could attend.

Siham did not much like taking us with her to the pictures because we talked and ate our way through the film as everyone would have done in Jerusalem. Roasted melon seeds were the favourite cinema nibble there. These are difficult for amateurs to crack, since there is an art, which all Arab children perfect by the age of five, to removing the shells in the mouth and extracting the seed inside. Everyone would be eating these during a cinema performance, and by the end the place would be littered with melon seed shells. Going against her better instincts, Siham arranged to take me and Ziyad to a film at our local cinema. They were showing an English comedy film called *The Lavender Hill Mob* (later to be lauded as a classic of the English cinema) at the Gaumont Cinema in Golders Green Road, opposite my convent school.

It was early evening and our mother had insisted we had supper before we went. She had made a delicious meat and potato dish in which she used large amounts of fresh garlic. Having eaten heartily and without a thought for the consequences we walked to the cinema to meet Siham. We joined her in the queue, talking and laughing and asking questions. But she shut us up angrily. "What on earth have you been eating?" she demanded, "Your breath stinks!" The people in the queue in front of us looked round, but we were speaking in Arabic. For the English, garlic was only mentioned in unflattering reference to the eating habits of foreigners like the Italians and the French.

"I've never been so embarrassed," said Siham afterwards to our mother. "Everyone in our row kept moving away and sitting somewhere else, and all because of them." "Well really," our mother said, "what a fuss over a bit of garlic."

Diversions like the cinema could not disguise the gloomy state of the country in the early 1950s. The effects of the war were still to be seen everywhere, in bomb sites and derelict places. It was in such a wasteland, the site of an old lead factory in Waterloo just south of the river Thames, that in 1951 the Festival of Britain took place. This great event, of which we understood little, celebrated British achievements and set out a vision of Britain's rosy future in a spectacular attempt to raise the country's morale after the war. The most memorable of its monuments was the Festival Hall where we went to hear concerts in the late 1950s and which of course still stands today. But at the time, no one in my family was interested in joining the huge crowds of English people who went to see the festival, for we did not feel in any way British nor did we identify with the future of a country which was not ours.

Neither of our parents wanted to integrate us into British society, even if they had been able to. Our father regarded our stay in England principally as a means of acquiring a good education. There was a widely held view in Palestine, to which he also subscribed, that the best education was to be had abroad, especially in Britain. This was a natural consequence of the fact that there were no institutions of higher learning in Palestine. The nearest universities in the region were in Istanbul or Cairo and after 1940 in Beirut. Even then, these were regarded as second-class choices after the universities of Europe, especially Oxford and Cambridge. When in the 1930s a few of the wealthier families in Palestine sent their sons to such places they were envied by the rest.

So now we found ourselves, *faute de mieux*, with the opportunity to have that same English education so prized by Palestinians, and our father's sole concern was that we would all go to university and gain degrees. Beyond that, he thought very little about the other aspects of life in England and what we would make of them. With our mother at home maintaining a traditional life-style, he assumed that we would naturally retain our identity as Arabs and Muslims without other help. As for the environment outside, if he thought about it at all he saw this as no more than a backdrop to the crucial work we must be doing on our education. He had little awareness of the psychological damage this attitude might have on vulnerable youngsters like us, striving to establish a new identity. Perhaps he clung to his mechanical view of us as a way of coping with a situation full of internal contradictions.

When in Jerusalem, a short spell working at the BBC in London, while we stayed at home with our mother, had been the furthest reaches of his ambitions outside Palestine. But now here he was, stranded with a family of growing children in an alien environment and no previous experience to draw on and no help from our mother. If anything, she was a hindrance. Rejecting every aspect of life in England, she was in no position to help us integrate either. If anything, she would try and pull us back every time she thought we were straying from our customs or our culture.

As a result, we were left to find our own accommodation to the schism in our lives between our Palestinian Arab origins, so zealously maintained by our mother, and the new society we had joined; between our identity as Arabs and Muslims and that of the European, Christian country around us; and above all, between the awareness of our bruised and dislocated history and the British indifference and hostility towards it. I resented my parents deeply for throwing us so unthinkingly into this cultural and political morass. In the years that followed, we were forced to feel our way forward uncertainly, trying to make sense of these contradictions and resolving them in our own different ways.

Seven

During those first years in England, the memory of Palestine grew ever more distant. No one talked about the past at home beyond the occasions when the news on the radio would provoke the odd exclamation or comment from one or other of our parents. Politics continued to form the subject of major concern to our father and his friends whenever they visited, and we might then pick up stray pieces of information about Israel and the Arab world from their discussions. However, there was nothing personal in any of this, no reference to our life in Jerusalem, no expression of sorrow over what happened except in our mother's deep sighs when someone reminded her of people or events there.

No one spoke about the circumstances which had prompted our departure from our home, or explained the history and politics of it. This was much at variance with what was happening in the refugee camps on the borders of Israel. There, Palestinian parents told their children every detail of the villages and towns they had come from, showed them the keys to the houses they had had to abandon, recounted stories of their past lives, such that in years to come these children knew Palestine as if they themselves had lived there. Not so in our case. What private memories, reminiscences, griefs our parents entertained, we never knew. Palestine had become a faded dream, a place of the buried past scarcely ever brought to mind.

This played directly into my own loss of memory. In some subtle, insensible way, I found that I had wiped out all remembrance of Jerusalem. If I ever thought about it, it was to realise with some shock that I could no longer recall the way our house had looked, or Rex, or even the features of Fatima's face. Those essential memories of my childhood had simply melted away, leaving only shadows and elusive fragments of feeling. Even our early time in Damascus became blurred, as if by extension of the amnesia that shrouded my earlier life in Palestine, and I lost the memory of that too. This was not a conscious process; I simply put away the past as if it had never been. But I wonder if my parents were trying to obliterate Palestine from all our memories, partly because they could not face recalling the pain and trauma of what had happened, but also for another, more hidden, reason. Perhaps it was a sense of shame for having deserted the homeland, for having left it defenceless to the hordes.

In any case, no one in England seemed to remember Palestine either. It is remarkable how quickly the word went out of general use. By 1953, when people asked me where I came from and I answered, "Palestine", they would respond with, "did you say Pakistan?" The country whose turbulent history had so frustrated Britain's government but five years before, simply vanished from people's consciousness. Instead, the talk was of Israel, "the new young plucky state which was making such rapid advances". Events there marched on apace; new facts were being established in our old country, despite all our mother's efforts to make time stand still in the Palestine of her young womanhood.

Two family occasions in Golders Green in the early 1950s

Zuhair wrote to tell us that all the land of Tulkarm up to the
railway line was now occupied by the Israelis. You could see the
Israelis working the newly acquired land with tractors and modern
machines, he said, an odd sight for the people of Tulkarm, who tilled
the soil with donkeys and mules. From time to time, he heard of
villagers who tried to go across the dividing line with Israel to visit
their houses or fetch some of their belongings; Aziza had been
tempted too, just to go over and pick a piece of fruit from what had
been her father's orchard. But this practice soon stopped when the
Israelis opened fire on the intruders and the rumour went about that
one or two people had been killed, though not anyone we knew.
Tulkarm was now under Jordanian rule and everyone had been given
Jordanian citizenship, but this did nothing to abate people's anger
against King Abdullah. They hated him for what he had done to
Palestine and held him responsible for a large part of its tragedy. It
was rumoured that he was still secretly negotiating with the Israelis
and preparing to concede more to them of what had remained of
Palestine.[1]

Some 200,000 Palestinians had been left in Israel, but no one heard
much about them. They seemed to have disappeared, swallowed up
in the waves of Jewish immigration that were flooding into the
country. The only Palestinians we recognised were those like us,
who lived outside the old borders. It was only when our friend, Adib
Khoury, married a woman from Haifa and brought her back to
England that we even realised there were such people as "Israeli
Palestinians". Adib had come to England in 1946 to study and so had

[1] The king was to pay dearly for his actions. In July 1951, he was shot dead as he went with his grandson,
the late King Hussein, to perform the Friday prayer at the Aqsa Mosque in Jerusalem. His assassin was a
member of the Jihad al-Muqaddas, although it was found subsequently that he had not acted alone, but
was part of a complex linked to the Husseini family. Nevertheless, Arab public opinion has regarded the
assassination as a paradigm for the fate that awaits all traitors to the Arab cause.

missed seeing the drama of Palestine. He supplemented his income, as many Arabs did at the time, by working for the BBC Arabic Service on an occasional basis, which is how he and my father met. In no time, he became a good friend, visited us frequently and was particularly attached to my mother and her cooking. He used to make gentle fun of me because of my habit of translating literally from English into Arabic.

By this time, I was exposed to considerably more English, since I spent most of my waking hours outside the house. In those days, there was no private Arabic schooling and my formal education in my mother tongue ended in Damascus at the age of nine. I continued, however, to converse in vernacular Arabic, since that was forced on us at home on account of our mother's total ignorance of English. But my literary Arabic was poor. In years to come, this would disparage me in the eyes of fellow Arabs visiting England who simply could not understand how I spoke Arabic fluently but could scarcely read or write it. And for years, this disability, which I put down to personal incompetence, used to fill me with shame.

One day Adib announced that his relatives in Haifa had arranged to introduce him to a prospective bride. The Arab world was technically in a state of war with Israel, which meant that people with Arab passports could not go there. Despite this inconvenience, Adib's family – and Adib himself – still expected him to marry a girl from his old home town, even though life had drastically changed for Palestinians, who had now become a small minority.

Many prospective couples could only meet on so-called neutral territory and Cyprus was a favourite place for such encounters. Adib did not need to do this, for he had acquired a British passport by then and could go directly to Haifa to see his intended bride. But he kept the news hidden from all but a handful of close friends. For the prevailing view amongst Palestinians at the time was that anyone who could ignore our history of British betrayal and bring himself to acquire British nationality was almost a party to that betrayal. It was for this reason that most Palestinians who had sought refuge in England, amongst them my mother and my sister, declined to apply for British citizenship.

For the same reason, when my father eventually did change his mind, he concealed the fact of his British naturalisation for years and urged me and Ziyad to do the same. This, of course, was another of the contradictions with which Palestinians lived. On the one hand, they hated what Britain had done to their country, but on the other, they clung to the security and advantages it provided them in exile.

But by far the worst treachery any Palestinian could commit was to contemplate going to Israel. This struck a chord of deep revulsion, for visiting Israel implied a recognition of Palestine's occupation and an acquiescence in what was seen as its rape and plunder. For decades after Israel's creation, scarcely any Palestinian or Arab who could legally have done so ever went there. It was a no man's land which for most ordinary Arabs existed only as a name on a western map (no Arab maps of the Middle East bore any reference to Israel), and, inevitably and sadly, the minority of Palestinians still left in Israel only existed in name as well.

On Adib's return, he brought his new bride to our house. I remember how we gazed at her with avid curiosity, for she presented us with a fascinating enigma. She was fair-haired and hazel-eyed and did not look particularly like an Arab. She wore a green knitted suit and low-heeled shoes – "Israeli clothes", I thought to myself with a shudder. But she spoke Arabic as we did and seemed normal. We knew that she was different from us, however, because she lived "there" with the Israelis, and I remember watching her for signs which might betray this otherness. But she never did, and when my father asked her what life was like for them in Israel, she only answered, "Well, you know how it is. They think it's all theirs now. They're in charge and they make sure we know it."

My primary preoccupation was in any case nothing to do with Palestine or the past. Unnoticed by my parents who were busy being Arab and while my mother carefully guarded our home from outside influences, I was relentlessly being absorbed into the English way of life. In 1952, Ziyad and I were naturalised as British subjects and became "citizens of the United Kingdom and Colonies". This meant that our father would no longer have to register us every year at the Aliens' Registration Office, a strange place in Lambs Conduit Street near Holborn where a register of all non-British persons resident in the country was kept. We went there with our father once or twice but it was a depressing experience, with dreary looking officials and a long queue of anxious people talking in different languages. My father was granted citizenship at the same time and his new British passport described him as Mr Hasan Effendi Karmi. The appellation "Effendi" arose from the Ottoman-style registration of his name on his (now defunct) Palestinian passport, where Effendi was the Turkish equivalent of Mr. He tried to persuade the British passport official to drop the Effendi, saying that one Mr in his name was quite enough, but to no avail. The man doggedly insisted that his name would have to be exactly as written in the Palestinian passport. And so it remained until it was renewed some years later.

Our mother, who did not wish to apply for British nationality, was nevertheless included on our father's passport as a dependent. Siham, being over eighteen, was not eligible for naturalisation and would have to apply for citizenship on her own account after five years of residency in England. She was not put out by this and said she would rather remain an Arab, making do with her British resident's permit. When, some years later, she left England, she was reminded by the officer at passport control that she would need to renew her permit while abroad if it was to remain valid. "No, thank you," she told him firmly. "Do you think that is wise?" asked the curious officer. "I don't care!" she responded gaily. "I'm leaving for good. I'm not English and never will be!"

But my feelings were quite different. By the age of twelve, I had become an avid reader of English literature. Our local library was to me a place of hidden treasures and delights. I could not stop marvelling at an institution which offered me free all the books of the world (or so it seemed). One could borrow four books at a time with the same ticket, and I sometimes took my sister's ticket with me so as to borrow more.

They're better than people, I used to think, they never talk back at you and never let you down. Our library was on Golders Green Road, next to Woolworth's store, where it still stands today. It had heavy glass and brown wooden entrance doors which swung back against your body if you were not careful to get out of the way in time. It was dark and sombre inside, but its atmosphere was old-fashioned and cosy. The librarians at the front desk all looked the same to me, men or women. They were old, wore glasses, had grey hair and spoke in low, hushed voices – out of respect for the books, I imagined. On the right was the children's section and the adult section was on the left. At first, I used to go to the children's library, which was light and colourful and was furnished for small people, with low round tables and small stools. All the shelves were likewise built low so as to be accessible. I quickly got through the children's books of E. Nesbit and Enid Blyton and graduated to the adult section.

Because I had no one to guide me through them, my father being more interested in Arabic than in English literature, I was much influenced by the books' external appearance, the colour of their covers and the size of print on the pages. I also went by the alphabet, so that I read nice-looking books under the A, then went to B and so on through the letters. In this way, I systematically worked my way through the English classics and tried some French classics as well. The books I read opened a world of the imagination for me which was all bound up with England and Englishness. I began to see London as it might have been in Dickens's time, exemplified in those pictures on Christmas cards which depict snow-covered carriages, men in frock-coats and top hats and snowy shop windows. Absurdly, I started to imagine myself as one of these nineteenth-century people, taking inspiration from the spate of gothic films set in a fog-bound Victorian London which were then popular.

My integration into European culture was rapidly taking place at other artistic levels as well. When I turned twelve, I began to take piano lessons. These had first started at the convent where I was given a weekly lesson by one of the nuns. Pleasant though this was, I learned little, since I had no chance to practise and the nuns recommended that I go to a private music teacher who lived off Bell Lane in Hendon. I was never good at the piano and felt nervous performing in front of this teacher, who was a diminutive and eccentric French-woman called Mademoiselle Jeanette Poussin.

She seemed to me very old; her face was criss-crossed by an array of lines and furrows and her lower lids hung down loosely away from her eyes like a basset hound. I had no idea what had brought her to England; she lived alone and I think made her living by giving piano lessons to people like me. Her front room where we met was furnished in a style which anticipated the much later fashion in England for the Indian look. Its one piece of furniture was a huge grand piano; the rest was given over to colourful mats, cotton hangings and cushions. She herself was often draped in strings of bead and amber necklaces, jangling silver bracelets at her wrists. She said the great French pia-nist, Alfred Cortot, at the Paris Conservatoire, had trained her. I have no idea what truth there was in this, but her stories of the time she had had there fired my imagination. I would beg her to play Chopin as

Cortot was supposed to have taught her. And frequently when she did this, sitting propped up on her stool before the grand piano, I would see tears gather in the pockets of her lower lids and spill down her lined cheeks, and I could only guess at what ineffable sadness or nostalgic memory gripped her. Although Cortot's training never filtered down from her to me, I owe much of my subsequent musical interest to her and to that strange acquaintance.

Siham and I started to visit art galleries when I was eleven. We went to the National Gallery and the National Portrait Gallery, to the Wallace Collection and to Kenwood House. The latter is an eighteenth-century mansion set in the midst of a beautiful country park in Hampstead and holds a small collection of paintings mainly by English artists. Because Kenwood House was near to where we lived, I often went there on my own or with Leslie. The Gainsborough and Reynolds paintings I saw there presented views of English eighteenth- and nineteenth-century life which, coupled with my concurrent reading of the English classics, imparted a sense of solid familiarity. I would gaze at ruddy-faced, bewigged men in breeches and women in straw hats and high-waisted dresses surrounded by fields and woodlands against a horizon of turquoise skies and fluffy clouds as if they had been a natural part of my own heritage.

Siham remained relatively unaffected by these westernising influences. Her appreciation of European art and music did not touch her inner core, which remained solidly Arab and Islamic. But my case was different. In my overt exposure to these cultural experiences and in a myriad other insensible ways, my inner sense of myself was irrevocably affected. At about this time, I began to write my own stories – private, hand-written compositions in a large, ruled school notebook. These were modelled on the classic books which I had read and from which I devised implausible, second-hand plots. They were all rooted in England and the English way of life which seemed to me far closer and more familiar than anything Arab or Islamic. The latter did not have the same reality for me and I mentally confined it to my mother's domain to which I commuted from England, as it were, in a form of daily ritual. Outwardly, I was the same Arab-looking, Arabic-speaking girl my family knew, but inwardly I grew ever closer to the society around me, identifying with its history and its norms in so far as I could understand them from the vantage point of an Arab household in Golders Green.

Our parents sensed nothing of this and blithely persisted with their assumptions, which held all of us suspended in their world, as if our world were only temporary and could be left behind at any moment. They heard me play Mozart and Beethoven on the piano (in fact helped to buy me a piano of my own, which sat for many years in our dining room), saw me go with Siham to concerts and art galleries, knew that we read nothing but English books, and yet none of this deflected them from the view that we were the same, unchanging Arab unit which had lived in Palestine. It was as if we had never left and, in that sense, it would have been absurd for them to think that we needed formal education in what was our natural environment. I suppose it was for this reason that neither of them told us much about our culture, customs or religion.

At first, my mother used to make me read the Quran out loud to her, but our formal education in Arabic, in the Muslim religion, in Islamic history, even in Arab social behaviour ceased from the moment we left Damascus. I knew how to perform the daily prayers, but I was ignorant of Islam's other dimensions. Of us three, Siham was least affected, since she was already mature when we reached London, but Ziyad and I fared differently. To this day and despite my attempts at self-education, I am still ignorant of customs, sayings and social attitudes which would be considered basic to Palestinian culture.

It would have been worse had not our mother kept us in an

inflexibly Arab environment at home. To her and to our father, our Arab culture was so strong, so natural and so right that no amount of Beethoven or Rubens or Thackeray could dislodge it. Our father held this attitude despite his extensive explorations of western philosophy, literature and religion; while this induced in him a tolerance towards my own similar intellectual inclinations, it went no more towards integrating him into western culture than our mother. In essence, his pursuit of western civilisation was a form of mental pastime, a complex scholarly façade beneath which he nevertheless maintained a total emotional and cultural separateness. Though he understood western cultural paradigms, for him, as for many Muslims, they could never be the norm. His adherence to Islamic philosophy, Arabic literature and, above all, the Arabic language ultimately took precedence, and the depth of this allegiance unconsciously communicated itself to us. Defective as my knowledge of these matters was, and in spite of my westernisation, I thrilled uncomprehendingly to the language of the Quran, resonated to the recitation of an Arabic sonnet, and felt an inarticulate reverence for classical Arabic.

My parents' cultural isolation should not be understood simply within the context of migration. Many migrant groups are known to maintain their previous cultures and lifestyles in their countries of adoption, often insisting that their children do the same. But this is by way of adjusting gradually to the new society and creating a bridge between the past they had chosen to leave behind and the present they had opted for. None of this held true for us. My parents did not choose to leave Palestine and they never willingly acquiesced in its loss. They did not see England as a place of the future, but only as a staging post on a route to where they could never go. And it could not have been otherwise, for abandoning that view was tantamount to accepting the irrevocable loss of Palestine.

And so, unlike the case of the conventional migrants who try to build bridges to the future, the only bridges my parents built were ones which connected them to the past – to Palestine and to the Arab world. My father's finest achievements, the dozen English-Arabic dictionaries he was to write and the reputation he earned as a foremost savant of the Arabic language, were in fact the bridges he built to return. And the large Arab social circle which my mother managed to gather around her was a bridge of the same kind.

Within our first two or three years in London, our mother had made our home into a communications centre, not just for Palestinians, but also for Arabs of every description. And this helped to lift her depression. Throughout the 1950s, her circle of friends widened as the number of Arabs in England, especially Palestinians, steadily grew. She went out or had visitors nearly every day. Although she spoke no English, she had mastered the London bus system and could recognise the roads and landmarks which led to the places she was seeking without the need to read road signs or ask for help. As is customary in many parts of the Arab world, where street names and house numbers are seldom employed, formal addresses meant nothing to her; she identified the houses of her friends by the colour of their front doors, the shape of their windows and other such features. After a while, though, she learned the names of most major areas in London and, much to our amusement, mispronounced them all – Hendo Wail (Hendon Way), Totteham Cot Ro (Tottenham Court Road), Rishmon (Richmond), Hammisted (Hampstead) – but despite our mirth and our scoffing her pronunciation never improved.

On days when she did not go out she busied herself on the telephone. Because distances were so much greater in London than she was used to she could not visit people on impulse as easily as she had done in Jerusalem, and so she compensated for this by making visits on the telephone instead. At times, her socialising became frenetic, but these bursts of activity were interspersed with episodes of the old gloom which still haunted her. It showed itself in the way she dressed. My mother was a good-looking woman with soft brown eyes and fine aquiline features who had taken considerable interest in her appearance in Palestine. She now hardly bothered and might go out wearing a dress with an uneven hemline or a clashing colour scheme. Siham was acutely embarrassed by this and would berate her for it. "Oh for goodness' sake, leave me alone," my mother would retort. "What does it matter here? No one knows me and no one cares."

Arab society was characterised by a very wide social network, where everybody knew everyone else, and fear of what people would say. To be the object of gossip was deeply shaming and much care was taken to avoid this by ensuring proper dress and behaviour "in front of people". My mother recognised no such strictures in London, where she felt anonymous. Of course, if she were due to see "real people", that is other Arabs, she was more likely to dress properly. But even then, she often did not bother, since she knew that many of them, especially fellow Palestinian exiles, were as isolated from the Arab world as she was, and however much they might gossip the word could not spread very far. When she went out shopping for the household she had a hunched way of walking, her head bowed and her face drawn, as if she bore a huge burden of care on her shoulders. If she was carrying a heavy shopping basket, she would frequently stop to rest and sigh deeply. School friends who saw her walking along the road in this way would ask solicitously if she were ill, and I would reply, "No, she's like that. There's nothing wrong, that's just how she is." Now, when it is too late, I look back with aching compassion for her. But at the time, I could only feel a slight guilt whenever I saw her like that, as if in some obscure way I were responsible for her unhappiness.

As she still shunned housework, Siham and I did most of it. We would take it in turns to dust, make the beds and clean the floor and sometimes, if she were out late with our father, we would cook as well. Ziyad, being a boy, escaped much of this, but he was roped in to help lay the table and dry the dishes from time to time. Siham and I also did the weekly staple shopping for the family, usually on Saturday mornings. We would take our ration books (rationing did not end until 1953) and go from shop to shop until we had bought everything we needed. At the same time, Siham would take the opportunity of looking at the clothes and shoes in the shop-windows. She sewed most of her own clothes and also mine, and she would look longingly at the flared skirts and the wide elastic belts and bell-shaped party dresses. I could not understand her fascination with clothes at that stage in my life. The whole thing bored me and I grumbled when I had to stand around waiting while she gasped and exclaimed over some blouse or scarf.

Our parents' lives were very different to ours. It is true that we had to join in when visitors came, mainly to help serve food or coffee, or occasionally go out as a family on return visits, but this was more of a duty than any real communal activity. Our father was fully occupied with his job, where he was now chief language supervisor. His old interest in books had revived in London and he spent much of his leisure time buying what he considered to be bargains from second-hand bookshops. This soon became an obsession, such that he scarcely ever came home without having one or two new books tucked under his arm. As the house began to fill up with these books, he had shelves put up in every room, including the kitchen, much to our mother's annoyance. She complained that her kitchen was being invaded, and he grumbled that the steam from her cooking pots was damaging his books. "Well, take the wretched things away then!" she would scream and sometimes add, "I've a good mind to throw them all out into the street!" At that point, he would take himself off to his tiny study upstairs and shut the door.

Neither of my parents seemed to take much interest in our lives, beyond our mother's commitment to cooking the daily meal and our father's concern about our achieving good marks at school. If our results were poor at the end of term he did not hesitate to show his displeasure and disappointment; even so, and like most traditional Arab fathers, he rarely helped us with our homework and expected us to be spontaneously bright and diligent. We accepted meekly the fact that virtually our sole aim in life was to be academically proficient. He was however responsible for the household purse; we went to him whenever we needed money for items like clothes or, in my case, spectacles frames when I was found to be short-sighted. I vehemently refused to wear cheap National Health Service frames, which were round and ugly. He often grumbled about such requests and gave in with bad grace only after much altercation and pleading. This was due not so much to our straitened financial circumstances – although these were barely adequate – as to his unspoken resentment of our mother.

In Palestine, she had spared him all such involvement, for he had given her most of his salary every month, keeping only a little for himself, and was content to let her deal with all the family expenditure thereafter. She was the one who bought us our clothes, furnished the house and paid the bills. Since coming to England, however, all that had changed. From the moment of our arrival, she made clear that her responsibilities extended only to the internal care of the house, cooking, cleaning and entertaining. Every other transaction would be our father's concern. Her chief excuse was her ignorance of the English language and hence her inability to deal with household bills, banks, the post office, clothes shops and the like. Since she managed never to learn English throughout her stay in England, this continued to be her excuse.

This new division of labour was only one of the ways in which they vented their frustrations on each other; in her case, an unforgiving anger at being forced to live in a foreign country and for which she blamed him, and in his, a mixture of guilt about this and resentment at the way in which she vilified him for it. When in 1950, barely one year after we had left, news of our grandfather's death in Damascus reached us, our mother wept inconsolably for days. She had not been close to her father, in fact had resented her strict upbringing, for which she held him responsible; but she grieved for being in England, so far away from her family at such a time. "He knew it when he said goodbye to us that terrible day," she sobbed. "He knew we would never meet again, he knew," and she eyed our father balefully, an unmistakable look of accusation in her eyes.

In this strained atmosphere, there was little concern for our griefs and our anxieties. We had no family life to speak of and few activities in common. Beyond the excursions of our first arrival in England when our father had taken us to see the sights of London, no further family outings of this kind took place. It was as if the sheer effort of daily survival left our parents no room for anything so relatively minor as organising leisure activities for us. On our major feast days, we went together to attend prayers at the Regent's Park Islamic Centre, which was then the only mosque in London. I found these occasions tedious, since the adults socialised with their friends and we were left trailing behind. There was not much festivity on these feast days either, although our mother still made special sweets, and we had visits from our Arab friends. But it was not the same here as it had been in Jerusalem or Damascus and since we did not celebrate Christmas or Easter either, even though we had done so in Palestine, we ended up with hardly any religious celebrations at all.

Gradually, we learned as a family to go our separate ways, as if we did not belong together. This was a new and depressing experience. For, although our parents had never "got on" in the romantic European sense – they had different temperaments, shared few outside interests and did not spend much time together – their marriage was in no way remarkable in our society. Few people expected to make love-matches and couples had limited romantic aspirations in marriage, no matter what other reality was represented in the sugary Egyptian films of the time. If love and companionship developed in the course of marriage, then that was a bonus. On the other hand, the ill effects of incompatible unions were ameliorated by the clearly differentiated roles assigned to men and women in society, ones which kept each busy in their separate spheres, and, not least, by the support of the numerous relatives who constituted the extended Arab family.

But here in London, bereft of the traditional structures and with few social outlets, our parents found themselves unrelievedly face to face, the fabric of their relationship cruelly put to the test. Totally unprepared for such an eventuality, our parents found themselves suddenly plunged into an alien environment. This was harder for our mother, since our father had many more escape routes. As a man, he had his daily job where he was part of a society outside the home. This was almost entirely composed of fellow Arabs who either worked with him or whom he otherwise met through his position. And though for years he complained that the people he had been forced to associate with were in the main banal and of low intellectual calibre – for him, people were worthwhile only if they met his rigorous definition of intelligence – he did in fact derive much enjoyment from their company. He made many new friends and joined what became a sort of informal Arab social club created by those working at the BBC. A few of these friends started to come regularly to our house and we sometimes met his more interesting contacts; it was in this way that Habib Bourguiba (later president of Tunisia) and Nizar Qabbani, the famous Syrian poet, as well as a number of Arab ambassadors came to visit us in the 1950s.

None of this impressed me. For by then, I had formed the opinion that anything Arab or connected with the Arab world was inferior and of no interest. These ideas were almost wholly derived from my English surroundings. Unwittingly, I had absorbed them together with the English culture which I was so eagerly embracing. I believe that it was for this same reason that I later found myself prejudiced against Indians as they started coming into Britain. Nothing infuriated me more in those days than to be taken for one, as frequently happened, for English people at the time had a tendency to define all dark-skinned foreigners, who were not obviously African, as being Indian. I sensed an unspoken insult in this attributed resemblance, since I could see that the English tended to regard Indians as rather fawning, unattractive and inferior.

Absurdly, I even adopted the pervasive English resentment against immigrants, as if my family and I were part of the indigenous population and these new arrivals were usurpers who had no right to be there. Accordingly, I wanted only to mix with English people, to emulate their society and to behave like them. I even wrote a piece about what I termed "the Arab mind", which was replete with colonialist ideas and phraseology. "The Arab", I wrote, "is naturally generous and hospitable but rash and unthinkingly impetuous." It never occurred to me in all this that I was myself an object of that same disdain the English meted out to my fellow foreigners, or indeed that, as a Palestinian, I owed the loss of my homeland ultimately to them.

The rest of the family did not share these anglophile sentiments, not even my father, who knew England and its culture better than any of us. Remarkably, he never made a single English friend throughout his stay in England or socialised with English people outside the formal requirements of his job. There was one occasion, however, when he invited two English colleagues to our house for dinner. My

mother did not approve, and in response to his plea that she cook
something bland and suitable for an English palate, she produced one
of her most Arab of meals. This was strongly spiced and heavily
flavoured with garlic. The two men, having expressed the view that
they were keen to try new tastes as long as these did not include
garlic, which they said they disliked, then proceeded to dine. They ate
so heartily that, as my mother said afterwards, they nearly ate the
plates with the food. "I told you not to give them any garlic,"
reproved my father. "Well!" she exclaimed. "If this is how they ate
with the garlic, God knows what they would have eaten if I hadn't
used any!"

Her social outlets, in contrast to our father, were limited largely to
the confines of our house. We, the children, provided her with little
alternative relief, as she understood nothing of our schoolwork and
had no dealings with our teachers or with other parents. Cut off from
our lives by language and our growing assimilation and having little
companionship with our father, she drew close to the Arab friends she
had started to make in London. In this, she was enviably successful
and cultivated around her a circle of devoted and loving Palestinians.
This was a motley group, single women, Christian and Muslim
families, rich upper-class people and simple, poor souls whom she
would not normally have befriended, widows and mixed couples. The
latter consisted of Christian Palestinian women long married to
Englishmen whom they had met in a variety of ways; one of them, for
example, had married a man in the Palestine police and had come out
to England before 1948. Most had not seen their families since then,
and for them my mother brought with her a breath of the old Palestine
they knew. They gathered around her lovingly, reviving the rusty
Arabic they had not spoken for years. She became something of a
Palestinian institution for the whole group.

And she herself clung to these friends in return, sometimes desperately, a dependence that grew with age. Perhaps reciprocally she felt them to be her new family, her new Palestine in exile. I often thought unhappily that she favoured the sons and daughters of her friends over us. As a child, I had little grasp of how she felt, or of the intricacies of our parents' situation, and yet, despite my resentments, I had no awareness that there was anything really wrong with our family, or any memory of it having been any different. Arriving in England had meant a total rupture with the past; the same rules did not apply here and I accepted every change as natural and inevitable.

Ziyad found his own diversion through his school friends and we saw little of him at weekends. He began to go to dances on Saturdays, but whether he had started to have girlfriends or not we did not know. It was tacitly understood amongst us that having girlfriends or boyfriends was not acceptable to our parents and that such things, if they happened, were to be kept secret. Siham studied hard preparing herself for university. She was anxiously applying to medical schools all over London. For my part, I read books and wrote stories and ate sweets (I was ecstatic when sweet rationing ended in Britain in 1953).

Although often busy with Siham on Saturdays, I found Sundays the dreariest, most tedious days of the whole week since no shops were open and no one did anything. I have never known anything more dismal, more numbingly boring than an English Sunday in the 1950s. It had a funereal quality, frequently aggravated by the weather, which seemed always to be dark and gloomy. I can still see myself standing at my parents' bedroom window during those dreary, interminable Sunday afternoons, surveying with dismay the red brick rooftops glistening in the steady rain and the wet pavements of the deserted street. Our mother would be sleeping in our dark kitchen, the radio close to her ear, and our father would be reading in his study. Ziyad would normally have gone out with one of his friends. Siham would be studying while I loitered about all alone.

I still had Leslie for my best friend and a few other school friends, but we spent little free time together. Siham had no English friends at all. "They're so cold," she would say. "I try hard to talk and be friendly, but it never leads anywhere." She found companionship instead in the newly formed Arab Students' Union. This consisted of a small number of young Arabs, nearly all men, who came from different parts of the Arab world to study in England. They formed the union in the early 1950s, and Siham became its active and energetic secretary. In this way, she was soon mixing with Arabs of her own age, but never formed a close relationship with any of them. As a result, she was more available to me than would have been the case normally for a girl of her age. And so, in the vacuum of our family life, I clung to her and entrusted her with my every childish secret, as if she had been Fatima reincarnated. My greatest fear was that she would one day leave home and I would remain alone.

࿇

In October 1952, just before I turned thirteen, I was made to move schools. I bitterly resented this, since I had by then settled into the convent with a degree of contentment. The nuns still indulged me and I felt warmly accepted into the convent "family". The England of that time had few dark-skinned foreigners of my type, for the influx of immigrants from the Caribbean and the Indian subcontinent had scarcely begun. Although I knew that I was Arab, I had no feeling of being essentially different from the other girls and identified with them and their aspirations in numerous ways. But my father and my sister, who had assumed responsibility for my education and that of Ziyad, had a view that I would benefit from a relocation to another, more "serious" school. This was to be the Henrietta Barnett grammar school in Hampstead Garden Suburb, a charming, leafy estate of rural-style cottages and village-like squares, quite unlike anywhere else in London.

The suburb had been designed during the early years of the century by the same Henrietta Barnett who had given her name to the school. It was a philanthropic effort to provide an estate where people of all classes, but especially the working class, could live together. No high walls were built to exclude one dwelling from another and houses were grouped together in artistic plots separated only by hedges. Sadly, this egalitarian social plan was never fully implemented. By the time I was going to school there the suburb was already an area of genteel housing whose residents were anything but working class. Today, it is considered one of London's wealthier and more exclusive districts.

I cried when I had to leave La Sagesse and the girls in my class gave me a parting present of six shillings to buy what I wanted. They wrote a farewell note, asking me to visit them at the convent. I bought Alexander Dumas's *The Three Musketeers* with the money, a handsome leather-bound dark blue volume into whose inside cover I carefully pasted their letter. I looked after this book lovingly for many years and determined that I would always maintain my link with the convent. The fact that I did not caused me agonies of guilt at the beginning, as if I had betrayed some sacred trust. I imagined the girls and the nuns day after day all disappointedly waiting for me to appear. Leslie remained my only link there for she stayed on up to GCE (general certificate of education) level. I continued to regard her as my best friend for a long time afterwards. And indeed, some nine months after I had left the convent, it was with her that I chose to share Coronation Day, that important national event, on June 2, 1953.

To watch the great occasion, everyone had to congregate in the homes of those few who had television sets. I went with Leslie to her grandmother's house, where there was a television with a large screen.

Across Britain, the shops were bursting with royal souvenirs and, to my delight, we had the whole week off school. I was not happy at Henrietta Barnett and had begun to see it as a kind of prison. When I walked there and passed normal people, like the milkman or the postman, I would feel like a prisoner let out briefly to gaze longingly at a sane, normal life I could not share in.

I preceded Leslie to her grandmother's house to find three French friends of the family, also Jewish, already there. It was pouring with rain and I remember feeling sorry for the Queen, who I thought would be drenched by the time she reached Westminster Abbey. But the bad weather did not deter the massive crowds who waited to cheer as she arrived in her gilded coach. To see her walk up the aisle of the Abbey, the long train of her dress borne by six maids, was a truly resplendent sight. All I could do then was marvel at the extravagance of the occasion and gaze open-mouthed at the golden canopy beneath which, mysteriously shielded from our eyes, the Archbishop anointed the new Queen; and wonder with everyone else at the way that even her husband, Prince Philip, had to pay her homage like any of her subjects as she sat on her throne, her delicate head now magnificently crowned.

Watching, I realised that I should have felt a foreigner on this most English of occasions, excluded from that special relationship being unfolded before me between a people and their sovereign, neither of whom was mine. But curiously, I did not. To me, the whole ceremony could have been out of the Georgette Heyer historical romances to which I was then addicted, and, as such, it was both magical and familiar.

The Coronation over, I was forced to return to the reality of my new school. It was utterly different to anything I had known before. I found it a grim, unhappy place with a humourless and disciplinarian band of teachers. It had a high academic reputation as a girls' grammar school and prided itself on producing "career girls", destined to become doctors, lawyers or other professionals. There was a marked emphasis on science subjects and on sport, both of which I loathed. I was forced to play hockey there, to my mind the dullest, most pointless game imaginable. Our sports teacher was a stereotype straight out of a 1950s British comedy film. She was hearty, had a large bra-less bosom, and was used to urging the more reluctant athletes amongst us along with a loud, booming voice like a sergeant-major. In revenge, some of these girls got together once and tied a huge white bra to the back fender of her car. Giggling and chortling, we watched her drive away, blissfully ignorant of the bra swaying and fluttering in the breeze.

Our headmistress was a short, stocky woman called Miss Leach. She had a plain, scrubbed-looking face and her short brown hair was neatly held in place with a fine hairnet. When she was angry, her neck flushed a deep red colour. As a result, we soon learned to watch her neck for this tell-tale sign. She was strict, but fair, and I remember that we both feared and respected her. Presiding over the morning assembly was amongst her regular tasks and it was here, at hymn singing, that I was first exposed to the Anglican version of Christianity. While in Palestine, we had come across the occasional Anglican in the shape of the few English people we met there and also amongst a small minority of previously Greek Orthodox Palestinians who had been converted by English missionaries. But we knew nothing about it and my time at the convent had only familiarised me with Roman Catholicism. Henrietta Barnett was a Protestant Anglican school and hymn singing was an essential daily ritual from which I was not exempt. I found some of the tunes pleasant and would hum them at home. "Immortal, invisible, God only wise . . ." I would sing until the others objected and told me to stop making those missionary noises.

Although I had to participate in this daily ritual of Christian worship, the Jewish girls did not. As Henrietta Barnett had a large intake of Jewish pupils at that time, arrangements were made for the Jewish girls to have their own religious assembly in a separate room off the main hall. The class I joined was at least fifty per cent Jewish, many of them the children of German immigrants. This was a wholly new experience, for until then my contact with Jews, apart from Leslie and her family, had been brief and for a defined purpose. I knew of course that we lived in a Jewish part of London. Golders Green first became known as the city's principal Jewish district in the period between the wars when it received thousands of Jews fleeing from persecution in Europe. In addition, from the East End of London, there was a small influx of Jews who had made enough money to afford Golders Green prices. The Jewish population was increased during the Second World War by more arrivals from areas of Nazi occupation, and, by the time my father rented our house, Golders Green had a number of synagogues, delicatessens, kosher butchers and Jewish patisseries.

Both our general practitioner and our dentist, who had a practice in the Golders Green Road close to that of Dr Seckbach, were German Jews. There was nothing particularly odd in this, since we were used to consulting German Jewish doctors in Palestine, where we did not regard them as Jews encroaching on our land but rather as proficient Germans. This remained our attitude in England. By the time I went to Henrietta Barnett, Ziyad had acquired more Jewish school friends, but this seemed a natural thing for him to do as there was a preponderance of Jewish boys at his school. We did not see these boys primarily as Jews either; they were just Ziyad's friends and we thought no more about it. In the North London Polytechnic where Siham enrolled in 1954 she also came across Jewish students.

In view of the prevailing anti-Semitism, many of these classmates were discreet about their Jewishness or tried to hide it – a situation quite unthinkable today. Frequently, their families had adopted anglicised names and they described themselves with reference to their national, not their Jewish, identity. One such was a young man called Eric Piers, who became a close friend of Siham. He told her his parents were Polish, but refrained until much later from saying that they were Jewish. Like the rest of us, this did not worry her unduly. She often said that she found Jews warmer and more companionable than English people.

For a Palestinian family to be in this Jewish environment was distinctly odd, yet I do not remember when I was growing up that we ever discussed our situation in these terms. We accepted unquestioningly our father's choice of London address. Our parents did not mix socially with Jewish people as most of our immediate neighbours happened to be Christians and the everyday shops we used were not Jewish either. Thus, we were largely oblivious to Jews. But when I was fourteen, a small incident occurred which highlighted the paradox of our situation.

I came home from school one winter afternoon to find a dismal scene in our kitchen. My mother was sitting in an armchair, her head thrown back and her eyes closed. My father was there as well, sitting uneasily on the edge of his chair and frowning deeply. As I came in and took in this grim scene, I said, "What's the matter? What's happened?" When there was no answer, I said in some desperation, "Has someone died?"

At this, my mother half opened her eyes and said with a touch of Arab drama, "If only she had!" and promptly fell silent again. Now thoroughly alarmed, I turned to my father.

"Please, tell me what's going on."

Still frowning, he sighed heavily. "It's the Dajani daughter" – referring to a Palestinian family who were close friends of my parents – "she's just told her mother that she's engaged to marry an Englishman."

"Is that all?" I cried with relief.

My mother cast me a venomous look. "What a stupid girl!" she muttered and closed her eyes again. "Please," I persisted, looking at my father, "what's wrong with it, why are you so upset?"

"Don't you know", said my father with some irritation, "that it's wrong for a Muslim woman to marry a non-Muslim man? This Dajani girl should have known better. I gather", he was now addressing my mother, "that he's offered to convert."

"Oh?" snorted my mother angrily. "Who's that supposed to fool?" She shook her head sadly. "After all that mother's done for them, to be repaid like this. And she a widow who sacrificed her whole life to bring them up."

No one noticed that I was agape with amazement. "Do you mean", I said to my father "that no Muslim girl, like me say, can ever marry someone who isn't a Muslim? That I can't marry Fuad, for example?" Fuad was a Christian Palestinian friend who worked at the BBC with my father.

"No!" my father shouted in exasperation. "You cannot. You should know these things without having to be told." But I didn't know, since no one had ever bothered to tell me. In those days I scarcely knew a Muslim of my own age from whom I could have learned what my parents never taught me. I found out much later that under Islamic law, marriage between a Muslim woman and a non-Muslim man was unlawful, but not the other way around. While conversion of the man to Islam would satisfy the legal requirement for a valid Muslim marriage, social custom meant that such conversions were dismissed as mere ploys designed in effect to permit an outsider male to have sexual access to a Muslim woman. "Marrying out" in such a way was regarded as a sin not ameliorated by conversion, and the people who contracted such marriages were usually either ostracised or spent the rest of their lives apologising for what they had done. In extreme cases, the woman was disowned, expelled from the family circle and regarded to all intents and purposes as having died.

In addition, the non-Muslim suitor might face direct threats or even physical attack from the men of the woman's family. In the Britain of the twenty-first century, very little of this would be news, but in the 1950s the country had not yet become home to the thousands of Muslim immigrants from the Indian subcontinent who settled later and made Islam a familiar creed.

I remember how on that dark winter's afternoon I went up to my bedroom, leaving my parents downstairs, and sat on my bed, thinking. I had a sense of revulsion and horror. "I am nothing to do with these people," I finally decided. "They're intolerant and primitive and I do not belong with them." I comforted myself with the knowledge that I was part of a higher order of being, liberal, free, English, where such bigotry would not be tolerated.

And there it was left until two or three weeks later, when I had occasion to go to Patricia's house one afternoon. Patricia Cohen was one of my three best friends at school and she and I were very close. She was a Jewish girl, pretty and petite with long blond hair, ivory white skin and china blue eyes. Patricia had joined the school one year after me and because she was shy and waif-like, I felt sorry for her and we soon made friends, telling each other secrets and visiting each other's houses after school. My parents grew fond of her and were especially charmed when she learned a few words of Arabic which she used whenever she saw them. Her family likewise took warmly to me and made me feel at home. Patricia's father was a businessman who lived in Jersey – "for tax reasons", they always said mysteriously – and came to visit the family from time to time. Her mother, a short, dark, homely woman of Romanian origin, maintained the family house in London on her own. She resented her husband deeply for this and, young as I was, I could sense the unhappiness and tension in Patricia's house from the first time I ever went there.

Not that her parents were ever anything but the soul of kindness and affection towards me in those days. Patricia's father was a witty, amusing man who looked and behaved like the stereotypical Jewish comedian. He would hunch his shoulders and move his hands about when he spoke – "Jewish hand signals", I was told – in a way which I found very funny. He always greeted me with a hug and a kiss whenever he saw me and he would usually say something to make me laugh. Patricia's mother was like a mother to me too. I used to eat in their house, stay the night, join them on occasions when the extended family – Patricia's aunts, cousins and their husbands and wives – got together, and became as intimate as if I had been one of them. Amazingly, I think looking back that I was the only "goy", or non-Jew, with whom they associated so closely and, ironically enough, the only Palestinian they ever met.

On that afternoon when I went to see Patricia I had forgotten all about the mixed marriage conversation at my home. As Patricia let me in, she put her fingers to her lips and, almost walking on tiptoe, ushered me into the kitchen where everyone normally sat. But, whereas I was used on such occasions to a warm greeting from her mother followed at once by tea and a large plate of cakes, this time there was no such welcome. I could see that I had intruded onto a tense family scene. I think I was there only because I was "family" too. Patricia's mother was pacing the kitchen floor, wringing her hands and looking more round and plump than usual, while Patricia's elder sister, Claire, sat at the table her eyes cast down as if in shame.

"How could you do it to me? How?" wailed the mother. "Oi, yoi, yoi, what a problem, what a trouble!" I looked at Patricia, mystified, who did not look back. "It's all your father's fault, of course. 'Take them to London', he said, 'they might meet nice Jewish boys there which they're not going to do in Jersey.' And I came, I believed him." She was now tearful. "And for this? We should have stayed in Jersey." She stopped by Claire's chair threateningly. "Look up, look me in the face and tell me what I did wrong? Didn't I give you girls everything, clothes, food, time to see your friends while I slaved here? And me all alone, your father never home, too busy enjoying himself to worry." She suddenly noticed me hovering just inside the room. "Sit down, darling," she said, "I hope you're never going to be a trial to your mother, like her." She jabbed an angry finger at Claire.

Claire spoke for the first time. "It's not a crime, we've only been out a few times," she murmured in a small voice. This invoked an instant redoubling of the mother's rage. "So, this is supposed to make me happy?" she demanded. "First, you go out, then he comes here, then I get used to the idea, then you speak to your father who's not here so he should worry, then you get married! Let me tell you, it's never going to happen." To my surprise, Claire suddenly burst into tears. She was older than Patricia, and had always seemed self-possessed, even hard.

"So you should cry!" said her mother relentlessly. "Just as you made me and your aunt Ruby cry. You better do a little thinking next time you want to go against your mother, your father, your whole family." And with that, her tough manner seemed to collapse and she also started to cry. In the small pause that followed, Patricia signalled to me and we both quietly slipped out of the room. Upstairs, as we sat down on Patricia's bed, I could hardly wait to find out what that scene was about.

"Well you see," she said, sighing, "it's this English boy my sister's been going out with. I knew about it, but Claire never told anyone else. And then my dear mother had to go and find out, because she picked up the phone when they were talking this morning."

"Well, so what?" I said. "Who cares? I mean why should it matter if she goes out with an English boy? And what's this about being English? I thought you were English."

Patricia looked searchingly at me. "We are English, but we're still

Jewish," she explained unhelpfully. "Don't you know about being Jewish? You're not supposed to marry anyone who isn't Jewish as well. Even going out with anyone who isn't Jewish is bad, because you might get hooked on him and get married. That's why my mother's so upset, and as my dad isn't here, I think she's scared he's going to blame her for it."

I stared at her in bafflement, memories of an earlier scene stirring in my mind. "Do you mean to tell me that a Jewish girl like you, say, can't marry a non-Jewish man?"

"Of course not, silly!" she said, "And the other way around. Didn't you know that?" But I didn't, any more than I had known about the Muslim version of the same story.

"And what would happen if Claire went ahead and married her boyfriend just the same?" I asked.

"Well, I'm not sure," said Patricia. "I know it can be pretty nasty. I suppose no one will speak to her or visit her. She won't be one of the family anymore."

"What about if he converts, you know, becomes Jewish? Is it all right then, can they get married?" I asked.

Patricia's brow puckered in thought. "I don't think so," she said uncertainly. "My cousin Ruth's friend married a goy who converted. All I can tell you is that no one likes him and her family doesn't let him visit. She always goes on her own, and I don't think they're very happy."

I fell silent, confused by what I had heard in both houses, hers and mine. The parallels were striking, the reactions disturbingly similar. And yet, Palestinians and Jews were supposed to be formal enemies. To us, they should have been alien, another species, with other customs and other ways and feelings. But apparently, they were not so different, at least in these respects. And my parents accepted without demur my friendship with Patricia and other Jewish girls like her.

They knew that I stayed with her family and they welcomed her into ours, although they themselves would no more have socialised with her parents than flown to the moon – a polite nod if they happened to come across one another in the shops was as far as either side was prepared to go. For my parents, the lines of demarcation were seemingly clear, but for me there was no such clarity.

They probably thought little about it. For, in a sense, they lived parallel lives to those around them; we could have been anywhere in England for all the difference it would have made to the atmosphere of our home. Since our parents did not engage in the life of the community London never acquired more than a utilitarian function for them. It was the place where our mother shopped and where our father bought his books, but little more. Although London meant more to us children, we also tended to see ourselves as inhabitants of a separate sphere. I do not know how this affected Siham and Ziyad, but to me it imparted a disordered sense of reality whereby at times I saw my Arab life at home as being the more real and concrete while at others it was my burgeoning life in London that came first.

This ambiguity was not helped by my experiences at Henrietta Barnett. As with most girls' schools, everybody formed cliques sooner or later. Because of the high Jewish intake, the preponderant cliques in my class were Jewish, leaving the rest of us non-Jews to befriend each other. If any of the Jewish girls joined us, they were the ones judged eccentric, like Patricia, or who otherwise did not fit in with the rest of the clique. One of these was an unprepossessing girl called Rachel Samuelson who wore thick-lensed glasses and was considered the class swot. Aside from her academic success, she distinguished herself chiefly by giving us what she described as illustrated sex lessons during lunch break.

Explaining that this was a part of our biology education, she graphically demonstrated to us with the aid of a fountain pen what sexual intercourse involved. But these sessions never lived up to their promise, for she giggled incessantly throughout and we suspected that she knew little about what really happened during sex. Susan Edelman was another one; she was fat and spotty, also wore glasses and had a huge bosom for her age. We all thought her dead common and when, during our next year at school, she fell pregnant, no one was surprised. Miss Leach, looking flustered and her neck a deep red colour, had to explain class by class what the whole school already knew, that Susan would soon be leaving due to her condition. Our chief interest in this event was to try and pump her for information about how "it" felt. At first, she was willing to give us a few tantalising details, but then, tired of our pestering, she finally snapped, "Oh, go and try it out for yourselves!"

After an anxious struggle to find my place in the class, I made friends with two Anglican girls, Josie and Sylvia, and one Jewish girl called Hilary Sternberg. She was the daughter of German Jews, an only child, and lived in a house at the top of the road above ours. When I started to go home with her after school, her mother at first regarded me with suspicion. But this soon disappeared and I was accepted as Hilary's friend, although never with the warmth I had known in Leslie's or Patricia's homes. Hilary looked rather like her father, short and stocky with wiry dark hair and fleshy, pink lips. He was the violinist in a string quartet, all of whose members were German Jews like him. They met regularly at his house. When they were playing, Hilary and I would stand and listen outside the double doors of the dining room where they sat around the table. They played Mozart and Brahms and Beethoven, and that seemed thrilling to me. When they stopped for a break, Hilary's mother would take them salami and smoked salmon sandwiches with pickled gherkins of which we also had a share.

Arab–Israeli politics did not feature in my relationship with Hilary or her family, or indeed with the other Jewish girls in the class. She visited me at home and her mother and mine nodded to each other politely enough if they happened to meet in the street. "I bet you've been to the Arab house again," Hilary's mother would often tease her. "You stink of garlic!" Other than this, no one on either side questioned our friendship with each other.

Which is not to say that my parents had no feelings at all towards Jews. One day, when my mother was out shopping, she stopped at the greengrocer's on Golders Green Road to buy some fruit. As she fingered the pears on display outside – a habit which used to infuriate the greengrocer who would shout at her from inside, "Don't touch me till I'm yours, love" – she found herself next to a foreign-looking, black-haired couple. To her amazement, they were speaking to each other in Arabic. "Are you Arabs?" she asked eagerly, as she was always looking for someone to talk to. The woman looked uncomfortable. "Iraqis", she answered. My mother suddenly understood. "You're Iraqi Jews, aren't you?" The couple nodded. "And what about you?" they asked. "I'm an Arab from Palestine," my mother answered. They looked even more uncomfortable.

"How could you do it to us?" my mother cried. "How could you throw us out of our homes and send us far away from our country?" When she said this, the couple seemed to get genuinely upset. "We would never have wanted that, believe me," said the man. "But we got there after the damage was done, and we haven't done well either. We should never have left Iraq. They cheated us with all sorts of promises, but we didn't fit in in Israel and we left."[2] "Now we can't

---

[2] From 1949 onwards, the Israeli government worked energetically to promote Jewish immigration to the new state. At that time, the Jews of Iraq numbered 130,000 people and formed a prosperous, successful community – the professional and commercial elite of the country – who made no move to emigrate. Consequently, the Zionists had to mount a vigorous campaign of persuasion and coercion to induce them to leave Iraq for Israel. The minority who did so found themselves undervalued and underprivileged in a European-dominated Israeli society and became disappointed and embittered. Many of those rich enough to do so left Israel for Europe or America.

go back to Iraq," said the woman, "and we're stranded here, like you." They invited my mother to visit them and were eager to find out where we lived. But my mother declined. As she said afterwards, "I know they meant well and I couldn't help feeling sorry for them. But what comfort could we of all people be expected to offer them?"

Despite this incident, she always maintained that she distinguished between "the Jews", that is those whom she held responsible for our plight, and individual Jewish people, for whom she felt no personal animosity any more than she had done in the Palestine of her youth – before the troubles started. I did not know until many years later that the major reason for our apparent tolerance of the Jewish presence in Golders Green was due not so much to this attitude as to something else altogether, one which should have called into question the larger issue of our whole presence in Britain. Although my father and many other Palestinians appreciated full well the Zionist plan for Palestine to which we had fallen victim, in a curious way he did not blame the Jews. He placed the primary responsibility squarely on the shoulders of the British who had betrayed us. "If you let a thief into your house and he robs you," he was fond of saying, "who is to blame, you or the thief? It was the British who were in power in our country. They had a sacred trust not to abandon us. And we believed in them right to the end." But when the time came, they did abandon us to our fate; and it was what he called their heartless, callous betrayal that rankled with my father. "If you ask me why I was not too bothered about the Jews of Golders Green when you were growing up," he told me later, "that was the reason."

As a schoolgirl, I knew little of this and unthinkingly adopted my parents' lack of hostility towards Jews. This stance was not difficult to maintain, for in my school – or so it seemed – we, girls, related to each other in an ordinary way. Judaism was not alien to me; quite the contrary, for Muslims it was a familiar and respected religion and I readily recognised Jewish rituals and holy days. Many of their attitudes to the world around them – family, children, friendships – were more recognisable to us Muslim Arabs than anything we found among the Christian English.

Furthermore, events in the Middle East did not feature in my life at that time. I did not listen to the news or read the newspapers and I took less and less interest in what my father and his friends talked about. I was unaware that Israel was rapidly building its institutions, developing a huge arsenal of arms, gaining international acceptance, and entrenching itself in the region. I did not know that the UN had set up the Palestine Conciliation Commission in 1949 to negotiate (fruitlessly) with Israel a way to compensate the displaced Palestinians for the loss of their possessions. We would have been included in such a deal had it succeeded, but no one mentioned such things at home. My parents never spoke about our material losses in Palestine – our house, our belongings, my grandfather's land – nor that we should ever demand restitution. I think, like many other Palestinians, they feared that if they ever did so and succeeded they would in effect have been bought off, would have sold a patrimony no money could buy.

My chief concern in the meantime was not any of this but how to keep running with the pack at school, terrified I would be left behind. I was oblivious as to whether those who made up the pack were Jewish or not, and I had no reason to suppose they felt any differently towards me. I recall no specific prejudice directed against me at that time from any of them, but that they merely preferred each other's company over the rest of us. Ironically, the instances of prejudice, if I can call it that, to which I was subjected came only from non-Jews. This racism was by no means extreme and could not be compared with the much cruder racial harassment that overtook British society later; but it shocked and hurt me to a degree that betrayed the extent to which I had come to believe myself a part of English society.

In Search of Fatima

The first incident occurred when at the age of fifteen I entered a reading competition at school. I joined eagerly because I loved literature and acting and reading out loud, as my poor sister knew only too well. In the event, there were only two finalists, myself and a girl called Catherine Willett. I had rehearsed my piece for weeks and recited it with all the skill and passion I could muster. But the adjudicator who came to judge the competition gave the prize to my rival. He said afterwards, "In point of fact, the little dark girl read best, but I cannot in all conscience give the first prize for an English recitation to someone non-English."

The second event happened during school lunch. This was quite a ritual at our school. It was served in a separate building, a ten-minute walk from the main school building. Choosing one's companions on this walk was crucially important for one's reputation. The most popular girls, those whom everybody aspired to walk with, were snapped up early on in the break, and if one were late starting out there was a danger of being lumbered with the school bores and other undesirables. I always cornered one of my friends before lunch to secure a walking companion, leaving nothing to chance.

More often than not, the lunch that cost me such efforts was unpalatable and served by a couple of surly, overweight elderly women who took evident pleasure in aggressively slapping rock hard potatoes and watery cabbage onto our plates. It was here that I acquired my abiding distaste for English puddings. These were either so bland and mushy as to resemble wet blotting-paper or so hard and sticky that our jaws were fastened together with each mouthful; the dinner ladies served these with the same malevolence which attended the first course. As there were no puddings in our cuisine at home, nor indeed any other English dish, I had no standard by which to judge what I was eating and decided that English food was to be avoided at all costs.

I was queuing for lunch with Josie one day; we were late and the queue was hardly moving. Two girls ahead of us seemed to be holding everyone up and I decided to push past them. Urging Josie to hurry up, I moved ahead. As I did so, I heard one of the girls mutter something at me. I did not catch it, but noticed that Josie had gone red and was looking embarrassed. When I asked her what was wrong, she said, "It's one of those girls we pushed past. She called you an FF." "What?" I asked mystified. "Don't you know what that is?" said Josie disbelievingly. I shook my head. "Filthy foreigner," she said slowly, "that's what it means." I remember feeling astonished and hurt. Why would anyone want to say such a thing about me? It gave me a sudden sickening feeling that I was somehow different, undesirable, contemptible. I could not reconcile this with my belief in my own assimilation and it preyed on my mind.

The fact was that during those first few years at school I lived in something of a fool's paradise. I resented, as we all did, the school's academic rigour and humourless discipline, but I had an illusion of friendship and harmony between us girls, Jewish or not, which I innocently cherished. I saw myself as one of them, an ordinary schoolgirl in an ordinary school. I knew of course that my family was different, but I did not think it any more foreign than the German Jewish families of my school contemporaries. Nor did I see my origins as an impediment to my personal integration into the society of my peers.

This illusion was soon to be shattered, the first stage in a painful process of realisation and discovery which would continue for the rest of my life.

Eight

By 1956, we had become truly embedded in London. Though our parents continued to live on the margins of English society, they succeeded in accommodating their distinctive way of life to the world around them. Our mother still stubbornly resisted the lure of modern household technology. While my friends' mothers began to acquire vacuum cleaners and washing-machines, our home remained reliant on brooms, floor cloths and handwashing. In fact, whenever my mother saw a washing-machine in someone else's house she would berate the owner severely. "Those things are useless," she would exclaim. "They don't clean. The washing comes out no better than when it went in. I wouldn't have one for anything." By this time also, our English neighbours had moved out and been replaced, to my mother's joy, with a Palestinian family. In fact, only the father was Palestinian, his wife was a Pakistani who spoke broken Arabic, and they had three young children. They had acquired the house through my father, since the man had come to work at the BBC and, finding that he was looking for accommodation, my father led him to the house next door.

In no time, the gap in the garden fence between our houses really came into its own, and there was a constant traffic of Pakistani and Arab dishes and of children and adults going back and forth. Siham had joined the Northern Polytechnic to study chemistry. Her strenuous attempts at entering medical school in London had all failed. She would go to interviews time after time, only to come back despondent. "I wonder where I'm going wrong," she would complain. "Perhaps I'm too honest." This came after an interview at St Thomas's Hospital, one of the most snobbish and prestigious of British medical schools, which my father had worked hard to arrange through his contacts. One of the men around the table who had been watching quietly while the others asked her questions suddenly said, "And what do you plan to do after you qualify?" Siham, thinking it best to be truthful, said, "Oh, I'd like to go back and work in the Arab world, where I may do some good." The man was not impressed. "I see," he said coldly. "So, you come over here, study at our expense, and then give us nothing in return. Is that the idea?" When at other interviews she had tried saying that she would find a job in England, they had commented, "And might you then want to get married and start a family? Rather a waste of an expensive training, don't you think?"

All this made her angry. "I don't believe any of their excuses," she said. "They're prejudiced against me because I'm a foreigner. If I'd been English, they would never have spoken to me like that." We were all deeply sympathetic and felt nothing but indignation. In some strange way and despite our attachment to our Arab roots, we really believed that we should have been treated indistinguishably from the English around us. This was not an aggressive expectation, but stemmed rather from our guilelessness and ignorance of the nature of British society. We mistook the civility, which characterised most public and official dealings in England, for genuine friendliness. What we took to be patient tolerance towards us was little more than phlegmatic indifference, in which, however, the English had no ambiguity about who was "us" and who "them" – a subtlety that escaped us at the time. Had we but known it, the civility which they displayed was a sort of social code and nothing to do with personal feelings; they understood its significance amongst themselves, but we did not. And so we deluded ourselves into believing that we were genuinely entitled to equal treatment with them in all spheres of life.

Though this belief was essentially misguided, it is not difficult to see how we might have been misled. For English society in the 1950s was largely homogeneous and had not yet had to come to terms with a large number of foreigners in its midst. It could therefore afford to ignore people like us and even treat us with kindness. Then there was the famous English sense of "fair play" which denoted a recognition of basic injustice in certain situations. This was what the English apparently meant by the expression that something was "not cricket", a phrase much heard at the time. We neither played nor even understood this game, but we soon realised that being "not cricket" had nothing to do with sport as such but referred to the same sentiment of British fairness. These qualities profoundly endeared England to us, even while we harboured a lingering sense of its betrayal of our cause.

Influenced by this appreciation of British fairness, Siham could not but believe that she would ultimately find acceptance at one or other of London's universities. But it was no use, and eventually she gave up and decided to apply to Ireland, where she had better luck. Trinity College, Dublin, offered her a place at its medical school, but in the event, our father decided it was too far away for her to go alone and she finally abandoned the idea of becoming a doctor altogether. Chemistry was of secondary interest only, but at least it was a scientific subject which accorded with her natural aptitude. The Northern Polytechnic was not a university in itself, but was considered a part of the University of London for the study of subjects like hers. I think that not attending a proper university disappointed her and I often wondered at the stoicism with which she pursued her studies.

Our gloomy house was no better decorated than when we had moved in; in fact it was rather worse because of the paraffin stoves our mother chose. She had long abandoned the coal fires of our early life in London for these heaters, tall, grey cylindrical objects, called, appropriately enough, "Aladdin". They were portable and could be carried by their curly wire handles which looked too thin to support their weight. A glass window in the base of their metal body displayed the flame when the stove was on and heat came out through openings in the circular top. Filling them with paraffin was a messy, smelly business, and not entirely danger-free. Father once slipped on a pool of the oily paraffin and fractured his right wrist.

Mother always overfilled the stoves and, though warned never to move them when alight, she was regularly to be seen staggering with one from one part of the house to the other. Each time the stove was disturbed it would belch forth black fumes to add to the damp and steamy atmosphere. To make matters worse, she took to toasting our bread on its top. God knows what amounts of toxic paraffin residues we must have ingested.

Eventually, her enthusiasm for this form of heating waned when the long-feared combustion finally happened. She was drying the washing around the stove one evening, as was her habit, when a pair of our father's pyjama trousers caught fire. The ensuing flame scorched her face, singeing her hair and eyebrows. I remember her coming through from the dining room where the accident occurred, her face black and her eyes starting from her head. "Don't tell your father, whatever happens," she begged, as if he could fail to notice her charred appearance. Thereafter, she was more careful with the heaters. But even so, central heating had to wait until the 1980s.

Though our home was dreary and old-fashioned, it never put off

our mother's ever-growing Arab circle from visiting. She now had
two groups of friends, the "regulars" and the "occasionals". The
latter were people who had come on short visits to England, or who
lived outside London and who did not stay for long, while the former
consisted of families and individuals who had ended up like us making
their homes in London. They were a motley group – "beggars can't
be choosers," as my mother used to say – and they formed a loyal
band around her. It was in fact one of these regulars who came to the
rescue the time our house was burgled. House robberies were
uncommon at the time and the general crime rate was low. This was
the era of the friendly bobby-on-the-beat, the police constable of
"Dixon of Dock Green" in his distinctive tall helmet who walked
along the streets looking safe and reassuring. Along with most people,
we viewed the police as being on our side and we had no hesitation in
approaching them for help of all sorts.

The majority of ordinary citizens in the Arab world did not normally expect to receive courtesy or respect from the police or any
other officials they had to deal with – not unless they were personally
acquainted or family-related, in which case they might hope to have
their business conducted pleasantly and speedily. The idea that official
dealings could be carried out just as satisfactorily without a prior
personal link between the parties was, from an Arab perspective,
unfamiliar and improbable. It took some time for many Arabs who
came to London to accept this state of affairs with confidence.

In a modest area like Golders Green, people did not fear burglary
and no one bothered to fit extra locks on their front doors or burglar
alarms; they might well leave the door on the latch while they went to
chat to a neighbour or run after the milkman. Our burglary happened
one Wednesday afternoon while we were all out. My mother was
returning home with Mrs Tibi, a friend whose family came from
Tulkarm and one of the "regulars", after a shopping trip. As they

drew up to our front door they saw that the glass window next to it was broken and a piece of newspaper had been stuck over the gap. "It's Ziyad!" exclaimed my mother angrily. "I bet you he's gone out without his key and broken the window to let himself in. And look, he hasn't even bothered to sweep up the glass on the floor." But as they entered it was obvious that something was badly wrong. A strange man suddenly appeared at the top of the stairs and, seeing them standing there, cursed loudly and came hurtling down. He wore a hat and was carrying two suitcases, one in each hand, which smashed into Mrs Tibi as he rushed past and out of the open door into the street.

"Quick," my mother screamed, "after him. Thief! Thief!" she shouted out in Arabic as they pursued the man down the road. A few doors opened as people peered out curiously at this spectacle and faces appeared at windows, but no one came to help. "Please", my mother shouted in the little English that she knew. "Please, look. Bad! Bad!" She had now caught up with Mrs Tibi and they both tried to pull at the man's clothes. He was well past middle age and rather weedy but could still run fast. As he rounded the corner, a small dog suddenly darted out from one of the houses directly in front of him, tripping him up and making him drop the suitcases. The dog's owner, a middle-aged Englishwoman in an apron, ran out after the dog and, seeing Mrs Tibi trying to stop the thief, joined in. Both women grabbed him while my mother started to drag the suitcases away. It was only at this point that a group of workmen, repairing a manhole in the road, stopped gazing idly at the proceedings and came forward to aid the women. They surrounded the thief who now shook himself free of Mrs Tibi's clutches and made as if to kick the dog.

"You don't want to take any notice of them," he said, appealing to the workmen and pointing at Mrs Tibi and my mother. "Look at them. Bleeding foreigners. Crazy, foreign women, you don't want to believe anything they say."

"Tell that to the police, mate," responded one of the men. The dog's owner had by now gone into her house and telephoned our local station. When the police arrived, they arrested the thief and then came to our house to take a statement. When they asked my mother about her age, she unblushingly replied, "Thirty-two". At the time, and despite the obscurity surrounding her exact birth date, she could not have been a day under forty. On hearing this later, Siham, who was twenty-four, laughed and said, "So, I suppose you were eight when you had me!" My mother ignored her.

The next day, our local newspaper reported the story of the burglary. Although Mrs Tibi featured in it, it was the English neighbour – "plucky Ada, the thief catcher of Golders Green" – who had pride of place. Our mother was scarcely mentioned at all, an omission that took her aback. A few of our friends put it down to the English prejudice against foreigners, but we were not so sure. However, not long afterwards, the Arabic press printed an account of it in the Arab world more favourable to our mother, describing her as the paragon of Arabs abroad, fearless and bold. And the matter soon subsided. A few weeks later, she went to attend the magistrate's court hearing of the case because Mrs Tibi was required to testify. Mrs Tibi was asked to swear on the bible, which shocked our mother. "Why didn't you tell them to give you a Quran? Didn't they have one?" she asked her later. "I think they did, but I felt too embarrassed to ask," said Mrs Tibi shamefacedly.

I saw Mrs Tibi as a heroine of this incident, especially as she was seven months pregnant at the time. With the exception of Mrs Tibi and a few others, most of my parent's friends held no interest for me. Sometimes, as happened with the Taji family, wealthy citrus farmers from Jaffa who, like everyone else, had fallen on hard times after 1948, there were children of my own age to whom I could relate. Of special interest for me was Ali Uthman and his wife. Ali's family originated from a small village outside Tulkarm. He had married an Iraqi Jewish woman in Jerusalem and come to England at about the same time as my father. Though she was ostracised by her family for having married an Arab, Ali's family and friends had accepted her. By the time that we met them in London, Israel had been established and a great deal of hostility to the new state had developed amongst Palestinians. But, for us, the distinction between the Jews of Israel and Jews elsewhere remained more or less clear and hence it was that my parents received her and her husband warmly in our house. "She's got nothing to do with it," said my father. "Israel's done no more for her than it has for us."

Ali and his wife visited us often. The main pleasure which such social visits entailed for me lay in the tasty leftovers which we had to finish. My mother excelled herself at such times, making delicious pastries and special cooked dishes, which she rarely made for us. But there was another effect of the visits which soon manifested itself in the shape of prospective suitors for my sister. By Arab reckoning, at the age of twenty-four, Siham was fast becoming old and ineligible. When suitors presented themselves they did so according to tradition and custom, in so far as that could happen in the alien environment where we all now lived.

Having no mother or female relative to speak on their behalf, as would traditionally have happened, they had to broach the subject themselves directly with our father. In Palestine, when a young man thought of marrying, his mother or sisters usually looked out for a suitable girl, whether or not the prospective couple knew each other. If he agreed, they would then approach the mother of the intended bride and put forward the proposal. Only when the negotiations between the two families were well advanced and the girl's agreement had been secured, did the couple meet. It might also happen that the womenfolk did not bother to wait until their kinsman expressed a desire to marry, but took the decision on his behalf. Unless he was headstrong, he normally submitted to the women's urgings and allowed himself to be married off. It was not unknown for daughters to marry off their widowed fathers in this way, and for many a sister to assiduously ensure that her brother did not remain unmarried for long.

Siham was attractive, tall and slim, with smooth dark hair and high cheekbones, and many young men admired her. Some amongst these were our Christian Palestinian friends who knew they had no chance with a Muslim girl. But, in any case, our father was dead against her marrying at this stage. To our mother's dismay, he shooed them all away. "My daughters are not for marriage. They have their studies to attend to," he would assert sternly. In this way, all but the most thick-skinned were put off. One of these, a Muslim man from Nablus called Jaafar Yassin, who was in England studying law, persisted in his suit. He was a regular visitor to our house, and Siham and I avoided him whenever he came. He was stocky and short with jet-black frizzy hair. Coarse black hairs curled thickly over each of the knuckles of his fingers and when he once came wearing an open neck shirt a mat of black frizzy hair could be seen jutting out at the top. Siham and I nicknamed him "the gorilla" and shuddered when we saw him. Our mother, however, was much encouraged by his persistence and spoke to Siham about it.

"Just ignore your father. What do you think of him yourself?"

Siham squealed in horror. "Ooh, I couldn't bear him! He's so ugly."

Our mother was put out. "And what have looks got to do with it?" she demanded. "A man's for being married to, not for displaying like an ornament!"

Though we burst out laughing, she was entirely serious. For, in that sentence, she had unwittingly epitomised the reality of Arab male–female relations, as she knew them. In the world where my mother grew up, and to a large extent even now, relations between the sexes were largely instrumental. When it came to marriage, men looked for a woman who was young, sound of body and who could keep house and rear healthy children, while women wanted a man of any age and almost any appearance as long as he was respectable and could provide for them and the children they would have. The marriageability of both parties was assessed primarily on the basis of these qualities; love and compatibility, though they might exist at the beginning or develop later, were not essential to this arrangement. Actually, many Arab men have a patronising attitude to women, whom they regard as inferior, while the power imbalance between the sexes in Arab society ensures that women see men not as individuals but as pathways to social status and financial support. With fundamental matters like these at stake, it is no wonder that the man's looks or personal charm are the least of their concerns.

One of the most striking examples of this that I ever saw was a couple whom I met in Syria when I lived there in 1978. He was a man in his late forties, a university lecturer who had been blind from birth. How, given the severity of his disability, he managed to carry out his duties I never knew, and he compensated for his affliction with such an exaggerated display of self-importance that it made him quite obnoxious, and people avoided him. He had never married and his family sought for years to find him a suitable wife. Eventually, they hit on a schoolteacher of twenty-eight who had been "remaindered", regarded as ineligible on account of her plain looks and advanced age. Both parties were given the essential facts about each other: in his case, that she was rather over the hill, but healthy and docile of character, able to look after a house and drive a car; and in her case, that although he was totally blind, he had a respectable job, a house and money put by, and, above all, that by marrying him she would no longer be a burden to her family – daughters are traditionally supported by their fathers or brothers until they are married.

By the time I met them, they had been married for a year and already had a baby son. Seeing them together was quite a spectacle. He ruled the house and her with a rod of iron, and she deferred to him obediently in all respects. He made a point of instructing her pedantically in everything she did, including the way she drove the car, as if she were the blind and he the sighted one. Being their passenger, as I once was, was an ordeal I did not repeat. She drove at a speed no grater than ten miles an hour, while he kept up a continuous monologue of admonition and injunction, punctuated by apologies to me about her nervous driving and poor car control. Her demeanour throughout was patient and long-suffering, and I wondered that she was never tempted to poison his soup and put an end to her suffering. Yet, in spite of everything, there grew a sort of tenderness between them. He would hold lingeringly on to her hand sometimes when she gave him something and show off the son she had given him with pride. And, behind her meekness, one could detect gentleness and pity for his bombast and pathetic boasts. Though indeed theirs was the most instrumental of marriages, the reality of such relationships in the Arab world is infinitely more complex than it might seem.

As things turned out, our father's anti-matrimonial tactics in furthering our welfare, as he saw it, worked. Neither Siham nor I in later years succeeded in landing an Arab husband in England. Siham kept her boyfriend Eric secret, not that she had any intention of marrying him, and Jaafar Yassin went off in a pique and, to our amazement, married a beautiful young woman from his hometown. "Silly girl", said my mother to Siham. "It could have been you in her place."

Meanwhile, our brother was no part of any of these deliberations and kept himself to himself. Had we been living in our own society, this lack of interest in his sisters' marriage prospects would have struck everyone as odd since brothers were expected to play a decisive role in such matters along with their fathers. But, living in Britain as we were, many of the old rules no longer applied. However, it was also the fact that Ziyad had begun to drift away. I am not sure at what stage this happened, but he was suddenly no longer a part of us as in the old days. He had made his own friends, spent most of his time with them and hardly entered our lives. Siham and I were largely home-based, but he was out dancing every Saturday night. He usually went locally with two or three of his school friends to a dance club in Golders Green Road. Or they might have parties at home (never ours of course) where they danced and drank beer and cider (they could not go to pubs as they were under age).

Our parents had a vague idea of what was happening but did not inquire too closely, since Ziyad was a boy and might be expected to do such things. The popular music scene was changing fast at that time and rock and roll and jiving were becoming all the rage. *Rock around the Clock*, the seminal film about rock music, crossed the Atlantic in 1956 and Bill Haley, its singing star, came over on his first musical tour in the following year. We were aware of this new musical fashion, and indeed Siham had started to go out dancing herself, but our first allegiance to classical music remained. She bought a gramophone, which we kept in our bedroom, and I remember the thrill of going out to buy records and bringing them home to play.

Ziyad did not concern himself with such things. He was part of the new youth culture which was overtaking the Britain of the mid-1950s. He was fashionably skinny, wore drainpipe trousers and Brylcreamed his hair; we thought he looked like Dirk Bogarde. He had started smoking when he was fourteen, a habit he carefully concealed from our parents, and became very interested in girls. How many girl-friends he had we never knew, but if his confidences to Siham were anything to go by, they seemed to be many. One Saturday afternoon, he had the temerity to bring one of them home for tea. She was a pale, young creature with straight hair done up in a ponytail. She wore a full skirt and an elastic belt round her skinny waist. I suppose she was pretty in a mousy sort of way and my brother made a great fuss of her, inviting her into the front sitting-room which was normally reserved for our parents' visitors.

He prepared the tea – since our mother was having none of it and had eyed the girl with undisguised disapproval when she first arrived – and had just brought this in with a plate of cakes he had bought earlier when the doorbell rang. As luck would have it, the Dajani family had come to call. Mrs Dajani was a great friend of our mother and, as she lived in Kensington and therefore at some distance from us, her visits were infrequent and eagerly awaited. Ziyad and his girlfriend suddenly found themselves up against our mother's competing demand for the use of the front room.

"Right!" she said briskly to him, barging in. "Take yourself and her out of here. I've got visitors." There was no arguing with this and so, in some embarrassment, he and the girl gathered themselves and their tea tray together and made a hasty exit. We saw no more of her after that and, from all accounts, Ziyad soon replaced her.

The girls he met were nearly all foreign au pairs who had come to work with families in Golders Green and nearby Hendon. They came from Switzerland and Scandinavia, but mostly from Germany, which we thought was odd since they worked mostly for Jewish families. Ziyad and his friends liked these foreign girls because, as he said, they were free. The choice of girlfriends in Golders Green was otherwise not encouraging; they were either Jewish girls who tended to be sisters or cousins of his friends and so unapproachable, or non-Jewish English girls who, according to him, were prudish and strait-laced.

He and his friends met the au pairs at the Bamboo expresso bar opposite Golders Green station, where young people hung out. These Italian coffee bars were very fashionable in London, and sitting down to order an expresso or a cappuccino was the height of cosmopolitan sophistication amongst the young at the time. Otherwise, they met the girls at dance clubs of which there were many in the West End. Ziyad did not go to the big dance halls like the Lyceum or the Hammersmith Palais; he said he could meet all the girls he wanted in local clubs. And indeed, he formed a serious attachment to a Swedish girl whom he had met in this way in the summer of 1956. He took her away for a weekend to a Butlin's holiday camp on the south coast. Wanting to ensure that they would share a double chalet, Ziyad registered in the name of Mr and Mrs Karmi. In those days the idea of an unmarried couple spending the night together was not acceptable. All went according to plan until a week after his return to London when a parcel in the name of Mrs Karmi arrived at our house. Our father, curious to know who might have sent something exclusively to our mother, opened the package to find a scarf inside with a note from Butlin's management to the effect that Mrs Karmi had left it behind at the chalet during the previous weekend.

Ziyad was summoned by our father to explain himself. It was not that our parents begrudged him the chance to sow his wild oats, as they would have us girls. The problem lay in the way he had so crassly broken the unspoken Arab family taboo where such improper actions, though suspected, were never publicised and could be ignored. "Well?" Our father asked frowningly. "Er, I know this girl," stammered Ziyad. "She's nice and I know I shouldn't have done it, but I really like her. In fact," he continued desperately, "I like her so much, I've even thought of marrying her."

Our father stared hard at him. "You may think what you like. But you will have to choose between the girl and your university education. If you imagine that I'm prepared to spend good money on you while you fritter your time away on girls, you're much mistaken."

If Ziyad was hurt or surprised by this, he never showed it. He could see, however, that it was futile to argue with our father, and we felt sorry for him. The matter was not discussed again, and in the autumn of 1956, Ziyad went to Glasgow University where he had a place to study civil engineering. Our father's endeavours to coerce Ziyad into studying medicine in place of Siham had met with little success. But he did not find this too serious, for my brother's choice of subject still fell within the context of acceptable careers for Palestinians like us. It was a training that allowed one to find work practically anywhere without being too weighed down by citizenship or residence requirements. For stateless Palestinians this was the overriding objective.

Now our father turned his attention to me as the last vehicle for fulfilling his ambition of seeing one of his children become a doctor. I had by this time shown marked aptitude for literature, history and languages and an aversion for science subjects; in other words, I had exactly the reverse profile of a potential medical student. This did not save me, however, from the career my father had set his heart on, nor did the entreaties of my Latin teacher, a certain Miss Sinclair, who tried to impress on him the error of diverting me from my natural inclinations. But to no avail. My father insisted that I chose those science subjects for my GCE Advanced Level examination which would best enable me to apply for entry to medical school.

Miss Sinclair's concern for my welfare was unexpected, since she was chiefly known at school for her cantankerousness and sarcasm. She would preside over our Latin lessons looking like an ill-humoured bloodhound, her jowls and eyelids drooping downwards and her chin supported on her crossed hands as her disapproving eyes roved over the classroom. She made clear that she found us unspeakably dull and ignorant, setting us odd tests, all of which we failed. The strangest of these was the time she asked us to comment on the date, which happened to be May 5, 1955. When no one answered, she cried, "It's 5.5.55 today. It will be 6.6.66 eleven years from now, and another eleven years after that it will be 7.7.77. And it means nothing to you? Not a flicker of interest? Truly, I despair!"

During the school holidays in the summer of 1955, Siham and I took the bold step of going on a holiday abroad. This was something new for us, our parents having no concept of holidays. No such institution had existed in Palestine or indeed in most of the Arab world. The idea that people would at some specific time of the year arrange to leave their homes and go to a different place for the sole purpose of getting away from their usual lives was to my parents quite strange. It was not that they had never left Jerusalem when we were there; indeed they would often take us to Jaffa or to Tulkarm, but these trips were either short-lived, picnic-style events or family visits whose primary purpose was to see our relatives.

We had no tradition of going somewhere in order to see what it was like, or simply to get away from our routine, everyday setting. Our mother had little interest in places which had no relation to what was familiar to her; like many Arabs, her concept of enjoyment was being with other people, not gazing at historical monuments which she scornfully referred to as "piles of stones". The only exception to this position she ever encountered in her life was when once, long after we were grown up, our father took her to southern Spain. There, agog at the splendid Islamic buildings of Cordova and Granada, where she could see the grand legacy of Spain's Arab past, she felt the thrill that piles of stones could impart. "What colour, what lightness!" she enthused. "How marvellous the Arabs were!" And she said that if we could not return to our own country, then we should live in Spain.

Siham arranged for us to go to Paris, because she had met a young Frenchman called Claude in London who invited her over. My views of France at that time were derived from a mixture of the romantic historical novels which I read and the francophobic attitudes I had picked up from my English surroundings. Despite my Arab back-ground, I still managed to share the English bias against the French as garlic-smelling, untrustworthy cowards who had succumbed to the

Germans during the Second World War. I adopted these stereotypes enthusiastically as if they had been part of my own history.

Much to my amazement, everyone in Paris took me for an Algerian, an experience that was to prove far from pleasant. Some nine months before our visit, the Algerian war of independence had started, and, when we reached Paris, the news was of little else. Not that we understood much of it. With my poor knowledge of French and Siham's total lack of it we barely managed to get by. No one could or would speak English to us in Paris and we had the distinct impression that they thought us beneath contempt for not speaking their language. Claude showed us all round Paris and all the time in the background the Algerian war rumbled on.

Until then, my knowledge of Algerian history and politics had been sketchy. This was partly due to ignorance and partly to the fact that we in the Arab Middle East viewed North Africa as a remote place. We also found it difficult to understand North Africans because the Arabic they use is considerably influenced by Berber (the original native language of the region), and is infiltrated with numerous French loanwords. This makes them well-nigh unintelligible to Middle Eastern Arabs and perpetuates the impression of difference and distance.

Even so, we regarded the inhabitants of the Maghreb (Arabic for "West", i.e. for North African countries west of Libya) as fellow Arabs and fellow Muslims; and as Palestinians we had a special bond with Morocco from where devout pilgrims had emigrated to Palestine for many centuries.[1] Many of them intermarried with Palestinians, and I remember that my mother's dressmaker in Jerusalem was a Mrs

---

[1] The Maghrebi Quarter in the Old City of Jerusalem was so called because of the Moroccans who settled there. It was built in 1320 and stood until the Israelis totally demolished it when they occupied the city in June 1967.

Aisha Maghrebi. Algerians on the other hand, having been dominated by France more deeply and for longer, seemed less familiar.

My father would often make declarations at home about the struggle of our fellow Muslims, as he put it, against France's occupation of their country. "These French are no better than barbarians," he would say. "They can do their worst, but it won't stop the Algerians from liberating their country. In the end, the people will win." The Algerian struggle, he said, was a shining beacon of inspiration to all Arabs in the fight against Israeli and Western colonialism. But in the summer of 1955, at the age of fifteen, I was far more interested in going on my first holiday abroad, like any English schoolgirl, than I was in the ebb and flow of Arab liberation politics.

And so it was with shock and a sense of humiliation that I found myself the object of leering, contemptuous Frenchmen who pinched my bottom at will. This happened most often in the metro, where bodies were packed tightly against each other, but also once in the street when I stopped to buy something at a stall. I was nearly sixteen and beginning to take on the shape of a young woman, although my bust remained depressingly flat. I suppose it may have been my curly hair, frizzy at the front, which gave me a North African look. But it was more the fact that, for the Frenchman in the street, Arabs meant only Algerians and other North Africans.

"Why do they do it?" I asked Claude.

"Oh, it's nothing," he laughed. "The men here, they see a pretty girl and they can't resist."

"They think I'm Algerian, don't they?" I remarked.

"Maybe," he replied, "and if they do, they won't care, because you wouldn't dare to do anything against them." Claude took us to see Gouttes d'Or, the North African quarter in the centre of the city. It was a self-contained ghetto, dilapidated, alien and totally out of place in the Paris we had been admiring. It was teeming with impoverished-looking Algerians and Moroccans, many of whom eyed us with suspicion. Claude stood nervously beside us, wanting us to leave because he said the place was dangerous. It had recently become a base for violent attacks against the French, as if the struggle back in Algeria was being waged here too.

There was a small, simple mosque which we wanted to see, although Claude advised against lingering too long. Inside, a man whom we presumed to be the sheikh or imam made us welcome. He spoke in rapid French while he showed us over the little building, and we wanted somehow to convey to him that we were not just tourists but Muslims like him. He looked strange, yet I recognised him as fundamentally an Arab. We told Claude afterwards that we would have liked to speak to him had we known any French.

"You don't think that was French, do you?" he laughed. "No verbs, no grammar, terrible pronunciation. These people are imbeciles, they all speak like that."

I froze and at that moment I had a sense of kinship with the man in the mosque as surely as if I had been Algerian too. My carefully cultivated Englishness was fragile and such incidents only served to make it more so.

꙰

At school the atmosphere had become more and more competitive. There was much rivalry about the number of GCE O-Level examinations people were taking. No one would be seen dead sitting for less than eight subjects and some boasted that they were taking eleven. As the New Year came in, thought of the coming examinations hung over me like an incubus. But I was also distracted by other things. Having turned sixteen, I had become increasingly interested in make-up and boys. Patricia and I had experimented with cosmetics for some time, but now we started to put them on every time we went out together.

Neither her mother nor mine permitted this, so we had to take our make-up with us and apply it in the ladies' toilet at Brent (now called Brent Cross), which was our nearest underground station. We would go in looking like schoolgirls and emerge like knowing young women with dark eye shadow and bright lipstick. On returning from our outing, we would reverse the process in the toilet and arrive back at our homes, looking as scrubbed and innocent as when we had left. This went well for some time until one day I returned home to a thunderous atmosphere. My mother looked me up and down most ominously.

"Anything wrong?" I ventured nervously.

She put her hand to her breast and shook her head mournfully from side to side. This was a bad sign and I braced myself for what might be coming.

"Anything wrong?" she repeated rhetorically. "You say, 'Anything wrong'? With your father having had such a shock?"

"What happened?"

"He saw you on the bus in Baker Street, made up like a tart, giggling with that girl. He couldn't do anything about it as he was walking along the pavement. But he came back here, really shaken. 'What a sight,' he said, 'I couldn't believe it was Ghada.'" She came up close and stared at my face. "Hmm. I can still see it. You didn't clean it off properly, did you?" My father said nothing, merely averted his gaze when I looked at him. They both made me feel guilty, but it only determined me to conceal the traces of the make-up more effectively next time. Meanwhile, Patricia had also been discovered because the remains of the eye shadow she had used still showed on her fair skin.

"So what're you going to be doing next, tell me?" her mother demanded. "Now it's make-up, then it's high heels, then it's boys I suppose. Well, let me tell you it's going to be nothing while your father's away in Jersey."

Boys were of course very much on our minds. Though making up was fun in itself, we were also quite clear that it was a bait for attracting young men. Our technique for doing that was not the most ingenious. We would get dolled up and then sit displaying our charms in the Marinella. This was Golders Green's second Italian coffee bar, opposite the taxi rank outside the station yard. Patricia and I would take the bar seats and chat to the Italian waiters over the counter while we had an ice-cream or a milk shake. I suppose we must have been eye-catching, both of us slender and petite, she with her pale skin and long flaxen hair and I with my dark eyes and thick brown curls. Our mothers scarcely ever came to that end of Golders Green, and we considered ourselves relatively safe. The fuss that my parents had made over the question of make-up was as nothing to what would have happened over the matter of boyfriends.

I cannot recall that this prohibition was ever made explicitly, but it was one that I had internalised unconsciously with my upbringing. I knew without asking that for me, as a girl, sex and men were taboo subjects. Going out with a boy, kissing and cuddling – or "necking", as we used to call it – were strictly forbidden, and anything beyond that was touching on the ultimate taboo, sexual intercourse. I assumed that this was lifted at marriage, but no one discussed these things in our family and I did not try to analyse them to myself. I simply side-stepped the whole issue and continued my explorations with Patricia in secret. When, every now and then at the Marinella, a boy tried to chat one or both of us up, we regarded it as a major triumph. We had not got to the stage of accepting to go out with anyone, partly because of the constraints of our upbringing and partly because we saw no one appealing enough. My ideal of masculine attraction at the time was Marlon Brando as he appeared in *On the Waterfront*. No one I met at the Marinella (or anywhere else) could have held a candle to this ideal. So, Patricia and I flirted and practised our female wiles on the waiters and the young men at the coffee bar. It was not until the summer of that year that she and I had our first boyfriends.

৵৵৹

Enveloped in my own small world, I had little space to think about what was happening in the Middle East throughout this time. But 1956 was to be a year in which events there could not be ignored and would intrude even into my consciousness. It was not Israel or Palestine that was the focus of interest at that moment, but Egypt. For the advent of Colonel Nasser, the Egyptian leader in the 1950s, brought about a profound change for the whole Arab world which extended also to Arabs like us outside and indelibly affected the international scene.

By 1956, President Nasser was seen as the embodiment of Arab nationalism. I knew nothing about this concept, but my parents understood it well. "We are all one Arab nation," they told me, "we have the same language and history and customs. And most of us are Muslims as well." I wondered about the Arab Christians like our friend Fuad in this scheme. "They're part of it too," explained my father irritably. "That's not the point. We've all been split up into states with artificial boundaries. Do you know, when I was your age, we could go from one town to another, say from Jerusalem to Damascus or to Cairo, without passports or permits?" I found the idea of my father and uncles travelling freely from place to place, like medieval pilgrims, rather appealing. "We were under Ottoman rule of course. But then, the Ottoman Empire fell, the West took over and look at the Arabs now!"

Yet, this did not destroy the feeling of Arab unity, he asserted; ordinary Arabs unconsciously sensed it without being able to articulate it. I remembered my strange feeling of kinship with the Algerian in the Paris mosque and thought I understood. Perhaps that was why my parents saw themselves and us as Arabs first and everything else second. Perhaps too it was why the Egyptian singer, Um Kulthum, whose voice my mother had virtually reared us on, had such ubiquitous appeal for Arabs. Even in England, I knew that her songs were uniformly appreciated throughout the length and breadth of the Arab world, as if in these she spoke to the Arab world in a universal language.

There was much talk in our house about Gamal Abdul-Nasser. Our parents listened to all his speeches from Cairo on the radio. Much of it was outside my sphere of experience and I was not sure I understood what he was saying. He spoke grandly about leading an Arab revolution that would recreate "the noble, united Arab nation". He announced that as a first step in this process, Egypt would explore the possibility of nationalising the Suez Canal. Hearing this, my parents gasped with surprise and admiration, but none of the parents of my English friends saw it in the same light. Britain's Prime Minister, Anthony Eden, hated and feared Nasser and declared that he saw him as an evil dictator like Hitler or Mussolini. I never normally read newspapers, but at this I started to look at the headlines in the papers Siham brought back with her every evening. They all called Nasser an "upstart". I can remember how this epithet made me wince; it was so contemptuous and arrogant that I felt as slighted as if it had been personally aimed at me.

In the summer of 1956, Nasser took the decision to nationalise the Suez Canal Company. Heated conversations at our house ensued. "You can see why he did it," said our neighbour Jiryis to general agreement. "He wouldn't have done it if the Americans had given him a loan to help Egypt build the High Dam at Aswan."

"Of course not! But he had no choice," said my mother vehemently. She had not taken such an interest in politics for years, but had become a fervent Nasser supporter because she said he spoke for her and all

Arabs. Apolitical teenager as I was, I could not help being swept along by her enthusiasm. Our friends said that the Americans wanted to deny Arabs any chance of independence. So, Nasser had to try and claim the Suez Canal's considerable revenues, of which Egypt had always received the smallest share ($3 million out of the canal's annual revenue of $100 million), to fund the Aswan High Dam project.[2]

But everyone was also keenly aware that he had another, nationalist, agenda for his action. The Canal stood on sovereign Egyptian soil. "Do you know," said my father heatedly, "that maybe 120,000 Egyptian labourers died building it, but it's been exploited entirely by foreigners?"

No Egyptian before had dared to challenge this outrageous state of affairs. We all viewed Nasser's determination to change history with admiration but also with trepidation because even I could see that his actions might provoke the wrath of the western powers who had hitherto controlled the Canal. But hardly anyone in Britain shared our admiration. Radio and TV quickly condemned the nationalisation. It was an "illegal and aggressive act which Nasser had no right to carry out". On July 26, the long-debated decision was made. Nasser announced the nationalisation of the Suez Canal Company when he addressed a massive crowd of some 250,000 people in Alexandria. It was one of the most rousing and eloquent of all his speeches and we heard it at home on my mother's crackly radio.

Through the irritating crackle we heard a voice attack western imperialism and accuse the West of trying to maintain its spheres of influence in the Arab world. One of these was Israel, the voice said,

---

[2] Egypt had never had a fair deal out of the Canal. It had no shares in the Suez Canal Company which ran it. Forty-four per cent of the capital provided by Egypt's ruler, the Khedive Ismail, was sold to Britian in 1875. Half of the company's privately owned shares belonged to the French and the bulk of its foreign exchange earnings was invested in Britain, France and the US, and did not contribute an iota to Egypt's national income.

which had been imposed on the Arabs. The imperialists wanted the Arabs to abandon the Palestinians and the Algerians in their struggle. But Egypt would never again bow down to orders from high commissioners and ambassadors. It would henceforth have an independent personality, and along with the Arab nation become a power in the world to be reckoned with. I found Nasser's voice hectoring and difficult to listen to, but I pricked up my ears when he ended his speech with these words:

> At this minute, some of your brethren, the sons of Egypt, are taking over the Egyptian Suez Canal Company and directing it. We have taken this decision to restore part of the glories of the past and to safeguard our national dignity and pride.

I could feel the hairs on the back of my neck stand up and I was imbued with a sense of pride in being an Arab such as I had never felt before. I do not know where the feeling came from, nor how it fitted with the English personality I thought was mine. Had I imbibed it, against the odds, from my father's scarcely heeded political conversations with his friends, or from my mother's unrelenting Arabness, which I disapprovingly dismissed and had done my best to ignore? Everyone in our house felt the same uplifting emotion, Ziyad and Siham, and our mother who cried openly. Even our father cleared his throat and nodded vigorously at the voice on the radio.

As news of the Canal's nationalisation broke, I thought naively that the justice of Egypt's case as I understood it would speak for itself. But it took only four days after the Canal's nationalisation for Britain to act. We woke up one morning to hear the radio saying that the British prime minister had told the House of Commons that the government could not stand by and see "this great international waterway" left under the sole control of a power which could "exploit it purely for purposes of national policy".

"Like having his finger on Britain's windpipe," screamed the newspapers. When Nasser turned to the Soviets for the aid that the US had denied him for the construction of the Aswan High Dam I could sense my parents growing alarmed. I started to pester Siham about what would happen. "Well it's a good thing she reads all their papers," approved my mother, hearing me. But Siham knew no more than I did. As we were to discover later, secret decisions were being taken at the highest level to arrange for the Suez Canal to be seized from Egypt, and an elaborate plan involving Britain, France and Israel was being drawn up for the purpose. But because all this was taking place during the school holidays, in the tense period between my taking the GCE examinations and waiting for their results, events in my own life were once more uppermost in my mind.

For Patricia and I acquired our first boyfriends that summer. We came across the two boys who were to provide us with our first romantic experiences at the Marinella. They were both French and, like us, in their teens. They had come to London for the summer to learn English. Within a short time, the taller and thinner of the two, Philippe, had settled for Patricia, while the short, dark one called Gérard chose me. Patricia, who was good at languages, chattered to them in French, but I was tongue-tied and would only speak in English. Consequently, Gérard and I could hardly communicate, while Philippe and Patricia were getting on well. We went out together for most of August before they returned to France. It was hot that year and we spent much time on Hampstead Heath, which suited everyone as it involved spending no money. It was here that I received my first romantic kiss. Lying in the dry, coarse grass, looking up at a clear sky, I tried inexpertly to reproduce the moans women made and the sideways head positions they adopted when they were being kissed in films. But all I could feel was the hard ground digging into my back and the insect bites on my arms and legs.

I remember that I was not particularly impressed with my boyfriend, who was noisy and gauche, and, when the four of us went out, more interested in shouting across to Philippe in French than in paying me attention. The only compliment he paid me was a playful insistence that I looked like Dorothy Dandridge. This was the black singing star of *Carmen Jones*, a Hollywood film version of Bizet's opera, *Carmen*, which was then playing in London. Though clearly of Afro-Caribbean origin, Dorothy Dandridge was more light brown than black. She was very attractive but much older and I thought looked nothing like me. When the time came for Gérard and Philippe to leave the country, I felt relieved.

When I restarted school at the beginning of September, the Suez question was far from settled. To my surprise, I found that it was a subject of discussion at school. I had always seen politics as something which was primarily concerned with the Middle East and which chiefly happened at home between my father and our friends. I had no grasp of British domestic affairs, scarcely knew the name of the Prime Minister, and had no idea about British policy anywhere except perhaps in the Middle East and, even then, the details were hazy. In this I was no different from the majority of my contemporaries, whose interests lay in spheres far distant from politics of any kind. This possibly explains the lack of friction over my origins which I had experienced with the Jewish girls in the class.

But the Suez affair was to change all that. On my return to school, I was struck by what I could only describe as a difference in attitude towards me. Being in the sixth form looked in any event to be a daunting and unpleasant experience. All my close friends, with the exception of Josie had left. Hilary Sternberg, who had been one of my group, had also stayed behind, but though we still saw each other out of school, we had been drifting apart ever since Patricia came on the scene. The rest of the form was made up of girls in cliques whom I had never mixed with and mostly did not like, and I feared I would be lonely.

It was Hilary, though, who first shocked me into realising that things were different. Of the two of us, she had always been the more diffident, always deferring to me, sometimes to my great irritation. She had few opinions of her own and usually kept quiet during most conversations. Almost as soon as term started, while I was in the classroom one morning organising my new desk, she came and stood in front of me. There was an expression of belligerence on her face which I had never seen before.

"Do you think it's all right what your Nasser did?" she demanded.

"What d'you mean, my Nasser?"

"You know, just go ahead and take something which wasn't his?" Her tone was accusatory, as if she held me responsible in some way. Hearing us, two of the girls in the classroom now came over and stood by Hilary looking at me. They were both Jewish and no friends of mine. I could feel myself getting agitated.

"It is his, I mean Egypt's", I retorted heatedly. "But ever since it was built, it's been run by other people for their own profit. It belongs to Egypt and they should run it, that's all."

Hilary pulled up the sleeves of her navy pullover. I could not imagine what had so emboldened her. "Don't you know that the Canal was created by us, by Europe, not by Egyptians? When you make something, you don't expect to have other people come along and just help themselves."

"And anyway," added one of the other girls, a certain Ruth Katzer whom I had never liked, "Nasser's broken the law. There's a law and treaties that say the Canal belongs to Britain and Europe. He's just torn up the treaties, he's an outlaw."

I wished fervently in that moment that I had listened more carefully to the discussions at home. I knew there was something wrong with the legal argument, but I was unsure of my ground. "Well, you're wrong, it is legal", I said, trying to sound firm. "But that's not the point. You've got to look at basic justice here. The Canal was built in colonialist times. No one was thinking about what the Egyptians wanted when it was built" – my nineteenth-century history was shaky and I was hoping that the others knew no more than I did – "and the fact is that the Canal is on Egyptian soil. It's only fair that Egypt should control it."

The audience was unimpressed.

"Don't you at least want to listen to my point of view?" I asked in some desperation.

They clearly didn't. "Nasser's a thug and someone's got to stop him," said Hilary giving me a contemptuous look. The others nodded in agreement and then moved off, leaving me shaken and confused. As if it had heard our exchange, the British government was indeed about to fulfil Hilary's wish. By the middle of September, there was open talk of war against Egypt in London and other European capitals. Britain and France were elaborating the actual plan of attack in secret, with Israeli participation. Strange as it may seem, until the Suez crisis erupted Israel had somehow slipped out of my consciousness. I knew that since we came to England it had totally replaced Palestine and I had learned to accept that most English people around me no longer remembered that there had ever been such a place as the country where I was born. My image of Israel was quite crude: it was enemy territory where unmentionable things happened. When there was talk of politics at home, it was about the conflict with Israel, but not about Israel itself, as if it had no separate existence outside the conflict. Thus I learned early on to dissociate Israel from Palestine and the rest of the Arab world and to ignore it.

But Israel could not so easily be ignored by those on its borders. In the early 1950s, while I was unaware of what was happening, my parents often talked of raids and reprisals between what were called Arab "infiltrators" and the Israeli army. These were the Palestinians my cousin Zuhair had told us about, refugees who had lost their homes and land and whom Israel refused to allow back. Mostly they crossed the border from Jordan, but others also tried their luck across the border from the Gaza Strip. Cairo Radio described the punitive Israeli reprisals against these refugees in painful detail, which upset my mother. But to my father, Nasser came up trumps here too.

"He's arming and training the Palestinians in Gaza" – this part of Palestine had fallen under Egyptian administration following the 1948 war with Israel and was home to 300,000 Palestinian refugees – "because he's going to use them in the war against Israel; you wait and see," he said. "Well, that suits us. It means our people will be able to fight for themselves at last." My father was right. Out of Nasser's plan to use Palestinians as surrogates in the Egyptian battle with Israel arose the guerrilla fighters or *fedayeen*. Their heads wrapped in check *kuffiyyas*, Kalashnikov rifles slung over their shoulders, these young fighters would become the hallmark of Palestinian resistance thereafter.

Now the British politicians we heard on the radio became even more worried about Nasser. Though my clever father and his Arab friends at the BBC argued day and night about the situation, they couldn't know that a secret plan to deal with Nasser was being concocted. "There's something cooking," said my father one morning over breakfast. "I don't know what it is, but I don't like it." And my mother said she wouldn't be surprised at anything the British did.

What was "cooking", of course, was an invasion of Egypt. As we were to find out later, there was a plot for Israel to unilaterally invade the Sinai and move towards the Suez Canal. Whereupon, Britain and France would intervene in the guise of peacemakers; though their real objective would be to wrest the Canal out of Egypt's control. If the plan succeeded, it would also have the effect of overthrowing Nasser or "cutting him down to size", thus putting an end to his "upstart" ambitions. We read later that to prepare for the coming war, France provided Israel with advanced military hardware, and the date of the invasion was set for October 29.

తించి

The new term at school was turning out to be just as bad as I had feared. The unfriendly atmosphere with which it had started had not lifted. I felt excluded from the clique of Jewish girls in my class who seemed to prefer each other's company and had no alternative but to stick to Josie as much as possible. But since she was taking different subjects from me we met less frequently than before. To make matters worse, the subjects I was being forced to study, physics, chemistry and mathematics, were difficult and held no appeal for me. Only zoology, my fourth subject, was interesting. I felt oppressed both by this and by the other girls who, it seemed, avoided me.

The worst time of all was school lunch. Josie, with whom I used to walk to lunch, now brought sandwiches, which meant that I had no one to walk down with. It never happened at our school that anyone, however despised, walked down alone to lunch. The lowliest, the least attractive girl could still find someone to go with. But who was there for me now? Hilary and I had not spoken to each other since the Suez conversation, the other Jewish girls now ignored me and I hardly ever mixed with the non-Jews. Excepting, that is, for one girl we used unkindly to nickname Goofy after the comic cartoon character. She was exceptionally tall, had carrot red hair, freckles and buck-teeth, and we spent most of the time making fun of her. She was friendless but for one other unprepossessing girl called Amy. This Amy had fair hair, glasses and large hips, and she was as short and squat as Goofy was tall and skinny. The two of them made a funny-looking pair whom no one would have been seen dead with.

But now to my horror, I found that I would have to contemplate the company of these two for lunch. It was that, or walk down alone. I thought desperately of the latter course, but my courage failed me. The humiliation either way was intense, but, on balance, walking alone was worse. Putting as good a face on it as I could, I asked to walk down with them and could almost feel the sense of triumph with which Amy condescended to agree. Goofy, on the other hand, was quite good-natured and looked genuinely pleased. It never occurred to me that I was being unkind to these girls; with the insensitivity typical of teenagers, I felt only for myself. To me, consorting with them was a climbdown, symbolic of the general wretchedness of my situation and I wondered how I was going to endure two such years in the sixth form.

In those early months of the new term at school, the Suez crisis intensified. At home, everyone was affected by it; Siham was so incensed by the anti-Arab tone emanating from the press and from some of her fellow students at the Polytechnic that she started talking about leaving England. Ziyad, who, like me, had never taken much interest in politics before, had also become involved. He tried to convince all his Jewish friends of the Arab point of view and when he went up to Glasgow University at the end of September he became active in the students' union with other Arab, especially Egyptian, students.

Suez was to become one of the great left-wing causes of the decade and a focus of passionate interest amongst students. Though we were preoccupied with politics, we did miss Ziyad. He had never left home before, not in Palestine or Syria or here, and, even though he had developed his own social life, there was a strange emptiness without him. I remember that first evening after he had gone when we sat down to have dinner. We were all silent and our mother looked bereft. She had cooked a dish that Ziyad particularly liked and she kept saying, "He would have so enjoyed this. God knows how he'll feed himself now. Oh, dear, if only he hadn't gone."

At the BBC, our father and his colleagues faced a problem they had not anticipated. The news, which was read over the air in all the overseas services, was not composed individually by each service but was translated into the different languages put out by the BBC from a standard bulletin, which was written in the central newsroom. This did not usually matter. Arabs considered the BBC an authoritative source of news and held it in high esteem. But in the autumn of 1956, the BBC bulletins which would have to be translated into Arabic reflected an increasingly anti-Egyptian national mood. And as the Suez crisis worsened so did the BBC's rhetoric. The tensions created by this were considerable, but were as nothing to what would happen when the attack on Egypt finally came, as everyone expected it to.

On October 29, the Israeli army invaded Sinai. And on the same date, we heard later, Israeli frontier guards carried out another massacre, this time at the border village of Kafr Qassem. My father, shocked, said it was a small, insignificant place, like many of Palestine's old villages. The Israelis suddenly announced a curfew, but gave the villagers so little notice that they were still hurrying home when the curfew came into force. The Israelis shot forty-seven of them, men, women, children, at close range. On the same eventful day, the Israeli army invaded Sinai.

My father came home late that evening, looking strained and tired. He and Cairo Radio became my mother's sources of eagerly awaited news. She talked of nothing else to all her friends. I would come home from school to hearing them discussing the latest developments. Within four days, the Israelis had captured much of Sinai, and the British and French governments duly issued an ultimatum to both sides to stop fighting. They then moved in a combined Anglo-French force, bombing the Egyptian army and airfields and going on to try and occupy the canal.

Total occupation never happened and the campaign was short-lived. At the UN, Britain and France were branded aggressors. "Serve them right!" exclaimed Siham and, in a confused way, I found myself empathising with her vehemence. Under strong American pressure, they were forced to cease hostilities on November 6.

The Suez war had a dramatic effect on the political scene in Britain. I appreciated it fully only years later. As a teenager, I was often peeved by everyone's preoccupation with politics, unaware that I was living in momentous times. The crisis divided the country into those who were for and those against the campaign. My family and virtually the whole of the Labour Party opposed it, as did the bulk of British middle-class liberal opinion. Siham and some of the Arab students went to join a huge and impressive public rally at Trafalgar Square on November 4, when the famous Labour politician, Aneurin Bevan, denounced the Suez invasion in fiery tones. Shortly after, the Arab students went out on a march to hand in a protest to the Prime Minister's office at Downing Street, but they were pushed back by police, some on horseback, and several of them sustained minor injuries.

We were bemused by the contradictions in British society. On the one hand, a ruthless and cunning duplicity, and on the other, a sense of morality and self-criticism. But uppermost in our minds was the depth of Britain's hostility towards our part of the world that the Suez adventure had unveiled. Where was the famous British sense of fair play in attacking Egypt three-to-one? And how could Britain encourage Israel to invade yet more Arab land?

Our home was now constantly buzzing with comment and reaction to the war. The family began debating our departure from England; Siham said that she had finally made up her mind to leave as soon as she took her final exams. "I always knew the English were our enemies," she said, "but this surpasses everything. I can't go on living here any more." There were anxious discussions about what should be done about me and Ziyad, where we would go and what work my father could expect to find. The Egyptians who worked in the BBC Arabic Service with him felt similarly. As the language of BBC news and political commentary had become stridently anti-Egyptian, the Egyptian announcers were outraged and held an angry meeting with the other Arab employees. They asked how they could be expected to read out material day after day which insulted their leader and their people. They declared that they would resign *en masse* and demanded that all the Palestinian employees resign with them. "Remember, Israel was your enemy before it was ours," they told my father.

There was much consternation and my father thought it best not to do anything hasty. "People need their jobs, they have their families to think of," he advised. As soon as the rumour got about that some BBC employees might resign their posts there was an instant queue of other Arabs waiting to take over. This dismayed everyone, but by then it had become an issue of conscience and honour and some Palestinians began to think they should resign. My father decided to take the matter to the authorities before something irreversible happened which everyone might regret. He sought a meeting with the head of the Arabic Service, a man called Geoffrey Thompson, and explained the concerns of the Arab staff. He asked that the BBC take account of their understandable sensitivities and consider ameliorating the pro-government tone in news broadcasting. He had expected to emerge out of the meeting empty-handed, but, to his surprise, Thompson took the matter seriously. He promised to look into it. My father returned to the Egyptians and relayed the message, but they were sceptical.

However, Thompson came back soon after and informed my father that a decision had been taken by the governors of the BBC to accede to the wishes of the Arab staff. They did not for a moment accept that the BBC was partisan and was anything but independent. However, henceforth, broadcast material which pertained to the Suez crisis would be carefully vetted. "I knew I hadn't got them because of any sympathy with how we felt," said my father afterwards. "It was the suggestion that they might be a government mouthpiece that really did it."

Whatever the real reason, the news material thereafter shed its stridency and became more neutral. But the change did not mollify the Egyptians who still resigned, maintaining that it was a matter of principle and calling on the Palestinians to do the same. None of the latter did and the Egyptians left the country in anger and disappointment. The moment they went, other Arabs stepped gratefully into their jobs.

"What happened to the Egyptians?" I later asked my father.

"It was very sad," he said. "They went back to Alexandria thinking to receive a hero's welcome. But no one took much notice and no one employed them for at least two years."

"And you, why didn't you resign as well?"

"I thought hard about it, probably the only time when I seriously thought to do such a thing," he answered. "But in the end, I came back to the fact that there were all of you to support and we had to live. And of course, there was the fact that those of us at the BBC who opposed the government didn't feel alone. The whole of the Labour Party and many others took the same view. That made it easier."

ॐ

When the Suez war started, life for me at school became harder. The antipathy I had thought I felt from some of the girls at the beginning of term was palpably more intense. It was fuelled by the weekly

sessions on something called "Civics", during which we were supposed to debate some political or current affairs topic to broaden our
horizons. Inevitably, given the stormy political events in which Britain
was implicated that autumn, many of the discussions related to the
Suez affair. Soon, the Civics sessions became a kind of purgatory for
me. They were not debates so much as contests in which I was on my
own in one corner, defending the Egyptian position, with everyone
else, including the teacher, against me in the other corner. Zoe Steiner,
a haughty, arrogant girl, who hardly ever talked to me outside these
sessions, led the opposition. After one heated debate, as we were
going back to the classroom, I walking alone in front and she behind
me with the band of cronies who accompanied her everywhere, I
heard her whisper loudly that Arabs lived in ghettos and were all
filthy; she had seen them when her parents took her to Paris, she said,
and everyone giggled.

I protested to the form teacher that I was being insulted during
Civics and that the girls said nasty things about Arabs. The teacher
said nothing but sent me to see Miss Leach. I did not mind this
because I knew Miss Leach was fair.

"I can see you're upset," she said, looking into my face. "But why
does it affect you so much? After all, you're not Egyptian, are you?"

"She doesn't understand," I cried at home to Siham. "She thinks
Egyptians are nothing to do with us." Siham was powerless to help.
Neither she nor my parents, who did not take my tribulations all that
seriously, knew how to complain to the school. Mostly, they said not
to worry and that the girls in the class were just silly.

But in late November things took a turn for the worse. Normally,
there was little friction in our classroom because we all attended
different lessons and spent little time together. But even there, I began
to sense a hostile atmosphere every time I went in, though I could not
have said exactly where it was coming from. Sometimes, when I

opened the door, it seemed to me that I heard suppressed giggles. When I walked to my desk the girls shot secretive glances at me. My school work was beginning to suffer; I was being told off for not concentrating in class and for handing in poor quality homework.

One day, just as the lunch break started, I found I had forgotten something and quickly went back to class to get it. My sudden return was evidently unexpected, for as soon as I entered I could see that I had interrupted something I was not meant to see. By the window, at the other end of the room, a strange scene met my eyes. Zoe Steiner, looking particularly pleased with herself, was seated on top of her desk surrounded by an admiring group of four or five other Jewish girls. As soon as she saw me, her lips curled in a knowing smile and she began slowly to close a notebook which had been lying open on her lap. They all looked round at me and sniggered, watching until I had gone to my desk, finished my business and gone out again.

This scene had me fascinated and confused. I realised that Zoe had been reading something to the others from her notebook, and that it was in some way connected with me. Though I had never been a friend of hers, I did not think she had anything against me. When Patricia Cohen was there, she used to comment about Zoe being a "Jewish princess", picking up the American term denoting someone spoiled and rich. Truth be told, we were also both a little jealous of her because her family was rich and she had beautiful clothes. But she had her own clique in the class, which she dominated, and we avoided her.

Inexplicably, however, now she seemed to harbour a sort of malice against me. I told Josie and asked her if she knew anything about this, but she shook her head. We decided to be more vigilant. And sure enough, there were several repetitions of the scene with the notebook. Josie, being a friend of mine, was not allowed to penetrate the group. All she could tell me was that Zoe did indeed read out something from her book which had the girls giggling.

There was nothing for it but to take a look at the notebook. We agreed that we should keep a watch out for when the classroom was empty and then rifle through Zoe's desk. The opportunity to do this came one morning when everyone was at school assembly. We were taking a risk by being absent from assembly, which was not normally allowed, but we had no choice. Going through Zoe's desk did not take long and there, at the bottom of a pile of exercise books, I found the notebook. I opened it tremblingly, afraid Zoe would come back before I had had a chance to look inside. There, scribbled in her large hand, was what seemed to be a story spanning more than half the book. It was about an Arab girl who lived in a place called "The Ghada Strip". Her father was a Bedouin who had four wives with heavy veils over their faces and twenty children. They all lived together in one large tent. They had goats and camels, and the goats lived with them in the tent. Everyone smelled like animals because they never washed, and they ate all sorts of revolting and peculiar things.

I did not bother to read on, as it all seemed to be in the same vein. Josie saw some of it with me, and then we quickly closed the notebook and put it away as unobtrusively as we could. I could see the story was about me, and even though I had experienced Zoe's antagonism towards me during Civics, I still felt stunned and uncomprehending. What had I ever done to Zoe Steiner? I agonised. Why was she so spiteful about me? I went home, deeply shaken, and bursting into tears, told Siham about it.

"Don't let it worry you," she comforted me. She thought that, since Zoe and her clique were all Jewish, it was somehow bound up with the Suez war and the role of Israel and the way people here had started to feel about Arabs. I complained bitterly to Patricia who was full of sympathy. "That Zoe Steiner, we always thought she was a real cow, don't you remember?" she said. "I know that type. Just ignore her and she won't think it's fun any more and she'll stop."

But I was deeply tormented at the prospect of having to go back to that classroom and face that spiteful girl and her hateful companions. How could I continue to pretend that I did not know what they were up to? My sense of humiliation was indescribable. Not since my first months in England had I felt so isolated and so helpless. I had no vocabulary to describe what was happening to me. Had I known, I would have recognised it for the bullying that it was. But I didn't, and no one at our school ever talked about bullying. We were supposed to be genteel, nicely brought up girls who didn't do that sort of thing. I felt vulnerable, exposed and utterly alone.

In desperation, I looked for a way to assuage my misery and put an end to Zoe's crude and bigoted prose. I had no thought of revenge at first, but only of some release from the dread that filled me every time I went to school, one which my pride prevented me from voicing after that first admission to my sister and to Patricia. I knew I had to do something to stop the fear. It preyed obsessively on my mind – until I came up with a bold idea. It was something wholly out of character for me, but I felt better as soon as I had taken the decision and told Siham about it. She was amused but, unaware of the depth of my misery, she did not take me seriously. "Do you really think you can do it?" she asked.

"Yes", I said with a confidence I was far from feeling. "If I can get her alone. Without her group, I think she'll turn out to be a real coward." At school, I took Josie into my confidence, since I could not carry out my plan alone. She agreed without hesitation, for she did not like Zoe Steiner or her clique any more than I did. She said they made her feel inferior because she was non-Jewish.

We planned carefully. Now, I was one of the smallest and thinnest girls in the class, but, fortunately for my plan, Zoe was even smaller. She was a shrimp of a girl and with a frame as slight as mine. My revenge – for that's how I thought of it now – would take place, we decided, in the changing room, since this was the least inhabited place outside gym hours and where we were least likely to be disturbed. We would have to find a time when the room was empty and then I would lure Zoe there with some excuse. Having got her alone, I would do my business with her while Josie, who was tall and big, would stand guard, ready to repel intruders.

The moment came one afternoon when Josie reported that the changing room was empty. It was a free period when we could do individual study, and a few of us, including Zoe, were working at our desks. As soon as Josie gave the signal, I went up to Zoe and said in a low voice that I should like to speak to her about something important. Even approaching her made me quake with anxiety. My heart was pounding and my throat was dry, but I could see that she suspected nothing. The novelty of my approaching her in this way after weeks of avoidance and mutual hostility was too intriguing for her to resist. She gave me a disdainful look that revived my fast-fading resolve. However, she agreed and I told her to follow me.

When we reached the changing room, Josie was already there. My heart was now thudding against my chest and a wave of nausea swept through me. Had Zoe but known it. I was more afraid of her than she would ever have been of me. It was a gloomy December afternoon and the sky was already darkening in the windowpanes, but we did not turn on the lights. Zoe stepped in confidently ahead of me but before she could realise that something was wrong, Josie had shut and locked the door behind us and stood with her back to it.

Beginning to perspire, I decided to go on the attack immediately. "Now", I said breathlessly, poking Zoe in the chest, "you can tell me why you've been writing a book about me." I was trembling with all the pent up anger and pain that she had caused me.

Zoe's eyes darted from me to Josie. She had gone deathly pale. "I didn't write anything about you," she stammered. "It isn't about you."

Fear and rage made me hysterical. "You're a liar," I screamed. "I've seen it. I know you've been reading it to the others and you've all been laughing at me. Calling me a dirty Arab." Infuriatingly, my eyes filled with tears. I swallowed hard to stifle the sobs rising in my throat. Blindly, I pushed her against the wall and her body got wedged between the clothes hangers all covered with gym clothes which bounced forward and hid her face. Shaking uncontrollably, I dragged her forward by her hair and grabbed her arms. I did not know what to do with her, since I had never hit anyone before, and for an instant I wondered whether I should stop.

"OK, I did write it," she gasped. "It wasn't so wrong, anyway. Everyone knows what Arabs are like. Smelly, filthy Bedouin!" This taunt instantly banished my tears and filled me with a cold anger. I slapped her face hard. How droll we must have looked, two small girls locked in a noisy, ill-tempered fight. But though I had been the one to strike the blow, I felt like a wounded animal, cornered and lashing out in pain. The ferocity of my attack was not all aimed at this Zoe, but at all the other Zoes in my school for the way they had excluded me and picked on me; for their superior airs and their self-confidence; for the years of unacknowledged humiliation at their hands, and the deni-gration of my past and history which they never spelled out, but which I sensed and brooded on. I was back in the loneliness of that orphaned childhood which I suppose had never left me.

I cast about in my mind for the most hurtful, the most terrible thing I could say about Jews that could parallel the crudeness she had used to dismiss me and my family as "dirty Arabs". The words suddenly came tumbling out of my mouth. "Hitler should have finished the job!" I shouted. "He should have killed *all* of you!" I did not really mean this seriously or even realise the import of what I had said. Nor was it some sinister indication of a latent anti-Semitism. I said it as one might say, "I hope you die". In fact, I knew little about the Second

World War and never thought about Hitler. The plight of the Jews in Europe was not something which featured high on the list of Palestinian concerns. If my parents ever talked about the war, it was always in connection with the British role in Palestine, never about the events in Europe. But I had lived in Golders Green long enough to know that, for Jews, Nazism had been an unspeakable disaster and Hitler the worst possible anathema.

At this, Zoe, already terrified, seemed to collapse. I should have felt vindicated, but I didn't. It was as if the table had been turned and suddenly it was I who was the bully. She started to scream at the top of her voice. "Help! Help! They're killing me. Please someone, help!"

Feet were running along the corridor. Through the frosted glass of the door the blurred figures of teachers and pupils could be seen, banging their fists against it and rattling the door handle. "Open this door at once!" ordered one of the teachers. Josie put her back stolidly against the door, but as the commotion increased and more teachers appeared on the other side, she shook her head at me, as if to say, "the game's up". Zoe meanwhile had collapsed on the floor, shaking and crying hysterically. Josie moved back and unlocked the door. As the first of the teachers entered, followed by a crowd of staring girls, she quickly took in the scene, Zoe overcome and me standing over her, red and flustered.

"Right", she said to the two of us sternly. "Go down to Miss Leach at once! You're going to have some explaining to do."

At home, my family was triumphant. They had never seen Zoe and imagined her as some Zionist ogre who had insulted me and been soundly punished for it. I became their plucky Arab daughter who had struck a blow for Palestine – a replay of 1948 with a different ending. My mother was instantly on the telephone, telling the story to all our friends with embellishments of her own. I had become a heroine overnight. An Arab journalist picked up the story and published it in a

Jordan newspaper from where it reached our family in Tulkarm. "Did you hear how Ghada beat up the Jewish girl?" they said proudly to everyone in the town, and when we visited them many years later, people were eager to meet me. "Tell us how you gave the Jewish girl a hiding," they all said eagerly.

Siham thought it funny at first too, but then she became uneasy. "I hope there'll be no repercussions at school." When Patricia told her mother about it, she was full of sympathy. "Poor child, what a terrible ordeal," she said. "I wonder why your parents put up with it. They should have complained to the school. Steiner? If it's the family I'm thinking of, I know the father and he's a real schmuck." She said this, knowing nothing of my remarks about Hitler, which Patricia had thought prudent to withhold.

Meanwhile, Zoe Steiner was reported to be sick as a result of the incident between us. She did not come back to school for two weeks and her parents lodged vociferous complaints about me with Miss Leach. They demanded that I withdraw my remarks and apologise formally to Zoe for what I had done. I could not back down and so I refused. But Miss Leach arranged for a meeting between us in her office, at which the matter would be dealt with. I had no choice but to attend. When I went on the appointed day, I found a tearful, pouting Zoe already waiting for me, her eyes downcast, flanked by her mother and father. She avoided my gaze, but her parents both stared at me, as if I had been a wild animal in a zoo. Miss Leach gave a brief summary of events.

"Now, I have seen the story which Zoe had been writing about Ghada, and I think that she was very wrong to do it. It was a naughty provocation. But at the same time, Ghada was very wrong to express her feelings in the way she did."

"A little story is the same as my daughter being beaten black and blue?" queried Zoe's mother in disgust. Zoe snuffled and kept her eyes lowered to the ground.

Miss Leach ignored this. "So, I'm going to ask you, Ghada, to say you're sorry for what you said and did to Zoe."

"I won't!" I said defiantly. "She's got to say sorry first for what she wrote about me." Miss Leach tried again to much tut-tutting from Zoe's parents, but I held my ground. Zoe gave in. "I'm sorry about what I wrote about you," she mumbled, not looking me in the eye.

"And I'm sorry for what I said about Hitler," I responded, even then unaware of the enormity of it. I felt I had scored a little triumph by not apologising for the rest of what had happened. To have done otherwise would have obliterated my moment of self-assertion and condoned the injustice I had suffered. Zoe's parents were patently not satisfied, but they said nothing and contented themselves with giving me venomous glances. There was little more to say, but when they took themselves off with Zoe, they did so with a menacing air of "you haven't heard the last of this". Left alone with Miss Leach, I looked round at her anxiously, fearing her displeasure. But to my surprise and relief I saw a flicker of something like compassion in her eyes.[3]

Not surprisingly, I had a poor academic report at the end of term. Siham, who had been worried for months by my obvious unhappiness, now came to the conclusion that I must leave the school. My father, who was largely unaware of such matters and had left my welfare to her long ago, did not argue. The decision came as a relief: the prospect of returning in the new term for a second round of fighting with Zoe, which no doubt would be joined once she had her supporters around her again, filled me with dread. Since the decision over my departure was taken during the Christmas holidays, I had no opportunity to take my formal leave of Henrietta Barnett. But I left

---

[3] Zoe and I met again by chance in 1983. She was a dentist and I a practising GP. We fell upon each other and embraced like long lost friends. She invited me to her home (also in Golders Green) where she introduced me to her Orthodox Jewish husband. Over a kosher meal, we reminisced over that incident in our childhood and shook our heads at the passions we had both felt.

without regret and with only the most miserable of memories. Whether my abrupt departure made Zoe and her parents think that they had won I never found out. And in the joy of my impending release, as if from a prison, I did not much care.

So ended an important and turbulent chapter in my life. But I cannot say, looking back, that I was able to make coherent sense of it at the time, or that I could interpret the complex messages it was giving me. The Suez crisis had challenged too many of my assumptions about Jews, about myself and about England, and I was lost in a welter of raw feelings and gut reactions, like the pieces of a jigsaw puzzle which I could not fit together. Had I succeeded, it is unlikely I would have liked the pattern that emerged. At the age of sixteen I was not ready to abandon the illusions I had worked so hard to build that I might reconcile the incompatible and contradictory sides of my life.

It would require another decade and yet another major crisis for my personal edifice to finally crumble. But without my knowing it, in the aftermath of Suez the process had already begun.

Nine

Increasingly, the issues which the events of 1956 had laid open began to haunt me. Was I Arab or English or a hybrid, and was there such a thing? I saw the Arab in me personified in my mother while, after so many years, my surroundings had also produced an English girl. Whereas until then, the English side of me had comfortably dominated, the experience of Suez brought back a compelling Middle Eastern dimension which I could not set aside. Impinging on these was a third element, the Jews and Israel and the separate challenge they posed. But I was too absorbed by the dilemma of my two selves to find a place for that at the time. I began to experience an internal conflict which grew worse with my increasing exposure to British society. London in the late 1950s was at last emerging from the austerity of the postwar years and it was exciting to be young. Against this background, my mother's frozen adherence to a traditional Arab way of life and her refusal to adapt to her environment struck a thoroughly discordant note with me. I wanted to reject what she stood for and yet I felt the pull of it because it was a part of me too.

At the beginning of 1957, I put Henrietta Barnett behind me as if it had been a bad dream and moved to join Siham at the Northern Polytechnic. Suddenly I was no longer a schoolgirl and found myself mixing with boys in a cosmopolitan atmosphere, thanks to the large number of foreign students at the Polytechnic. I acquired a boyfriend briefly, a young English boy called Robert. We did no more than hold hands as we walked along the corridor, but it made me feel that I was really in the swing of things.

Somehow, I managed to overcome my resistance to the subjects I was studying and passed the examinations in the end. Numerous applications to medical schools – prompted by my father – yielded nothing but rejections, just as my sister had experienced. Each time this happened, my heart lifted as his sank. Just as it seemed I would not be studying medicine after all, I received a late acceptance from the University of Bristol. My father was overjoyed and I knew with resignation that, as an Arab daughter, I had no choice but to obey.

I castigated myself many times over the years for this supine acceptance of a destiny not of my choosing. Had I the courage, I would have firmly refused to enter medical school from the start and directed myself towards a career I preferred. But that would have risked my father's displeasure and, what was worse, I could have found myself alone outside the group. In the situation of isolation in which we lived, closely interdependent and cut off from the wider society, such a course would have been unthinkable. It would have lost me the support of the family without providing a substitute. In addition, defying my father in the context of our traditional Arab family was something I could not have contemplated. Despite all my intellectual pretensions to having adopted a liberal, non-authoritarian European paradigm, when it came to confronting my father or opposing his wishes, the cultural imperative prevailed.

Miserably, I prepared to go to Bristol in October 1958. My mother was unexpectedly sympathetic. She had once tried to point out to my father that I had a literary bent and was not cut out for medicine – as she said, "Look at her, she's either writing or telling stories the whole time" – but he had ignored her. "Never mind," she told me as I packed my case. "It's a good and honourable profession. You won't regret it, you'll see." Siham came with me to Bristol to help me settle in. We went up by train and then found our way to the lodgings which I had been assigned by the University accommodation office. Because I had been accepted at medical school so late, all the places in the university halls of residence were already allotted. However, there was a number of so-called university approved lodgings where students lived with a family, usually in twos or threes. It was to one of these that Siham and I were directed, a house in the Redland part of Bristol, within walking distance of the University. And it was here that I got my first real taste of English xenophobia.

The landlady was a portly, middle-aged woman called Mrs Briggs. She had a thin, insignificant husband and was clearly the power in the home. With me were two other women students, one studying to be a vet and the other taking languages. I shared a room with the latter, which was quite comforting, since it was what I was used to at home, and she and I got on reasonably well. Both girls were English, which made me conspicuous to Mrs Briggs. Siham told her that I had never been away from home and asked her to look after me. When she left, I felt desperately frightened and alone. I had never learned to be independent, partly because such qualities were not cultivated in a typical Arab family such as ours, and partly because of the legacy of my uprooted childhood. Leaving me to the tender mercies of Mrs Briggs was an unhappy decision in the circumstances.

She never lost an opportunity to refer to my foreignness. Often, when I came into the sitting room, she would break out into song. "Maybe it's because I'm a Londoner, that I love London town ... "

With her broad Bristol accent, she was anything but a Londoner. "I don't suppose you have anything like London where you come from?" she would remark with seeming innocence. At other times, she would ask if I had got used to the cold yet. "Have you ever seen snow before? It's really hot in your country, isn't it?" Clearly there was something inferior about a hot climate and anyone with no experience of cold temperatures was somehow substandard. When I told her that it often snowed during winter in Jerusalem, she looked at me in disbelief and with disapproval, as if I were trying to usurp some distinction reserved only for the English climate.

One evening, I came home late, which meant half past ten at night, in the company of a theology student I had got to know. We stopped by the gate and he kissed me. We lingered for a minute or two whispering and then he said a respectful good night. I let myself into the house, unaware that I was being watched. The next morning Mrs Briggs said she hoped I was not going to carry on outside the house as I had done the night before. "Only it upset Mrs Dickens opposite something rotten. She says to me, 'hot country, hot blood, my dear, that's what it is'." Then Mrs Briggs, giving me a knowing look, added, "I know you can't help it, but we all have to try and control ourselves."

My room-mate, who didn't like Mrs Briggs any more than I did, chiefly on account of her awful cooking, left at the end of the first term. I wanted to do the same but had nowhere to go. So Zandra, the veterinary student, and I stayed on until the summer. In that time we became good friends and decided to find our own accommodation. In the autumn, we moved into a small basement flat off the Whiteladies Road, which was dark and indescribably damp. But we hardly cared, since we were now free of Mrs Briggs, and our new landlady, a retired English nurse married to a Chinese, a most unusual combination in the overwhelmingly English Bristol of the time, left us alone. We had our own entrance at the front and the back, and a small overgrown garden for our use.

For the first time since I had come to Bristol I began to enjoy university life. My first year, spent completing a pre-medical course, was undemanding. I had a leisurely timetable and few lectures. Zandra and I kept house together, cleaned and shopped for food and cooked. She soon discovered that I ate no pig-meat and had never drunk alcohol. "Not even cider?" she asked, amazed. Such Muslim dietary traditions are commonplace in Britain today, but were wholly unfamiliar at the time. Someone like Zandra, reared in Norwich, would never have come across either the Muslim or the Jewish prohibition about pork. "You're not going on like that, are you?" she asked.

This struck a responsive chord in me. The truth was that my previously warm relationship with Islam had changed. My devotion to religious ritual, which had started during my time at the convent, had largely dissipated by the time I was sixteen. I had by then become enamoured of humanist philosophy and spent hours discussing God and religion with my Jewish friend, Leslie Benenson. But this was a form of intellectual conceit and neither of us connected it with everyday life. However, I continued to mull it over and by the age of eighteen felt ready to take a conscious decision about religion and the existence of God.

I decided that as there was no evidence for God's existence I could not logically believe in him and I was not bound by any religious system to which he was central. By extension, I could not accept any of the ceremonies and rituals which accompanied a belief in God, whether they belonged to Islam or any other faith. So I stopped praying and fasting. Nevertheless, the effects of my Islamic dietary conditioning regarding pig-meat and alcohol lingered.

The eating of pig-meat is totally prohibited by the Quran, and

Muslims are brought up to adhere to this injunction. The case of alcohol is slightly different. The Quran did not forbid its consumption in the same way, but only at the time of prayer. Since Muslims pray five times a day, this meant in effect a near-total ban. The Prophet followed up the Quranic dictum with a clear and absolute prohibition, since when the drinking of alcohol became forbidden to all Muslims. How far these laws were obeyed in practice depended on a number of factors. By and large, the prohibition on pig-meat was more strictly adhered to than that on alcohol. Many a Muslim who broke the ban on drinking nevertheless baulked at eating pig in any form. This was possibly because the aversion to the meat was constantly reinforced by references to the animals' unclean habits and omnivorous appetite. People who were considered ugly or dirty were frequently compared to pigs, reminiscent of such English sayings as "eating like a pig" or "making a pig of oneself". But whereas the latter expressions can be light-hearted and even a little humorous in the English context, in the Muslim case they are always censorious.

On the other hand, adherence to the prohibition on alcohol depended on such things as class, educational level, exposure to the West and gender. By and large, poor, uneducated people observed the ban faithfully and, conversely, the wealthy, sophisticated classes did not. Those who had studied in Europe and were exposed to western society also picked up the habit of drinking. And women in any of these categories were more likely to adhere to the ban. This was not only due to the fact that women in most societies tend to be more conservative, but also because of the position women occupy in the traditional Muslim family. A moral licence which these families permitted to the males was usually withheld from the females. Many a girl might grow up seeing her brothers drinking alcohol, making sexual liaisons and indulging in behaviour which would never be allowed her. My own family was essentially no different, for we all knew that Ziyad drank alcohol and went out regularly with girls. But Siham, and later I, had to keep any boyfriends we acquired secret. And neither of us was supposed to drink.

But now I found myself psychologically ready to break these taboos. I would embark on eating pig and drinking alcohol, but I did not look forward to the regime I had set myself with any relish; these were not to be pleasurable indulgences but deliberate acts emanating from the intellectual stance I had adopted about their significance. On Zandra's advice, I tried bacon first, found it tasty, and moved on to ham and finally pork, which I enjoyed least.

Next came alcohol. This proved more difficult, for I disliked the taste of every form of drink I was offered. Eventually, I settled for cider which I found tolerable. At least it meant that I could hold my own in the pub and thereby break another taboo. Pubs were a core English institution; every neighbourhood throughout Britain had them, but I had never gone into one before. There was a cultural horror at the idea of places whose sole *raison d'être* was to provide people with intoxicating liquor. My mother used a derogatory term for them, *khammara*, literally meaning "winery", but implying a place for drunkards. Even today, pubs excite feelings of revulsion amongst devout Muslims, who see them as temples of the forbidden.

The remaining taboo related to sex. Throughout my adolescence in London, I had conducted my excursions into the world of romance, such as they were, with the utmost secrecy. In this matter, my sister was no less vigilant than my parents. Although she herself had a boyfriend she judged me too young to do the same. And she had no hesitation in showing her feelings. One night, after I had been at the Polytechnic for a year, I went out one night with a group of new friends I had made; amongst them was a boy who had shown a marked interest in me. I knew it and was thrilled. When the others went home, he walked me to the tube station. But we dawdled along the way, holding hands and leaning against each other. When we reached the station, he put his arms round me and we kissed.

In the excitement, I had forgotten the time and saw to my horror that it was after ten o'clock and much later than I had intended. The train took a long time to arrive and by the time I got to Brent station it was just after eleven. I walked the short way home from the station panting with anxiety. As I drew up to the house, it was dark, and I thought with relief that everyone was already in bed. All I had to do was go in quietly and no one would be any the wiser. But as I turned my latchkey gently in the lock and pushed open the front door the hall light suddenly came on. There, standing before me in her nightdress, was Siham, an unmistakable look of wrath on her face. I started to say something, but she slapped me hard across the cheek. The blow caught the side of my ear and made me go temporarily deaf.

"Where have you been?" she said in a harsh whisper. "You said you'd be back at nine. I've been worried sick."

We went into the kitchen where we could speak without waking up our parents. I stammered something about the tube being late. But she was having none of it. "It's that boy, isn't it?" she said balefully. "I've seen you giggling with him. Now, understand that we don't want any of that business. I don't mind you having mixed friends, that's all right. But not this sort of thing."

I could have asked what she meant by "this sort of thing" and what she thought I had been up to, but of course I understood her in the same implicit way in which I understood my parents' moral restrictions. No one in the family had ever said, "You cannot go out with boys, even if you just hold hands, because you might end up having sexual intercourse with them. And that is the worst thing imaginable for any unmarried daughter of ours." But that is what they meant and I instinctively knew it. Siham's admonition was only in line with this attitude, but I was shocked and hurt. I had expected her to understand

my adolescent romantic explorations and not see them as some pre-
lude to a life of promiscuity. My cheeks smarted with the beating and
the humiliation, and I knew that so long as I remained in London, I
would have to lie and dissemble in front of her just as I did with my
parents.

It was the only realistic policy I could think of at the time. But its
effects on my sexual development were far-reaching. Because in
families such as mine the subject was hedged about with secrecy, no
one taught me how to conduct myself with men. I had no experience
or guidance to help me navigate sexual relationships and developed no
psychological antennae with which to pick up danger signals. Thanks
to my parents' fears for my chastity, I ended up more vulnerable to
the very thing they feared than if they had prepared me for it honestly
and openly from the beginning.

However, I was unaware of these things as I sat in Bristol happily
alone and far away from what I considered to be my family's stifling
prohibitions and constraints. And I was determined to tackle this issue
just as I had the others. Of course, it would not be so easy, since I
could not simply pick up a boy as easily as I had picked up a glass of
cider. I went out a couple of times with the theology student, once to
the pub and once to his hall of residence where he showed me the
textbooks he would be reading for his course. But he was by way of an
experiment and I went on hoping someone more exciting would turn
up.

In those days, girls were expected to be passive, waiting for the call
of the "right man"; the knight on the white steed who would storm
into our lives and transform us forever. To have approached a man
first or shown interest in him before he himself had made advances
was considered fast or even tarty. So Zandra and I shyly put ourselves
about, hoping to be noticed.

To my breathless excitement, someone took the bait at last. The young man who asked me out was a third-year medical student, which put him into a desirably senior and sophisticated category. I remember that he was dashing with a slim, lithe body and striking blue eyes, and I thought him very attractive. He invited me to his flat for dinner, saying he was a good cook and did I like spaghetti? He said he had three flatmates, but they were all going to be out that evening. I was madly flattered, dying to accept but nervous to go because we would be alone in his flat, and I wondered what that would mean. Of course I had no idea how to handle such situations and did not want to ask for advice, since it would reveal the true extent of my inexperience. My dilemma was simple: if I went, might he think me cheap and easy for agreeing to be alone with him the first time he had ever asked me out, and if I didn't, would he ever contact me again? I decided that what I needed was some ploy which would permit me to accept his invitation but put a brake on any "intimacy" during the evening.

So I remembered my knitting. In my last year in London, Siham had taught me to knit and although my skills never amounted to much, I would sporadically have spurts of enthusiasm when I embarked on making a jumper or a scarf, more often than not left unfinished. When Zandra and I moved into our flat I started knitting again, this time to make a cardigan. I usually kept my knitting in a beige linen bag and as I looked at it, with its bulges and needles sticking out at the top, it struck a note of such homeliness that I felt it would surely dispel the hottest ardour.

On the appointed evening I dressed as well as I could, which was not easy since my clothes were drab and unexciting. This too was a legacy of my conservative upbringing, where the power of dress to seduce men was well recognized, and exposing the body as required by fashion was taboo. It was not that my mother covered herself or us in the manner so commonly seen amongst Muslim women today, but we had a strong awareness that certain parts of the body were private and must never be displayed. The colour black was regarded as especially dangerous, a view not confined to my family. In my fourth undergraduate year, I recall being taught by one of our senior gynaecologists that women patients dressed in black underwear were usually up to no good. "With that sort of woman," he would say darkly, "you can expect anything."

When Derek, as was his name, came to pick me up, I made sure that I had tucked my knitting into my bag. It was a short walk to his house, a large Edwardian property on several floors, all let to students. The flat he lived in was on the first floor, with spacious rooms and large windows. The sitting room he showed me into was inordinately cluttered and untidy. He sat me on the sofa and offered me a drink. He told me he had prepared everything in the kitchen beforehand and I must say as soon as I was hungry, because it wouldn't take a second to cook our meal. All the while I imagined he was eyeing me with a mischievous smile.

No sooner had he gone to get the drink than I quickly took out my knitting, reasoning that if I introduced a prosaic tone early on in the evening it would serve to halt any undesirable advances. There was no doubt about its effect. When Derek came back, he stopped dead in his tracks and stared at me knitting placidly on the sofa. His flatmates were likewise mesmerised. As they came in, one after another, and he introduced them, they looked from me to him with ill-disguised astonishment. As they quickly excused themselves, I heard them burst out laughing on the stairs.

Zandra too burst out laughing when I told her. "I can't believe you did such a thing," she said. "How could you be such an idiot?" I felt stupid and gauche and, needless to say, the affair with Derek went no further. The incident affected me deeply, the more so when I saw others of my peers going about confidently with boys and making what appeared to be easy, unflustered relationships. I tried my luck again, first with a student reading English and then with another who was not at the university at all and whom I met in a pub. Each of these also ended in disappointment and a feeling that it was due to some failing of mine.

I began to look back with resentment on the constrained upbringing and inhibited childhood which had thus disabled me. Until then, I had accepted the uncomfortable, joyless environment of my home in London with resigned equanimity. Privately, I used to call my parents "the Anti-Life League", but more by way of a joke than in anger. Otherwise, I scarcely ever questioned their behaviour towards us, which I took to be as natural to them as the colour of their hair or the sound of their voice. But now, away from home and trying to adapt to the norms of a new society, I began to feel differently. I dwelled on the assumptions with which I had been reared and found them severely wanting. I could not accept my mother's confined traditional thinking or my father's conservatism. Siham's watchfulness over my morals, *in loco parentis*, was no better.

The taboos about sex, food and drink I had been taught were all part of what I saw as a war on the body. Those who advocated such absurd prohibitions were crass and myopic. Such life as we are given is short, I reflected; to hem it all about with rules and strictures, to denude it of its fleeting pleasures by denial and abstinence struck me as the most oppressive folly. So extreme were my feelings that I wanted to dissociate myself completely from what my family stood for. I could see no possible compromise between their position and mine. And since I put it all down to their Arabness, I rejected that too and all Arabs along with them. But such radical thoughts also frightened me. I had a sense of disloyalty and a yearning to be back in the family fold, as if they had divined my thoughts and already expelled me.

During my first term at university, I used to feel homesick and went to London as often as I could. I missed Siham and my mother's cooking and the familiarity of the neighbourhood. I still saw Patricia and her family whenever I went and occasionally Leslie, who was now at art school. But as the year progressed, and I became more engrossed in my new life, my visits lessened. When I went back for Easter I felt that I had grown distant from the others. Siham complained that I had changed – "not as docile as you were," she said. Ziyad had come down from Glasgow at the same time and I wondered whether he had changed too. But he was apparently the same as before, fun loving, carefree and always out with his friends. When the long summer vacation arrived, I wondered how I would be able to stand the long months at home.

Throughout this time, my mother, happily unconscious of my dawning doubts about her, my father and our origins, behaved in a way almost designed to increase my disaffection. Every time I came back from Bristol she would berate me for being late.

"Where have you been?" she would demand at the front door before I had even entered the house. "I've been standing at that window this past hour, looking up and down the road for you."

"For God's sake," I would retort, "why can't you ever once say, 'Hallo, how nice to see you?' "

She would then grumble at me and mutter something to the effect that I had changed since I left home. "We never should have let you go so far away. What an affectionate child you were. We used to say, the others will all go on their way, but not this one, she'll always be at our side. And now look at you."

Such pronouncements, which she made often in different forms, had the unfailing result of making me feel guilty, as if I had uniquely let her down and was the sole cause of her unhappiness. When her accusations enraged me, Siham would say, "Don't take any notice, she always tries it on. You know what she's like."

Much of her anxiety derived from her impending fear of being all alone in the house. Ziyad was still away in Glasgow and now Siham was preparing to leave. She had completed her chemistry degree and had decided to return to the Arab world. This was no surprise, since she had intimated as much ever since the Suez war. But her resolve hardened after the union between Egypt and Syria took place in 1958. This "United Arab Republic", as it was named, with Nasser as its first president, was a remarkable event in the Arab world. For two Arab countries to come together in an area previously so divided, was a momentous happening. The fact that it had been instigated by the Arabs themselves and not in accordance with imperialist wishes had reversed a historical trend. But the Union also signified the first step towards the fulfilment of a dream: the beginning of an age of Arab unity, ushered in by Egypt's mighty, charismatic leader to whom everyone looked for the attainment of this cherished ideal.

On assuming the presidency, Nasser declared that the Union would work to create an all-embracing Arab unity to include the people of every Arab country and that it would strive to free the Arab nation from imperialism and its agents. This touched a wildly responsive note amongst the people of the whole Arab world (to the alarm of pro-Western Arab governments). When he made his first visit to Damascus after the Union had been declared, huge crowds surged out to greet him choking the streets and climbing onto the rooftops. When my uncle Abu Salma, on his way to a political conference, visited us briefly in the summer of 1958, he gave a graphic description of this spectacle.

To see him in London was a strange experience. He belonged to the past, which I had put away with the other memories of childhood in a far-away place where I never went. We had last seen him in Damascus on that fateful day of our departure for London in September 1949. How distant that time seemed now; another century, another planet. Abu Salma had lost his hair and wore unbecoming black-framed glasses. He told me I was pretty in that indulgent, flirtatious way I chiefly remembered him for. But we drew no closer. I was not totally at ease with him, nor he with me and it made me sad; he belonged to another world and so now did I.

Hearing him talk about Nasser, Siham was thrilled and uplifted. She wanted to be part of the fast-moving developments in the Middle East. "For the first time, I've really begun to feel that we stand a chance of beating Israel," she said excitedly. "Disunited as we were, we could never have done it." Nasser himself nurtured such sentiments by often recalling that glorious time in Arab history when Saladin drove out the crusaders from Palestine. If he implied by that an identity between him and the great conqueror, he also intimated that, just as it had taken a hundred years to expel the crusaders from Jerusalem, so it would be a long struggle now with Israel. But few Arabs heeded this implicit warning, preferring to see him as an instant second Saladin who would deliver the Arab world from its foreign shackles.

By contrast in Britain, where Harold Macmillan was now Prime Minister, distrust of Nasser was as strong as ever. Far from regarding him as Saladin, Macmillan saw him only as a second Hitler "in a fez". "Do you wonder", said Siham, "that I want to leave this country? I know that however long I live here, I will never be accepted, I will never belong." She determined to go to Syria, since it was part of the new Union and a country she had regarded as home ever since our stay there in 1948.

When she announced to the family that she had arranged to go and live at our uncle Abu Salma's house in Damascus and find a job there, neither of our parents agreed to her leaving. "Please don't go without us," begged our mother. "We came here together and we should leave together. Wait until Ghada finishes her studies and then we can all leave."

Freezing on an outing to Brighton in 1959 (top), and with Siham on a trip to Oxford in 1960

"Your mother is right," said our father. "It's not right for you to break ranks like this. We should stay together."

But Siham shook her head. With a note of prescient certainty in her voice, she said, "No, I'm not waiting for you. Whatever you say, I don't think you'll ever leave this country."

This angered our father so much that he warned her he would not pay for her travel ticket. But Siham did not care. She got herself a job at the BBC doing freelance work and saved up the money for her ticket. I marvelled at her determination, her ability to defy our father in contrast to my own craven incapacity to do the same. But she had an unshakable conviction that there was no future for her outside the Arab world.

She left in July 1959 just as I started my summer holidays. I never really believed she would do it until the final moment. On that last day in London, we went to see her off at Victoria station where she was taking the train to Genoa and from there the boat to Beirut. Ziyad was doing a holiday job in Genoa as part of his engineering course and she was to see him there. She took one suitcase with her and asked us to send on her trunk with her books and other clothes in the event of her not returning within six months. I hoped wildly that she would weaken and come back. Six months was not a long time, after all. We went back sadly to the house, my mother weeping and my father silent.

I went up to the bedroom we had shared for so many years and wept inconsolably. I could not explain Siham's departure in spite of my awareness of her Arab sentiments and of the alienation in Britain she had often expressed. All I could feel was that she had callously abandoned me. We had been so close, had lived through so many traumas together; she should have waited for me, as I had always believed she would, to share that final experience of returning to the Arab world. But she had chosen to undertake it without me. I had a sense of emotional, but also intellectual, betrayal of the Western acculturation that we had both experienced.

Although I had absorbed Western values much more deeply than Siham I knew that England's special culture, its liberalism, its intellectual values and sophistication had affected her too; they had opened new horizons for her and introduced her to thoughts and ideas she could never have had in the country for which she was now so eagerly heading. To throw away the gains of all that precious experience for the sake of embracing Syria's narrow, conservative society in its place struck me as reckless, even immoral. I passionately deplored what she had done and was overwhelmed with grief and disappointment. Echoes of my parting from Fatima came back, painfully mingled with the fear of uncertainty. Siham had been there all my life, close behind me. Without her now I was truly alone and would have to face in solitude the complexities of my future life.

After Siham's departure, I felt increasingly alienated from my parents and their friends, as if they existed on another planet, utterly incongruous with me and the England I was now part of. I was moving on, changing and developing, while they stood still, frozen in a sterile and fossilised world. Such thoughts were not new to me; I had felt estranged from my background before, but never with such force. It was as if the dichotomy of cultures which had tormented me was beginning to find a resolution. Between the newly discovered freedoms of Bristol and the stifling discomfort of home, there was scarcely any contest, and I was unconsciously glad of it, for it helped ease my transition from my Arab self into my English one. Siham's departure and Zandra's appearance in my life added the final touches. While I was growing up and trying to deal with the new society around me, Siham had acted as the mediator through which I received Arab culture; in a sense, she interpreted for me what would otherwise have become increasingly alien and exotic. Because she understood the

Arab world and yet was familiar with Britain she enabled me to make contact with Arab norms in a language I could understand – unlike my mother, whose uncompromising style and attitudes made no allowance for my evolving Anglicisation. With Siham's departure, I felt that the last link with my Arab origins had gone.

At the same time, I had forged a close friendship with Zandra who, in a way, replaced my sister. By strange coincidence she was as thoroughly English as Siham had been Arab. She was one of four daughters and I met them all during the winter holidays when Zandra invited me to spend Christmas Day with them. My family of course did not celebrate Christmas; in fact my mother noted it chiefly because it upset her usual routine. When, one Christmas Eve, our milkman advised her to make an extra milk order, as he wouldn't be back for a couple of days, she looked at him in some surprise and said, "Why you no come?" He laughed and said, "Christmas. You know? Heard of Christmas?" "To hell with you and your Christmas!" she muttered back in Arabic. Misunderstanding her, he said cheerily, "Thank you, missus. And the same to you too. Happy Christmas!"

I was glad to accept Zandra's invitation, as this was the first English Christmas I would experience, and indeed the first English family I would get to know. I found everything about that holiday enchanting. Her family lived in a large terraced house on the edge of Norwich. I arrived on Christmas Eve and found Zandra's family which included her aunts and uncles, her grandmother, her cousins and all her sisters, congregated in the house. They were all eating mince pies, still oven warm, and drinking sweet sherry.

There was a large decorated Christmas tree in the sitting room, all lit up, with a heap of wrapped presents at its base and looking like the trees I saw on pretty Christmas cards. That night, we sat up late with Zandra's sisters and cousins eating sweets and nuts and mince pies, and the next day when I got up they were already making

Christmas lunch. Zandra's mother had been up early to put the turkey into the oven and Zandra was now preparing the Brussels sprouts.

I helped her sisters lay the table and when we sat down to lunch, there were fourteen of us. After the turkey, Zandra's mother brought in the Christmas pudding, also homemade. It was decorated with holly leaves and Zandra's uncle splashed it generously with brandy and then set it alight. A bluish flame sprang up all over it but, to my amazement, did not burn it. As they gave me my helping, Zandra's father told me to look out for the sixpence. I learned that a coin, a sixpence or a threepence, was always embedded in the pudding and whoever found it could expect good luck.

There was nothing exceptional about any of this. All over England many English families were celebrating Christmas in exactly the same way. Zandra's home was ordinary and her family's means modest; there was nothing special about their circumstances. But to me, that Christmas was magical. It seemed that here at last I had discovered what it meant to be English, and I wanted to be part of it. I wondered what they made of me, but everyone treated me as if I had been one of the family. I found this odd but Zandra saw it as entirely natural, although she jokingly used to refer to me as "that Arab"; if we were walking along the road and I dropped litter onto the ground, she would pull me up sharply. "Here," she would say, "pick that up. You're in England now!"

I knew that these were affectionate rebukes, but one day, when she came home and called out, "Rada!" – as she pronounced my name – "Rada! Where's that Arab got to?" I remarked, "You're right, I am an Arab."

She looked at me in astonishment. "What do you mean?" she demanded.

"Simply that it's true, I'm not English."

"Don't be so silly," she answered briskly. "You're just a dark-skinned English girl, that's what you are."

I was pleased to hear this and yet uneasy. I knew that her description did not encapsulate the whole of me, although I could not have said exactly what did. However, for the time being, I was not going to argue. To be taken at face value for English was good enough.

∽◦∾

In the second year at medical school, I finally came together with all the students who would form our group until we qualified.[1] There were sixty of us, of whom only ten were girls. This gender disparity was quite usual for the time, and only one English medical school, the Royal Free in London, operated an admissions policy favourable to women. Of the sixty students there was a handful of foreigners, including one Palestinian like me. He and I became friends, but for me, at least, it was not on the basis of our common origins.

I had by then become remote from all of that. This harmonised with the prevailing English ignorance about Palestine, which was now even more total than it had been during my schooldays. Knowing this, I would hesitate when people asked me where I came from, and then I would answer awkwardly, "Somewhere in the Middle East". At the same time, Israel was as solidly established in the popular mind as if it had always existed. But the whole subject seemed irrelevant in Bristol, where I hardly came across a single Jew. None of my fellow medical students was Jewish and, with the exception of Professor Yoffey, our head of Anatomy, none of our teachers either.

---

[1] It was more usual for students of medicine to start the course at this so-called second MB stage. I was amongst a small minority who had done a first MB year beforehand.

In any case, I had no interest in Middle Eastern events and I generally shunned Arab company. There was an international students' society at the university which included a number of Arabs. I would come across them at the student refectory and some of them would try to talk to me. But I treated them all with such disdain that it was a brave man indeed who would approach me again. Once, when one of them, an Egyptian doctor who was visiting the medical school, asked me if I were fasting, I looked at him as if he had come from Mars.

"Well it is Ramadan," he stammered, seeing my expression, "I just thought . . . " he trailed off. "No, I'm not," I said witheringly. What outraged me was his assumption of a common bond between us, as if I, with my English consciousness, could be equated with a simple Arab like him. How could he be unaware of the difference between us and just see me as yet another dreary Muslim like him? Following this exchange, he did not try to speak to me again.

I threw myself into university life eagerly. Britain on the threshold of the 1960s was an exciting place to be. The Prime Minister's famous slogan, "You've never had it so good", was a reality. The economy was booming and the country was enjoying a prosperity it had not known since the end of the war. Pop music had exploded onto the scene more so than even in the rock and roll craze of the late 1950s that had seized my brother. We raved about the Beatles when they appeared in 1962. I hummed their tunes and sang their songs like any other young English person. I had no sense of myself as being any different and wanted to emulate my English peers in every detail. When Zandra introduced me to the records of Frank Sinatra and Ella Fitzgerald, singers of a much earlier era, I took to them with the same undiscriminating eagerness.

Many of the girls we knew were sleeping with their boyfriends, not waiting until they were "going steady" or married. Some were even "sleeping around", which in the early 1960s meant little more than having two boyfriends. Zandra and I thought we could identify the girls who engaged in this. Nearly all of them were Arts students and they had a certain "promiscuous" look – long, straight hair, heavily made-up eyes, pale lips and a jaded expression. They all smoked cigarettes and drank black coffee. Despite my bold determination to abandon the sexual taboos of my upbringing, I still found this behaviour rather shocking, but would have died rather than admit it. Furthermore, Zandra and I had both started smoking ourselves; for me this had begun merely as a desire to look sophisticated at parties. I would puff inexpertly at my cigarette, hoping I looked exciting and mature. After a few months, the puffing gave way to proper inhalation and I became as hooked on smoking as anyone else.

Clothes and fashion now became more exciting. We kept up with fashion by progressively shortening the hems of our skirts. I bought impossibly pointed high-heeled shoes, not caring how I tottered about in them. I grew my hair so as to wear it in the fashionable beehive style like the other girls. I backcombed it so that it stood in a high dome above my head with the ends flicked inwards or outwards at chin level. I kept all this in place with a heavy dose of lacquer which made my hair feel like straw.

With the miniskirts came the new nylon tights. For a young woman like me, released from the constraints of a strait-laced upbringing, no more exhiliarating attire could be imagined. Suspender belts and stockings became a thing of the past. No more struggling to hook the suspender belt at the back, or pushing the stocking top through its buckles at the thighs, or with the chilly draughts that blew up one's skirt and straight through one's underwear. No need to worry about the seams at the back of one's stockings staying in the centre and not swivelling to the side as mine always did. Wearing tights was not only warmer but also made it possible for skirts to ride up high over the thighs without this looking brazen. I could now display my legs without a twinge of embarrassment.

Did I wonder then what a Muslim Arab girl with a conservative upbringing like me was doing in a skimpy miniskirt and heavy make-up? And, if we had stayed in Palestine, would I have had such licence? If I wondered this, then it was so far beneath the level of consciousness that I was unaware of it. For, at the time, I truly believed myself to be a "dark-skinned English girl".

Meanwhile at home – a place that was beginning to hold less and less reality for me – Ziyad had returned from Scotland and found himself a job with a firm of consulting engineers. He had graduated in the summer, though, no one from the family attended his graduation ceremony. "Scotland?" my mother had said. "That's like going to the ends of the earth." But she was much relieved by his return to live at home once more; she had been lonely since Siham left.

But she had also become involved with the new Palestinian neighbours who had moved in at the bottom of our road. Whenever I went to London, I would find her happily engrossed in their affairs and living a life ever more remote from the reality of her presence in Britain. They were an unmarried couple with a complicated, unhappy relationship. The man, who was called Jiryis, originally came from Haifa. When the city fell in 1948, he fled to Cyprus where many Palestinians went at the beginning of the exile. In 1959, he gained a position at the BBC Arabic Service in London. An amusing, witty man, he and my father had known each other briefly in Palestine and, on the basis of that acquaintance, he had rented the top floor flat of the house in our road.

Some short time afterwards, Sophie, another Palestinian, rented a room in the street round the corner from him. Gossip had it that she had been in love with him for years and had pursued him on all his wanderings. At one point in Cyprus, they had lived together as man and wife, something unheard of, even amongst Christian Palestinians like them. But in the anonymity of exile, it passed relatively unnoticed – not of course amongst her family or those who might have been her suitors. She could be said to have sacrificed her reputation for his sake and with it any hope of a decent marriage. And yet, Jiryis did not marry her in all the years they lived together, and when he got his job at the BBC, he left her behind and came to London. But, as in the past, he did not escape for long and she soon followed.

Their relationship was stormy, and my mother, who had become a friend to both, was often drawn in to arbitrate. Christian Palestinian friends like Fuad and Adib Khoury and his wife also became involved. In no time, they had formed a small, close-knit group who got together regularly over Sunday lunch, invariably cooked by Sophie. It was rumoured that Jiryis provided the money and she did the work, but he was no more committed to making an honest woman of her than he had been before.

"What a silly woman," said my mother, "ruining her life for a man like that. She could have lived with her younger sister, Marie, and kept her self-respect."

"Did you suggest it to her?" inquired my father, who found the story more engrossing than shocking.

"Of course I did. Do you think she wants to listen?" snorted my mother.

"Poor woman," said my father, "she's given up so much for him, she might as well stay where she is."

My mother agreed. In fact, the arrangement was a godsend to her, for it recreated for her something of the neighbourly atmosphere she had known in Palestine. All she had to do now was walk a little way down the road and simply ring the doorbell of Jiryis's flat, where Sophie was usually also to be found. "Come up and have a coffee," they would call out, and my mother would join them for a friendly gossip, just as had happened in Palestine. But things were not always congenial. It frequently happened that the members of Jiryis's group fell out with each other, usually over something trivial. These quarrels could become quite heated and then they would stop talking to each other for days or even weeks.

A particularly bitter squabble broke out one day over the matter of Adib Khoury's father-in-law. The Khourys and Fuad were due to have their customary Sunday lunch at Jiryis's flat. Sophie had been cooking all morning, when Adib telephoned to say that they had received news of his father-in-law's death in Haifa. Jiryis offered him his condolences but omitted to speak to Adib's wife. Sophie later spoke to her, to find her cold and distant. Adib followed suit and all relations were abruptly terminated.

"What on earth is wrong, Adib?" asked Fuad, who had been deputed by Jiryis to find out the reason for this *froideur*. "Jiryis has no respect for my wife," responded the other. "He could not even extend her the common courtesy of offering her his condolences in person. It's an insult. He's no friend of ours."

"Come on," said Fuad, wanting to mollify him, "don't take it so seriously. After all, her father was an old man."

"What?" Adib now turned his wrath on Fuad. "You too want to insult my wife? Well, you're no friend either!"

Fortunately, they all remained friends with my mother as she was seen to be a neutral figure, firmly outside the fray. Whenever I visited London, I made sure always to find out what was going on before I talked to any of them, since too warm a commendation of the one who had offended was liable to annoy the rest. "Tell me," I'd say to my mother, "what's the state of play down the road?" And she would laugh and put me in the picture. For my father, who was now busy compiling his first English-Arabic dictionary, her daily bulletins about the state of play provided a relaxing break.

An outsider would have found himself baffled by these quarrels. He would not have known that they were mere accentuations of tendencies characteristic of Arab society. Traditionally, when two parties fell out, everyone rallied round to bring them back together, and frequently what had been the bitterest hostility would turn into the warmest amity in the twinkling of an eye. The difference here was that there was no larger social group to conciliate the parties, and hence disagreements tended to persist and rankle to the point of acrimony.

Siham and I corresponded. Initially, she had missed London more keenly than she had expected. She wrote that she wished she could listen to "The Archers" again or read *The Observer* on Sundays or drink afternoon tea. She missed going to concerts at the Festival Hall, listening to the Third Programme, and even visiting our local library. I wondered about all the other things she had experienced in London that she never mentioned, the freedom she had enjoyed here as a woman, the boyfriend she had known, the independence she had exercised. Our parents were not paragons of liberalism, but they had interfered little in her life by comparison to the stifling restrictions which would be placed on her as a woman in Damascus. Not surprisingly, it took her nearly two years to settle down there. She found work as a chemist in the public laboratory service and eventually started to describe herself as happy at our uncle's house where she was closely in touch with the rest of our family in Damascus.

When she first arrived, she also went to see our relatives in Tulkarm. Our grandmother had died in 1953, leaving our aunt Zubeida and our father's twin brother Hussein and his family in the house. Zuhair and Aziza had left for Kuwait, where they were both working in the government education system. The oil economy had taken off in Kuwait and the native Kuwaitis, whose training was unequal to the demands of their rapidly expanding economy, needed expertise of all kinds. Thousands of impoverished Arabs flocked there, many Palestinians amongst them, to make a living in the newly affluent state. It was a grim place to be in those early days, without any of the modern amenities which were to come later; only those in dire economic need were prepared to tolerate its pitiless summers and unwholesome, humid air. Zuhair tried to tempt Siham to join them, since her qualifications made her eligible for a senior, lucrative position. But she declined vehemently. "I want to be in a place where I can belong," she said. "That's why I came back. Where on earth does Kuwait fit into all that?"

No one in Tulkarm spoke of Israel. They seemed unaware of its existence, and the only time they saw Israelis – or Jews, as they still called them – was on the trains which passed along the old Hijaz railway taken over by Israel in 1948. Since this railway now formed

My cousins Zuhair and Aziza in the early 1950s

the border between the West Bank and Israel, it was only the people working in the fields in that area who saw the trains. Life seemed otherwise normal, our uncles and aunts concerned with everyday matters. Before leaving, Siham went to visit Jerusalem.

Only the Old City and its immediate environs remained in Arab hands. She went up to Sheikh Jarrah, which had been the place of our old school, and as she tried to walk there, found herself in the vicinity of a line of rubble and barbed wire with heavily armed soldiers on either side of it. This was the so-called Mandelbaum Gate which separated the two halves of Jerusalem, the eastern part under Jordanian rule and the western part occupied by Israel. Fearlessly, she went right up to the partition but was ordered back sharply by the Jordanian soldiers. The Israelis, meanwhile, had turned and were staring in her direction. "But I used to live on the other side," she protested, "I just want to visit, that's all." "Get back! We don't want any trouble," shouted the soldier.

I remember that I felt nothing when she wrote to me about this incident. It brought back no memories and no emotion. When I translated the letter to my mother, she sighed and said, "May God curse the Jews for what they have done." It was no less than I would have expected her to say, for I had grown up with the fact that every mention of Palestine, the Jews or Israel was unfailingly associated in our home with some mournful or angry pronouncement. Remote as I now was from all of that, I was untroubled by any of the same emotions and could not wait to return and resume my life in Bristol.

Ten

"I say! Anyone fancy my body?" called out one of my fellow medical students, laughing raucously, and one of the girls answered, "Anyone interested in my vagina?" This repartee took place in the dissecting room and was intended to shock those listening. Each cadaver was usually shared between four of us, and students were on the lookout for people to complete the numbers. As some of the bodies were male and some female, when it came to "the organs of generation" it was necessary for those working on the body of one sex to change over to the other. I did not find my colleagues' humour amusing and in fact thought little of any of their other attributes.

This was as much to do with my rejection of the medical training I was being forced to undergo as it was to do with any specific dislike of my colleagues. I found the boys almost uniformly brash, crude and uncultivated. There was a masculine culture in English medical schools at the time which encouraged beer drinking, football and the lascivious pursuit of nurses. By contrast, girl students were considered dreary bluestocking figures, boring swots who could be relied on to take lecture notes which the boys, sleeping off their hangovers, would use afterwards. Rarely would any of the male students dream of taking a sexual interest in their female colleagues.

This culture flourished at Bristol. It was strongly nurtured by our teachers, nearly all male, who joked with the boys, but were uncomfortable with us females. Not everyone was happy with our teachers and I managed to form a small number of friends amongst my colleagues. These were virtually all foreigners, Zarin Khan, a Pakistani, Subhi Zabaneh, the Palestinian, and Cleeve Mathews, who was South African. I had some friends amongst the girls as well, but, having spent most of my life until then in female company, I was less interested in them.

No one in the year designated us as foreigners. I recall no awareness at that time of such ethnic differences. We had one student from Africa and another from Ceylon (as it was known then), both of them extremely black. But, as far as I could see, there was no prejudice against either of them on that basis. My English colleagues put down differences they saw in me to my being "a sophisticated Londoner", and none of them had any idea that I spoke Arabic. As for Subhi, who had come over to England from Jordan where his family had lived since 1948, they found him simply confusing. This was mainly due to the fact that he was a Christian, and no one seemed aware that there were such people as Arab Christians. This used to annoy me. "You don't think Jesus Christ was English, do you?" I would say, suspecting that many people secretly did. As a result, no one knew how to place Subhi, and so he became an honorary Englishman with foreign overtones.

On the periphery of this circle was a student called John Thornley. He was older than the rest of us as he had joined the army after doing National Service. The army paid for his education and gave him a salary, in return for which he would have to serve in the army's

My class at medical school in Bristol (I am roughly centre second row from front; John Thornley is far left on the same row)

medical corps after he qualified. His finances were a good deal better than those of the rest of us; he had a car and was always smartly dressed. At first, I thought little about him beyond noting his dark, brooding good looks. Cleeve once said he was like Heathcliff in *Wuthering Heights*. With his brown eyes and dark hair, it was difficult to believe that he was English.

And yet, he could not have been more so, the son of a farming family who lived on the edge of Bath. He was a quiet and serious student and we regarded him as somewhat aloof. On the face of it, he and I could not have been more different. I was as lively and talkative as he was taciturn and we had no interests in common. His friends were amongst what I called the uninteresting set in our year. And yet, when he began to pay me considerable attention, I was flattered and also strongly attracted, as he was the handsomest and maturest student in the class.

The fact that John looked foreign and could have passed for an Arab even, but was neither, was crucially important to me. For at that time, I could no more have had a sexual liaison with an Arab than flown to the moon. The thought of any form of intimacy between me and such a man was unbearable. Living in London with my family where the opportunity for sexual adventure was limited, I had remained comfortably unaware of this idiosyncrasy. But now in Bristol, where I was free to experiment, it became noticeable.

I realised that for me, all Arab men were like my father; if any made advances to me, it would be like an invitation to have sex with him. It was this which lay at the root of my revulsion for, and my rejection of, Arabs as sexual partners. This confusion was perhaps not surprising; for, growing up in a family which had been isolated from Arab society for years, the only representatives of the Arab male sex I was close to during my adolescence were my father and my brother. As my strict upbringing prohibited me from mixing with non-Arab men, my father became the only model I had when I tried as a teenager to visualise Arabs as husbands or lovers. It was therefore not surprising that I viewed all Arab men as dangerous and forbidden, and even the thought of such relationships made me shudder.

Back in London, my Jewish friend Patricia had become engaged to a young man called Melvyn, a physicist with a promising career – "a nice Jewish boy", as her mother inevitably said. She had feared that Patricia might not make it. "How you're going to get a husband when you can't keep a kosher kitchen, I'll never know," she used to grumble. He struck me as intelligent and smart, but rather cold and incompatible with Patricia's vivacity and warmth. I was not sure why she wanted to marry him, and when I voiced my doubts to her parents on one of my visits to London, her mother said, "A girl's got to get married in the end. And pray God you will too. Don't leave it too long or you'll go *meshuggana*, like all those spinsters." "Rubbish!" said Patricia's father, kissing me on the cheek. "Lovely girl like her, she'll be fighting them off. That is," he added winking, "when she can spare the time from running the Clinic!" Since I had started studying medicine, whenever he saw me, he would greet me with, "Well, how's the abortion business going?" This was in the days before the 1967 Abortion Act where there was money to be made out of back-street abortions.

The wedding took place in June of 1962 and I came to London especially to attend. This was the first occasion since I had gone to Bristol when I found myself in the company of Jews once more. The reception, a quite lavish affair, was held at a special hall in St John's Wood. All Patricia's family was there, many of whom I knew, and all her friends. Her sister Claire, whom I had not seen for some time, was there with her husband (she had also married "a nice, Jewish boy" in the end), her hair puffed up into a tall beehive and looking extra smart in a matching coat and dress. The gathering, which included the groom's relatives and friends also, must have come to over a hundred people. I was seated amongst the friends, most of whom I did not know.

In the buzz of conversation around me, I could hear Yiddish being spoken, and I felt distinctly uncomfortable and an outsider. I suddenly realised that despite a childhood spent in Golders Green, I had never been in such a large Jewish gathering before. In my own mind – and it was entirely in my own mind – I suddenly felt a sense of menace and insecurity. I was sitting among people whose kinsmen had thrown me and my parents out of our home and country. What was to follow sharpened my unease.

After we had all been settled in our allotted places and before the

Patricia, with her parents either side of her, and me, far right, at her wedding in 1962

meal commenced, the Master of Ceremonies asked us all to be upstanding. Thinking this was to be for some speech or toast, I stood up with the rest. But to my dismay, the strains of the Israeli national anthem suddenly filled the air. I was seized with consternation. How could they do such a thing, I thought angrily. Even though I had tried obligingly to forget it, it was as if they were pushing my Palestinian identity down my throat, forcing me to react. I thought, "I cannot stand up through this. I must sit down." But as I looked round and saw that every single person in that room was standing, including those who were elderly and could barely manage it, I felt too embarrassed to do otherwise. So, I stayed awkwardly on my feet though leaning forward over the table as if to make myself look invisible and inwardly cursing my own cowardice.

The Master of Ceremonies then asked everyone to raise a toast to Israel. At least, I did not do that. When I saw the glasses raised and heard the murmur of voices saying, "Israel!" all around me, I felt baffled. "Why do they do it?" I wondered. "This is a wedding of British people, not a political rally for a foreign state." Every person in that room was originally from Romania or England or Eastern Europe; not one of them originated in Israel. They were all British subjects and now lived in England. And yet, here they were celebrating the national anthem of another country, as if they had been expatriates. I wondered who they believed they really were, and if they themselves understood the significance of playing Israel's anthem in the heart of England. "It's like a fashion," said Patricia when I queried her afterwards. "Everybody's doing it at bar mitzvahs and weddings and God knows what. I don't think it means anything."

உ~௭

Earlier that year, Siham had married a Palestinian engineer by the name of Isam Kamal who approached her through our uncle. His family originated from Jerusalem, but they had ended up in Lebanon during the exodus of 1948. His eldest sister, who lived in Damascus, had spotted Siham and considered her a suitable match for him. Abu Salma put no pressure on her to accept and left her to make her own decision. The couple liked each other and decided to marry within a few months. She wrote to tell our parents and our uncle assured them that the suitor seemed a respectable man. Our father then gave them his blessing and Siham was married in Damascus in April 1962.

This is a legal ceremony when, according to shari'a law, the marriage contract is signed between the parties, the groom and two witnesses on one side and the bride with her two representatives on the other. The contract deals with such matters as the dowry and the bridal settlement. The latter is a sum of money which the groom pledges to the bride in case he divorces or deserts her in the future. Its value usually reflects his financial circumstances, but also his esteem for the bride. In Siham's case, the figure was put at 10,000 Syrian pounds, which was a handsome sum in those days. At this time the groom also usually presents his bride with a present, traditionally a piece of gold jewellery. This derived from ancient custom where gold was given in lieu of money. The woman keeps it as a monetary guarantee against non-payment of the bridal settlement by the man. In my sister's case, the bridal gift was a diamond solitaire ring.

Following this, in July, they held the wedding party. Since the legal contract is all that is required for a couple to be man and wife, any additional wedding celebration is optional and may take place at any time after the contract has been drawn up and signed. It was however customary to hold such weddings, often highly festive and elaborate. But Siham decided on a simple dinner party for close friends to be held at our uncle's house. We attended neither event. It was not even a point of discussion at home, and I was surprised, waiting in Bristol,

Siham and Isam at their wedding celebration

to hear no suggestion that the family should travel to Damascus either in April or in July.

Siham was disappointed when our father wrote that the travel costs prohibited us from coming, and our mother said nothing. Siham eventually put it down to some strange aberration. But I could see that it was neither and I wondered whether this was due to a barely articulated conflict which her marriage had provoked in our father. He said afterwards that he had not really approved of the match. But I wonder whether it was the quandary he feared would confront him if he went back to the Arab world, one which he preferred to avoid, the choice between the uncertainty of life there and the certainty of life in exile. And perhaps also a sense of shame that he, unlike his daughter, had abandoned the Arab homeland.

Who knows that perhaps our mother had her reasons as well? Despite her rejection of life in England, she had found some compensations. In Palestine, she had been simply my father's wife, expected to entertain his friends and attend to her domestic duties, but with no status of her own. Although there was no formal segregation between men and women in our Jerusalem home, it was not customary for the woman of the house to spend any time in male company. This was the social order for everyone and, knowing nothing else, she had accepted it. Here in London, however, she was a person in her own right, popular amongst the Arab community and able to mix freely with the many bachelors who regarded her as their mother by proxy. This gave her a sense of fulfilment and importance that she could not have admitted to. Going to Damascus, seeing her family, she anticipated the pressure they would put on her to return. And if that happened, it would force her, in her turn, to confront some unpleasant choices. At the very least, it would evoke feelings of guilt at what seemed to be her own self-indulgence. I felt little empathy with her at the time, filled as I was with my own anguished resentments, but years later, I looked back with sad compassion for my poor mother's predicament. Even when she had managed to find some release from the melancholy of her disrupted life, she could not feel free to enjoy it without shame and guilt.

Siham and her new husband, visiting us in London, spoke excitedly about their future plans. They would be leaving for Somalia once they returned to Beirut, as Isam was to start work on a major engineering project there. They talked of finding a place for my brother in the same project.

Watching Siham animatedly talking and planning, I suddenly felt bereft. I could see how she had changed from the Siham who had been "ours", to this confident, vigorous woman who seemed to have left us far behind. I was envious of her certainty about herself, her comfortable sense of her own identity. It seemed to me that while my parents played absurdly at being Arabs in an English land and I floundered trying desperately to fit myself somewhere in between, she had truly found herself. When she and I were growing up, it was our parents who had been our ultimate reference point for Arabness; we deferred to them in such matters at every stage. But the positions were now reversed. By returning to the East and sharing in its life, it was she who was the authentic one and we who were out of touch and out of date. I doubt that our parents understood much of this, or, if it had been explained to them, whether they would not have rejected it out of hand, believing doggedly in their own superior authority. But for me it was clear, I knew that our old relationship with her had ended.

Such thoughts inevitably stirred up anew the conflict of my two identities which I thought I had started to resolve. In Bristol, where I now longed to return, there was little of this to trouble me. My life there with Zandra and my other friends posed no existential riddles and made no psychological demands. It was being in London that was the problem. I determined that I would come back as little as possible.

࿇

The early months of 1963 were bitterly cold. There were prolonged snowfalls that year and we were glad that we would spend the worst of the weather in lodgings in Southmead Hospital. Our consultant teachers varied; a few were gentle, but the majority were capricious egoists. It was on the "firms" – study groups of ten or so students – that we were closely subjected to their paternalism and their arbitrary exercise of power over us. Anxiously, we studied their every vagary because the medical world operated on a system of networks and personal recommendations and it was important not to offend. Everyone dreaded the fate of the mythical house man (junior hospital doctor) who, having completed his first house job (as pre-registration hospital appointments were known) received a reference from his consultant to this effect: "Dr So-and-so tells me that he has been my houseman for the last six months." Or, in a variation of the story, the reference went: "This man has been working for me over the last six months to his own satisfaction." The reign of terror we lived under merely reinforced for me the paternalism and prohibitions of my childhood.

Nor were the patients any more protected from these medical prima donnas than we were. On one of the medical firms, I remember that we came into contact with the senior chest physician, a Dr Pearson. He was a dapper, well-dressed man who had the air of an aristocratic younger son. His speciality brought him into contact with a large population of patients, mostly men with chronic bronchitis. They were inexplicably devoted to him, for he treated them all like old family retainers, never addressed them by anything except their surnames and was remarkably unsympathetic to their plight. If patients, wheezing and coughing, and so short of breath they could scarcely walk, ever complained of their condition, he would say briskly, "No use complaining, Smith," – or Jones or Wilson – "you're living on borrowed time, hmm? Realise that, do you?"

And they would answer, "Thank you very much, sir, thank you." One day, while taking us on one of his ward rounds, he stopped by the bed of a patient with a collapsed lung. The patient's chest had been fitted with a tube, connected to a positive pressure appliance which helped him to breathe. The tube ran down the side of the bed and, as Dr Pearson stood beside the patient explaining the case to us, he leant unthinkingly against it. His weight shut off the tube and the patient, who was already having difficulty breathing, started to protest feebly. But Dr Pearson, looking towards us and unaware of the problem, mistook this for another of the complaints he usually dismissed.

"Quiet, Dickson, there's a good chap. Lucky to be alive, hmm?" But the man's distress increased and when his face turned blue we could no longer stay silent. "Sir," said one of us timidly, for consultants were never to be interrupted or corrected, "sir, I think the patient's tube is shut off." At this, Dr Pearson started and, looking down at the constricted tube, jumped away smartly from the bed and called the nurses. As the patient was revived, he patted him over the head and said, "Terribly sorry, old thing. Didn't mean to. Better now?" And, to our surprise, the man nodded with no hint of reproach.

That same winter at Southmead, a group of us went on the obstetrics "firm". We continued to "live in", as it was known, since we had to be available at all hours to deliver the babies who, as we discovered to our annoyance, more often than not arrived at night. Our firm included my good friends Cleeve and Subhi, but it also included John Thornley. The rooms we were supposed to occupy were crammed together with partitions between them hardly thicker than cardboard, and we had the impression we were all living together in one large room. And it was here, due to this proximity, that what had been an interest from afar on his part and a sense of flattery on mine started to develop into something more. By the time we left Southmead, John and I had begun to go out together.

I enjoyed these times with him; he had generous habits and behaved like a gentleman. Until then, I had only known impoverished students or boys of limited means. It was a new experience to be treated like a lady. He took me to country pubs and restaurants. These were usually in the countryside outside Bristol, places with names like Chipping Sodbury, Chipping Norton and Norton St Philip that evoked memories of the Shire in *The Lord of the Rings*. The inns in these hamlets represented the best in the English country pub tradition, which I had until then only seen in photographs. Often, they were thatched cottages or old stone buildings covered in ivy, with large open fires and oak beams.

Nothing could have been been further from my memories of Tulkarm, Qatamon, Jerusalem or Damascus. But it enchanted me and gave me a new sense of intimacy with England. I was so enthused by my new life that I would chatter happily away to John, not minding that he scarcely spoke in return. After a few of these outings, he invited me one Sunday to meet his family at lunch.

They lived in an old farmhouse, part of it dating from the eighteenth century, which was just off the Bristol–Bath road. It was a long, low grey stone building which opened onto wide lawns and a large rose garden. Beyond this was rolling countryside as far as the eye could see. John's father, who had died, had farmed the fields round about, and they owned cattle, sheep and poultry. His two brothers had taken over from their father and were both farmers with houses nearby. Of the three of them, John was the only one bound for a professional career and the apple of his mother's eye. Visiting his home for the first time, I was overwhelmed by its charm and character. His mother came out to greet me with great warmth. I did not know what he had told her about me, but she behaved as if I had been an old friend. She was a large woman with a generous bosom and a finely wrinkled, lived-in face. Her manner was strongly matriarchal and from the first, she seemed to take me under her wing.

Before lunch, John suggested that we take the dogs out for a walk. We cut across into the woods. It was overcast with a fresh wind blowing and a dampness in the air. The wood smelled of peat and dank leaves, and when we came out from its dark enclosure into the open, we found ourselves suddenly on the crest of a hill overlooking undulating, grassy fields. "It's so beautiful here," I said.

"It's nothing special, not when you see the rest of Somerset."

I shook my head. "You're wrong. It is special here, it's the privacy, the fact that it's yours."

"This isn't ours," he laughed pointing back at the wood and the extensive lands in front of us. "Nothing to do with my family. It belongs to the local squire."

"I don't mean this specific bit," I said, impatient that he did not understand me. "I mean that you can walk out into your garden and your fields and know that it's yours, your land, your country. Do you know John Pellowe?" He was a medical student in the year below ours. John and I used to exchange the odd friendly conversation from time to time, but for some reason at that instant he came compellingly into my mind. John shook his head. "Well, he comes from Devon, near Dartmoor. He once told me that the thing he loves most is to run across the moor and open his arms to the wind and say, 'It's mine! This land is mine!'" I paused. "Well, there's nowhere I can do that. Nowhere on earth." John looked uncomfortable. He cleared his throat, waiting politely for me to continue. But when I didn't, he took my arm and said, "Anyway, shall we go back for lunch?"

I had never had English roast lamb before. My mother's version was overcooked and highly spiced and served with rice and pine nuts. She never learned or cared to learn the art of the English roast joint, since this was not part of traditional Arab cuisine. Here now was the real thing, to be served with fresh mint sauce from the garden. As I took my first mouthful of that moist, tender meat, slowly cooked in its own juices in the Aga since morning, it gave me a lasting taste for English roast lamb. New potatoes and cabbage, also fresh from the garden, complemented a perfect meal and I was so impressed that I imagined I would never again eat anything so good. I saw nothing odd in it. Yet, here I was, an Arab reared on spices, my palate finely attuned to my mother's rich savoury cooking, now inexplicably seduced by the unchallenging cuisine of an English Sunday meal.

When lunch was over, we went into the sitting room, prettily furnished with chintz curtains and floral armchairs, evoking memories of the home of Mr and Mrs Heathcott-Smythe all those years ago. A large log fire was burning in the grate, the dogs sleeping exhaustedly in front of it. How familiar their sleeping posture seemed; the faintest memory stirred inside me. But these were English dogs and the memory quickly receded. John brought us all tea, made as his mother liked it, very strong and very sweet, in delicate, patterned china cups. Only then did his mother come in and sit down with a deep sigh of contentment. "Best moment of the day when you have a hot cup of tea, I always think," she said, sipping at her cup and smiling at me. I smiled back at her, but it had nothing to do with tea. I was thinking that I had fallen in love, with her, her son, the house, the roast lamb and the Englishness of everything I had seen that day. And I wanted to keep coming back.

By the summer of 1963, John and I had been paired off in the eyes of our colleagues. I moved out of the house I had shared with Zandra, who had by then qualified and left Bristol, and took a bed-sitter in another house, this time sharing with Subhi Zabaneh, my fellow student from Jordan. John liked him and the three of us often did things together. Subhi and I met on common cultural ground over certain matters and we introduced John to some simple notions of Arabness. Meanwhile, Cleeve Mathews had met the girl who was to be his future wife and we saw less of him than before. And the whole time, my involvement with John and his family was growing. I was now invited to spend occasional nights at the farm. His mother gave me a pretty bedroom to stay in with stunning views of the back garden and the fields beyond. She would bring me morning tea in bed and spoil me all the time that I stayed with her.

From time to time, she would take me for outings into Bath. We would drive into the city in her large Ford Granada and then we would go for afternoon tea at Jolly's, Bath's largest, smartest department store, where she had an account. Before we had tea, we would walk round the pretty store looking at all the beautiful clothes and elegant accessories. Many of the assistants knew her and chatted pleasantly to us. I felt flattered to be included with her, as if I too were an English country lady out for the day.

As our friendship grew, I never knew what she thought about my background, for living in the depths of the English countryside she had scarcely ever rubbed shoulders with a foreigner, let alone had one in her house. She was a pillar of the local church, entertained the vicar to tea regularly and ran the Christmas jumble sale for the handicapped. I must have seemed utterly incompatible with her world, and I never understood how she was able to find a place for someone like me in her archetypally English West Country life.

The only time the issue of my foreignness came up was when I started to make the odd Arab dish, which I had learned by watching my mother, as an hors-d'oeuvre for Sunday lunch. It was then that Mrs Thornley discovered in herself an un-English taste for savoury food she had never suspected. Of all the family, she devoured to the last morsel the garlicky aubergine salads and fried cauliflower I made. Once, I even cooked them stuffed spleens. This Arab delicacy consists of fried sheep spleens (or melts, as they are known by English butchers), stuffed with raw garlic, hot peppers and fresh coriander. Not all Arabs liked them and, to a certain extent, they were an acquired taste. To my surprise, Mrs Thornley loved them, while the rest of the family either declined to have any or visibly grimaced on taking the first mouthful.

I was by now quite taken up with my new life. I enjoyed being a "normal" young woman, as good as my peers. I had a steady boyfriend who took me out and whose family liked me, for I had now made friends with John's youngest brother Peter and his wife Yvonne. Increasingly, as I went to Willow Farm, I felt it was home, certainly more comfortable and welcoming than my own home in London had ever been. John and I had developed a social life in Bristol with our small group of medical student friends and in Bath too where we often went out with Peter and Yvonne. They invited us to dinner-dances organised by the Young Farmers' Union. I did not enjoy these functions, since I had never been taught ballroom dancing, and I felt clumsy and awkward each time I was dragged around the dance floor to the tunes of a quickstep or a foxtrot. I would hang tightly onto my unfortunate partner, clenching my jaws and sweating with embarrassment, until the music came to a stop.

Meanwhile, I had entered my final year at medical school and was due to qualify in the summer of 1964. My studies appealed to me now even less than they had done before, for the demands of clinical work were daunting and, at times, positively frightening. We were having to encounter death on the wards for the first time in our lives and to attend post-mortems, which I never found anything but sinister and distasteful. The first death on the wards I ever saw is deeply etched on my memory. One night, I was made to sit with a young woman patient on the medical ward at the Royal Infirmary. She was twenty-seven years old, not much older than I was myself at the time. Because of her grave condition, we medical students were made to keep a twenty-four-hour watch by her bedside. My turn came in the evening, and I was fearful and reluctant to do it, never having nursed anyone before. She was restless and delirious, her lips cracked and caked with dry blood and saliva.

"I am the Queen of the Jordan," she raved over and over again. And our medical registrar, who had come in to see her, turned to me and smiled. "Did you hear that? Go on, talk to her in Arabic. Go on, try it!" I found his flippancy in the face of this awesome scene repellent. But he was young himself and maybe this was the only defence he had against it. Feeling foolish, I said a few words in Arabic. She stared hard at me, her eyes full of alarm and focused for the first time, as if she had just come to. I wondered for a moment if, by some crazy chance, she understood Arabic. She suddenly sat up on her pillows and tried to say something, as if she had an urgent message to impart, but no sound came. The registrar told me to hurry and get the sister, but I stood frozen, staring at her. In that second, she fell back, her sudden spurt of energy gone, her neck extended onto the pillows and her eyes closed. No one needed to tell me what had happened. I had never seen death before, but I knew it instantly.

I had an overwhelming need for fresh air. As I ran down the hospital stairs, I nearly collided with her husband coming up to see her. He took one look at me and I saw the awful recognition in his face. I could not bring myself to speak to him and, feeling a coward, went on running down. Outside in the air of a cold October night, its sharpness stinging my face, I found the bus which normally took me home waiting at the depot. I jumped on, shivering with the memory of what I had just seen and somehow expecting that other people would know about it too. But the bus conductress and the driver were having a chat and were in no hurry to go anywhere. The conductress was in the middle of a story. "I said to her, I said, you do go on. Why don't you put the kettle on and shut up. You should be glad you've got a husband at all." Her words were like music to my ears. I nearly hugged her. That's right, I thought, put the kettle on, have a cup of tea, do all the homely, familiar things that meant being alive, normal, healthy. Thank God I was me and not that poor sad corpse stretched out on the bed up there.

෫ঌ

The threat of the final exams hung over us. Fortunately, John was one of the best students in the class, and I copied his work shamelessly. In the midst of these anxieties, London seemed very far away. My visits there were as infrequent as I could make them. My mother never ceased to complain about this, but when I suggested she and my father come to Bristol to see me instead, knowing her reluctance to entertain such an idea, she held her peace for a while.

In October of 1963, however, I went to see Siham, who had come over to have her first child in London. To the disappointment of all, this turned out to be a daughter, for, of course, a son would have been infinitely better. Siham was a happy, busy new mother and my parents were gratified by their new role as grandparents. Her husband had come with her and when she left the hospital, they all stayed in the house. Ziyad had left that year to work in Aden. Seeing them all together, the new parents and grandparents, I was struck by the distance there was between us. I was certain that this was imperceptible to them, for I must have looked and sounded the same as before. But inside I knew that I had moved away so far and so profoundly that I was a virtual stranger in their midst.

This was not a passive personal change; it was more that I had turned my back decisively on their culture, their customs, their society and all that they stood for. And Siham and her husband, who were an integral part of that too, were not exempted. We now had nothing in common, and though I went through the motions expected of an Arab woman, it was like acting a part. And I was quite successful, for I could see that none of them or, for that matter, the friends who came to congratulate my sister on her baby's birth, expected anything else of me.

This left me disbelieving and angry. How, I wondered, could my parents and now Siham be so crass as to imagine that a childhood spent in England, a five-year stay at an English university with scarcely an Arab in sight, and an entirely English education, would leave no mark? It was as if Englishness to them were a form of clothing, a coat or a dress which you wore when you went out into English society, but which you removed as soon as you were back with Arabs. So they expected me to behave indistinguishably from any other Arab daughter, as if I had arrived but yesterday from the Arab world. The corollary of that view was of course that they had no sympathy with a position of dissent. Had I been able to reveal my true feelings about England, I would have been judged disloyal to my heritage, misguided or even mentally unstable.

Needless to say, I remained silent, most of all in regard to my relationship with John. How, even if I dared, would I ever be able to explain this to them? How could I hope for them to understand that in John and his family I had found affection, acceptance for what I was, and not for what I should be, and a sense of belonging? That with them, I could lay aside the conflict which rent me and be free of the shackles of a complicated and half-remembered history which I felt obscurely responsible for? That in my newly discovered life, I could say I was a "dark-skinned English girl" and hope to be believed?

Of course I could not speak of such things to anyone. But at the same time, I carried an awesome weight in concealing my involvement with John, only made possible by my geographical distance from my parents and their friends. The taboo that forbade me, a Muslim Arab girl, from making a sexual relationship with a non-Muslim man was as potent now as it had been with the Dajani daughter during my childhood. Though nothing was ever said, my parents had laid upon me a burden of responsibility to observe the taboo and not betray their unspoken trust.

As the final year at university commenced, my mother came up with a new source of pressure. Having lamented for years our enforced stay in England, she now started to talk about her hopes for a return to the Arab world as soon as I qualified. Siham always said unkindly afterwards that our mother no more wanted to give up her life in London than fly to the moon. The plan was that after I had gained my medical degree, I would find work in some Arab country, and then, Siham and Ziyad being already out of England, she and my father would go back with me. Needless to say, this was not done in consultation with me and indeed I only found out about it by chance after she had been broadcasting the news to her friends. When I confronted her with it, she was quite unabashed.

"Why not?" she said. "There'll be nothing here for you once you've got your degree. Your father thinks the same." When I tried to speak, she held her hand up. "No, no. It'll be best for all of us, you'll see."

I did not know if this was a serious intention or whether it was meant as a way of consoling herself for the guilt of her continued residence in England. With the passage of time and loss of contact with the Arab world, my mother developed an ambivalence towards her return there. Though, over the years, she spoke less and less about going back, the fantasy of return she had harboured since 1948 was still alive within her. But she saw her enjoyment of her life in London as a kind of betrayal of her roots and felt ashamed. So she sought a way of resolving her conflict by channelling it though me. The plan she had devised sounded real enough to induce in me a sense of dread that I might be asked to conform to her wishes. This did not accord with the shape my life was taking and, though I myself had no coherent plan for the future, I did not feel prepared to think about it as yet. Even so, I feared that some such fate awaited me, and when people in Bristol asked me what I would do after qualifying, I started to say, "Oh, I expect I'll be going back to the Middle East." What I meant by "back", even I did not know.

For there was no return to Palestine and hence nowhere to go "back" to. But everyone assumed I meant Jordan, for I had stopped saying, "somewhere in the Middle East", whenever people asked me where I came from and now said, "Jordan". There were several reasons for this. By then, I had held a Jordanian passport for many years; our family's town of origin, Tulkarm, had been part of Jordan since 1950 and it could be said that if I went "back", it would be to

Jordan; but in addition, I had unconsciously picked up my family's reluctance to admit to having British citizenship, as if by doing so, we had disowned our Arab origins; in order to reverse that impression, my father would always say firmly that we were Jordanians whenever the subject of nationality came up.

I had no thought about the future, but merely wanted for life to continue as it was. In this, I reckoned without John. In the time we had known each other, he had become increasingly attached to me. He said he was in love with me, though I never quite knew why. He was not an emotionally articulate man and I thought he observed rather than partnered me. When I mentioned this to his mother, with whom I now felt able to be intimate, she smiled. "Ah," she sighed sentimentally, "just like my dear husband. Never said very much, but it never mattered, I always knew what he was feeling. Maybe not what you might call exciting, but loyal and true. And that's my son all over, just like his father."

John treated me with fond indulgence. He spoiled me and gave me presents. He went along with all my ideas and tolerated my changeable moods. In contrast to me, he was calm and phlegmatic, apparently content to let me take the lead in every area of life, except for medicine. This he took with extreme seriousness, was a diligent student and everyone could see he would become a dedicated doctor. Aside from the attraction of his handsome looks, what I felt for him in return was not love, but a need for him to love me and make me feel secure. I relished his indulgence of me, his devotion and the stability his presence had introduced into my life. I could see that he did not share my artistic tastes or the breadth of my education and might make a dull companion. But beyond that, I never saw him very clearly as a man in his own right. For to me, he was inextricably entwined with his situation, as if he came as part of a package that included his mother and her dogs, the house, the Somerset countryside, those china cups. It was all *that* I wanted; I perceived John as no more than an appendage to an idyll.

Of course, I did not see any of this with such clarity at the time. In the first flush of my relationship with him, I knew only that it seemed right for us and that we should continue going out together. I had little experience of men and no way of judging whether he was a suitable companion or not. And so it was that I found myself quite unprepared for his proposal of marriage. We had been together for some time, he explained, long enough for him to be sure of his feelings for me and he wanted us to be married.

He had intimated the idea of marriage between us before, but never directly, and I had always managed to ignore him. This time, I could see that he was serious. I started to feel panicked and tried to persuade him that we should wait a little longer. But he was not to be deflected. "I don't see the point in waiting," he said stubbornly. "I've been waiting ages and you've always fobbed me off. But I'm not having it this time." Looking me straight in the eye, he said, "I'll give you till the end of Easter to make up your mind. If you say no, then that's all right. But it'll be over between us."

In a flash, I saw myself alone, without a boyfriend, like all the dowdiest girls in our class whom I pitied. Never again to be able to visit Willow Farm, or to walk the dogs, or to see Mrs Thornley and be a part of her family. Never again to be someone's special person, cherished and desired. Viewing life in such absolutist terms, as I did then, I found the prospect I had conjured up too appalling to contemplate. I saw with a sense of shock the full extent of my dependence on John; how in the years we had known each other, he had become a solid anchor in my life. Perhaps I should have loved him more for himself. Had I done so, my coming sacrifice would have made more sense.

But for me at that time, something more vital than love propelled me towards him. Through him, and for the first time in a fractured life, I had found a new place for myself, which felt comfortable and happy. If I gave all that up now, what did I have to put in its place? The thought of London and my family flashed through my mind. The alternative was them and our dreary home; the obligation put upon me to be a conventional Arab woman with all the prohibitions that that implied; and, lately, the duty imposed on me to take my parents back to a place that I neither knew nor wanted to live in. The gulf between what my Arab origins had to offer and what my present life promised was too profound to ignore.

During the Easter holidays I deliberately went back to London to confront my new dilemma. Of course nothing had changed as I cast a merciless eye on our damp, dark kitchen with its bare floor and steamy windows; the freezing hallway and upstairs corridor which one crossed speedily to get into the malodorous warmth of a paraffin-heated bedroom; and the ancient, unpainted bathroom with its rusty, dripping taps and ill-fitting linoleum-covered floor. My mother had laid on a welcome for me full of complaints about the fact that I never phoned home or asked after anyone. She eyed my new clothes and long earrings with ill-disguised disapproval. She used to criticise Siham for buying so many clothes, which she called rags, and me for my love of jewellery, which she dismissed as a foolish taste for "jangling trinkets".

"What's that you're wearing?" she said, fingering the new skirt that I had painstakingly saved up to buy. It was made of black wool and hugged my figure closely. When I pulled the material away from her hand with irritation, she stared at me and laughed. "Silly girl! Spending your money on rags and trinkets, just like your sister." I suppose in her odd way, she was glad to see me, but no sooner had I been home for an hour than she was on the phone to her friends, arranging visits and outings with them. When that evening my father came home, we talked about my medical studies and how he hoped that I was working diligently.

"Of course she is," said my mother, laying out dinner. "She's going to pass her exams and then find a good job and we'll all go back with her." My father ignored this and asked about my friends. He knew Zandra who had come home with me on several visits during our first years at university.

"Has she got herself a boyfriend yet?" he asked. Surprised at this question, since he never normally discussed such matters, I told him that she was engaged to be married. "Oh, good," he said. "I know English girls like to have boyfriends. They don't feel normal otherwise. Though, come to think of it, all girls probably feel the same." But whoever the "girls" he had in mind were, they certainly did not include me, as confirmed by his next statement. "Anyway, let's talk about you. When do the final exams start?" He listened intently while I explained. And then he said, "Make sure now that nothing distracts you from your studies. It's of the utmost importance that you don't waste your time and that you concentrate on getting your degree. One must work hard, establish a firm basis in life, and then other things can follow. There will be time enough."

For one panicky moment, I wondered if it were remotely possible that my father knew something about me and John. But of course he didn't. "Look at me," he continued. "I work on the dictionary every evening and most weekends. I'll let nothing distract me until it's finished. And once that happens, I'll have something solid to show, something firm and concrete. And you must do the same, get yourself established, not dissipate your energies."

Having delivered himself of this advice, my father changed the subject. I have no doubt he meant well, but to him the question was a simple one of diligence and academic results. His one-dimensional view of me, and possibly of all of us, had remained essentially the same over the years. He knew nothing of the world that I inhabited and if he had, I believed that his apparently benevolent concern for me would have rapidly given way to a harsh and unforgiving anger. I could see that the gulf between us was unbridgeable and I felt more fearfully isolated than I had ever done before.

No, there was nothing here for me, I concluded, and no dilemma to resolve. With trepidation, but also with a sense of inevitability, I made my decision. I would leave my parents to their world and embrace wholeheartedly my English husband and his English life. If Palestine still lingered somewhere in my memory, it cast no shadow and meant nothing. To all intents and purposes, the transition from the Arab child who arrived in 1949, knowing nothing about England, to the miniskirted young woman at home only in England, was now complete.

Eleven

Our friends all got to hear of our engagement, but not my family, whom I could not face telling just yet. I shuddered every time I though of what would happen once they knew. I started to have troubled dreams, full of longing to revert to the time before I knew John, only to wake up to the reality of my situation with a feeling of awful dread. With the final examinations drawing closer, however, there was little else to do but revise and I managed to immerse myself in work and put other things aside. John and I saw less of each other, as he studied at home and I remained in Bristol.

When the results came out and we found that we had passed, all the indignities and embarrassing moments of our student days were rapidly forgotten. Having qualified, we felt different, suddenly grown up. People would call us "doctor" and that was thrilling. For me this was especially important because I thought it would give me the confidence I needed to deal with my parents, as I soon must. I decided that I would bolster up my courage further by waiting until I had started my first house job.

Before being able to practise medicine, newly qualified doctors had to complete a year of so-called pre-registration hospital work which were called "house jobs" and consisted of six months medicine and six months surgery. Medical schools usually produced more graduates than could be absorbed by their own teaching hospitals and they had to go elsewhere. John and I did not have to stray far from Bristol, for we found jobs at St Martin's Hospital in Bath. These would commence soon after graduation. My parents, having failed to attend Ziyad's graduation ceremony and having been spared Siham's, as she herself had not bothered to invite them, decided to come to mine. It was a fine summer's day, warm and sunny, and they took the train up from London. I found their presence in "my world" strange and disorienting. But there was no doubting the pleasure and pride they took in me and in the occasion. I rarely remembered seeing my father beaming so continuously and looking around him with such intense interest. I introduced them to my friends and finally to John.

He and I had prearranged the meeting with the idea that, although they did not know who he really was, he would at least have a chance of seeing them for himself. He looked exceptionally smart that day in his dark suit and polished shoes. But I could see that he was nervous and anxious to please. As I introduced him, saying lightly that he was another of my fellow students, my parents smiled warmly at him and shook hands. My father chatted to him for a while and congratulated him on getting his degree. When he went to fetch them some tea, my mother said, "What a pleasant young man. But he's very dark. Is he English?" I replied that of course he was, but did not dare to say any more. John's mother was meanwhile at a safe distance away from where we were standing, and John had had to explain to her why she and my parents could not meet yet. We took many photographs that day, and when the formal portrait of me in my graduation robes came out I gave it to my parents. They displayed it on the window ledge at home in the sitting room so that when people asked after their children, they could point to the picture and say, "And that's our youngest, Ghada. She's a doctor!"

With my parents on graduation day, 1964

By September, when I had been in work for two months, and with John pestering me, I decided reluctantly that the time had come to tell them about us. Ironically, my parents and I had been getting on better since I qualified, and my father had given me my first car as a graduation present. This was a grey Morris Minor which I drove around with much pleasure and I dreaded the moment when I would have to throw his generosity back in his face, as it were. I talked about it to friends and colleagues in the hope of finding an easy solution. Cleeve said, "You want to tell them that you're marrying a black Jew, and when they pass out, you say, 'only joking, he's an Englishman!' Whereupon they'll be so relieved, they'll welcome him with open arms!" Roger Wood, a senior house officer I had got to know at St Martin's, did not find it funny. "I think it's monstrous," he said. "How can they expect you to marry people according to categories? They've no right to interfere. It's your life. Just go ahead and do what you want." But our medical registrar, who was a Pakistani, thought differently. "Take my advice, never let it be known. There is no other way, believe me." "But how can I keep it hidden?" I protested. He shrugged. "I don't know, but you've got no choice. They will never accept it."

John's mother found the whole affair bewildering. She behaved as if she thought my parents were suffering from some chronic ailment and needed careful handling in case their condition worsened. Her obvious sympathy with me indicated that she thought them unreasonable, but she was also piqued at the suggestion that her son might be considered less than desirable. Although I explained that it was not aimed at him in particular but at any non-Muslim she remained unconvinced. She started to wonder whether John and I should not wait longer in view of the difficulties, and that somehow decided me to take the plunge.

I sat down there and then and wrote two letters, one to my father and the other to Siham. These were confused compositions, half apologetic, half defiant, in which I explained that I had known this classmate of mine for five years and that we had become friends. But recently, it had developed into something stronger and we wanted to get married. I knew that the news would upset them and especially my mother, but I hoped they would understand. I then told them how respectable John and his family were and how kind they had been to me. I wrote in English as my written Arabic was poor. But because I never spoke to them except in Arabic the letters looked alien and unnatural.

There followed an ominous silence. And then, at the end of the month, I heard from Siham that she and Ziyad were coming to London in early October and would like to see me. He had left Aden by then because of the Yemeni rebellion against the British occupation and was working with Isam in Somalia. On receiving my letter, Siham had become alarmed and decided to come and see what she could do; and Ziyad, who had a business trip to London coming up anyway and was equally alarmed, accompanied her. She recalled her husband's warning to her after he had met me in London, "I've got a feeling your sister's going to give all of you one in the eye with some Englishman if you're not careful. We must try and get her away before that happens." He had suggested finding me a medical job in Beirut to tempt me out of England. Siham thought back on that and wished they had acted on his advice.

She and Ziyad arrived in London to find our parents, especially our mother, in a state of intense agitation. The family conferred and decided to send them to see me and John with the aim of dissuading us from proceeding further with our plan. Siham telephoned to arrange a meeting between the four of us in Bristol. John received the news with dismay, and I with trepidation and then with resentment. I had thought that Siham might sympathise, but I was clearly wrong, and Ziyad, who I saw to be playing the untypical part of the heavy-handed Arab brother, filled me with irritation. We met them at the university entrance on Park Street and took them to the Berkley coffee house opposite. It was midday, but I said I had already eaten and ungraciously did not offer them lunch. It was an awkward, unhappy meeting, and thankfully did not last long. They earnestly explained our family's distress and begged that we reconsider going ahead with the marriage. They stressed it was nothing personal against John but that we came from different backgrounds and would face many difficulties. "When all's said and done," said Siham, "Ghada's an Arab and a Muslim."

John held his ground. "She's more English than she is Arab," he said, "and we're neither of us religious." Ziyad shook his head as if to say that there was no point going on. I remained virtually silent throughout.

"Look," said John. "I'm prepared to go with her and work in the Middle East, if that would help."

"That's very nice of you," replied my brother, "but you really mustn't jeopardise your career." He looked at Siham with an air of finality and said, "Shall we go?" It seemed they had both concluded that we were determined to go ahead and further attempts to dissuade us were futile. However, our mother would not accept it. She urged Siham to try again and this time to speak to John's family as well. When Siham got in touch to arrange this I felt a renewal of hope that perhaps I could make her understand my position. John's mother thought the whole thing extraordinary but was willing to meet my sister and invited her to stay. This trip, however, proved no more successful from my parents' viewpoint than the one before it. Everyone was polite, and the night went pleasantly enough. Siham took me aside, on our own this time, and tried to show me the error of my ways.

"He's a nice man, I can see that," she said, "but he's got a very different temperament to you. He's very English and you're not." And then she said, trying another tack, "What if there was to be some enmity between the Arabs and the English, as happened at the time of Suez, what will you do then?" Finally, she asked the question which must have been uppermost in her mind. "Have you thought about the children you might have? What are they going to be? Arab, English, Christian, Muslim or what?" "My children will be English," I replied firmly, "because I am English. I know you find that difficult to believe, but I've grown up here, I have no other country. My life is here, my friends are here and my future will be here too." But my bravado was only skin-deep; inside myself I was desperate with fear and defiance and an apprehension of how alone I was.

When Siham returned to London, she was resigned. "You must leave her alone now," she told our parents. "Her mind is quite made up. And at least, he's a decent, respectable man, a doctor, and he has a nice family. It could be worse." "What?" cried our mother furiously. "We sent you to get her sorted out and this is what you come back with? You're useless!"

John suggested we go and see my parents. The prospect filled me with anxiety, but I nevertheless telephoned to arrange it, anticipating that one or other of them would refuse to speak to me. Siham and Ziyad had left by now and, though my father sounded strained on the telephone, he agreed. Feeling wretched, I took John to our house on a Saturday afternoon as arranged, thinking how shabby he would find it by contrast to his own home. My father let us in awkwardly and showed us into the front room. My mother was nowhere to be seen. I sat down on our sofa next to John, absurdly feeling like a guest and so full of agitation and embarrassment I hardly heard what they were saying. My father was explaining to John, whom he said he remembered meeting at our graduation ceremony, that our marriage would be unlawful in Islamic law. At this, John offered to convert to Islam, but my father pressed on. He described my mother's distress, saying that our marriage would be blighted from the beginning. He stressed, as my sister and brother had done, that it was nothing personal against him and he had no doubt that John was an excellent young man, but that there were wider issues at stake. John tried to explain that he and I loved each other and, though he respected the family's feelings, there was also my personal happiness to consider. I knew this cut no ice with my father, who had no sympathy with the view that, in personal relationships, the wishes of the individual superseded those of the collective. This essentially European concept was unlikely to appeal to

a man reared as he was in a powerful tradition of family and communal obligation.

And then, just as I was beginning to think that I must go and find
her, my mother came in with a tray of Arab coffee in the traditional
small cups, which I knew John had never tasted before. As she could
not communicate with him she nodded and smiled and then asked my
father what they had been saying. Both of them ignored me, as if I did
not exist. My father said in Arabic that John had offered to convert.
But my mother shook her head bitterly and turned towards John.
Unexpectedly, she addressed him.

"Please," she appealed in a pitiable voice and suddenly burst into
tears. "Please, please," she kept repeating as the tears streamed down
her face. "You no for Ghada, no." I tried to get her to stop, but she
shook me off and went up to John and made as if to touch him,
begging and pleading. If there was a moment in her life when she
wished she had spoken English, I am sure it was then. The meeting
turned out infinitely worse than I had imagined.

Later, as we sat at a café in Golders Green where my father had
suggested we go following this scene, he said, "I am sorry about my
wife's behaviour, but you see how this affects her and all of us.
However," and he sighed heavily, "if you are both set upon this
course, then I will not shirk my duty towards Ghada. I will do what is
proper, and you must let me know how you will proceed and what
you will need me to do when the time comes. But that applies only to
me. I cannot vouch for my wife."

In the next few months, as our extended family got to hear of my
impending marriage, two of my uncles wrote to me from Tulkarm.
They pleaded with me not to go through with it. One of them said his
wife had a weak heart and the shock might kill her. Others of our
family were said to be in similar states of distress. My parents did not
communicate with me at all and I did not attempt to visit home after

that autumn of 1964. I buried myself in planning for the wedding, which we had decided was to be in May. On an impulse, I chose May 15, the exact anniversary of the loss of Palestine in 1948. It was not a conscious association, for I never thought of the past and Palestinians at this time did not commemorate that painful date in their history. I remember only that I felt it was significant. Perhaps in choosing that date, I was drawing an unconscious parallel between my original country and my family. And hence, the loss of the one symbolised the loss of the other.

The wedding took place on a day of fine weather and brilliant sunshine, the ceremony first at the Bath Register Office and the reception afterwards on the lawns at Willow Farm. Zandra had come up the night before and stayed at the house. She helped me dress and make up on the morning of the wedding. Mrs Thornley's friend, the vicar, drove me and my father, who had come to Bristol earlier that day with Fuad and my second cousin, Muhammad Said, to the register office. My cousin approved of my marriage no more than did the rest of the family, but he lived in London at the time and felt it his duty to support my father. My mother refused to come or to recognise what was happening and told my father that if he insisted on attending then he should know he would not find her on his return. Fuad, who was driving him and my cousin in his car to Bath, was alarmed by this. But my father said, "Don't worry. The furthest she'll go will be the garden."

My mother likewise refused to recognise the Muslim marriage we had gone through in London the week before. John had duly converted, to his mother's enormous disquiet, and we had gone to the Regent's Park Islamic Centre where the sheikh married us according to shari'a law. This impressed no one in my family, as John was not an authentic Muslim, and everyone knew he had gone through the conversion and Islamic marriage process only to appease them.

That car journey to the register office, in which my father and I sat awkwardly next to each other on the back seat, was one of the most difficult of my life. Neither of us spoke of what was about to happen, as if we were going to a funeral rather than a wedding. Desperate for something to counter the heavy silence, I chatted brightly about my work and how I had been thinking of moving to a London hospital for my next job. My father listened gravely, making the odd comment about hospital work and my future career. I could not imagine what the vicar was making of our solemn conversation in Arabic, interspersed with the occasional mention of English hospital names.

As my father had promised, he did his duty. He witnessed the marriage along with Muhammad Said and then returned to Willow Farm, where our friends and the rest of John's family started to arrive for the reception. There he stood dutifully alongside Mrs Thornley to receive people's congratulations as they came in. To my sorrow, Patricia could not be there for she had left for New York with her husband six months before. They had met John once in London and she had told her mother of my forthcoming marriage. Mrs Cohen had received the news gloomily and soon after, when she was walking through Golders Green, she bumped into my mother. They normally exchanged nods and smiles only, but this time Patricia's mother squeezed her arm warmly and said, "Believe me, my dear, I know what you're going through. What a terrible business, she should have gone for one of her own." My mother did not understand any of this, but she responded gratefully to the other woman's obvious sympathy.

Mrs Thornley had brought in caterers from Bath and there was a great deal of food and champagne. My father and his companions did not stay long, but before leaving, he took Mrs Thornley aside and asked her to let him know what the reception had cost. He understood that it was customary in England for the bride's family to meet the expenses of the wedding (unlike the practice in Islamic marriages, where it was the other way round). He said he would send her a cheque for the amount as soon as he heard from her. He then shook hands with John and coldly let me kiss him on the cheek. I noticed that at no time in the proceedings had his mood lightened or his frown lifted. He had maintained a dignified, but solemn, stance throughout as befitted a man who was witnessing what to him was a shameful spectacle which would reflect badly on him in the eyes of his family and friends. Although I tried to enjoy the reception after he had gone he left a dark cloud behind him which hung over me. Zandra said, "To hell with your bloody family! If I were you, I'd have nothing to do with them ever again."

After a few hours we left everyone still drinking and went and changed into our travelling clothes. We had arranged to go on honeymoon the next morning and to spend that night at a hotel near the airport. Zandra and her husband Raymond drove us away with ribbons flying and tin cans clanking from the back fender of our car, and our friends waving us goodbye at the gate. We reached the hotel by evening and Zandra and Raymond kissed us and wished us a wonderful honeymoon. And so at last we were alone.

We had a quiet dinner together and then went up to our room. I put on my new nightgown and negligée set, a luxurious lace outfit in sea-green and chocolate brown, bought at one of Bristol's most exclusive stores. I looked at John who was waiting for me and thought, we've made it, survived the difficulties, and we're actually married. Despite the tensions of my father's presence at the wedding, I could not help feeling exhilarated to be embarking on this new life. I went to bed with John that night in relative contentment.

When my father returned to London that day it was to find an empty house. My mother had gone. He called all her friends but no one had seen her. And as I slept that night, dreaming of the future, she was found by the police in the early hours, wandering the streets, distraught and weeping.

My marriage to John did not go well. Portents of the troubles to come were already apparent on our honeymoon. We went to Tangiers and stayed at a splendid hotel with a blue-tiled courtyard and luxuriant gardens. Morocco was not quite the Middle East, but still part of the Arab world, and I tried to interest John in some of the features, which I thought similar to what I remembered of Syria and Palestine. These were few, as North Africa differs considerably from the eastern Arab world, but I found myself hunting for similarities between the two with a strange nostalgia. I sought to speak in Arabic to waiters in restaurants who did not understand me and preferred to speak in French. From time to time, as we walked along the streets or by the seashore, I would suddenly be gripped by moments of anguished remorse. I spent time in the souk, looking for a present for my father, driven by a compulsion that I had to do something to make it up to him. Finally, I found a gold signet ring which I had the jeweller engrave with his initials HK.

I gave it to him on my return, and for a long while he could not wear it in case my mother asked him where it had come from. Even meeting him had been a secret rendezvous, for, to my mother, I had become *persona non grata* since my marriage. She would not talk about me, refused to hear me mentioned in front of her and never so much as spoke my name. And my father, whom she watched like a hawk, was not allowed to be in touch with me either. She was angry with him for attending the wedding and, as it were, implicitly condoning my marriage. If I telephoned home, which I tried to do at the beginning, she would put the phone down as soon as she heard my voice. Though my father was less ferocious in his condemnation and we were able to keep up an intermittent form of communication despite her vigilance, I knew he basically agreed with her and had not forgiven me either. Siham, who had not been able to attend the wedding, but had sent us a large bouquet of flowers, tried to talk sense into our mother. "It's happened now," she wrote. "I know none of us wanted it, but you must learn to accept it."

My mother did not heed her and nothing changed. In August of 1965 John and I went at my insistence to work in London, he at St Thomas's Hospital and I at the Westminster Hospital. We shared a small, uncomfortable bed-sitter between the two hospitals and both our jobs were demanding and unpleasant. There was no reason in the world to have gone to London except for my blind need to draw near to my parents. All the time, I was aware of how close their house was, just a tube's ride away, and my father's office at the BBC was even nearer. Yet, they might have been in darkest Africa for all the difference it made. I knew I could not see them or even hear my mother's voice, and that made London feel like a foreign country. For my perception of the city was inextricably bound up with their presence in it; I had never known it otherwise.

The boycott lasted for a full six months. My mother finally allowed herself to respond to my phone calls, although she remained cold and distant for months thereafter and there was no question of us meeting. My husband was never mentioned in any of our conversations, as if he had been some unspeakable affliction with which we had been blighted. All of this had a curiously debilitating effect on me and, overwhelmed by a crushing weight of guilt, I felt nothing would ease it except their forgiveness. I wondered where my independence had gone, the defiance I had felt so strongly when I turned my back on them and all they stood for. And where was my new English identity and my determination to lead a totally English life without regret? Hard as I tried to tell myself that my parents were harsh, unreasonable and unfair, I still felt like a criminal who must atone for her crime.

Inevitably, all this took its toll of the marriage. In trying to deal with my anguish, John was out of his depth and could only look on helplessly. Our relationship was not made to withstand these pressures and we began to bicker and quarrel. The basic incompatibility between us, which had been suppressed by the events leading up to our marriage, began to resurface, provoked by the tensions with my family. I knew that John was not and never had been a suitable match for me. The fact of my having married him, not for himself, but in pursuit of a sense of belonging, now became painfully obvious. And from then onwards it was a downhill course. We moved back to Bristol at the beginning of 1966 and rented a flat off the Whiteladies Road in a turning opposite the one Zandra and I had shared. I tried to pull myself together and make a home for us, and matters improved for a while. But hovering over us continuously was the shadow of my family and our unresolved difficulty with them.

By 1967, we had separated twice for a few weeks each time, he staying with his mother, and I living alone in Bristol. I remember that on the first occasion, when we parted at my request, he suddenly put his face in his hands and wept. It was a disquieting, poignant sight and I was powerless to console him. I felt responsible for his unhappiness, but to have added the guilt he inspired in me to that I already had in abundance about my family was more than I could bear. In that time, ironically enough, my mother had relented somewhat and I had gone home for an uncomfortable, desperately apologetic weekend visit. In the spring of that year, Siham came over with her small daughter to stay with us at Willow Farm. John unburdened himself to her.

"Your parents still do not accept me. What more am I supposed to do?"

"What did you expect?" said Siham. "We tried to tell you how we all felt before you got married. Now that you have, most of us have adjusted to it, but my mother will always find it difficult." He looked sullen, and Siham said, "Look, it won't always be so bad. Ghada may have told you, we have a cousin who's also married to an Englishman, and my mother has accepted it. Please be patient, it's only a matter of time."

❧

But time was not on our side. On June 5, 1967, Israeli warplanes attacked Egypt and destroyed its airforce. They also invaded Syria, Jordanian-controlled Palestine and East Jerusalem. Israel and the Arabs were again at war and this critical event swept aside all other considerations. I was working at that time as a senior house officer at Frenchay Hospital in Bristol and was so obsessed by my problems that the war took me by total surprise. I had not followed events in the Middle East for years, why should I have? After all, I was English and had put all of that behind me. I had therefore not foreseen the fact that hostilities must sooner or later have broken out between Israel and its Arab neighbours. The last time I had taken any interest in Middle Eastern politics proper was in 1956, during the Suez crisis. I made brief contact again when Siham went back in 1959 during the era of the United Arab Republic. But thereafter, and being at Bristol, away from my father's political conversations at home, I heard little more about the Arab world. Even so, I was aware of the virulent and continuing hatred for Nasser around me. Epithets like "Nasser the new Hitler" and "Arab Nazis" were in common use. At the same time, Israel was portrayed as small and vulnerable, trying pluckily to stand up to its nasty, menacing Arab neighbours who constantly threatened its annihilation.

This was such a pervasive image that I scarcely thought about it, not because I believed it, but because I had grown used to it. In the same way, no one in England questioned Israel's right to exist. It had been the ancient land of the Jews and there was a natural logic about their wishing to return to it. In doing so, the argument went, they had only reclaimed what was rightfully theirs, and anyone who disputed that was seen as wrong-headed and hopelessly out of step. I had understood this almost instinctively and without knowing it had already acquired a sort of internal censorship which ensured that I never embarrassed anyone by speaking of Palestine, or the Palestinians who had lived in that same land for many centuries. This was made more possible by the fact that the rest of the world observed the same self-censorship. The original inhabitants of Palestine were called "Arab refugees" who lived in designated camps and who were only heard of in the context of international aid or UN statistics. Those not in camps, like us, were "Jordanians", or "Syrians" or other nationalities that gave no indication of their real origins.

It is strange to think now of that vacuum in Palestinian history and how we all accepted it. Certainly I, living in Bristol and married to an Englishman, had no awareness of myself as Palestinian and I never gave the matter any thought. I felt distant from the Arab world as a whole, but Nasser was such a British obsession that one could not avoid hearing the news. When he became a close ally of the Soviet Union, which helped him construct the Aswan High Dam and also train and equip his army, the newspapers became hysterical. Ordinary people in Bristol said it was two devils in harness. It recalled for me the time of Suez and with it I started to feel the beginnings of an unease about my surroundings.

When Nasser sent units of his revamped army into Yemen in 1962, to help the revolutionaries who had staged a coup against the monarchy there, British opinion was outraged. To me, Yemen was a faraway place that barely registered as an Arab country like Syria or Jordan. But Britain ruled over Aden and saw Nasser's army as a dangerous threat. How different from the way Arabs saw it. For them, Nasser was a hero. The same British newspapers that castigated Nasser were just as scathing about this Arab reaction. Few British people could understand why he had such prestige in the Arab world.

Although Egypt's union with Syria, which was supposed to usher in a new age of pan-Arab unity, lasted only till 1961, Nasser had become the undisputed leader of the Arab world.

My feelings towards all this were inchoate. Like almost everyone else in Britain, I had little curiosity about what was happening to the Palestinians. And so I missed the early stirrings of a Palestinian resistance movement that would change everything. In the late 1950s, just as I was getting to grips with university life, a small political movement called Fatah was beginning to take shape amongst Palestinians in the Arab world. Its founders included a young Egyptian-trained engineer called Yasser Arafat. No one I knew thought this was important and I had no awareness that my fellow Palestinians were mobilising.

In Siham's letters to me, she sometimes said how sad it was that we, Palestinians, had been forgotten. After 1948, the world saw us (if they ever thought about the problem at all) as either refugees in camps, to be pitied, or as scattered individuals and groups trying to survive. We played no part in politics or in mainstream society. Though Arabs, like those who worked at the BBC with my father, talked incessantly about Palestine, it was an abstract cause, and the real people were generally ignored. So Palestinians, fired by the ideal of Arab unity, looked to Nasser to achieve it and, through it, the liberation of Palestine.

If anyone in Britain had ever mentioned this, I might have become interested. As it was, the only Arab struggle we heard about was the Algerian revolution. "Only because France is involved," my father would comment. "One colonialist power sympathising with another." When France was defeated and the Algerian Republic came proudly into being in 1962, Subhi Zabaneh and I were the only ones to be excited. I knew as little about the Algerian struggle in 1962 as I had done on that schoolgirl visit to Paris years before. But I still felt it had been a victory for the whole Arab world. I later understood that for all Palestinians it was a great inspiration and a supreme model to be adopted in their own struggle with Israel.

By 1964, Arafat and his fellow revolutionaries had established the beginnings of a guerrilla organisation around them which attracted fedayeen from the refugee camps and Palestinian sympathisers in exile. My cousin Zuhair, now in Kuwait, said that everyone was giving the organisation money. Arab students, even those abroad, offered ideas and enthusiasm. Many eventually joined as fighters as well. Subhi said he thought he knew one or two Arab students in the Bristol University Union who had done so. They went to train in the new Algeria, which also gave them arms.

When I looked back to that time I thought it sad that, caught up in my own narrow world, I should have been so oblivious to these defining moments in Palestinian history. On January 1, 1965, while I was making preparations for my wedding, Fatah mounted its first guerrilla operation against Israel. Though it was a short-lived, abortive raid into northern Israel and damaged no one except the fighters themselves, it was the event, much celebrated by Palestinians afterwards, which launched the process and the concept of the Palestinian armed struggle against Israel.

I was too detached from these events to share the enthusiasm which now gripped Palestinians. They adopted the new guerrilla movement as authentically their own and one that would at last give expression to their frustrations. Even in distant Somalia, Siham and her husband and the whole of the Palestinian community felt the same excitement. When Yasser Arafat's brother went to Somalia in 1965 to ask them for funds, they turned out in strength to welcome him. To loud applause, he said that Fatah would not rest until the homeland was totally liberated and all Palestinians could return.

No one in Britain had heard of him or his brother at the time. The one Arab leader the British did know and admire was the young and handsome King Hussein of Jordan. He came across to them as a British-trained officer and a gentleman, more English than Arab. But to my family and their friends, he was no hero, since the Jordanian authorities, fearing Israeli reprisals, made every effort to obstruct guerrilla attacks against Israel from Jordanian land. Other Arab countries followed suit. And there, possibly, the Palestinian struggle might have ended, marginalised and insignificant, with me none the wiser as to when it had started or ended had it not been for the Six-Day War of 1967.

This dramatic and seminal event in Middle Eastern history came suddenly, as if out of the blue. When it started, the family heard about it in London before I did. Siham was still with our parents at the time, and on that fateful morning of June 5, as the family was finishing breakfast and listening to the radio, they heard news they could scarcely credit. The BBC relayed the information that at a quarter to nine that morning Egyptian time, two hours ahead of London, Israeli planes had swooped down on the Egyptian airfields. The Egyptians seemed to have been taken completely by surprise, their radar systems bypassed and their anti-aircraft missiles made impotent. In three hours of intensive bombing, the Israelis had demolished nearly all of Egypt's aircraft and rendered the runways unusable. This brilliant manoeuvre deprived the Egyptian army of defensive air cover and meant in effect that the war was all but won, not in six days, but in the first three hours.

So flabbergasted was everyone that my mother said quickly, "It can't be true! Quickly, tune onto Cairo." To her relief, the news from Cairo radio was good. Lofty pronouncements announced an Egyptian victory and an ignominious Israeli rout. "There you see?" she said. "The BBC was telling nothing but a pack of lies." However, as the day wore on, more dire information emerged. Jordan, which had joined the Egyptian front, reported that a large number of Israeli aircraft had mounted an attack on its territory. Meanwhile, an Israeli land attack had commenced across the Sinai pushing against the 100,000 Egyptian soldiers stationed there. They put up a fierce fight, but without air cover they were doomed. By the end of the first day of the war, Israel had captured El-Arish, Sinai's major town, and cut off Gaza. Cairo Radio was still broadcasting news of victory until my father, exasperated and angry, switched it off.

At lunchtime on that first day, while I was on the ward examining the new patients, someone mentioned that war had broken out between Israel and Egypt and that Israel had the better of it. It gave me a strange lurching feeling in the stomach and I could not wait to finish my afternoon ward round. But it was not until early evening that I was able to join a number of my colleagues avidly watching the news on TV. And it was there that I saw unforgettably the painful story of Arab defeat unfolding before my eyes.

As images of jubilant Israeli soldiers in tanks and a grinning General Dayan, the defence minister, with his unmistakable black eye patch came into view on the television screen, a cheer went up from those around me. "Hurrah!" they cried. "Good for Israel! That's right, give them all a good licking!" I looked at their rapt faces as they stared at the screen. Many of them were friends of mine, yet not one was on my side. All gawped with admiration at what Israel had done and an equal contempt, as it seemed to me, for its Arab adversaries.

The next day, it was no better. The Egyptian army started a mass withdrawal out of Sinai. The Israelis pressed on into Jordan and, after a massive offensive, invaded East Jerusalem. At the same time, they occupied the Gaza Strip and pushed their forces down towards the Suez Canal, taking Sharm al-Sheikh on their way. Calls at the UN for both sides to observe an instant cease-fire went unheeded. The Israelis seemed unstoppable. They overran the whole of the West Bank, causing a refugee exodus across the Jordan of some 200,000 Palestinians, or a fifth of the population. Some of these were refugees twice over, having first fled their homes in 1948. By the third day of the war the Israelis had captured the Old City of Jerusalem.

Along with the others, I watched in fascination the scenes of wild rejoicing as Israeli crowds swarmed all over the Wailing Wall.[1] Israel's leaders announced that Jerusalem would be theirs forever. What a curious, disturbing sight, I thought, to see the gleaming Dome of the Rock, one of Islam's most famous shrines, become the backdrop to this alien horde of black-robed rabbis and soldiers. To my horror, the Israeli flag was hoisted over the top of the Dome, the most sacrilegious, most inflammatory act of all. Even they could see that and it was brought down after a few hours.

Memories, dormant for years, of visiting my aunt's house in the Old City and playing with other children in the giant forecourt of the mosque on hot, still afternoons stirred inside me. The vast tiled courtyard in front of the Dome of the Rock used to make a perfect playground for hopscotch, and the historic arches, pillars and holy sanctuaries were ideal for games of hide-and-seek. As there were no parks or open spaces in the Old City where children could play, the mosque compound was the only place available. As the memories came back, I felt a dull ache, as if an ancient wound, which was thought to be long healed, had just been re-opened. I had a sense of deep perturbation and the first stirrings of anger at what had befallen us.

On June 8, Egypt accepted the UN's call for a cease-fire, but the Israelis pushed on regardless. By the next day, they had reached the

---

[1] The so-called Wailing, or Western, Wall is part of the mosque complex known as the Haram al-Sharif, which the Israelis call the Temple Mount. For Muslims, the Wall is a *waqf*, that is an Islamic endowment which is under the care and protection of the Muslim community.

eastern bank of the Suez Canal and could have gone on to Cairo for all the Egyptian resistance there was left. In that short time, Egypt lost over 10,000 men and over 5,000 soldiers were taken prisoner.

It was now Syria's turn and, on the fifth day of the war, Israel began pounding Syrian positions on the Golan Heights. Though Syria asked for a cease-fire, the Israelis ignored it and pressed on with their tanks to storm the Heights. They reached the topmost point and occupied the Syrian town of Kuneitra. Only at that moment did they accept the cease-fire. When the Six-Day War ended, Israel had destroyed three Arab armies and was in occupation of the whole of Sinai; the Gaza Strip; the whole of Jerusalem and the West Bank; and the Syrian Golan Heights. And it had done so with the whole-hearted approval, the loud applause even, of those amongst whom I lived.

At home, our family and friends were in a state of shock. I telephoned them every day during the war, our differences temporarily forgotten, to find consternation and a deep sense of shame. "The Arabs are totally useless!" exclaimed Siham bitterly. "They're like a house of cards. At the first push, they all came tumbling down." She had been considering a return to her home in Somalia, but when the war broke out, her husband cautioned her to wait until it was over before travelling to the region. No one had anticipated that the war would only last six days and end in total defeat for the Arab side and jubilant victory for Israel.

But no one around us at the time was in a mood to analyse the causes. The questions they put were despairing and rhetorical and the overwhelming feeling was one of shame at the Arab armies' abysmal performance. In Somalia, Ziyad, who was working with Russian engineers, felt too ashamed to face them. "We trained, armed and supported you," they said. "What went wrong?" In Britain, matters were aggravated for us by the florid, public display of pro-Israeli and anti-Arab sentiment which appeared in the wake of the war.

Numerous adulatory descriptions and editorials extolling Israel's
bravery and military skill appeared in the newspapers. They applauded Israel's victory as "the triumph of the civilised" – over the hordes
of Arab barbarians, they might have added.

Until then I had little understood the depth of sympathy which
Israel evoked amongst people in Britain and in the rest of Europe. Its
image of brave vulnerability as it faced annihilation from superior
Arab forces (an image that was far removed from reality) touched
people's hearts. The sufferings of the Jewish people at the hands of the
Nazis were fresh in the public mind and made what the Arabs were
allegedly trying to do all the more insupportable. "It's not so long
since they lost six million. They've suffered enough," was a common
view. And it was the Arabs who were the villains of the piece.

They were scorned and derided just as if the years of pent up
hatred for Nasser and the fear of the threat he had posed could now
find release in a virulent derision of all Arabs. There was public
delight at the humiliation which Israel had inflicted on him and the
Arab armies. Cartoonists in British newspapers published caricatures
of Arab soldiers, depicting them as shifty, cringing and cowardly. By
some mad psychological inversion, the Arabs had taken the place of
the Jews in popular scorn and what had been an ancient tradition of
European anti-Semitism was now converted into a racist anti-Arab-
ism. All of this made a deep impact on me, not least because in the
midst of this onslaught I felt undesirably prominent and at the same
time alone. I imagined that people saw me in the same light as they
saw the rest of the despised Arab nation. And I had no defence to
proffer, for the defeat of the Arabs by Israel was so thorough and so
devastating that there was nothing to be done except to hide one's
head in shame.

Siham in London experienced the same thing. She avoided English
people for fear of their contempt, although many assured her they had

no ill will towards her. Similarly in Bristol, colleagues comforted me with such remarks as, "You're different. We don't see you as Arab anyway," or, "Don't get so upset, it's Egyptians we can't stand." This only made me angry and I started to argue the Arab case passionately, just as I had done all those years before at the time of the Suez crisis – to as little effect. I saw with increasing shock and dismay the extent to which the *idea* of Israel had entrenched itself in the English mind.

This was not only to do with its supposed Biblical associations in the region, but also with the question of anti-Semitism which the Six-Day War had brought to the fore. When I argued furiously that whatever had happened to the Jews at the hands of Europeans was not the fault of Arabs, I met blank stares. "Why should we pay for what you, Europeans, did to the Jews? It's not fair!" I would exclaim. "If you're so sorry for them, why not have them all here or give them a part of Germany? That would surely be just, wouldn't it? And why didn't you and the Americans take them in when they were in trouble in the 1940s? Why ease your consciences at our expense?"

In delivering these diatribes I was giving voice to a widely held resentment amongst Arabs. It was not to do with anti-Semitism, in the European sense, which, for Arabs, was an alien notion. Jews were a part of Arab history, not another species to be subjugated and ghettoed. That was a European refinement, foreign to Arab thinking, and Arabs rejected being tarred with the same soiled European brush. But this left everyone I spoke to either cold or indifferent. Far from convincing them, I seemed only to affirm the prevailing opinion that Arabs were undyingly hostile towards Israel. Friends regarded me as emotional and overwrought, which I despairingly knew from long experience to be the ultimate English put-down. For to argue from emotion, something that foreigners were said to be especially prone to, exposed one to accusations of being irrational and unstable. One's views could thus be dismissed as unreasonable or hysterical. I remember one of the consultant physicians for whom I worked at that time saying, not unkindly, "I can see that you feel strongly, but you should understand that many of us over here wish Israel well. It's not blind prejudice, as you might think, but that after all the Jewish people have suffered we wish them well."

On the evening of June 9, Nasser announced his intention to resign. In a speech televised from his home he took full responsibility for the Arab defeat. As I looked at his haggard face and drawn features and heard the start of his halting words a lump came into my throat and I was filled with unutterable sadness. No one around me was moved in the slightest and I was quite alone in my sorrow. When, even before he had finished his resignation speech, it was reported that the people of Cairo were pouring out of their houses in hysterical grief at his departure, no one in Britain could understand it. By the next day, millions of Egyptians had converged on Cairo, clamouring for Nasser to stay.

"Strange business," concluded one of my colleagues. "You'd think, given the disaster he inflicted on them, they'd be glad to see the back of him. Funny people, Arabs." But I had no difficulty in understanding why Egyptians wanted Nasser to stay. He was the man who had taken back the Suez Canal, had stood up to foreign domination and had given Arabs a sense of national pride which had reached out even to those such as I, growing up in a foreign country, far away. I could see that to lose him now would spell the demise of the Arab world's unique historical opportunity to achieve independence and would offer the ultimate succour to its enemies. I longed to speak of these new insights to those around me but it was impossible. The war, brief as it was, had made me realise that I was alone. My community of friends, as I had thought of them, no longer existed, perhaps had only ever existed in my wishful imagination. I wanted them to understand and accommodate my sense of dual loyalty, to being English but also to being one of those "funny people". And more than anything, I wanted an acknowledgement of the wrongs committed by Israel against me and, by extension, all Arabs.

In expecting this, was I asking too much of Bristol's provincial English society which in the 1960s had little experience of foreigners, or of the conflict of identity that would only surface amongst young immigrants in Britain twenty years later? Was it reasonable to demand of Protestant Christians like them, reared on Old Testament stories which familiarised them with the Jewish link to Palestine and ignored everyone else's, that they recognise the Arab claim to the same land? And especially when those same Arabs were routinely presented in unflattering stereotypes and denigrating images? Perhaps, looking back, I did ask too much, but at the time I only felt depressed and misunderstood. I thought that my husband at least would take my side. The war had uncovered a political dimension to my life more important than I had ever suspected, and I assumed that he would understand it.

John was, however, guarded from the beginning. I noticed that even on that first day of the war, when the shock of it had hit me hardest, he was quiet and non-committal. As the situation worsened for the Arabs day by day he made none but the most anodyne of comments. This disturbed and bewildered me. Finally, I had it out with him.

"What do you think about it all?"

He looked uncomfortable. "You know what I think. I've said so."

"I don't think you're being frank. Please tell me what you really think about the war and about the Arabs and about Israel," I persisted.

To my surprise, he said, "I don't want to discuss it, if you don't mind."

"Why on earth not? You must have a view, surely. Why don't you say what it is?"

He shook his head. "You'll only get upset and we'll quarrel." This alarmed me further. I looked hard at him.

"I know you're Arab and all that," he said slowly, "but to be quite honest, I can't help admiring Israel. I mean, they fought well against enormous odds and they deserved to win." He paused, seeing my expression. "I'm not the only one who thinks so, you know," he said defiantly.

I thought: doesn't he understand how I feel or doesn't he care? It was true that we did not normally talk about my origins or indeed about politics, but he knew enough of my personal story to have formed an opinion of its rights and wrongs. To find him now slavishly following the pro-Israeli line of those who did not have his special insight into the problem was astounding. I remembered the times I had confided to him some small incident of my early life, some sad remembrance that came back from the past, and felt he had betrayed me.

Cleeve Mathews said afterwards that John's offence was not that he had a different view of Israel from mine, as couples often disagreed about politics, but that he should have been more aware of my personal feelings. Cleeve did not understand either. For me, the dissonance between us was not just a simple matter of tactful behaviour. It went to the heart of my relationship with him. If he could see nothing wrong in supporting Israel, which had usurped my homeland and been the cause of my expulsion from it, and which had caused yet another exodus of my countrymen in this war, then he was quite simply not on my side. And since he was not, on this most crucial of issues, how could I continue to live with him as if nothing had happened?

I now felt doubly alone. It was as if the week of the war had exposed me. I wondered who exactly I was. For years, I had wrestled with the impossibility of being two opposing personalities, Arab and

English. Eventually, I had settled for being predominantly English, although I knew underneath that I was not. But it had not seemed to matter, except for the difficulties caused by my family over my marriage. In marrying John and in numerous other ways, I had sought to belong to England, to fit seamlessly into English society, to adopt English culture as my own and to rebuild my fragile sense of identity along English lines. But the Middle East war put paid to all that. The polarisation that it caused forced on me the question, "If I am not one of them, then who am I?" And my husband's rejection of my side in the conflict exacerbated this dilemma.

I was crushed by the thought that my life had been nothing but a sham. The sense of belonging I had nurtured was only a pretence that I could no longer support. I may have become English in culture and affinity, but in all the ways in which it mattered I was not. And my sense of isolation amongst my colleagues forced me to face another melancholy realisation. Even had I wanted their acceptance they would never have given it. Their opposition to my stand on the conflict between Israel and the Arabs meant I could never be one of them. But then, whom was I one of? And could I go back to being the split personality that had caused me such anguish?

My marriage to John finally broke down one year later, in the summer of 1968. But before that he and I had parted temporarily in the wake of the Six-Day War. When we resumed living together we were both guarded and tense. Siham had started a charitable society in London to help the refugees and other victims of the war. Word had reached us that the Palestinians who had flooded into Jordan were desperate for clothes, food and money. She set up her society with the help of the Arab League office in London and raised funds and donations from many people. I visited her on the occasion of a charity bazaar she was running and invited John to go with me in the forlorn hope that he might be persuaded to see my point of view. When we met my sister he behaved politely enough; but he bought nothing, and she could not draw him out on the subject of the war.

We struggled through that final year together until July, when we decided on yet another temporary separation. By this time, John's mother appeared to think the blame for our matrimonial difficulties was mine.

Strangely, in that final year my mother resumed normal relations with me. She even came to Bristol on an unprecedented visit and stayed with us for a week. This was a considerable strain for she insisted on everything being done in the way she was used to. She took over the kitchen and the cooking and rearranged all the pans and crockery. She criticised my housekeeping endlessly – haven't you got this or that, what sort of a home do you call this? I suppose in her own way she had finally accepted the fact of my marriage, and her visit to us was an indication of that.

But it came too late. In August of that year, after John and I had been living apart for a few weeks, he telephoned and asked to see me. I wondered whether he wanted to tell me that we should start again, perhaps on a new basis. Lonely and depressed as I was by a sense of personal failure I wondered whether I should give it another try. Perhaps, I thought, we could make it work after all. We met in a hotel in the centre of Bristol. I thought this odd, but there was also something exciting about it. The first thing I noticed when I saw him was how well he looked. For months he had been pale and drawn, but now his skin gleamed and his dark eyes had regained their shine. For the first time in some years I found that I was enjoying his company. The thought that we might have dinner together later on flickered across my mind.

"What did you want to see me about?" I asked eventually.

I was totally unprepared for his answer. "I want you to give me a divorce," he said. "I've met someone else. I couldn't believe it would ever happen to me again, but it has."

I was momentarily struck dumb. A yawning sense of loss too terrible to describe gripped me. Why did I feel so bad? Did I love John after all or was this a replay yet again in my life of leaving, of abandonment, of neglect?

"Who is it?" I asked, numb with shock and not really wanting to know.

"You wouldn't know her," he said, trying not to smile. "She's an anaesthetist. I can't really believe it, but she's in love with me and we want to get married." He radiated happiness. Thoughts raced though my head, about him, about our doomed marriage and its sad ending. Though its failure had been inevitable, perhaps from the start, I felt agonisingly empty and bereft, the more so when I suddenly realised that John had come not just to end our marriage but also to take some sort of revenge – on me, on my family, perhaps on all of us because no one appreciated what he had endured in order to marry me. His triumphant manner, as of someone holding a trump card, gave him away.

And in truth how much had we considered what it had cost him to convert to Islam? Or the pain it had caused his devout Christian mother? Or the years he had spent trying fruitlessly to appease my guilt for marrying a non-Muslim and please my family?

"And that's it?" I said. "That's why you wanted to meet?" He nodded. I waited, wondering if he would say more, explain, express some sorrow or regret. He had always found it difficult to express his feelings, I knew that. Even so, it could not end like this, I could not accept it. But there was no discussion of the past, of where we had gone wrong, or of his feelings during our marriage. He did not tell me how he had met his prospective bride or how long they had known each other. He only wanted to talk about the practical details of our divorce. He was on another plane, buoyed up by his new-found love and unreachable. Nothing I said or did would have affected that excited optimism.

I asked that we postpone discussion of the divorce practicalities to another time. I felt defeated and sick at heart. I had lost my way. Unhappy though my marriage had been, it had at least given me a context and a social structure. For all our difficulties, John had been a constant, reassuring presence in my life. Parting from him brought back echoes of a previous parting, long ago in childhood, when the world I knew slipped away from me, irrevocably out of reach. What would happen to me now? He had found a solution in another love affair. But what about me? Where was the love affair for me?

And looking at John's contented self-satisfied smile, I suddenly knew the answer. I suppose it had been shadowing me all my life. John may have found happiness with his anaesthetist, perhaps for now. But the tortured love affair that waited inescapably for me, as for all Palestinians, was the one with Palestine. And, for good or ill, it would last a lifetime.

Part Three

In Search of Fatima

Twelve

In 1969, the Israeli prime minister, Golda Meir, made an astonishing pronouncement. "It was not as though there was a Palestinian people in Palestine considering itself as a Palestinian people and we came and threw them out and took their country away from them," she said. "They did not exist." Had it not been for statements like this, the changes which the defeat of 1967 had stirred in me might never have progressed further.

I knew that Mrs Meir's words sprang out of a new Israeli self-confidence as a result of the Six-Day War. Indeed, I had seen it spread to England in the atmosphere of glowing pro-Israeli approbation, which rose to a crescendo after the 1967 war. Thereafter, and although Israel's occupation of Arab land acquired in that war was illegal, any question over its right to exist in what had been Palestine was heresy; the concept of "Israel proper" – the state within the 1948 borders – was born to affirm this Israeli title to the country; any notion of Palestinian rights to the same land was absurd; and any criticism of Israel was anti-Semitic.

At the same time, Jewish people in England "came out". They were now overtly proud of their Jewishness and their links to Israel as never before; gone was the nervousness which had caused many to assume English surnames and English identities. There was a noticeable increase in the number of Jewish men wearing skullcaps, and the identification of British Jews with Israel was striking. A few days before the 1967 war started, Akiva Orr, an Israeli living in Golders Green who was later to become a close friend, had a strange experience. As he came home to his lodgings he bumped into his landlord, an elderly German Jew who had lived in England since before the Second World War and was a British national. Looking genuinely worried, he said to Akiva, "Well, what do you think? Will they destroy us?" Who is "us", Akiva wondered, since his landlord was originally German, lived in England and was not even religious. But of course, the man had meant "us Israelis".

In this climate of opinion there was no room for Palestinians. It was not that the Israeli point of view had no dissenters in England; indeed the 1967 war spawned a small number of British organisations and individuals who strenuously put forward the Arab case,[1] but that the support and sympathy for Israel was overwhelming. As I had recognised earlier, much of this was due to a cocktail of guilt about the Holocaust, a long and dishonourable history of European anti-Semitism, and Israel's Biblical associations, which influenced many Christians.

But it also derived from a staggering ignorance of the events which had led to the creation of Israel and which governed its subsequent behaviour. In addition, a new overt Jewish hostility towards Pales-

---

[1] One of the best known of these, the Council for the Advancement of Arab-British Understanding, or CAABU, was founded directly as a result of the war. Its founders comprised a number of concerned Britons and Palestinians and it aimed to present the Arab and Palestinian point of view to the British public. It is still functioning today.

tinians started to appear. When I left Bristol for London after my divorce in 1969 I took up a post at the Central Middlesex Hospital. One morning, while on my ward round to see the new patients who had come in during the night, I came across a Mrs Ruth Daniels. She was a middle-aged housewife from Willesden and had been admitted with pneumonia. Despite her state of illness, she eyed me warily from the start. After I had examined her, during which time she never took her eyes off me, she suddenly inquired where I came from. Without thinking, I answered that I was Palestinian.

"Ah!" she exclaimed angrily. "So, you're our enemy! And they've sent *you* to look after *me*?" I remember the sense of shock I had at her unexpected hostility; but I also felt somehow apologetic in case my national origins should serve to delay her recovery. Such was the aggressive thrust of pro-Israeli propaganda in those days that I unknowingly internalised some of its attitudes. I found myself applying an unconscious censorship to what I said and did, in case that dreaded accusation of "anti-Semitism" should be levelled at me. The effect of this was to make meeting Jews an uncomfortable experience; I would take scrupulous care not to reveal who I was or express my true opinion of Israel in case this introduced a discordant note into the relationship. It was as if, for all the world, it were they and not I who was the wronged party. Because of this, my experience with Mrs Daniels subsequently prevented me from disclosing my real identity to any more Jewish patients.

Not that such encounters were always so grim. When running my first out-patient session at the hospital in a clinic for neurological patients who had to be followed-up regularly for chronic ailments, I met a Mr Isaacs. Some months before, he had been paralysed from the waist downwards and confined to a wheelchair. But he had made a good recovery and could now walk with the aid of a walking stick only. As soon as he saw me he said, "You're new here, doctor? I never met you before." I smiled and asked him to sit down. "Not that I mind," he continued, making much of finding a place to rest his stick and groaning loudly as he lowered himself into the seat. "New face, new hope, that's what I say. Where d'you come from, doctor?" The memory of Mrs Daniels fresh in my mind, I thought for a bit and said, "Persia". (The country was not then popularly known as Iran.) "Very nice," he said, "very nice. Maybe they know to make me well in Persia. You know, doctor, I used to think that money was everything, but since I had this, I say to myself, 'Money, what's money when you haven't got your health?'" He flicked his wrist downwards in a gesture instantly reminiscent of Patricia's father.

I was new to the clinic and inexperienced in dealing with such patients. So, thinking it best to assume a brisk and jovial tone, I wagged my finger at him and said, "Now, now, Mr Isaacs, you're actually doing very well. Have you seen all those poor people out there in their wheelchairs? Think, you could be like them."

He looked at me for a second and then, hunching his shoulders, he said, "But on the other hand, I could be like you!" At this, we both dissolved in laughter and he and I became friends. We met at the clinic several hilarious times after that but I never felt able to tell him where I really came from.

Due to all these factors, by the beginning of the 1970s I felt invisible as a Palestinian. Worse still, my side of the story was unacknowledged and illegitimate. What had previously most angered me amongst my Jewish fellow pupils at school now resurfaced with virtually everyone I met. No one wanted to hear what I had to say or to give validity to my experience. No newspaper or magazine would have printed my story or that of any Palestinian, no radio or TV station would have spared a moment for a Palestinian view. No matter what my personal memories and experiences had been, or those of countless other Palestinians, only the Israeli version was valid.

It was clear that, whatever the cost, the Israeli project was determinedly to flourish, untrammelled by the embarrassing human detritus entailed in its creation. The Palestinian account of how Israel came into being could not be allowed to spoil the idyllic picture of a new young state built by fearless pioneers who had "made the desert bloom". This left me with the bitter realisation that I had not only lost my country, but that I had no right to grieve over it, or resent the fact that it was seized by others. The unvoiced implication was that we, Palestinians, had been no more than squatters on someone else's property, and, it was sometimes hinted, I was lucky to have found a home in England.

Meanwhile, other Palestinians, feeling as forgotten as I did, were determined to reverse the situation dramatically. In September 1970, the Popular Front for the Liberation of Palestine (PFLP), a group affiliated to the PLO, carried out a spectacular series of hijackings to a disused RAF wartime airstrip in the Jordanian desert called Dawson's Field. Three aircraft, two American and one Swiss, were seized by the hijackers and taken there. On the same day, another attempted hijack of an Israeli plane failed; one of the hijackers was killed while the other, a woman called Leila Khaled, was handed over at Heathrow airport to the British police.

The hijackings were indefensible; yet, watching events in London, I and many other Palestinians could not help but feel impressed. Suddenly, everyone was talking about the Palestinians, a subject long deemed buried in obscurity. Leila Khaled, though described repeatedly as a terrorist, clearly held a special fascination for people in Britain. Young and good-looking in her black and white check *kuffiyya*, she came across as defiant and mysterious. The journalists who covered her story were intrigued and attracted by her and there was something undeniably exciting about an exotic young woman who seemed so dedicated and so fearless. I remember that I admired her, not for her hijacking exploits but for her passionate dedication to Palestine.

When I met her in London many years later she had lost none of her charisma or her devotion to the cause. "Did you ever regret what you did?" I asked. She looked at me earnestly and said, "We never wanted to harm anyone not involved in our conflict. That was not the aim. But we had to publicise our cause. One hijacking did more for us than twenty years of patience and waiting." Even so, the terrorist label stuck to her and I wondered that Israelis, whose history had encompassed far worse terrorist acts in the service of their own ideal, should so condemn the likes of Leila Khaled.

No matter that the world denounced "Palestinian terrorism", the whole episode had returned the issue of Palestine to the international agenda. That had of course been the aim of the whole exercise. As George Habash, the leader of the PFLP, said at the time, "When we hijack a plane it has more effect than if we killed a hundred Israelis in battle. For decades world opinion has been neither for nor against Palestinians. It simply ignored us. At least the world is talking about us now."

That was certainly true, but what relief this action might have brought to the forgotten Palestinians was short-lived. The Western world found little to sympathise with in the Palestinian reappearance on the international stage. There was scant regard for the patient, passive twenty years in which Palestinian refugees had quietly endured their awful lives, awaiting a solution, and little understanding for the frustration of Palestinians forced to resort to acts of terrorism in order to have their case heard. But if they had hoped thereby to persuade Western powers of their position they were sadly mistaken. On the contrary, they gave Israelis and their sympathisers a perfect weapon to level at the Palestinians, who were now dubbed "terrorists" and marginalised even more.

Patricia's parents were amongst those to be influenced by this. To my chagrin, I found that they had begun to avoid me, and if we ever met by chance they would look nervous and embarrassed and try to make the meeting as short as possible. At this time also I recall being in Oxford Street one day and bumping into a German woman who worked for Lufthansa airlines and whom I had met through friends. As I smiled at her in greeting she shrank away from me. "What's wrong?" I asked. "Don't people like you ever think of the damage you do?" she hissed and walked on hurriedly. Fear, however, was not the only emotion I inspired, as I soon discovered.

❧

In my second year as medical registrar at the Central Middlesex Hospital I acquired a young house officer called Jeremy Stone. It transpired that he had an Israeli father and a Christian, English mother. As such, he was a non-Jew according to Jewish religious law which recognises as Jews only those who have converted or been born of a Jewish mother. In his case, however, this made no difference and he was passionately attached to Israel and Jewishness, as if he had been the most pure-bred of Jews. In appearance, he was strongly Aryan, blond and blue-eyed, with a very light complexion. Barry Fink, my other house officer, who had two Jewish parents and was thus the "genuine article", thought him bizarre. Barry had been disowned by his family for "marrying out", and cared little about it. "I couldn't wait to get away from all that 'eat your chicken soup and listen to your mother' crap," he said. "And look at him, stupid sod, that's all he wants!"

Jeremy had stayed on a kibbutz in Israel and in the process had acquired an Israeli girlfriend called Tamar who came to see him whenever he was on call for the hospital. It was in this way that I got to know her and noticed how she used to stare at me. Jeremy was aware of my origins and we occasionally spoke about the conflict, a pointless and irritating exercise, as his partiality for Israel was so total as to render him incapable of even listening to another point of view. I had grown familiar with this kind of reaction in England, and it usually enraged me. But I tolerated it in Jeremy, whose exaggerated feelings for Israel I deemed to be linked to some emotional problem he had rather than to any reasoned position. Perhaps he hated his mother, I thought, and rejected the English side of himself she represented by attaching himself to another people and a foreign country. Whatever the truth, his social life included none of his compatriots but revolved entirely around visiting or immigrant Israelis; he had also decided to marry Tamar and move with her to Israel once his medical apprenticeship was over.

None of this need have mattered had it not been for my meeting with his Israeli group. One day, to my surprise, he and Tamar invited me to meet their friends. These were to be several young Israelis who had expressed the wish to meet a Palestinian. It was the beginning of 1971, when several hijackings had taken place and when Palestinian political action, frequently dubbed "terrorism" by Israel and the West, was already notorious. I am not sure what decided me to accept Jeremy's invitation. I had a vague idea that I might succeed in conveying something to his friends about Palestine and, in addition, I was curious about them too. Though I knew many Jews, I had scarcely ever met Israelis. In deciding to go and see them I certainly had no suspicion that their intentions might have been anything but benign.

A lifetime spent in England had conditioned me to the gentlemanly view of things, that, however badly people felt about each other, there were still basic decencies to be observed. It was a version of the "not cricket" approach to life which I had learned in childhood and had come to expect as a matter of course. We met at an address in Hampstead which turned out to be a flat above a shop called "Chic".

This was a smart and expensive boutique which sold French lingerie. I had often lingered before its windows when walking down that road, having no suspicion that its owners were nothing whatever to do with France.

They were in fact Israeli, relatives of the group I was to meet. When I arrived, Jeremy opened the door to my knock, looking awkward. I followed him up a dark, narrow staircase which ran alongside the shop. It led to a small upstairs flat whose sitting room directly overlooked the street. Here, I found a roomful of people crammed together on the few chairs, some sitting on the arms of sofas and some on the floor. Perhaps I anticipated that they would look "Israeli", whatever that meant, but they had no recognizable features in common. Some were fair, others dark; the shapes of their faces varied from Slav to Nordic. None looked remotely Middle Eastern and they could have originated from anywhere in Europe.

As I entered they all went quiet and stared at me, as if I had been a strange animal. There were slightly more men than women amongst them and, like Jeremy and his girlfriend, they all looked to be in their twenties, not much younger than myself. Too late, I realised I had been set up, deliberately brought there to satisfy an idle, prurient curiosity, without even a nod to any intrinsic interest I might have had as a human being in my own right. I had an urge to walk straight out and should have done so but for a misguided sense of courtesy towards them.

Someone made room for me on a chair and asked me to sit down. Jeremy offered me a drink but I declined. One of the young men introduced himself as Dan and said they'd heard a lot about me from Jeremy. The others all nodded. Then he asked me where I came from. I sensed this conversation was pre-arranged and that I was meant to fall into some trap. I thought again of leaving, but was held there, as if mesmerised.

"Palestine", I answered.

"You mean Israel," he said.

"No, I mean Palestine. That's what it was called when I was born there."

They started to laugh. "You don't like Israel, do you?" This was Tamar, who had always seemed mousy and timid, but was now clearly emboldened by the presence of her colleagues. "That's right, isn't it, Jeremy?" He had the grace to flush and look embarrassed. He mumbled something unintelligible.

"Would you expect me to like Israel?" I asked.

"Why not?" she asked.

"Well," I answered, "what you call Israel was once called Palestine and is my homeland. However, people like you came over from all kinds of places, took it over and threw us out. How about that for a reason?"

One of the boys, who had been silent until then, now responded. "It's Jewish land, it's our land from thousands of years. We wanted the Arabs to stay, but you all ran away."

"Fine. Suppose you're right, why don't you let us come back then?"

They looked at each other and then changed track. "Do you think it's fun to hijack planes and kill people?" This from a girl sitting at the back by the door. They all stared hard at me. The atmosphere had slightly changed; in addition to the discomfort I was already suffering, I began to feel an obscure unease, as if they might actually attack me physically. I looked round at their hostile faces – some wore jeering expressions – and decided I had to leave. I got up.

"You must answer," said Dan, who I realised by now was a sort of group leader. "I don't do hijacking and I don't kill people," I replied angrily. "It's a pity you brought me here just to be nasty. It's a pity you didn't take advantage of the opportunity to be with an actual Palestinian and try to find out how we feel and what really happened."

They laughed again and a few lit cigarettes. I looked at Jeremy, expecting him to help me. But he looked back at me coldly and put his arm round Tamar. I got up and said, "Excuse me, I'm going." "Of course," retorted the girl who had mentioned the hijacking, "you're all in it together. Call yourself a doctor? Did you know that doctors are supposed to save lives, not kill people?"

I pushed past her and out of the door. As I ran down the stairs, they all started talking at once, and I was glad to slam the street door shut behind me on the babble of their voices. I was shaking with anger, frustration and self-recrimination. How could I have subjected myself to such an experience?

In the weeks which followed that night I came to a decision. The accumulated frustrations, humiliations and sense of being misunderstood as a Palestinian in Britain had reached a climax. I was determined to reverse this dismal fate by action that would counter such ignorance and contempt. At first my feelings were inchoate. My political experience was non-existent. I longed to start, but didn't know how. I began to look for what I thought were like-minded Palestinians, but with little result. The small Palestinian community which lived in Britain in the early 1970s was politically inactive.

Amongst them were people like my parents, whose energies had been exhausted by surviving the trauma of 1948 and then acclimatising to a life in England, far away from home. They lived on their memories and consigned Palestine to an irrevocable past which it would be futile to reincarnate. None of that generation ever considered visiting Israel, though, technically, they could have done so using their British passports. My parents even shunned seeing pictures of Israel and avoided any mention of travel there. For them, it was a place frozen at the moment of their departure in 1948, like a photograph – an Arab country with Jews in it, not the other way around. They could not have borne seeing its familiar landmarks, the nostalgic haunts of their youth, despoiled, as they would see it, in Israeli hands.

The other Palestinians in Britain were short-term visitors, mostly students or people who had come for professional specialisation. Their presence in the country was often precarious and conditional on the good offices of the British authorities and so were unwilling to jeopardise their opportunities by engaging in political work. The Palestinian sense of statelessness and fear of dispersal which underlay this behaviour died hard. It is still present today and remains a bar to effective action. Outside of the small Palestinian students' union, there were no Palestinian societies, no cultural or lobbying groups and no organised communal activities. The contrast with Britain's highly efficient and organised pro-Israeli lobby could not have been greater.

Every gap in public information on Israel, its history, invented or real, its conflict with the Arabs, its tourist sites and other attributes was plugged by this lobby. The Arab side of the story was absent by default and the vacuum it left was rapidly filled by Israel's friends. To me this was Arab and Palestinian defeat in action. Not all the military exploits of the PLO or the flamboyant hijackings of its extremist cadres could make up for these defects – they actually exacerbated the problem. The Arab side was in retreat and had been since the defeats of 1948 and 1967. And it meant that in this conflict, victim and perpetrator, right and wrong, were turned upside down to the extent that it was now up to the native Palestinians to prove their history and their title to the land they had lost, not the newcomers who had displaced them.

Eventually, I found a small group of sympathisers, none of them Palestinian, to help me establish Palestine Action in 1972. This was before Yasser Arafat's historic appearance at the UN General Assembly in 1974 and before there was any PLO representative in Britain. We were all amateurs, filled with enthusiasm and a confident sense of the justice of the cause we were promoting. The fact that we were the first political group solely concerned with the Palestine issue added piquancy and excitement to our work. We invited Andrew Faulds, the Labour member of parliament, to be our president.[2] He was a strikingly handsome man who had been a well-known actor before he entered politics. But his chief importance for us was his unflinchingly brave and principled stand on the Palestine question. He was amongst a small minority in a political party which was over-whelmingly pro-Zionist in the misguided belief that Zionism and the Israeli Labour Party were both socialist.

I raised money for the organisation by going to Arab embassies in London and begging for it. My astonishing success in doing this emboldened the group to embark on a programme of great daring. We wrote to world leaders, requested meetings with the British Prime Minister and made contact with radio and TV. I am not sure that this had any effect, but we had the illusion of being important in a heroic struggle.

As the organisation grew it started to attract a few Jewish sym-pathisers who came to our meetings. They were an odd collection of left-wingers, communists and genuinely confused Jewish people, unhappy about Israel's oppression of the Palestinians. The rest of the Jewish community disowned such people as traitors to the cause of Israel and Zionism and called them perverse, "self-hating Jews". At this time also I made my first contacts with sympathetic Israelis. These represented a tiny constituency in Israel, scarcely more than a handful of people with extreme Marxist or communist anti-Zionist ideologies. They had no political influence in Israeli society but they made a profound impression on me. It was then that I met with Akiva Orr and Moshe Machover, founder members of a fringe anti-Zionist Israeli organisation called Matzpen.

Akiva was a funny, lovable man with a bald head like the actor Yul

---

[2] He remained a lifelong friend of Palestine until his death.

Working with Palestine Action in the early 1970s: demonstrations (top and right) and a press conference with Peter Hain

Brynner and a strong German-Israeli accent. Born in Berlin, he had emigrated with his parents as a child to Palestine. Like other European Jews at the time he grew up a committed Zionist and served in the Israeli army. However, he became attracted to communist ideas in the 1950s and eventually turned away from Zionism which he viewed as a settler-colonialist movement, incompatible with the ideas he supported. His openly anti-Zionist stance made it difficult for him to remain in Israel and he ended up living in London. Soon, his small house in Kilburn became a centre for radical political discussion and a meeting point for dissenters. I regarded him as my first and most important political mentor and indeed he became something of a guru for many of us aspiring Palestinian and Israeli activists.

Through Akiva, I met a new young generation of radical Palestinians and Israelis and in time also a number of committed anti-Zionists like him. In the climate of the time, contacts between Palestinians and Israelis were highly unusual. Despite the fact that the

Palestine National Council (PNC), the Palestinian parliament-in-exile, had called in 1970 for a state in which all Jews, Muslims and Christians would live in equality,[3] Israelis were generally regarded as enemies and most Arabs did not distinguish a "good" Israeli from a "bad" one. The handful of Palestinians like me who undertook such contacts at the time were a valiant rarity which unknowingly anticipated much later events. I had, of course, to be discreet about my political friends with my family, although I once introduced Akiva to my father who took interest in him for his socialist views. My mother never found out and neither did our friends, but I did not otherwise bother to conceal what I was doing.

Emboldened by my new role of activist, I wrote to the Israeli embassy in London under an assumed name, saying that I was Palestinian, that I had family in Israel and was applying for permission to emigrate. This was done deliberately as I knew that Israel practised a so-called Law of Return which gave the right of emigration to any Jew anywhere in the world but denied it to non-Jews, which included Palestinians. For example, Mrs Daniels, my Jewish patient from Willesden, could have gone to Israel the next day, but someone like me and really entitled to "return", was barred from entry. The embassy wrote back, predictably explaining that I could not emigrate although I could visit on a tourist visa like anyone else.

Many Arabs disapproved of my mixing with Israelis. But I didn't care. I was young and inexperienced enough to believe that the sheer existence of an organisation like Palestine Action and its activities were enough to promote the Palestine cause. Furthermore, the justice

---

[3] The Democratic Front for the Liberation of Palestine (DFLP), one of the groups affiliated to the PLO, first introduced the idea of "secular, democratic state of Palestine" in which all citizens, irrespective of their religion, would have equal status. The proposal, which was a remarkable invitation for Jews and Arabs to live together, was contemptuously dismissed by the Israelis and also rejected by most Palestinians.

of the case spoke for itself, I believed. Professionally, I carried on part-time general practice, which supported me; but my heart and soul were entirely taken up with my political work. The years of neglect of my cause, the ignorance and misunderstanding of what Palestinians had suffered and the humiliations meted out to me by countless insensitive people in Britain drove me like a demon.

My father was horrified. His ambition to keep all of us shielded from the conflict that had caused our exile and see us settled in safe and respectable occupations had been thwarted. I did not know whether Siham and Ziyad approved of my new life. They both lived in the Arab world and seemed immeasurably remote. Ziyad had met a Danish woman while working in Somalia and, much to my mother's dismay, married her. I did not meet her until later and each of us was so embroiled with our own lives that we were rarely in touch.

By the mid-1970s I had latched passionately onto the cause of Palestine as an inspiration, an identity, a reason for living. I felt part of a lofty enterprise – to put right a huge injustice of which I was also victim. Grandly fired by this sense of destiny I embarked on adventures that would have been unthinkable in my previously staid and conventional English life. In 1976 I went to Beirut and met Yasser Arafat for the first time. By then he had acquired mythic status for me and all Palestinians; a hero and patriot to us, a shrewd and canny statesman to the Arabs, but a terrorist to Israel and to the part of the world where I lived

We met in the Fakhani district which the PLO had made into their empire in Beirut. It was a poor area, abutting onto the large Palestinian refugee camps of Sabra and Shatila (later to be the scene of a horrible massacre in 1982 perpetrated by Christian Lebanese gunmen, who entered the camps under Israeli protection) and consisted of several apartment blocks where the various PLO factions had their offices and housed their families. The buildings covered an area of about one square mile. Everyone regarded it as "Fatehland", since its largest faction, Fatah, dominated the PLO. In 1976 I was seeing Palestinian power in the country at its zenith.

The PLO controlled the whole of the western, Muslim part of Beirut; it was responsible for maintaining communications, disrupted by the civil war, and was the sole power responsible for people's protection from aggression and crime. Yasser Arafat was said to be hunted wherever he went and so had no fixed place of work or residence. He was constantly on the move, without a home or wife or family, and no allegiance beyond the cause of Palestine.

For me, that first meeting with him was unforgettable. A new and amateur recruit to the world of Palestinian politics as I was, I could hardly believe that I was actually there, in the flesh, looking at that face, which I had seen so often on TV and in the papers, the face of a man who had inspired such hatred, such obloquy and at the same time such admiration. He was wearing a black and white check *kuffiyya* on his head and an open khaki shirt and trousers. When he stood up to greet me I was struck to see how short he was, scarcely taller than myself. He put his hands on my shoulders and, to my amazement, he kissed my brow. He had thick lips, but they were extraordinarily warm and soft. I was uncomfortable and yet flattered by the familiarity of this action.

As I described my organisation in London and the most prominent of our activities he doodled idly on a piece of paper in front of him, as if he were not listening. But I could see that he did not miss a word, darting sharp looks at me out of his piercing, intelligent eyes. I remember thinking what charisma and presence he had, and, despite his physical ugliness, how attractive he was. When he finally spoke he revealed an Egyptian accent which he had acquired over the many years he had spent in Egypt. He talked about the struggle on two fronts, diplomatic and military, and said that we must not flinch from warfare when it was needed.

"Never forget that it was our heroic fedayeen and our martyrs who made the world sit up and recognise the cause of Palestine once again," he said gravely. "When the Zionists took our country, they used force to get what was not theirs. Can anyone expect we should do less to get back what is ours?" I stared at him, wanting him to continue. But he suddenly smiled at me and reiterated the famous Fateh fighting slogan, "Revolution until victory!"

As I got up to leave I realised that he had offered me nothing tangible for my organisation or any promise of a formal link with him; in fact, none of the things I had promised my group I would try and obtain. And yet I felt strangely satisfied, as if the mere contact with him had given me something more important, a sense of specialness and inclusion. To me, he seemed a hero and the true leader of our people.

I could not imagine, looking at him then, that there would come a time when I – when many of us – would feel differently; a time when he would lay down his arms and would strike a deal – the Oslo Agreements of 1993 – that guaranteed so little for us and so much for our enemy; would call an end to that "revolution until victory"; and, in spite of all of that, would be reviled as a terrorist.

Several months later, in the Libyan capital of Tripoli, baking in the mid-summer sun, I was at an international conference on Zionism. Eight months before, in November 1975, the UN had passed a resolution branding Zionism a form of racism, much to the anger of the Israelis and their supporters. The Arabs welcomed it and there was a flurry of meetings and conferences in the Arab world to affirm the UN decision. Libya, a well-known supporter of the Palestinian cause, had convened this conference on the subject. Many participants were Palestinians like myself living in different countries abroad and it was a rare opportunity for us all to meet. When someone asked if we would like to see the guerrilla training camps outside Tripoli, a few of us eagerly agreed. For me, it felt like getting to the very heart of the excitement and the danger of what it meant to be Palestinian.

Out in the desert I met the camp commander "Abu Zaki", his *nom de guerre*. (All fighters in the revolution have *noms de guerre* whether or not there was an eldest son to justify the title; the most famous *nom de guerre* of this type was of course that of Yasser Arafat who was known to everyone as "Abu Ammar".) Abu Zaki told us about his life, that he spent many years as a diplomat travelling between different countries before he became a full-time soldier. He seemed to enjoy our company and even consulted me regarding his chronic indigestion. But when I suggested he give up smoking he shook his head vigorously. He described the training "the boys" received in guerrilla warfare and how it was based on military models in Algeria, China and North Vietnam, all supporters of the Palestinian revolution. In this camp the guerrillas were given only basic training before they were sent out on missions. I had the uneasy feeling that the boys in his charge were more like cannon-fodder to feed the revolution than valued soldiers.

Having drunk the coffee he offered us, he told us it was time to visit the boys.

"Just say a few nice words to them," he said, "something about your lives abroad. It's nice for them to hear news from the outside world as they never see anyone except us and those who train them. Remember," he continued matter-of-factly, "once they're sent on an operation, we never know which of them will come back." I found this chilling, although I knew of course that Palestinian guerrillas were trained for the sole purpose of military attacks on Israel.

As such, they had mounted hundreds of raids since 1967 and had become a *cause célèbre*, attracting thousands of non-Palestinian recruits, mostly other Arabs but also many Europeans, to the ranks of the PLO. By the 1970s, some of the operations were aimed at targets outside Israel and were called terrorist. The most shocking of these was the attack on the Israeli athletes at the Munich Olympics in 1972[4] and this labelled all Palestinians thereafter in the West as "terrorists". No one any longer distinguished one type of Palestinian from another, and even I was regarded with suspicion.

Among the trees behind Abu Zaki's hut, we came to a clearing, where, lit by several camp lights, we saw a dozen men with rifles wearing camouflage uniforms and army boots. They were sitting on the ground, smoking and talking. As we approached, they struggled to stand up, but Abu Zaki motioned them to sit down again. They greeted him warmly and some reached up for his hand.

"These are the foreign visitors I told you about, boys," he said, introducing us. They all smiled and nodded, and some murmured, "Welcome". I was amazed at their youth. I don't know what I expected, but I was shocked to see how young they were and how thin and vulnerable many of them looked. We asked them about themselves and learned that they all came from the refugee camps of Lebanon. Most were too young to remember Palestine properly and knew no other life than that of the camps. They had been taught at the UNRWA camp schools and had never travelled anywhere before. This assignment in Libya was their first and they were being prepared for missions to take place quite soon, although none would enlighten us about the details.

It seemed somehow banal, even frivolous, but I told them about my

---

[4] This was carried out by Black September, an extreme PLO faction set up in the wake of the massive anti-PLO attacks by Jordan in 1970 which the Palestinians could not forgive. Black September fighters took the Israeli athletes hostage and made a series of demands for their release. In the armed attempt by the German police to free the hostage, all the athletes were killed along with several of their Palestinian captors.

political work in London, the demonstrations I organised for Palestine and the fact that I lived in a small flat by myself. I knew that none of them could even begin to imagine what a place London was like, so totally was this outside their experience. They looked at me with fascination and, as I talked to them, I remembered England, its safety, its prosaic tranquillity, shopping at Sainsbury's, listening to "The Archers", drinking tea in bed with the papers on Sunday mornings – and I felt ashamed.

I suddenly saw that my life there was nothing but an act. I was playing at being Palestinian, unwilling to soil myself with its reality. It was these poor boys, these "terrorists", with their wretched lives and the certainty of their violent ends, who were the reality. All else was hollow, self-indulgent pretence. My having left medical practice to devote myself to political work in England seemed suddenly a shameful abnegation of responsibility. I decided that the only honourable course open to me was to leave my comfortable, but dishonest English lifestyle, and make a genuine contribution. I would take my medical skills to the refugee camps where I could truly serve my people. It was a defining moment and I felt healed, cleansed and at peace with myself.

࿇

The refugee camp, with its miseries and its strengths, is at the heart of the Palestinian problem. In the summer of 1977 I went to the biggest and most turbulent, Ein al-Hilweh, near Sidon in Southern Lebanon. As I walked amongst the crowded rows of cement-built shacks, narrow alleyways snaking between them, all identical, I wondered how people knew their way around. Small, grubby children skipped deftly over the rivulets of dark liquid which flowed down through the open sewers in the middle of the alleyways. People peered at me curiously from their doorways, the women shouting to the children to come away. But when I smiled at them and my guide said, "This is Dr Ghada. She comes from England", they responded warmly and invited me into their homes.

One of the women was particularly insistent. She was carrying a child of two years or so who stared at me from beneath his mother's chin. She was so thin and pale that I wondered she had the strength to carry the child. I followed her into the one-room shack where she lived with her husband and three other children. She looked too young to have had such a large family and, when I said so, she explained that like many of the girls there she was married at fourteen. Her husband supplemented the rations they received selling scrap metal.

Few of the men – this is still true a quarter of a century later – had any form of regular employment. Many of them resorted to occasional work like car repairs or helping out in the fields at certain times of the year when extra labour was needed. Several also ran small shops in the open area outside the shacks, selling fruit and vegetables, sweets and cheap plastic goods. The inside of the shack was dark and bare. A floral curtain in the corner enclosed the "kitchen". There was no bathroom or toilet and when I asked how they managed she said they used plastic bags which she took every day to the cesspit outside.

It turned out she wanted to consult me about her son whom she tried to put down on the floor. But he cried listlessly and she had to pick him up again. She said that he was constipated and would not eat and I could see that the child was ill. He had an unhealthy colour and black shadows under his eyes. I told her that he needed to see the doctor, but she said that the doctor had sent her away. I turned inquiringly to my guide, a cheerful-looking young man, born and bred in this place, wearing jeans and a T-shirt saying "I love California". "Now, that's enough," he admonished the woman firmly but not unkindly. "Dr Ghada is here on an important visit. She doesn't

want to be bothered with your troubles, she's here to help all of us. I
told you before to go to the clinic if you're worried. It's open every
morning."

The woman looked dejected at this and I started to protest in
sympathy. But the young man took my arm and drew me away.
Outside, he said, "They can be a real nuisance here, moaning and
complaining. If you listen to them you'll never hear the end of it,
believe me." He guided me to the building which housed the kindergarten and left me with the headteacher. But I was troubled by the
encounter and went on wondering about that poor woman and her
sick child.

All my experiences that day left me shaken. I had never visited a
refugee camp before and did not know what to expect. Up until then I
had visualised them as an assembly of tents in some empty wasteland.
I was taken aback to see the reality which more closely resembles the
shanty towns sprawling on the edge of large cities, self-contained
entities that have a separate existence from the place they stand in. A
moment's thought should have made me realise that it could not have
been otherwise, since these camps had been standing here for decades,
ever since the Palestinian exodus of 1948.

Ein al-Hilweh means "sweet water spring", a cruel mockery of the
place's squalid reality. When I saw it in 1977 it housed some 20,000
people. (There are double that number now.) The inhabitants were
predominantly Palestinians who fled from the Galilee area in the north
of Palestine. They had lived here all their lives dependent on
UNRWA food rations, education and health clinics. But since 1967
there was also the PLO, which provided the refugees with funds and
an additional network of health and social services. As in the other
refugee camps of Lebanon, the young men and some of the young
women were the fighters whom the PLO recruited in its war against
Israel; I immediately remembered Leila Khaled and thought of the

boys I met in Libya. Seeing the bleakness of their lives, I did not wonder at what drove them to fight Israel. When they died in these operations the PLO adopted their orphaned children, who from that time onward belonged to the Revolution and were trained to be fighters in their turn when they grew up.

Zahra, the headteacher, took me to see the kindergarten. Each classroom was known by the name of a different Palestinian city. She paused outside the door called "Haifa". "Do you want to come into this class? The kids here are four years old but should be able to tell you where they come from." I was puzzled. "We teach our children all about Palestine," she explained proudly. "By the age of four, they all know their exact place of origin and they can show it to you on the map." She put her head round the classroom door and asked if we could come in. It was a sparse, clean room. There were several round tables with six to eight children seated at each. They were all dressed in identical uniforms and they all looked scrubbed and neat. They were also surprisingly well nourished and as they looked round at me their faces were full of bright curiosity.

The classroom walls were hung with childish drawings of hills and trees and each one was inscribed with the name of a place in Palestine. Also on the wall were pictures of a benignly smiling Yasser Arafat and his two popular lieutenants, Abu Jihad and Abu Iyyad (both later to be assassinated, the first by Israeli agents). One child was pushed over the edge of his chair by another and started to cry, but their teacher, a young girl with a fresh, pretty face, hurried across and comforted the child.

"Now, now," she scolded, "is this the way to welcome our visitor?" All the children shook their heads solemnly.

"No," continued the teacher, inviting me in, "it isn't, is it? So, what do we say to the visitor?"

"*Ahlan wa sahlan* [Welcome]!" chorused the children.

"And where do we all come from?" she prompted.

"Palestine!" they answered in a great shout.

"And when we grow up," continued the teacher, "where are we all going to?"

"Palestine! Palestine!"

The teacher looked pleased with her efforts and Zahra suggested we go on to the next classroom, where, she told me, it would be exactly the same. I was filled with indescribable feelings and wondered what on earth Palestine can mean to these poor toddlers. What future could they possibly have, refugee children born in the camp of refugee parents born in the camp? Today, twenty five years later, I find the same scene replicated, the same Palestine remembered, its liberation just as distant.

❧

By 1975 and in consequence of my frenetic activities, I had attained a certain prominence with the PLO. I met with their officials in London, Beirut and Damascus and they invited me to visit refugee camps and guerrilla bases. There was a romantic aura to those times, a seductive mixture of danger, excitement and secrecy, as if I were taking part in a film about wartime resistance. On the one hand, I saw myself engaged in an epic fight between good and evil, battling on the side of the righteous and, on the other, I felt it was a vindication of the doubts and frustrations of an unsatisfactory past.

In fact, I was embroiled in a game I did not fully understand. I saw the attentions of the men of Fateh as a reward, thrilling and flattering, for what had been years of lone political activism. I looked to them for acknowledgement and acceptance, but found instead puzzlement and not a little titillation. A few wanted to have affairs with me, my single status and anonymous London flat apparently an irresistible draw, especially to one or two of the married men who saw in this a chance of making a convenient and discreet arrangement with me. Their logic was quite simple: I was unmarried, which meant automatically that I was also companionless and so would be grateful for male attention, no matter what its source.

I continued working in Palestine Action until 1978, when it seemed that its role had become redundant. By then, the world (except for Israel and America) had recognised the PLO as a genuine liberation movement and accorded its leader, Yasser Arafat, legitimacy and respect. There was a PLO representative in London, and the Palestine case was no longer an obscure, forgotten subject, confined to the ranks of political analysts and crude sloganisers. I could have regarded my role as also redundant and, perhaps, given my sense of unrequited devotion, I should have seen it as the end of a chapter. Indeed, there was at the time some reason to think so.

As we wound up the organisation I remember being filled with optimism that a new and hopeful future was about to begin for Palestinians – and perhaps even for me.

Thirteen

I was wrong. The hope I had had in 1978 came to nothing, neither for Palestine nor for me. In that year, Israel invaded southern Lebanon in order to control Palestinian guerrilla attacks across its northern border and stayed on. Four years later, it thrust deeper into Lebanon and chased the PLO to its Beirut headquarters. The Israelis besieged the city and cut off its supplies. Faced with vastly superior Israeli military power and widespread civilian suffering, Arafat and his fighters were forced to abandon the base they had held for more than twenty years. The Palestinian leadership was exiled to Tunis, and many fighters were sent even further afield, to Yemen.

The PLO's departure was a catastrophic blow, not just to the organisation and its standing, but also to the thousands of refugees who depended on its services and protection. But even for people like us the PLO was indispensable. For all its shortcomings, it had embodied the aspirations of a whole generation of Palestinians. We were unaware until then of how much we had come to see it as a substitute for Palestine, how we had invested our thwarted pride and dignity in it.

My personal fortunes meanwhile fared no better than those of Palestine. In the turmoil that hit me after the breakup of my marriage it was by no means clear where I would end up. For a long while I had only the most inchoate of emotions – about my duty to Palestine, my lonely future, the response of my family to my divorce. My mother made no secret of her delight with this outcome of what she never ceased to believe had been a disaster. When I took myself off to London in that autumn of 1968 and miserably told her and my father of the failure of my marriage she could scarcely hide her satisfaction.

She did not spare my father her frequent reminders that had it not been for our presence in "this cursed land", none of this would have happened. She accused him of a secret attachment to the English that was at the core of our remaining in their country. This was a new form of attack and sprang from my father having been awarded an MBE that year.[1]

He was due for retirement in 1968 and was recommended to the authorities for an honours award in recognition of his long and distinguished service to the BBC. He was rather gratified by this and saw it as an expression of appreciation for a job he had done diligently and well. But my mother thought differently. "I trust you won't dream of accepting it," she said severely. "You don't want anything from the English or their queen." My father did not agree; but she made him feel uneasy. "After what they've done to us," she pressed on, "how could you want their honours or their awards? For what? So that they can pretend we're all friends now and that all is forgotten? Have some pride." This stung him, and he tried to explain that the MBE had nothing to do with our history in Palestine and that it was only a

---

[1] The British Government ran an annual so-called Honours List, whereby individuals who had given exceptional service were recommended to the Queen for a merit award. These were ranked in order of importance, ranging from the top, a knighthood, to the bottom, becoming a Member of the Order of the British Empire, or MBE, such as my father was offered.

gesture of respect for him. But she was not convinced and, in the end, he had to force her to go to Buckingham Palace for the award ceremony. I accompanied them and had to endure her ceaseless grumbling, which started with a shopping trip to Golders Green to buy her a suit smart enough for the occasion, all through the morning of the ceremony, when she had to dress, and for the whole duration of the taxi ride that took us to the palace.

Once there, my father was taken away through a separate entrance reserved for those who were to receive the honours, and we went into the section reserved for their families. Despite herself, my mother was impressed. To penetrate into the interior of a building that throughout our time in London had been a closed façade gawped at by tourists was a remarkable event. The long gallery we walked through to reach our seats was thickly carpeted in deep red, its walls hung with huge gold-framed paintings and illuminated by long windows through which the sunlight slanted. We were awed by its grandeur. When we took our seats overlooking the arena where the Queen would shortly appear I saw my mother looking around her with undisguised interest.

A line of those who were to receive the awards came in through one door and the Queen came in through another. At her appearance we all stood up for the national anthem, then watched while each person came forward in turn to stand before her. Afterwards, when we had witnessed her pin my father's MBE medal on his lapel, which she did standing on tiptoe because she was so short, my mother said, "I've never had anything against their queen. She's got dignity and breeding."

Outside, we found my father waiting for us, looking extremely pleased. He was unusually voluble. "You know, the Queen's got the most beautiful colouring," he said. "You don't realise it from just seeing her in photographs or on TV. She's got a really clear complexion and such blue eyes. She talked to me about the BBC and seemed to know a lot about my career." My mother shot him a sour look, and when he beckoned over one of the professional photo-graphers who was hanging about outside the palace gates, she refused to have her photograph taken with us. After some cajoling, she acquiesced with a reluctance that was graphically caught on camera. The photograph shows my beaming father as he holds an open velvet box, which displays his MBE medal, flanked on one side by me and on the other by my mother, the corners of her mouth turned down and her expression deeply mournful.

Throughout the exciting years of activism in the 1970s, I had managed somehow to put my private life on hold. I had a number of restless relationships, all with Western men, and all without lasting significance. I dragged each of them along with me in my work for Palestine, a pointless and ultimately futile activity, and we usually parted disappointed and dissatisfied. I began to have a conviction that only a relationship with an Arab would do. This idea grew, despite all the years spent in England, my sexual aversion to Arab men and the fact that I had met no one who remotely interested me. Undeterred, I started to muse longingly over the day I would meet some imaginary Arab who would make an idyllic companion, marry me and take me into the bosom of his family. And there would be acceptance and belonging at last. This illusion derived from seeing happy young Arab couples whom I had met in the course of my work, but much more from the almost desperate need I had by then to find my roots.

I decided there was nothing for it but to go to the Arab world, a world closed to me since my childhood and latterly only seen through the perspective of short working visits and political conferences. With a mixture of eagerness and trepidation, in 1978 I went to work in Syria and then to Jordan, where I thought I would fit in best, since most of the people there were Palestinian. Siham was by then living in Damascus, in a beautiful villa where I used to visit her at weekends from time to time. She had four children and was a busy wife and mother. But she and I still had our old rapport, although her children found me eccentric and quite outside their range of experience. Isam, her husband, disapproved of my Western ways and made no secret of it. When once the British ambassador to Syria, whom I'd contacted as a British subject – what an anomaly that seemed – came to visit me at Siham's house, he frowned and said, "Your sister's too liberated. She's a bad influence."

But I was unperturbed. The sentimental idea that I would somehow "find" myself amongst my fellow Arabs and settle down with them happily, perhaps for good, had taken firm hold. But to my dismay it soon became clear that I was as alien to them as they to me. I looked and sounded Arab, but in myself I was not, and they sensed it. I did not understand their cultural norms and was thus prone to commit social indiscretions and *faux pas* that might have been forgiven a genuine foreigner, but not someone like me. For, although my identity was ambiguous and they found me strange, I was still regarded primarily as an Arab and expected to behave as such. Astonishingly, no one understood the human effects of exile or displacement; what I took to be a self-evident case for sympathy left them indifferent. The fact of my having spent most of my life in England was simply an item of information, devoid of personal significance. People would often ask me when I was "coming back" to live in the Arab world, as if my thirty-year residence abroad had been no more than a foreign holiday.

My naïve eagerness to join in with them and belong was misinterpreted, and some even thought it suspect. They found my halting Arabic surprising and difficult to justify; my father being such a well-known Arab linguist and man of letters, they assumed he must have automatically handed on his skills to me. For all these reasons, I did not fit any category they recognised, and both men and women felt uncomfortable with me. My manner in mixed society, which I regarded as normal, but which they saw as unusually bold and direct and no way for an Arab woman to behave, was a cause for comment, especially in the comparatively unsophisticated Jordanian circles. It led some of the men to make passes at me on the assumption that, as I was "different" and had been reared in the West, I would be sexually available, unlike their own women. A number of them had studied abroad and had had relationships with foreigners which they now sought to recreate with me.

I found the approach of these men, whom I met predominantly in Jordan, unbearably crude. They would seize any chance to make a pass, which they did in the urgent and hungry way of the sexually repressed. I remember one of them pressing himself against me at a party once – these occasions were meant to replicate the Western environment many of us were used to. He was an engineer who had gained a Master's degree from the US, and I had found him a reasonably Westernised companion. We were supposedly dancing, but no sooner had he put his arm around my waist and taken my hand in his, than I felt myself held in a grip of steel. He crushed himself against me, panting and red-faced, and pressed a drooling mouth into my neck. An elderly Swiss colleague, who was watching, had virtually to prise him off me. Or there was the other man, an archaeologist who had studied in Germany and whose wife and children I liked. Coming to pick me up for a lecture one day, he grabbed me in the doorway of my flat and pinned me to the wall, rubbing himself against me and muttering ardently in English (as if that made it somehow more acceptable), "Oh, I like that, I like that."

Had I been a true Arab woman, I suppose I would have screamed, slapped his face and complained to the authorities, whatever my sense of outrage. The fact that I did not counted strongly against me and must have egged on others to try the same thing. One night, I found that I had lost my keys and was locked out of my flat. The administrator who normally took care of such things also lived on campus and I sought his help. He was a burly, coarse-looking man in his fifties with a balding head which he tried to conceal beneath a carefully combed lock of hair from the side. When I presented myself at his door, he invited me in and asked me to wait while he found the master-keys to the flats. On returning, however, I found that he had exchanged his trousers for the bottom part of his pyjamas. I burst out laughing, which evidently did not put him off, for he proceeded to draw me towards him, muttering and sighing. "It's all right," he said, breathing hard. "You don't have to worry. I've had a vasectomy. Probably the only man in Jordan who has."

Even had I thought to be flattered by such advances, I soon realised that none of these men had any real interest in me. They saw me merely as a vehicle for the discharge of their pent-up desires. None would have married me, for however attractive they might have thought me, my previous life and experiences suggested that I was fatally tainted by corrupting Western influences. Arab men, I discovered, had a split view of women: there were those they married and those they liked to sleep with. Western women belonged to the second category and, in so far as I was Westernised, so did I.

Aware of the moral niceties in Arab society, I had kept the matter of my previous marriage hidden. But that made no difference to their perception of me as a woman of questionable morals and potentially loose behaviour. I slowly began to realise that, even had I wanted to, I would find no husband there. My mother's fond hope that I would bury my "shameful past" in a respectable Arab marriage was likely to be frustrated, and my own quest for a suitable partner seemed doomed. The Westernised Arabs, who should have been my natural consorts, were worse than the natives. Most had acquired the trappings of Western culture, but not its essence. They spoke atrocious English and patronised the local people, as if they themselves were a cut above. Underneath the whisky drinking and the liberal-sounding conversation, they were as conventional and narrow-minded as those they affected to despise. Unused as I was to such societies, I found all this bewildering and disheartening. I was lonely and could see no future in staying any longer.

Perhaps, given my social disadvantages in Arab society, the only options open to me were liaisons with married men, or worse still, to end up as someone's second wife. While in Jordan, I met a man married to two women, in itself not unusual in Arab society, since the Islamic law of polygamy was and still is operative. But the extent of its application varied from one Arab country to another and also between classes – educated and wealthy people being the least likely to have more than one wife. In this case, however, the man was a well-respected architect who had spent some years training in England. He was the head of a firm of architects in Jordan and a frequent traveller abroad, in fact, a man whose education and experience should have made him an unlikely candidate for polygamy.

However, it appeared that his wife was infertile. This was at a time when in vitro fertilisation was not available, and the couple were consequently faced with unpalatable choices. They could either abandon the idea of having a child altogether, or the husband would need to remarry. In traditional Arab society, these were not real choices. Due to the importance accorded progeniture, especially for men, an infertile marriage was unacceptable. In these cases, the husband's family would urge him to put aside his barren wife and find another. Such was the situation here, and the man found himself increasingly pressurised by his female relatives (usually more vociferous than the men in such matters) to abandon his wife. He longed for fatherhood, but he also loved his wife and could not countenance the thought of leaving her for something not her fault. It was an impasse, until he hit on an ingenious solution.

He decided to marry a second woman for the purposes of pro-
creation only, while keeping his first wife – a sort of surrogate
motherhood arrangement long before it had become a recognised
practice in the West. Accordingly, he cast around for a suitable
woman and found a widow living alone with her child. He proposed
and was accepted with alacrity, for, as a respectable, well-to-do
architect, he was a desirable catch, no matter that he was already
married. Within a year, she had produced a child which was presented
to the first wife at birth. She was allowed to keep the second child, but
the third went to the other wife as well. The fourth and last child
remained with her.

When I met them, they all lived in one large house with a floor for
each of his two families. Each woman was bringing up the children
allotted to her, and he divided his time between the two households,
though he maintained that his first wife remained his only true love.
"Don't you think your two wives mind about this arrangement?" I
asked him when we had got to know each other. "What's the alternative?" he replied. "This way, I don't have to divorce my first wife and
consign her to a life of loneliness. At the same time, my second wife is a
decent woman who was struggling to bring up her child alone before I
married her. And I would have been miserable without children of my
own. Is it not better that each of them now has half a husband rather
than none and I have the children I always wanted?" I had no ready
answer. I knew that his predicament was genuine and only possible in a
society which functioned primarily for the benefit of its male members.

Without the architect, the women's alternatives were bleak indeed.
Marriage provided them with a passport to respectability, status and a
role in society. To be without it was to be marginalised and socially
irrelevant. If he had left his first wife, she would have suffered a
double disadvantage for being both discarded and infertile. And his
second wife, though a widow, had been "used goods". Worse still,

she had been lumbered with a child that any prospective husband would always regard as someone else's and not wish to take on. Given this situation, it was not difficult to see why all three in the architect's household had opted for his solution. It should be said, however, that some divorced and widowed women do manage to remarry, but this is uncommon.

Imbued with Western notions of sexual equality and the rights of women as I was, I found the whole story repellent. Many of the women I met who knew about it were no less disturbed than I was and pitied the wives, especially the first one. Some of them criticised her, however. "Should have had more self-respect and walked out on him," they said. "She could have lived with her old mother in dignity and to hell with him and all men." But most were grateful they had been spared such a plight. "It's easy to talk, but what life would she have had without a man?"

"Surely," I said, "it would have been better than sharing one, wondering what he's doing and saying every time he's with the other woman. It must be hell for her. Of course, it's all to do with women's unequal status here. In Europe, for example, such a situation could never arise."

Too late I realised that I had made a *faux pas*. I must have sounded patronising and colonialist. They looked at me unsmilingly. "What's so good about the way they do it in Europe?" one of them asked. "They certainly don't respect women there. All the men have mistresses, but the difference is the wife doesn't know and the mistress has to be kept hidden. She has no rights at all. At least here, the other woman is married to him and her children are legitimate." The rest of the gathering nodded in vigorous agreement. "Look at you, for example," continued the same woman. "You live in Europe, but what good has it done you? You're not married, you've got no children and no one to care for you. Wouldn't you be better off with someone like this man, even if he's not all yours?" I remember feeling confused for a moment. Was she right? What happiness had my single life in London really given me?

I came back to England in the summer of 1980 with a feeling of despondency and failure. In that year, my uncle Abu Salma died and was buried with great ceremony in Damascus in recognition of his inspiring nationalist poetry and his lifelong devotion to Palestine. It had been his dearest wish to find his last resting place in the land where he was born. But this was not to be, since Israel, which did not permit the return of any Palestinian living, refused the same to any Palestinian dead. This pointless act of Israeli spite further dejected me. With the closure of Palestine Action, I had no organisation and no political work to return to. All my previous political contacts seemed to have disappeared and I heard from no one in the PLO. All my devoted activism had apparently counted for nothing.

Two years in the Arab world had not helped me find my roots. Rather I began to fear that I had none to find, at least not in the places where I had sought them. And yet, the time spent abroad had distanced me from England too. I began to feel that I did not belong there either and found myself missing the warmth and sociability of Arab society. My old friends had somehow disappeared. Patricia was living in America, married and divorced for the second time and with two children. We had never lost touch, but she was far away. I did not know what had happened to the other school friends I had once been close to, Leslie and Hilary. Hilary became a doctor like me, but we never met again. My fellow students at medical school had not featured in my life for many years. I lost touch even with Cleeve, who had worked for a while in his native South Africa, but was now back in England. As for Zandra, who had meant so much to me, we scarcely ever met. After her marriage failed and a subsequent long-term relationship as well, she turned in on herself. Living alone in a windswept village outside Cambridge, she fell victim to a vicious form of rheumatoid arthritis. I saw her a few times after her illness had taken hold. But she became progressively more embittered and paranoid and refused to see me again.

I was wretched and desperately lonely. The English struck me more than ever as cold, self-contained and impenetrable. And the Palestinian exiled community in London, which might have provided an alternative, was little better. The majority were recent arrivals and had formed themselves into a series of cliques. Like my mother before, but with far less excuse, they sought to recreate an Arab milieu in London. They socialised only with other Arabs, maintained Arab lifestyles in their homes and, it seemed to me, spent much of their time gossiping about each other.

Unlike British Jews, who seemed cohesive and loyal to their community, Arabs did not help each other, and if anyone became especially prominent, the rest were more often jealous than supportive. This played into the worst of Western notions about the Arab world, classically seen as hopelessly divided and quarrelsome. The Arabs' reference point was Palestine and the Arab world to the exclusion of the new society they were actually living in. And yet this did not prevent them exploiting its obvious advantages which they soon learned to use – but only instrumentally – without absorbing the culture that had created them. This jarred on my own sense of integration and respect for that same culture. Consequently, we had little in common and I mixed as little as possible with them.

I was beginning to see that, in effect, I had no natural social home in England or in any other place. Did we all feel the same? Siham, who had made her home in the Arab world so determinedly all those years ago, had come back to England. Her marriage had broken down and in 1983 she left her husband in Saudi Arabia, where the family had gone after Syria, and returned to London with her children. Ziyad was living with his wife in Copenhagen, but had taken years to learn Danish, and was not part of Danish society. What and where was their real home?

Perhaps, I concluded desperately, I would have to go to the source, the origin, the very place, shunned fearfully for years, where it all began in order to find it. The truth I could not face as yet was that I was truly displaced, dislocated in both mind and body, straddling two cultures and unable to belong in either.

Fourteen

For me, Israel had always been the forbidden place, the country my parents refused ever to visit or let us see, their phobia becoming ours: a place that was out of bounds, a bizarre entity, without a concrete existence and nothing to do with "our" Palestine. Israel was a hostile political construct whose sole relevance was that it posed a problem for the Arab world; but above all, it was an illegitimate place, created by sleight of hand, its history fabricated, its population imported.

Now, in August 1991, I was here. The first intifada[1] was in its last days, the "peace process" had not yet started and the encounters between Arabs and Israelis that were to become so commonplace by the end of the 1990s were still unfamiliar.

---

[1] The popular Palestinian uprising against the Israeli occupation that started in 1987.

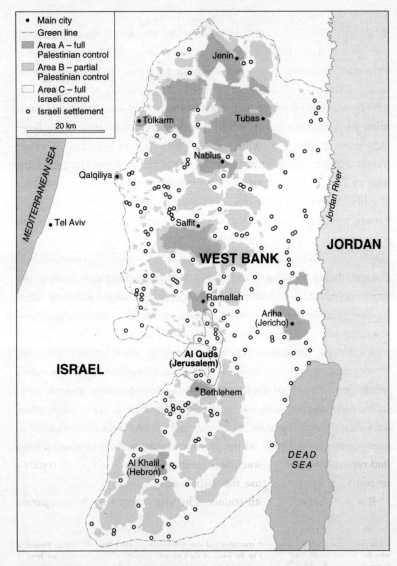

The West Bank in the 1990s, at the time of my visits there

Day 1: Ben-Gurion airport, Tel Aviv

The same Ben-Gurion whose name I had first heard mentioned with fear and anger at home in Jerusalem as a little girl. He was then the head of the Jewish Agency, building the bones of the state that would usurp us as Palestinians. It was a notion then; now I was seeing for the first time concrete proof of the existence of this alien state and these alien people. The airport building with its flag fluttering and a large sign over its entrance which read "Welcome to Israel" – I could barely repress a shudder at the sight of the Hebrew lettering. Like the Star of David on the flag, it had symbolised the Enemy throughout my life. Standing in the queue at immigration inside the air-conditioned building I surveyed the young officials, mere boys and girls, looking self-assured and healthily tanned by the sun that should by rights have tanned me. The queue I stood in was for "Non-Israelis", mostly Jews from other countries, all looking as diverse as those in the adjoining queue for "Israelis". The girl who examined my passport looked half Arab and half European, evidently the product of a marriage between Sephardi and Ashkenazi Jews.[2]

I asked the girl not to put an Israeli stamp in my passport, for this would make it unusable in Arab countries. In 1991 all these countries, with the exception of Egypt, were in a state of war with Israel and hence did not admit anyone who had been there. I was also worried that, in view of my past political activities, she would find my name on some security list and send me for interrogation. Akiva, who by then had returned to live in Israel, was meeting me and had come prepared to contact a lawyer in case this happened.

But she obliged on both counts. The visa stamp went on a separate

---

[2] The Sephardim are Jews from Arab countries and also descendants of Jews from the Iberian Peninsula who fled during the fifteenth century to the lands of the Ottoman Empire. The Ashkenazim are Jews of European origin. Traditionally, these communities were separate in Israel, but mixing and intermarriage has occurred with increasing frequency.

Arrival at Tel Aviv airport, 1991

sheet of paper without any argument and, much to my surprise, she waved me through and told me to have a nice holiday. Perhaps it was that "Karmi" was a common Israeli name, said Akiva afterwards, and she thought I was Jewish. "This is nothing," he said, seeing my shocked expression. "Listen, it's much more serious that no one in security stopped you. What an insult! I remember when they started letting me through without a fuss I knew I was finished!" When I came out of airport immigration I found him waiting for me with Rami Heilbron, an Israeli friend from London. As soon as they saw me, they held up a large welcome-home placard. I looked round at the crowd of other Israelis there that day and wondered if any of them had the slightest idea what that meant, and I felt myself close to tears.

Day 2: The beach at Tel Aviv

Stiflingly hot and humid. The place teemed with swimmers and holiday-makers, not an Arab in sight. With its skyline of tall modern buildings and skyscrapers it could have been anywhere in Europe. The Hilton Hotel overlooking the sea is built on the site of a huge Muslim cemetery, which was bulldozed flat. Next to the hotel was a heap of rubble and broken gravestones from the cemetery, still there, walled off and overgrown with shrubs and weeds.

The centre of Tel Aviv was a slice of Europe, shops, cafés, many people chatting in English. I met a couple from Finchley who had emigrated there. A ten-minute drive away lay Jaffa. In my childhood Jaffa had been Palestine's foremost city, to which Tel Aviv had been no more than an annexe. Now it was a depressed, dilapidated slum. Its streets and buildings were in disrepair, its Palestinian inhabitants reduced to poverty. Here and there fine Arab houses were still in evidence, and the hospital which had belonged to Mrs Dajani's husband, Fuad, was there also.

On the sea front, however, I found a very different scene. Here the beautiful old houses which had belonged to Jaffa's Arab notables in their heyday, their owners long since fled, had been renovated and restored. They now looked like a Hollywood film-set, a picturesque tableau framed by the azure sky and the white-flecked waves of the Mediterranean. But their inhabitants were all Israelis, and they were no longer homes but an artists' colony on show to visitors and tourists. There were many such people that day, clutching glossy brochures, which said, "Come to Tel Aviv-Jaffa, Israel's Holiday City on the Mediterranean!" and taking photographs of each other set against the renovated Arab houses. I mentioned it to Fahmi Gharib, a native of Jaffa with a fine old Arab house in the centre of the town. He was a man in his sixties and reminiscent of all the friends who used to come to see my father in the old days.

"I never go there," he said. "I can't bear to see the houses where our friends used to live made into this circus." He was an angry, bitter man. "They took us over in 1948, but I've never accepted Israel and I never will. You were luckier than you know, going to England. You never had to live through the things they did to us. The government schools they set up for our children to be taught about Jewish history and Zionism and nothing about our own history or literature. All the teachers are vetted in case they are a "security risk", meaning they might teach the children some self-respect." He paused to draw breath. "They don't belong here. All they've done is spread strife and misery amongst us and throughout this region. Look at this city, the Bride of Palestine, we used to call it. Look at it now, dying on its feet. It breaks my heart." His wife, who came in with a tray of coffee, tried to calm him down. "Don't get yourself so worked up," she admonished. And then turning to me, she pointed to the left side of her chest. "Heart trouble", she said, shaking her head at him.

But he was not to be deterred. "Believe me, I often thought of getting up and leaving when things got too bad. But then I would say to myself, 'why should I?' Do you know that this house was built by my great-grandfather? Tell me how many of them can go back that far in this country. Pah!" he spat. "It's not me that should leave but them!"

It made me sad to see him. What difference would his anger make to anything? There he sat defiantly in the house of his ancestors, his rage and passion burning inside him, but no one, aside from his wife and neighbours who must have heard it a thousand times before, knew or cared.

৵৽৹

Day 3: A picturesque restaurant between Tel Aviv and Jaffa overlooking the sea

At night-time, in a cool breeze and under a magnificent, star-studded sky, the clients were mainly Israelis, the restaurant owned by an Arab with Arab waiters serving. Bending over deferentially to lay our table, they thought I was Israeli too. I spoke to them in Arabic, trying to claim a national commonality, but they looked nervous and confused, as if I had been an Israeli secret agent sent to trap them. The restaurant owner came over and greeted Akiva heartily in Hebrew, ignoring me. The uncomfortable waiters slipped away. It was strangely destabilising to hear a fellow Palestinian using the language of Israelis. "How many Israelis speak Arabic?" I suddenly asked. "Very few", answered my companion. We ordered a variety of Arab hors d'oeuvres – *hoummos*, *mutabbal, tabbouleh* – such as I had been brought up on; food, they said, now favoured and claimed by Israelis as their own.

The waiters reappeared with that same fawning, deferential air and started to lay out the dishes before us. "Coolies", I thought, "and these are their masters." It gave me a sense of unutterable shame to see them, colonised and colonisers alike. Even Akiva, I noted to my dismay, betrayed a certain condescension in his attitude towards the restaurant owner and the waiters. But what had I expected? How could it have been otherwise? I realised then how I too, no less than my parents, had preserved an internal picture of this country as the Arab place it had been, but currently forced to house these aliens whose stay would be temporary. In this frozen scenario I expected my fellow Arabs who lived here to hold exactly the same view. Just as for me Israel had no concrete reality, so I thought it must be for them. It was an absurd, naive notion, which was rapidly to crumble away in the face of the contrary evidence I saw all around me.

❦

Day 4–5: Haifa, a bustling, hilly place with stunning views over the Mediterranean
This city reminded me of Beirut until I saw the Israelis in their baseball caps and T-shirts, which made it seem more like Florida. The

lower part of the town houses the Arab sector, more like a ghetto.
Hardly any Israelis lived or visited here, in the dusty, ill-kept streets,
dilapidated houses, people sitting on stools in front of their shops,
chatting to each other and passing their worry beads through their
fingers. It was a sight to be found in all Arab cities but incongruous
here against the proximity of the men and women in shorts, some
playing Mozart on the promenade, others drinking scotch or swigging
beer out of cans. It was hard to believe that here once was a thriving
Arab community whose wealthy had built their houses on the Carmel,
the steep hill that overlooks Haifa's harbour. Though the Carmel was
still exclusive, it was now reserved for the city's well-to-do Israelis,
some of them living in the self-same Arab houses which had been
abandoned by their owners in 1948.

Yet another incongruity was Samira, a young fair-haired, European-
looking Palestinian woman. Now working as a laboratory technician
in the main hospital, she had been born and bred in Haifa and spoke
fluent Hebrew. People often took her for Israeli. We sat in her flat in
an apartment block on the Carmel, hardly any other Arabs around. "It
was very difficult getting this flat, believe me," she said. "They don't
want Arabs here. It's only for Israelis, and if you buy into one of these
blocks, the other residents start to think the value of their flats will go
down. We had a lot of opposition, but we paid the owner a pile of
money. The neighbours have only just started to say 'Hallo', and
we've been here three years!" I asked why she had bothered.

"Why shouldn't we live wherever we want in our own city?" she
demanded. "I tell them all at work, 'You're guests here, that's all.
This is not your place'." "And they take it from you?" I asked
disbelievingly. She nodded. "You see, they think I'm like them. I look
and sound like them. I suppose it might be different if I were dark or
if my name had been Fatima."

Though they did not know it, there was another reason why Samira was more like them. Her mother had been a Polish Jew. It was a sad, wartime story with a happy ending. A young orphan girl of seventeen, recruited by the Zionist organisation in her native Poland and persuaded to leave for Palestine, Samira's mother had arrived in Haifa in 1945 to find herself more or less abandoned in a strange country. Brought up as a communist and seeking like-minded companions, she joined the Haifa communist party, one of the few organisations which had both Arab and Jewish members. While there, she met the man who was to be Samira's father, a Palestinian communist and political activist called Jamil. He was so touched by her plight that he persuaded his mother to take her in. She lived with them in one of those same houses which I had seen in the Arab ghetto earlier that day but which at the time was a respectable and well-to-do quarter of the city. The family grew to love her, as did Jamil, and adopted her as one of their own. And in time, she married Jamil, lived with him happily and gave him three children.

When Samira was sixteen, her mother took her and her brothers on a visit to Poland to show them her native land. She never accepted the claim of Zionism that Palestine was her real place of origin nor what Israel had done to the Palestinians because of it. Before they left, she made them visit Auschwitz, because she said they must see the site of man's greatest inhumanity to man and the place where her whole family had perished. If what had happened there had any purpose or meaning, she told them passionately, then it must be that people would learn never to do it again or take out on others the evil that had been done to them. For years, Samira thought no more about it. And then one day, she met a Jordanian woman at a dinner party when she was on a visit to London. Israeli Arabs, like Samira, never normally saw such people except outside Israel. When the Jordanian woman found out where she came from, she said: "How can you bear them all around you?"

"You get used to it," replied Samira.

"Well, I never would," said the other woman. "They make me sick and if you ask me, they should all have gone to hell."

"I suddenly thought," recounted Samira to me, "she's talking about my mother. I wanted to tell her and all of them that night about who I really was, but I just couldn't. The woman was hateful, vulgar and dolled up, gold jewellery everywhere. What did she understand about anything? What had she ever suffered that could compare to that?"

There were tears in her eyes and all I could do was reach out silently and hold her hand. How much better it would have been if none of it had ever happened: neither what was done to them nor what they did to us.

༄

Day 6: A gnarled and ancient olive tree just off the side of a road in the Galilee
Hundreds of years old, its bark holed and pitted and grooved, its convoluted roots spread about its base like Medusa's head, the tree fronted a large mound of rubble, broken concrete, the odd piece of furniture and twisted electricity wires. And just a few yards away a tent flapping in the breeze; inside it, a woman and small children. Outside it and sitting on his haunches, a dark, leathery-skinned man with a *kuffiyya* wrapped around his head. Balancing a coffee pot on top of a small camp stove. "You see that man," said Dr Hatim, pointing to a "1948 Palestinian", one of those who had not been evicted and a native of Galilee – who was showing us round. "He's been living in that tent for three months." In fact, ever since the authorities came one day without warning and bulldozed his house to the ground, the pile of rubble all that was left of it. He had built the house without a licence, they said, and the routine punishment for that was demolition. Like others guilty of the same crime, all of them

Arabs, no one had bothered to give him advance notice of the order to destroy his house. And when they had flattened the house before his eyes, they then presented him with a bill for the cost of demolition. "What will happen to them now?" I asked. Dr Hatim shrugged his shoulders. "Who knows?"

In a small Arab village on a hill we found the inhabitants had no running water, no electricity, no public services of any kind. A huddle of run-down shacks for homes, on barren, rubbly ground, chickens running about and a few goats grazing on the few tufts of grass. This was one of the hundred-odd so-called Unrecognised Villages, places which the Israeli State ignored as if they did not exist. On the hill immediately adjoining, there sat a prosperous Israeli village with large electricity pylons, street lamps and TV aerials, and its own fat, shiny water-pipe running along the ground just a few feet away from the unpaved path leading to the arid, unrecognised Arab village. The people came out to greet the doctor, whom they knew well, and welcomed us into the most presentable of their shacks. Everything here was stamped with their poverty, and yet they insisted on offering us glasses of warm Fanta and coffee, all they had. A glance through the gaps between the shacks and we could see the well-built homes of the Israeli village across the hill, its neat playgrounds and shady trees, its large range rovers driving in and out. I wondered how its people could bear to look across and see the deprivation of this place and turned to Dr Hatim.

"Ah, but they don't see it," he said. "Like they don't see us. For them, we are of no account at all, sub-human. You must understand that the only people who count in this country are Jews. And it shows in all the statistics, they have better health, better education, better housing, better towns, more amenities, more wealth." He had studied in the US and had returned to practise public health to help his community. He had had to work his way up in the Israeli ministry of health and had attained a senior position. But after a few years he left to set up his own health organisation with foreign funding. "I had got as high up in the ministry as it's possible for an Arab to get. And I couldn't go on being obsequious in the way they like you to be. So I left."

Did it have to be like that? Had he made no Israeli friends at the ministry?

"How could I? How could any of us, when you think of what they did and how they still behave? Of course we have relationships with them, but they're on a formal basis or for some specific purpose. Otherwise, we don't socialise with them. Many of them would like to make friends and want us to accept them, but only on their terms."

He took us to Nazareth and I saw for myself the disparity he had mentioned. A dilapidated town, potholes in the streets, uneven pavement stones, run-down buildings, very like impoverished cities all over the Arab world. But on the hills above it, something out of a Hollywood film. Another town, modern, prosperous, Israeli, called Nazaret-Illit, or Upper Nazareth. Wide, well-paved streets, tree-lined avenues, large houses. An American-style shopping mall, young people indistinguishable from their peers in the West lounging about drinking from cans with Walkmans in their ears. I was told that some amongst them were Palestinians who had come up from the lower town, trying to emulate the same style. The contrast between the two places could not have been more glaring. "You know," said Dr Hatim, "Israeli taxi drivers often take people asking for Nazareth to this place. If they insist on going to our town, the drivers say, 'you don't want to go to that place. It's filthy and full of Arabs.'"

❧

Day 7–8: Tiberias

On the road before reaching the town, the twin horned-hills of Hattin, the site of a decisive battle in 1187 between the great Muslim leader Saladin and the crusaders. In a crushing victory here, the Arabs destroyed the Frankish army and Saladin retook Tiberias. Within two months, he had recaptured Jerusalem, in crusader hands for a hundred years. By 1189, he had overcome nearly all the other crusader strongholds of Syria-Palestine as well. Here was a proud Arab history and a dazzling Arab heritage which belonged to us and meant nothing to the people who lived here now: Israelis from the various corners of the globe, many here on a poor man's holiday, rather like the summer holiday-makers of Florida who could not afford wintertime peak prices.

Tiberias was shabby and dirty, the Israelis here of a different class from those I had seen before. Here and there, beautiful Arab houses were still preserved, but along the main street there was a row of old Arab shop fronts with Hebrew lettering all over them, as if to try and obscure their real origins. And standing directly behind them was a group of hideous, modern, high-rise blocks, dwarfing the small shops and totally out of place in what had once been a charming Arab street.

Just off the centre, a square of shabby cafés and dowdy shops with litter on the ground. In the middle of the square a mosque, dating from Ottoman times, shut up and abandoned. No Muslims left in Tiberias to use or care for it. The mosaics on its walls overlaid with grime, the marble pillars black and pitted, it stank of urine and neglect. Empty packets, old newspapers, detritus all around it, a place of utter irrelevance to the Israelis who now sat at the cafes, eating ice cream and shouting across to each other. A dead building in a dead place, the saddest I had yet seen in all that sad country.

*Day 9–12: Jerusalem: Driving out of Tel Aviv towards Jerusalem along a
busy dual carriageway*

Trying to absorb the scenes of Palestine's geography, denied to me
since 1948, as we headed for that most important place of my childhood, I saw the terracing on the hillsides, so typical of the Levant, an
ancient, indigenous agricultural system that had long preceded the
arrival of this modern state. The road signs were written in Hebrew
and English, but not in Arabic – ostensibly Israel's other official
language – except in some places where the Arabic script was so small
as to be virtually invisible. This, like the occasional remnant of an
Arab building on the side of the road and the Arab houses dotted
about in the Israeli cities I had seen, was a ghostly reminder of a
presence not quite buried, "present-absentees", as the Israeli phrase
has it.

By the roadside I noticed the wreck of an old tank dating from the
1948 Arab–Israeli war, preserved with pride by Israelis celebrating
their first victory over the Arabs, over people like me. Rounding a
corner and suddenly having in full view the hills that surround Jerusalem, a view that should have been breathtaking, I found it hid-
eously deformed by serried ranks of tastelessly built, featureless
apartment blocks covering the hilltops like fortresses and crawling like
a rash of boils down their sides. They had flat roofs, unlike the houses
of the West Bank Israeli settlements where the red-brick roofs sloped,
built as if for rain and snow and more appropriate to a place like
Switzerland. But both were eyesores in this soft Mediterranean
landscape.

I visited Tulkarm, our town of origin, the day before. I had last
seen it on a brief visit in 1960 when it was part of Jordan and had
found it a largely unmemorable place, drearily rural and quite alien to
my then burgeoning identification with England. It was a very different experience seeing it now under military occupation and subject

to frequent curfews, its people cowed and nervous. I ate lunch at my cousin's house trying to ignore the Israeli soldiers on the rooftop opposite the house, striding about with their loaded rifles and walkie-talkies. We watched afterwards a huge march of people bearing the coffin of one of the townsmen shot by the army. It was a common occurrence, they said, especially during the intifada. Many families had lost sons that way. Sometimes the bodies were never returned to their relatives for burial, without any explanation given. But everyone said it was because they had been tortured before they were killed. The walls along the main street were still daubed with patriotic slogans and declarations of support for the PLO, evidence of a former defiance, which the heavy army presence in the town had now managed to subdue.

Leaving Tulkarm I passed through the town of Taybeh, from where Mrs Tibi's husband came. It looked little different from Tulkarm: all these Arab places were dusty, arid, and bleached by the sun. Yet across the West Bank border into Israeli territory, hardly any distance, it was another country: lush scenery, green lawns, flowering orchards, luxuriant trees and bushes, reflecting the gross imbalance in water supply between the two bits of land that had been indistinguishable before 1948 – the one now replete with water at the devastating expense of the other. "You can always tell when you've crossed the line into Israel," said our Arab taxi driver. "It's like coming to the edge of a green carpet laid on sand."

We were now driving through the outskirts of Jerusalem and seeing the walls of the Old City looming up on the horizon – the wildly incongruous juxtaposition of this medieval Arab place with the modern Israeli city created around it in less than fifty years. The next day, I went on foot to the Old City, down Salah al-Din Street and into the noisy traffic and bustle in front of the Damascus Gate. Palestinian peasant women, the first I had seen in the flesh since I said goodbye to

Fatima all those years ago, dressed in their familiar embroidered caftans, were sitting on the kerbside to sell the vegetables they had brought from their villages that morning. Just like the village women who came to our house when I was a child, they displayed huge, fat radish heads, taut-skinned, shiny aubergines, aromatic bunches of fresh mint, dill and coriander as could never have been found in Britain. For a crazy moment I searched for Fatima amongst the peasant women, staring into their faces, longing to see her again, oblivious to the passage of time.

These women would have to sell their produce that day, for the money each made most likely supported a large family who anxiously awaited their return. A couple of Israeli soldiers passing by, their rifles swinging against their sides, suddenly stopped and kicked their boots into the carefully heaped-up vegetables to send them sprawling into the gutter.

"You are not allowed to be here. Out!" one of them said to the peasant woman in broken, heavily accented Arabic, while she scrambled to get back her damaged vegetables. She smiled at him placatingly, but he repeated in tones not totally devoid of humour, "Come on, old woman, out!" I gathered it was a common occurrence and the women usually waited until the soldiers had gone out of sight before setting out their wares all over again.

Despite the army presence everywhere and the proximity of the modern Israeli buildings just in view, this was still an Arab place. I tried to remember that it was here, in this busy street with its village men and women, its buses and taxis, that many years ago I had stood clinging to Fatima and saying goodbye to her for ever. But no memory or feeling came back from that special moment as I stood amidst the crowds, and I gave up and crossed over into the Old City.

Walking down its winding streets towards the Haram al-Sharif, past the small shops on each side, I noticed how dirty and unkempt it was. The shopkeepers were desperate for custom, saying that Israeli tour guides had scared the tourists off by claiming the Arabs would rob them. On the way down, I saw a strange discordant sight. It was a large menora atop a typical old Arab house and armed guards outside it: the house of Ariel Sharon, Israeli political leader, soldier and hero of the Lebanese invasion, of Sabra and Shatila,[3] who had acquired the house here in the heart of the Old City. He never used it but kept it there in order to make a point, just like the black-coated, ultra-orthodox Jews, swaggering about aggressively, going in and out of the Arab houses they had taken over, as if to say, "This is our place, not yours."

I took the approach to the Haram, past the special route built after 1967 to link the Jewish faithful directly to the Wailing Wall, an underground tunnel, forbidden to Arabs and guarded by soldiers. Looking up at the golden Dome of the Rock, I felt an ineffable joy and pride in its solid, unchanging beauty. What had those who claimed this city and this country for their own ever made that could compare to this? Ascending to the massive, part-tiled courtyard, I looked back through the pillars that bounded one side of it to the Aqsa Mosque below, trying not to see the brash, modern apartment blocks crowding the skyline behind, as out of place here as if they had been dropped from another planet. It was shocking to find the peace and tranquillity of the Haram shattered by something unheard of in a place of such sacredness: the presence of armed soldiers, raw young men crashing about, stopping people, checking IDs, asking questions. No doubt obeying orders, but without regard or feeling for the majesty of the place they had traduced.

---

[3] Sharon was the commander of the Israeli army at the time of the 1982 massacres in the two refugee camps. He was subsequently found indirectly responsible for the action by an Israeli judicial commission of inquiry.

The next day, I visited the Knesset, the Israeli parliament, built on the flattened and now unrecognisable land of the Palestinian village of Lifta. A huge menora stands opposite the Knesset's gates, a present from the British government – no doubt wishing Israel well. Looking at the fortress-like building, I suddenly remembered *The Lord of the Rings* which I had read in childhood and thought of Minas Morgul, the tower that was the headquarters of Sauron, the Lord of evil. The crowd of tourists milling round the gates saw none of this, admiring the view and taking photographs.

The Holocaust museum nearby was also built on confiscated Arab land. Inside, there was a brilliant and affecting exhibition of tragic European–Jewish history, skilfully interwoven with the creation of modern Israel; a seemingly logical progression from the gas chambers to Palestine, not omitting pictures of the Mufti of Jerusalem negotiating with the Nazis. It was a deliberate statement about the right of world Jewry to this country. Crowds of European Jews milled reverentially around the photographs and exhibits. Outside, a humble Palestinian gardener in shabby, soiled clothing pulled weeds and dead flowers from the beds, making the place pretty and neat, oblivious of its significance.

On day 12 I called on an Israeli couple, friends of friends, he a left-wing writer, she an artist, both introduced to me as "progressive" Israelis. They lived in an Arab-style house which they assured me had belonged to Yemeni Jews, not Arabs, at the turn of the century: trendy, ethnic furnishings, embroidered cushions and rugs on the floor, she wearing long Palestinian-style silver earrings. The atmosphere was relaxed, civilised and European, Bach playing softly in the background. We could almost have been in Hampstead. The conversation we had purported to make me feel that I was among friends. They had no time for right-wing Israelis, disapproved of all religious groups and individuals, deprecated the military occupation of Gaza

At the Haram al-Sharif, 1991

and the West Bank and had several Palestinian friends. They were Labour Party supporters and might be described as Zionist doves.

I found out that she was the daughter of a Polish immigrant to Palestine who had become a member of the Irgun gang in the 1940s. I recalled that it was the Irgun who had blown up the King David Hotel in 1946, just yards away from my father's office. There was not a hint of shame or apology in her voice as she said this, as if having a terrorist for a father was the most natural thing in the world. Nor did she seem to have any awareness that he might have shared in acts which could have maimed or killed my family or friends. The most she conceded was that she did not share her father's political views.

When they asked me for my impressions of Israel, I cast about in my mind for some pithy way to summarise the range and complexity of what I had seen in the last week. Only one word came to mind: apartheid. As I said so my hosts looked visibly shocked. They did not agree because, for a start, they said, there were people like them in Israel who were making links with Palestinians, developing a movement of solidarity and cooperation. They were trying to understand, trying to build bridges.

"I realise that," I persisted. "But the fact is there are two peoples here, unequal in every respect because the one considers itself superior to the other. It's clear for anyone to see that Arabs in this country live separate, excluded lives. In the rest of the world, we call it racism." They were both uncomfortable. "I must say I don't understand how decent, civilised people like you can bring yourselves to live in such a society."

"By trying to change it!" exclaimed the husband. But she, looking me straight in the eye, said coolly, "I live here because I belong here. This is my country."

Her country? I thought. By virtue of what? That fifty years ago, one Polish immigrant had brought himself, uninvited, to what was my country and bombed and plotted his way with others like him to steal it from its rightful owners? And now it was this man's daughter, who was telling me that she belonged here?

∂∞⊛

Days 13 and 14: Qatamon: Looking for my house with Akiva and two other friends from London

I had directions and a map of sorts taken from Siham before I left England. But the landmarks by which I was to recognise our road had long gone or been renamed. We stopped one man to ask our way, but he turned out to be a recent immigrant from Golders Green, of all places, and we exchanged a few pleasantries about the strange coincidence. It was stiflingly hot and things did not look promising. All the people we met had come to Qatamon after 1948, and one woman we approached actually asked for directions herself, speaking to me in

Hebrew. We were running out of landmarks to guide us, the last of which was to be the Semiramis Hotel. Although it had been blown up in 1948, it had stood in the road directly behind ours and its site might still be known to someone here.

I was bitterly disappointed to find that I remembered so little. From the moment we climbed the Qatamon hill which I knew led to our road somewhere near its top, I had tried to summon back remembrance. For this part of Jerusalem had been more or less preserved because, like the German Colony just below it, it was considered to be quaintly old-fashioned and appealing. Middle-class Israelis had taken over the best Arab villas, but many post-1948 buildings had been added, some of them for the elderly. In addition, and especially in the parts that were run down, there was a large number of orthodox Jewish families and a few religious schools. All the Arab villas looked familiar to me and many of them could have been replicas of our old house. Standing for a moment on the hill underneath the trees, I could feel that same tranquil stillness of long ago, just as it had been on summer afternoons when all the adults were sleeping and we were playing, wide awake. As I walked past each turning off the hill, I stared into it, hoping that it would be the one I was looking for. But I found nothing and no one had heard of the Semiramis Hotel. After a while, thirsty and overheated, we gave up.

We returned the next day to try again. Now that I had decided to confront the past, I could not bear to leave without seeing, knowing, breaking open the magical seal set in childhood and left undisturbed for forty-three years. I must find the house. This time, we took a Palestinian with us who used to live in Qatamon, a sad old man who had never set foot there since his expulsion in 1948. Though he had lived for all those years on the other side of Jerusalem, barely a mile away, he had never once been back. Encouraged by my quest, he came with us, saying that he remembered the Semiramis Hotel and also probably where our house had been. I did not find this unlikely, since Palestinians traditionally knew their neighbourhoods by the site of other people's houses. But when we drove him into Qatamon, he was confused and could barely find where his own house had been. He walked along the streets in a daze, his eyes full of tears, touching the walls of the villas we passed and pausing every few minutes to stare silently into the distance.

And then, just as I was about to give up again, Akiva found an old newsagent at the top of the hill who had come to Palestine before 1948 and did remember the Semiramis. He seemed glad to talk to someone about that time and walked out of his shop with us to point us in the right direction. He showed us an unremarkable house on the corner which he said had replaced the hotel. From there we located the road immediately below and parallel. This then should have been our road. By now I was so impatient to get there that I hurried towards it, leaving the others behind. Entering the road, I began to count the houses from the end, just as Siham had told me: not the first, not the second, but the third. This should have been our house and the end of my quest. Akiva had now caught up with me and we both stood silently on the pavement and stared at it.

We found ourselves looking at a modern, square building, nothing like the beige stone Arab villas of the area, and certainly not my old house. It had a small forecourt where a few small children were playing, boys with ringlets at the sides of their heads and skullcaps. A few women in wigs stood about, presumably their mothers. The scene could have come from the orthodox Jewish part of Golders Green. It turned out that this was a kindergarten for religious Israelis in the neighbourhood, but the people in the adjoining houses did not know when it had been built. It must have replaced our house at some point; an old man in the first house in the road thought he remembered that there had been an Arab villa there before, but he could not recall when it was knocked down. Unutterably dismayed, I walked back and stood staring at what had been the site of our house. I squeezed my eyes shut to banish the present from my consciousness and recall the memories of childhood, the echoes of laughter of those other children long ago, and the scents and sounds which had once been homely and familiar.

But I could not. There was nothing here to which I could attach my longing for home. This was not my house, nor were the structures on either side of it our neighbours' houses. They were unfamiliar places in an unfamiliar street, filled with strangers. Silently I turned away and we walked back to the car. I had a sense of frustrated hopelessness. Flotsam and jetsam, I thought, that's how we ended up, not a stick or stone to mark our existence. No homeland, no reference point, only a fragile, displaced and misfit Arab family in England to take on those crucial roles. And even that family, now also dispersed and fragmented: Ziyad neither inside nor outside society in Denmark; Siham, struggling with her four children in the country she had so firmly rejected; and our parents, who in old age had felt the urge to go home and, being unable to, had settled in Jordan, the nearest thing to Palestine there was. My mother, already gravely ill, would die there a year later and be buried in a large cemetery outside Amman, neither her original home nor my father's. And what of me? Disillusioned, restless, without a place to settle and destined to remain so for the rest of my life.

"Have to face it, Akiva," I said. "Your side has won and we have lost. Whatever is the point of struggling now? I look back on all that we did in the seventies and all that I went on to do for years afterwards, all that picketing and demonstrating, the letters to great people, the TV appearances, the meetings, the travelling – all for nothing in the end. I and others like me were lone voices crying in the wilderness, no one now remembers what we did or cares. It made no

In Search of Fatima

impact on events and things for the Palestinians have only gone downhill since then. Might as well accept we're finished, the new Armenians of the world, doomed to be fragmented and dispersed for ever."

Akiva listened quietly. And then he said, "I'm going to tell you a story my father told me years ago. He said there was once a young frog and an old frog who fell into a jug of milk. They struggled to get out, but they couldn't, and the old frog said to the young frog, 'Give up, my boy. It's no use struggling. We'll never make it. We're going to drown, might as well accept it.' And with that, the old frog sank back into the milk and sure enough, he drowned. But the young frog could not accept it. Despite himself, he went on scrabbling and pushing against the sides of the jug, so hard and so long that he churned up the milk, which curdled and turned into butter. And when that happened, he climbed out and survived." He paused.

"Don't be like the old frog," he said.

Epilogue

It wasn't true. The house was still there. I found it in June 1998, the
year of Israel's fiftieth anniversary. The Jewish State flamboyantly
celebrating its success, not a mention of the human cost it had
entailed. Another hot day, another companion, Rami Heilbron this
time. And better directions this time too, from Siham who had finally
made it to Israel in 1996 and found the house. And there it was. The
one with the brick-red roofed veranda, our house without question.
The spell was broken, the mystery at an end. An ordinary house,
much smaller than the one in my imagination. An upper storey built
on its roof which had never been there before. The iron gates and
railings painted black. They used to be grey. No Rex to wag his tail
behind them. On the wall a plaque that read Ben Porath. The steps
going up, so huge in my memory, really quite small, and the veranda
where they led but a modest rectangle. The windows on either side of
the front door not half so tall as I remembered them. The whole place
a fraction the size it had been in my child's memory.

I went up to the gate. There was an old woman in a rocking chair on the veranda. Children's toys lying around. The black and brown mosaic floor was exactly as I remembered it, though here and there the colours had faded. In a flash, I saw Fatima resting on the floor, her eyes closed. No resemblance to the woman now in the rocking chair, white-haired, European-looking. I pushed the gate open and went up the steps, Rami following. She looked up surprised. I smiled. He started to speak in Hebrew. She held up her hand.

"I'm sorry," she said, "I don't understand. I'm American. Do you speak English?" We nodded.

He said, "Sorry to bother you, but she used to live here many years ago. This used to be her house and she has never been here since. She just wants to look around a little. Do you mind?"

She looked bewildered. "I must ask my daughter-in-law." She went into the house through our front door which had not changed an iota. She came back with a younger woman, plump, in a dark wig, with a toddler clutching at her skirt. "It's OK with me," said the younger woman, also in an American accent. "But my little boy is sleeping inside."

"I just want to go in the garden and maybe a little into the house," I said. Both the women stared at me. I walked down the steps, turned right into the garden. Again, much smaller than I remembered. The lemon tree under my parents' bedroom window, still there. But the vine had gone and so had the apricot trees. At the back, more trees, but everything overgrown, untended, unloved. Windows which opened onto rooms no longer ours. The clothes line where Fatima hung out the washing had gone. In the top right-hand corner, the shed where Rex slept reluctantly at night, also gone. Then down the other side of the house. A child, my earlier self, playing under the mulberry tree, now also gone. Against the wall and spoiling the symmetry, a staircase leading to the upper storey that someone had thoughtlessly added on. A large palm tree which had never been there before.

On the veranda of our house in Qatamon, 1998

I came back to the foot of the steps and went up to the veranda. The old woman watched me. I pushed open the front door, my heart pounding. Inside, it was dark, the floor still retained the old tiling here and there. The *liwan*. My father in his chair in the top right-hand corner, reaching for a book from the shelves on the wall. The room was now distorted by a staircase going up to the upper floor. The woman in the wig motioned me to be quiet. Her son was sleeping there. I tiptoed towards the back, which should have opened onto the dining room, the kitchen, our bedrooms. But now unrecognisable. A large modern kitchen, a Filipino maid who looked round at me in surprise.

I wanted to stay longer, to go into the room kept for visitors where my mother had had her *istiqbals*, into my parents' room, into the room where we had slept. They were no longer there, knocked down at some time to make a larger central space. But more than anything, I wanted to be alone so that the memories could seep back. So that the ghosts could return and let me touch what I had buried for so long. God knows when there would be another chance, when I would ever be allowed in here again. But the woman was uncomfortable. She had regretted letting me in and clearly wanted me to go. I steeled myself to speak.

"Would you tell me what you know about this house? Is your name Ben Porath?"

"No. That's the owner. We're just renting here."

"Do you know when he got the house?" She shook her head. "Well, would you let me have his telephone number so I could talk to him myself?"

She looked alarmed. "I don't know. I'll have to phone my husband. He's at work."

I waited while she went into the back of the house. She returned very quickly. "I'm sorry, but he says we don't want anything to do with it. It's nothing to do with us."

I hid my disappointment as well as I could and thanked her. She followed me outside. The old woman was back in her rocking chair. They waited for me to go down to the gate and then shut it behind me. I crossed over to the opposite pavement to get a better view. To the right, the Muscovite's house, as it used to be. To the left, I saw that our old neighbours' house, the Jouzehs', was also still there, better preserved and its garden better kept than ours was now.

But of course it wasn't ours any more and had not been for fifty years. Our house was dead, like Fatima, like poor Rex, like us.

∂∽∽

I lay on my bed in the hotel near the Old City where I was staying. My limbs were leaden, my mind a blank. Inside me was a numbing emptiness. Then suddenly a sound, familiar and evocative. It was the call to prayer, beamed forth from the Haram al-Sharif, spreading through the Old City, travelling over the houses, over the cars, the modern office blocks and passing on to the hills beyond:

Allahu akbar – God is great!
Allahu akbar – God is great!

I testify that there is no god but God and Muhammad is His Messenger ...

As the sound hit my ears, I sat up, wide awake. Mesmerised, I went to the balcony windows and threw them wide open, the better to hear it. On it came, over the Wailing Wall, over the huddle of poor Arab housing, over Israel's brash buildings, its luxury hotels, its noisy traffic. The unmistakable sound of another people and another presence, definable, enduring and continuous. Still there, not gone, not dead.

I closed my eyes in awe and relief. The story had not ended, after all – not for them, at least, the people who still lived there, though they were now herded into reservations a fraction of what had been Palestine. They would remain and multiply and one day return and maybe overtake. Their exile was material and temporary. But mine was a different exile, undefined by space or time, and from where I was, there would be no return.